ACCLAIM FOR *Rebecca Solnit's*

Savage Dreams

"One of the finest new books. . . . The product of a stunningly original and expansive imagination, *Savage Dreams* ties together the histories of Yosemite National Park and the Nevada Test Site—the country's Eden and Armageddon—to illuminate the political stakes of how we think about, and act upon, the landscape."   —*SF Weekly*

"Solnit's intelligent meditations may awaken us from our self-congratulatory coma. [Her] mind is fertile, wide-ranging and capable of integrating the bewildering deluge of fact, political delusion, flights of genius, inconceivable danger and cunning deceit that [have] characterized the nuclear age. . . . *Savage Dreams* is a historical travelogue, a memoir that rounds out stories of Solnit's own travels with geographical and anthropological anecdotes."   —*Los Angeles Times*

"Reckless courage. . . . *Savage Dreams* summons us to the campfires of resistance."   —Mike Davis, author of *City of Quartz*

"*Savage Dreams* is about many things: despoliation and restoration, finding a voice between contemporary noise and silence, making friends and enemies. Most of all, though, it may be about a journey into history: about how understanding history and making it are not really very different. 'To know a place, like a friend or a lover, is for it to become familiar,' Solnit writes; 'to know it better is for it to become strange again.' That is the outline of the map *Savage Dreams* fills in."   —Greil Marcus, author of *Lipstick Traces*

BOOKS BY *Rebecca Solnit*

Secret Exhibition:
Six California Artists of the Cold War Era

Savage Dreams

Rebecca Solnit

Savage Dreams

Rebecca Solnit is the author of *Secret Exhibition: Six California Artists of the Cold War Era*. She has written a number of essays for museum catalogs and magazines. She lives in San Francisco.

Rebecca Solnit

Savage Dreams

A Journey
Into the Landscape Wars
of the American West

Rebecca Solnit (signature)

UNIVERSITY OF CALIFORNIA PRESS
Berkeley · Los Angeles · London

University of California Press
Berkeley and Los Angeles, California

University of California Press, Ltd.
London, England

First California Paperback Edition, 1999

Reprinted by arrangement with the author.

Library of Congress Cataloging-in-Publication Data

Solnit, Rebecca.
    Savage dreams : a journey into the landscape wars of the American
West / Rebecca Solnit.—1st California paperbacks ed.
      p.   cm.
    Originally published: San Francisco : Sierra Club Books, c1994.
    Includes bibliographical references (p.   ) and index.
    ISBN 0-520-22066-8 (pbk. : alk. paper)
      1. West (U.S.)—Description and travel.   2. Landscape—West
(U.S.)—History.   3. Yosemite National Park (Calif.)   4. Nuclear
weapons—Testing—Environmental aspects—Nevada.   5. Indians of
North America—West (U.S.)—Wars.   I. Title.
F591.S6685   1999
978—dc21   99-20034
                                                        CIP

Manufactured in the United States of America
08 07 06 05 04 03 02 01 00 99
      10 9 8 7 6 5 4 3 2 1

Contents

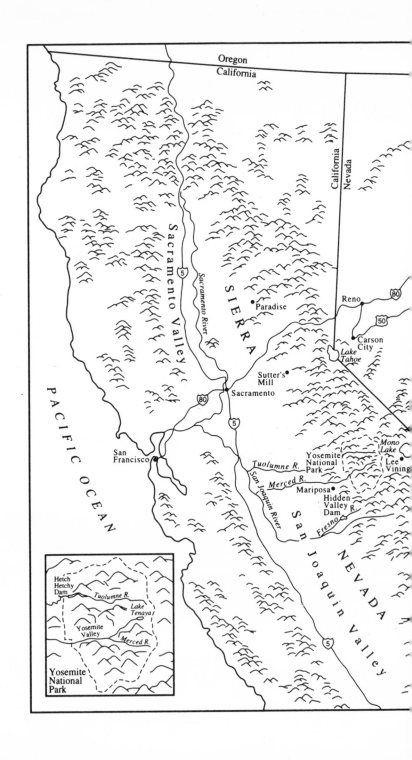

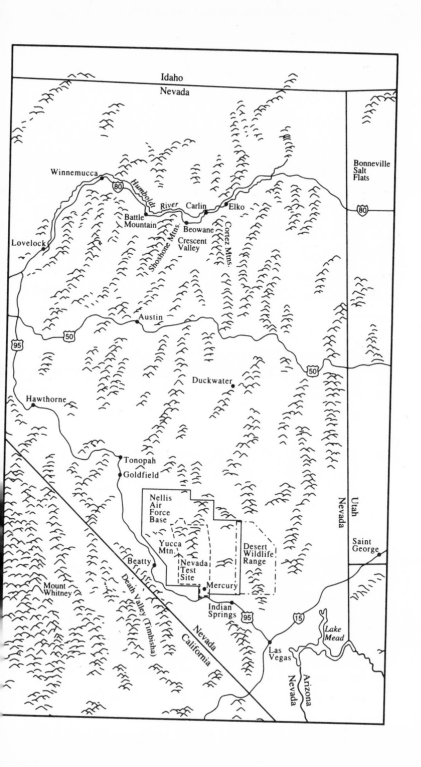

Acknowledgments

This is a book about trying to come to terms with what it means to be living in the American West, learning as much from encounters with landscapes and people as from readings. Much of what I was interested in was the border territories between disciplines—how the way we picture landscape affects how we treat it, how what we believe blinds us to what is going on—and how the nuclear war that was supposed to be our future and the Indian wars of our past are being waged simultaneously, without attracting much attention from those not directly affected. The results herein are by no means meant to substitute for the many histories they draw on (which are given in the Sources section at the back).

This book is dedicated to the people who move through its pages and across the landscapes described here:

—firstly to my brother David Solnit, who drew my attention to nuclear issues, the Nevada Test Site, whose political conscience has always been a spur to my own, and who has been a good friend through it all

—and to the many generous, dedicated people I met in Nevada, including Bob Fulkerson, Bill Rosse, Pauline Esteves, Rachel Gertrude Johnson and her fellow princesses, Carrie and Mary Dann and their family, Corbin Harney, Bernice Lalo, Lauri Di Routh; to Dana Schuerholz, Sarah, Doug, Lillian and their fellow Seattle activists; to Heidi Carter, Raymond Yowell; to Grace Bukowski, Heidi Blackeye, Chris Brown and the staff of Citizen Alert, Kairot Umarov and the other activists from Kazakhstan's Nevada-Semipalatinsk An-

Acknowledgments

tinuclear Movement, Stephanie Fraser, Reinard Knutson and the long-suffering staff of American Peace Test, Father Alain and Sister Rosemary of the Franciscan nonviolence organization Pace E Bene, Lisa Belenky, Jodie Dodd, April, Jason, Lone Wolf, and the other hardcore supporters at the Western Shoshone Defense Project, the many downwinders and atomic veterans who shared their stories, particularly Janet Gordon
—to my cousin Mary Solnit Clarke for her inspiration and friendship and for the glorious example of my friends, including the women of Women Strike for Peace
—and to my friends who travelled with me on the occasions described herein, particularly Tim O'Toole, Diane Driscoll, Catherine Harris, Jesse Drew, and David Dodge
—to Logan and Angela for their hospitality and conversation the night my truck slid into a ditch during a flash flood near Zion National Park
—and to the artists whose work and friendship has been the core of my education about landscape, Linda Connor, who came first, then Richard Misrach, Meridel Rubenstein, and Lewis deSoto

Thanks also to the Yosemite Park employees who took time to talk to me, particularly Jay Johnson, Sue Fritzke, Linda Eade, and Craig Bates
—and the other people who discussed Yosemite's issues with me, including Kat Anderson, Zandra Bietz, and Elmer Stanley
—and to the people who generously took time to read portions of this book, including David, Bob, Dana, California ecological historian Grey Brechin, and the scholar of Yosemite-region indigenous issues, Dave Raymond, who provided many valuable suggestions and documents from his own research

—and to the marvelous editor Barbara Moon, who first worked with me at the Banff Centre for the Arts in Alberta, where we improved the chapter "Lise Meitner's Walking Shoes," and who then read and commented on the whole manuscript

—and to the Banff Centre for the Arts for a residency there in the Arts Journalism Program in the summer of 1993 and to the National Endowment for the Arts for a literary fellowship for 1993–94, which greatly eased the research and writing of this book

—to my Sierra Club editors Annie Stine and Jim Cohee, whose faith in my work has been pleasantly startling.

It is the innocence which constitutes the crime.

James Baldwin, *The Fire Next Time*

*And he never was in Eden, because coyotes live
in the New World. Driven forth by the angel with
the flaming sword, Eve and Adam lifted their sad
heads and saw Coyote, grinning.*

Ursula K. LeGuin,
"A Non-Euclidean View of California
as a Cold Place to Be"

DUST, OR ERASING THE FUTURE:
THE NEVADA TEST SITE

From Hell to Breakfast

✠ DAWN WAS ONLY A FAINT GLOW BEHIND THE BLACK CRESTS
of Skull Mountain and the Specter Range when I swung off Highway
95 and arrived, ten hours hard driving away from home. It was still
too dark to pitch a tent, so I bundled my sleeping bag around me
and curled up on the car seat. An hour later, groggy and aching,
sleeping bag strings imprinted upon my cheek, I gave up on sleep
and ventured out with my tin cup in hope of coffee. Someone who'd
seen my little brother up at the gates of the encampment sent me
his way.

In the morning light everything looked familiar again, the hard
pale ground paved with rocks and the roads kicked into dust, the
evenly spaced tufts of thorny grasses and scrubby bushes—the almost ubiquitous texture of the Great Basin, the plateau between the
Sierra and the Rockies. The explorer John C. Fremont named it the
Great Basin in the 1840s, when he realized that this vast expanse
doesn't drain into either side of the Continental Divide. For one
thing, there's hardly anything to drain. The major river in this place,
the Humboldt, doesn't go anywhere at all; after flowing most of the
way across northern Nevada it fades away into an alkali flat. Range
after range of mountains, each separated by a flat expanse like the
one the camp was in, rise for hundreds of dry miles across the state
of Nevada into Utah, stretching north into Oregon and Idaho,
hemmed in on the south by the Colorado River. It was the lowest,
hottest, driest southwest corner of the Basin that I woke up in, and
across the Funeral Mountains to the west, the Basin ends, and California, Death Valley, and the Mojave Desert begin.

I remembered to be afraid of the dust, the dust that might be radioactive, the dust that over the next few days would powder everything to biscuit color, the dust that might be the dust of the hundreds of nuclear tests conducted somewhere across the highway I'd just driven in on. At first I hadn't been alarmed by the dust here, and later it became second nature to fear dust everywhere, but this dust didn't look like anything special to the naked eye. Most studies suggested that the background radiation at the Peace Camp wasn't any worse than that in Las Vegas, seventy miles to the south, since they were both upwind of most of the nuclear tests—though that wasn't comforting, especially if you lived in Las Vegas. It wasn't the background radiation but the fallout mixed into the fine, pale, silky powder that posed most threat, however. "I will show you fear in a handful of dust," said a poet.

But to see mortality in the dust by imagining in it the unstable isotopes of radioactive decay took an act of educated faith or perhaps of loss of faith in the government. It looked like ordinary dust, and perhaps it will be, so far as the health of most of those who camped here are concerned. And people were living in this dust I had driven into, in a place called the Peace Camp, the gathering place for thousands who came every spring to prepare to invade the Nevada Test Site. The particular basin we were in is sliced in half by Highway 95, and across the road, along with Skull Mountain and the Specter Range, is the Nevada Test Site, the place where the U.S. and Britain have been setting off nuclear bombs for four decades, more than 900 so far in the hot secret heart of the Arms Race.

✦ The Nevada Test Site (NTS) is big on a scale possible in few parts of the world, and in a way that only the West of the United States is big. The Test Site hewn out of Nellis Air Force Range in

1951 is 1,350 square miles, which makes it bigger than Yosemite National Park or Rhode Island. Nellis is a little over four times as big—5,470 square miles—bigger than Connecticut, a place that approaches one of the world's smaller nations in size—Israel, say, or Belgium. And if an army were to depopulate Belgium for half a century and explode hundreds of nuclear bombs on it, people would probably notice. Yet this has happened in the Great Basin, and few Americans know it has.

Before the bombs had gone underground, the public had been more aware of the goings-on at the NTS. The flashes were many times brighter than the sun, and those who were out before dawn could see the light of atomic fission from as far away as the mountaintops of northern California and southern Idaho. Strangely colored clouds drifted east across Nevada and Utah from the predawn explosions, and pictures of mushroom clouds sometimes appeared in the news. Nearby, the bombs felt like earthquakes. Since 1963, all of the tests here have been underground, but they have still been colossal explosions and they still leak radiation into the atmosphere. Since 1963, even most antinuclear activists haven't paid much heed to the Test Site. Nuclear war, whether you are for or against it, is supposed to be a terrible thing that might happen someday, not something that has been going on all along.

Test is something of a misnomer when it comes to nuclear bombs. A test is controlled and contained, a preliminary to the thing itself, and though these nuclear bombs weren't being dropped on cities or strategic centers, they were full-scale explosions in the real world, with all the attendant effects. I think that rather than tests, the explosions at the Nevada Test Site were rehearsals, for a rehearsal may lack an audience but contains all the actions and actors. The physicists and bureaucrats managing the U.S. side of the Arms Race had been rehearsing the end of the world out here, over and over again.

Even those who didn't question the legitimacy of the Arms Race sometimes questioned the necessity of testing. There were other ways to ensure the efficacy of existing nuclear weapons, and tests were only necessary for developing new weapons. The bombs set off in Nevada seemed instead a way of making war by display and displacement, as some cultures and species do—demonstrating their ability to attack rather than actually doing so. For every bomb set off in Nevada was potentially a bomb dropped on Odessa or Tashkent, and every bomb signified the government's willingness to drop a bomb on such a place, to pursue such a policy. And even if the bombs were invisible to most people in the U.S., the Soviets watched and took warning.

Other nations besides the U.S. and the U.S.S.R. had tested nuclear bombs, but only these two were rehearsing the end of the world, for they alone had developed enough bombs to annihilate not specific targets, but possibly whole continents of people and with them the natural order, the weather, perhaps the genetic codes of most living things. The bomb at Hiroshima was the end of a war, but the bombs on Tashkent and Odessa would have been the beginning of one, and the beginning of the end. The rehearsals were largely invisible, and so was the damage. Radiation is invisible, and the effects of radiation are invisible too. Although many more people are born with defects and die of cancer and other metabolic disorders in places affected by atomic fallout, the effects can only be calibrated statistically, with exhaustive research. There are already atomic epidemics, previews of what would happen to those who didn't die in an atomic war. And genetic damage—the scrambling of the codes—is as invisible as cancer, and as hard to trace to a cause. Radiation can make cells lose their memory, and loss of memory seems to be one of the cultural effects of the bombs too, for Americans forgot that bomb after bomb was being exploded here. Or perhaps people never forgot we were testing bombs, rehearsing the end of the world, but learned it so well and so deeply that the bomb-makers no longer needed to terrorize children with bomb drills, or adults with civil defense scenarios and mushroom clouds on TV. Perhaps the bomb came to affect us all as an invisible mutation in our dreams, a drama we could watch in our sleep instead of the Nevada skies.

The Test Site was a blank on many maps, a forgotten landscape, off limits to the public and swallowed up in a state which itself seemed sometimes to be overlooked by the rest of the country. Even though Nevada is growing rapidly, its population is still not much over a million, half of it in Las Vegas and most of the rest of it in the Reno–Carson City area. There aren't many people living in all that open space, and few artists and writers have celebrated its qualities. Not very many people were displaced when the land that became Nellis was sealed off in 1941, when the population of Nevada was around 110,000, and not many people objected, because this landscape is widely thought to be worthless already.

Space itself isn't an absolute, or at least the spaciousness of landscapes isn't. Up close, aridity means that even the plants grow far apart from each other; for people and animals, this sparseness means that they too have to spread out to make a living off the land. In the East, a cow can live off a few acres of grass; out here the land is often overgrazed at only a few cows per thousand acres, and where they overgraze the soil erodes back to dust and rock. It is rock—geology—that dominates this landscape. In lusher landscapes, it is as though the skin and bones of the earth are dressed in verdure; here the earth is naked, and geological processes are clearly visible. It is geological time and geological scale that dominate this landscape, dwarfing all the biological processes within the uplift of ranges, the accretion of basins. The very rocks on the ground have lain in place so long around the Test Site that their tops and bottoms are different colors, and any disturbance leaves a lasting scar. Every act out here has to be measured against this scale of change and scope. It is this apparent geology, this bare rock, that makes newcomers read the desert as a dead or barren landscape, though if you spend more time in it, you may come to see the earth itself lives, slowly and grandly, in the metamorphoses of geology.

✦ ABOUT HALF A MILE DOWN THE ROAD TO HIGHWAY 95, I found my little brother and eight of his friends piling into a station wagon, and when they urged me to join them, I crammed in. They were on their way down 95 to blockade the workers coming from Las Vegas to Mercury, the industrial town within the Test Site. They were merry inside the car, burbling inconsequentialities, joking, drinking out of water bottles, bota bags, and canteens, clad in Levis, flannel shirts, T-shirts advertising other actions and causes, in army surplus, bandannas, shawls, ethnic oddments, tights and thermals. That spring morning, the desert was cold. We passed the main gate to the Test Site, the gate on the road into Mercury, and kept going south. By day Mercury is a faint glimmer of dust-colored buildings five miles into the Test Site, but by night it looks like a quilt of fallen stars, the only electric light visible anywhere from the camp. These days most of the Mercury workers live in Las Vegas, and we were apparently planning on preventing them from getting to work. If there was a nuclear war going on, then there was a war against it as well, and this morning of March 30, 1990, these scruffy young people were the people who were fighting it most directly.

There were times when the conflict between government and activists became deadly serious, dangerous, even fatal for the activists, but there were more times when it was a neatly staged conflict in which both sides played by the rules. The rules on the activists' side were first and most crucially those of nonviolent direct action, often called civil disobedience. Nonviolence means not merely refraining from violence, but of working for change without violence—which means embodying the ideal you work for. Some political theorists call it "the politics of prefiguration," which means that it attempts to realize within the movement what it seeks to bring about on a grander scale. By making such change part of their means rather than simply their end, such activists have already begun to realize their goals, whether their action causes further change or not. Nonviolence also makes a qualitative rather than merely a strategic distinction between sides: To take violent action is to endorse violence as a means. And nonviolence disrespects violence, undermines force and might as arbiters of fate.

The theory of nonviolent direct action, first articulated in Henry David Thoreau's "Civil Disobedience," is a noble one. The practice is far more complicated. Many religious people, notably Catholics and Quakers, commit civil disobedience with quiet fervor; a lot of anarchists and other young radicals commit civil disobedience with an insurrectionary verve that is harder to associate with Gandhi and Martin Luther King. Like civil obedience it requires a tacit cooperation with some form of governmental authority—that's the civility of it. If Thoreau hadn't let himself be hauled off to jail and hadn't stayed there (until his aunt bailed him out), he would have been a tax cheat, not a civil disobedient. Every once in a while, the governmental body in charge gets wise and doesn't show up, neutralizing the civil disobedience and diluting the impact of the demonstration. Sometimes the civil disobedients get crushed—as they were in Tiananmen Square in 1989—and the government then wins the battle, but loses the support of the public. And sometimes the force of un-armed people in public places is enough to topple governments, as it has in Eastern Europe and other parts of the world in recent times.

Here nonviolent direct action most often gets trivialized, by the general population as well as by the media and the courts. At the trials, defense of necessity, prevention of a crime, and Nuremberg principles are almost never allowed to be introduced into court. The Thoreauvians are tried for acts stripped of political meaning—ob-structing a public thoroughfare, trespassing, damaging property, al-though unlike criminals, nonviolent direct activists take action publicly with readiness to deal with the consequences of their acts.

Civil disobedience has a proud directness to it, unlike all the sup-plicatory lobbying and petitioning that somehow endorse the im-balance of power they seek to redress. People who are shocked by others who break the law and challenge the government seem to re-gard government as a parent, to which we owe respect and obedi-ence (and they tend to confuse the country, which includes land and people, with the government that regulates them; "I love my country but I fear my government," says a bumper sticker that tries to straighten out this muddle). The government is not a finished work, and it must constantly be re-created, maintained, improved, cor-rected for the well-being of the land and people, and in this sense it is also a child.

Then, too, those who are shocked conceive of government as an inalienable whole. But the government as an ideal—the law and the source of justice—is often distant from the government as individ-uals engaged in specific acts, and citizens must often choose between the ideals and the individuals. There have been many illegal govern-ment acts in recent decades, and many questionable ones. And then there are higher laws: international laws, human rights, and natural law. The right to protest by speech and public assembly is in the First

Amendment. But the need to commit it is often an issue of natural law, of adherence to an idea of justice that transcends lawbooks. And the duty to commit civil disobedience is implicit in the international laws of the Nuremberg Principles, which signal the end of obedience as an adequate form of citizenship. The Nuremberg Principles are abstracted from the Nuremberg trials of Nazi war criminals who justified their acts as following orders, a justification the world refused to accept. "The fact that a person acted pursuant to an order of his government or of a superior does not relieve him of responsibility under international law, provided that a moral choice was in fact possible for him," says the fourth Nuremberg principle. The principles cover crimes against peace, war crimes, and crimes against humanity; the testing of nuclear weapons violates all three. These principles remove us from the shelter of authority—of doing what we do because we are told to do it—and put us in the roofless territory of individual conscience.

There's a nice symmetry between Thoreau's night in Concord jail in 1846 and the activity around the Nevada Test Site. By refusing to pay taxes, Thoreau was protesting the U.S.'s war on Mexico, which was a war for land. The land acquired through that war included Nevada and most of the Southwest, from Texas to California, though no one paid much attention to Nevada at the time; it was until 1861 part of Utah Territory anyway.

The morning after his night in jail, Thoreau took a group of his fellow citizens out huckleberrying.

✛ About three dozen people took over the two northbound lanes of Highway 95, which is a divided road as it approaches the Test Site. Luxury cruiser buses full of Test Site workers, pickups, Winnebagos, and four-wheel drives began to back up for blocks, then for half a mile. The arrests that began at seven that morning were rowdy. Activists were expected to wander into the Test Site, but not into oncoming traffic, so the sheriffs, thick and red-faced in tight, shortsleeved uniforms the same color as the dust, were irate. Most of the people sitting in the road used passive resistance—they didn't struggle, but they didn't cooperate with the people arresting them. They had to be carried off the road. Some of them entwined arms with each other and then linked their own hands beneath their knees, making a human chain. This was a surprise action and there was no place to take the blockaders away to until requisitioned buses came, so the handcuffed activists were put down by the side of the highway.

The crowd on the road thinned and the crowd by its shoulder thickened, then everyone suddenly rushed back onto the road and sat down again. Supporters standing on the gravelly freeway divider yelled at the sheriffs to treat the blockaders with care whenever they saw an arm being twisted or a body being dragged instead of carried. Other than these cries of care, it was as silent as a pantomime. Only rarely did a stopped car honk, a protester or sheriff speak. There was no way I was going to get arrested until after I had a cup of coffee, so I just watched. All the shadows that filled the hollows of the mountains were gone, chased out by the rising sun, and the landscape already had the flat, stark brightness of midday. As I watched the burly men picking up blockaders by arms and legs stiff with resistance, I saw their frail forms as *bodies,* as potential corpses and as pathetically vulnerable objects to put between the landscape and the military, and my eyes filled with tears.

Finally, the buses came and took all the handcuffed people away, including my little brother. (I fell into calling him that to distinguish him from all the other Davids, and all my other brothers, and I should add that he has been a little over six feet for the last decade or so, though he was smaller than me once.) He is an anarchist, and a key organizer for the antinuclear movement, and though he was initially an anarchist in the sense that innumerable punks were in the eighties, he has read his Bakunin and Kropotkin and is now very seriously an anarchist. Anarchy, I should explain, means not the lack of order but of hierarchy, a direct and absolute democracy. Voting democracy, as anarchists point out, simply allows a majority to impose its will on a minority and is not necessarily participatory or direct. They themselves continue the process of negotiation until all participants achieve consensus, until everyone—not merely a majority—has arrived at a viable decision. Anarchy proper usually works out to mean excruciatingly interminable meetings, rather than the mayhem the word evokes in most American imaginations. The Peace Camp and American Peace Test, which organized the camp and the actions, were run on anarchist lines: Each affinity group—the basic organizing unit of direct action—deliberated over the issues and then sent a spokesperson to represent its decisions at a spokescouncil.

During the Spanish Civil War, the writer Sylvia Townsend Warner once said of anarchy—the prevailing ideology of the Spanish antifascists—that "the world was not yet worthy of it, but it ought to be the politics of heaven." During the season that the movie *Reds* came out, my little brother, then still a teenager living at home, was so inspired by John Reed's extravagant Bohemian anarchy in the early part of the century that he imitated him, tacking a sign to our mother's front door that said, "Property is theft; walk right in," an ideal he put on hold when he moved to the city. I myself am not yet worthy of anarchy, or at least I have never found the patience and tolerance necessary to work with group consensus for extended periods. During the several years we both lived in San Francisco, however, my brother and I worked out a beautiful symbiosis: He was much better at going to meetings, and I was much better at spelling, so he organized, and I pitched in on the publication projects he took on and showed up for the demonstrations. Occasionally, like Thoreau's aunt, I paid his bail.

So many Americans seem to think that activism is an aberrant necessity brought on by a unique crisis, and then throw themselves into it with an unsustainable energy brought on by the belief that once they realize some goal or other, they can go home and be apolitical again. I always admired my brother for the steady nonchalance with which he approached his work, recognizing that political engagement was a normal and permanent state, and because however much he idealized direct action and populism, he never lost his ability to see the ludicrous aspects of the movement. He was the force that got me to Nevada the first time, though it was the desert and the bomb that kept me coming back again and again.

✛

After the bus pulled away, I went back to camp and pitched my tent beside three yuccas and crawled inside. Around noon I stuck my head out and looked up into the sky, which had filled with clouds while I slept. Rain fell straight into my eyes, a few light drops in a shower that lasted only a minute or so, and left the landscape as dry as before. I took out my water bottle and stove and made coffee, sitting in the door of my tent, bemused by the reduction of my domesticity to a bagful of gear, my privacy to a tube of ripstop nylon, to find myself drinking coffee in solitude in the middle of all the bustle of the camp surrounded by all the silence of the desert. That utter abstraction the Arms Race and its sister the Cold War only became believable for me when they acquired a location, a landscape: this landscape. This was the place where the end of the world had been rehearsed since 1951, and this was my third spring at the camp. We were living closer to nuclear war than anyone but its technicians and its victims, which should have been devastating, but we were doing something about it, which was heartening.

The present large-scale actions had begun in earnest a few years earlier. An annual Lenten vigil had been held out here since 1977—a remarkable Franciscan nun named Sister Rosemary had initiated it—and the spring actions had grown over the years, bringing together Quakers and other religious denominations with the Franciscans, then nonreligious activists (and pagans). Around the equinoxes was the only time most people could bear to live out in the desert at all, because the heat of summer and cold of winter were both fierce. Even in spring, the nights could be freezing and the days could climb into the nineties. Secular antinuclear activists decided that it was time to turn to the very heart of the Arms Race and held a thirty-day protest out here in 1985, organized by the direct-action task force of the national nuclear freeze movement. When the movement decided to quit sponsoring direct action, the task force split off into American Peace Test, the central organization in coordinating the mass actions since. This year, 1990, attendance was down a little, probably because so many Americans took the peaceful changes in the Eastern Bloc countries as a sign that everything would turn out all right without their participation. The Cold War, popular wisdom had it, was thawing. France had said it would stop testing if the U.S. and the U.S.S.R. did, and forty-one nations were clamoring for a comprehensive test ban treaty at the 1991 U.N. conference. And the U.S. was testing, despite the moratoriums of the U.S.S.R., and so we were here.

✚ ON A FEW OCCASIONS, PEOPLE ACTUALLY STOPPED NUCLEAR tests. Most people hadn't the stamina or conviction to do more than a ritual act of civil disobedience, a symbolic interference with the Arms Race, but some had walked to Ground Zero and prevented tests from taking place. Walking to Ground Zero meant carrying seventy-pound packs with gallons of water, walking by night and sleeping in gullies and mesa shadows by day, for three days or so. In 1986 a Greenpeace team showed up at Ground Zero and disrupted a scheduled test, but the team's announcement and photograph hardly made the news when it rushed them out over the wire services. In 1988, a woman walked to an observation tower at Ground Zero and locked her neck to a steel pole there. The precautionary guidelines American Peace Test published for such actions were terrifying in themselves: "The Nevada Test Site is a highly radioactive place with many hot spots, dumps, and storage areas. . . . There is little that can be done to protect your body from beta and gamma rays which are unseen and penetrate your body. Alpha particles, however, may have more longterm effects. They are found on dust particles that can be breathed in or ingested. Cover your face when walking in the wind. Do not eat food dropped on the ground. Don't use bare, dirty hands for eating. . . . A large test can throw someone three meters into the air at Ground Zero and kill them. There is a rippling of ground motion that goes out from this center. Detonations create limited earthquakes. The Nellis Air Force Base surrounds the Test Site on the east, west and north. Depending on which part you venture through, you will have to deal with ammunition strafing, falling bombs, unexploded bombs on the ground, maneuvering around targets, and Stealth bomber security. At the time of arrest, it is vital that team members make no sudden moves that might be considered threatening to the security forces. They are very well armed and quite capable of shooting if they feel threatened."

A lot of people hadn't gone all the way to Ground Zero, but had reached surprisingly far into the Test Site. Some Western Shoshone people had simply disregarded the fences and signs and continued to walk across the land, visit traditional sites, and hunt and gather on it during the decades after its withdrawal from the public domain in 1941, and Pauline Esteves, an elder from the Timbisha Shoshone community in Death Valley, remembers her uncle going deer hunting there in the 1940s. Presumably the place where all our nuclear weapons are tested should be a major national security area, but the government has always counted on the remoteness of the place and indifference of the people to shield its actions. In practice this place was liable to be overrun at any time, was an area without much security at all, even against a bunch of loosely organized pacifists.

The night that I first got arrested at the Test Site, something else happened there. I didn't hear the real story until years later, when I was driving one of the participants back from Nevada to San Francisco—another all-night drive on the route that had become a roster of familiar landmarks. On the last leg of the journey, past the white windmills of Altamont Pass and down through Livermore, California, where nuclear bombs are designed and the H-bomb was conceived, as daybreak came like a postcard in my rearview mirror, Rachel told me about the Princesses of Plutonium. The year before, at the Mother's Day 1987 action, two of the future Princesses had succeeded in reaching Mercury and had been cited and released with everyone else, and somehow going to Mercury became their goal. They talked about what they could do when they got there.

Rachel came up with the mask she had been using for another project, so they all acquired expressionless silvery robotic masks and white paper coveralls that looked like radiation suits.

At night, after the big arrest action in 1988, the Princesses of Plutonium took off for Mercury. "And we really were princesses. We travelled in comfort, with thermoses of coffee and tea and chocolate-covered espresso beans, and every time we had to hide, we had a little snack," Rachel recalled. They took a leisurely approach to the forbidden city, hiding and refreshing themselves frequently during the night. The last time they thought they were seen, they hid in a ditch, and during that halt they donned their rad suits and masks and waited, then climbed a fence at the eastern side of Mercury and began to walk around. "And we were there for a long time, ten of us, in the early morning on a Sunday, we stuck together and we put up stickers and things: We were really visible and we couldn't believe we were just free to walk around. Finally a Wackenhut came up, a red-faced senior guy I see at the cattleguard all the time now, and I'll never forget how shocked and scared he looked. He couldn't tell by looking if we were men or women or what.

"And they took us into custody and interviewed each of us alone for a long time. They were pretty cool; we all gave our name as Priscilla, after a particularly dirty balloon-dropped nuclear test in 1957, and the interviewer was saying that it certainly was a coincidence that there were so many of us with that name. Then they took us to Beatty, and we started to have problems. Some of the people who had never been arrested before were really scared, and got upset at others for leading them into this. They took us to jail and kept us till Tuesday [from Saturday]. We had to give our real names then; they took away our possessions and clothes, gave us jail uniforms, the works. But the peace camp was great. They came and did support actions outside the jail and some men went to Mercury in solidarity with us, and we could yell and sing at them in the jail. I tried to drink as little water as possible because the water there's really radioactive. When we got home, things started to fall apart with the Princesses. There was disagreement on how to handle the case and things. We worked on it for months, and then they dropped the charges."

✛

Priscilla exploded on June 24, 1957, fifth in the Plumbbob series of twenty-four large bombs. Unlike most Test Site bombs, this one was set off in the southeast corner of the Test Site, at Frenchman Flat, a few miles north of Mercury. Near Ground Zero were live pigs dressed in specially tailored military uniforms to test the fabrics' abilities to protect against thermal radiation. The explosion was bigger than expected, and the remote-control camera captured the pigs writhing and squealing as they died in what proved to be a pointlessly cruel exercise. Slightly further away were soldiers in trenches, one of whom wrote an account of Priscilla. Marine Lieutenant Thomas Saffer wrote, "A thundrous rumble like the sound of thousands of stampeding cattle passed directly overhead, pounding the trench line. Accompanying the roar was an intense pressure that pushed me downward. The shock wave was traveling at nearly four hundred miles per hour, pushed toward us by the immense energy of the explosion. The earth began to gyrate violently, and I could not control my body. Overcome by fear, I opened my eyes. I saw that I was being showered with dust, dirt, rocks, and debris so thick that I could not see four feet in front of me. . . . A light many times brighter than the sun penetrated the thick dust, and I imagined that some evil force was attempting to swallow my body and soul. . . . The metallic taste in my mouth was foul and would not go away." The Plumbbob tests dropped fallout from Oregon to New England.

✚ I CAME TO THE TEST SITE FOUR SPRINGS IN A ROW, AND THE third spring, the spring of 1990, the place began to make sense to me. The first year, the afternoon before the Princesses set out, I walked with friends into the arms of the waiting guards. We had simply climbed through the fence a short distance away from the road entrance to the place, and they had come to get us. The boundary of the site is marked by a barbed-wire fence, and the point at which one is trespassing on the road is the far side of the cattleguard (cattleguard, easterners and urbanites: a set of thick bars running the length of a trench across the road, easy for human feet to cross by stepping on the bars but impossibly treacherous for hooves). It seems typically Western that all the Test Site boundaries are designed to obstruct livestock rather than people, for no serious walker is halted by a cattleguard in the road or a fence across the land.

My second year at the Test Site I went in with a bunch of anarchist women from San Francisco and Seattle. Two of the northerners became friends of mine later, but I didn't know any of them well at the time. We'd agreed that we would pair off so that no one got abandoned or left at the guards' mercy without a witness, and then we'd hiked northwest up 95 about a mile north of the main gate, so that we'd have time to cover some ground before we were interfered with. I'm not sure what our purpose was—curiosity?—but my own desire was always to walk as long as possible across the land that was off limits. "Reclaim the Test Site," the big American Peace Test action of spring 1988 had been called. Walking claims land not by circumscribing it and fencing it off as property but by moving across it in a line that however long or short connects it to the larger journey of one's life, the surrounding roads and trails, that makes it part of the web of experience, confirmed by every foot that touches the earth.

Actually, that spring afternoon in 1989 the dozen other women and I only got about a quarter mile in, walking in a gully that made it hard to see us from the land, before the helicopters found us, swooping low overhead with men in paramilitary uniforms leaning out ready to jump. If we were conducting our war as a picnic meander, they were conducting their job as a military maneuver. But when the hovering copter got low enough to pelt us with gravel spat from the ground by its gust of air, we ran, and the men leapt out and ran after us. I ran madly in the bad footing of the desert, with its soft patches of sand and crusted-over dust, cobbled stretches, boulders, loose rocks, and low bushes, only slowing down enough to keep pace with the woman with whom I'd paired off. The anarchists were all wearing vivid colors, and I in my dusty khaki regretted that we were so visible. I wondered this time, as I did so many others, whether I could disappear from view if I walked by myself, but solitude was discouraged here—it could be dangerous.

I ran for a ways without looking back, and then I turned my head a little and saw a man in camouflage all but close enough to grab me, far closer than I expected. He must have decided to join another chase, because it seems unlikely that I actually outran him. And running was one of the things that we usually agreed not to do, as it wasn't in keeping with the spirit of nonviolent direct action. Urgent, unpredictable, quick actions threw the security forces into a panic, made it possible for things to go astray.

I gave up easily, letting them handcuff my hands behind my back, but my companion resisted, letting the two guards know why she was here and by what laws she had the right to be here. She cited the fact that the land was stolen from the Western Shoshone in the first place, and that we had permission from them to be here, that she was following the Nuremberg Principles they were violating. Now I can't even remember which of the women she was, only the unwavering conviction with which she refused to cooperate. She refused to walk, too, and so they herded the two of us into another gully and handcuffed us ankle to ankle. One stood guard over us while the other went for reinforcements. The other women were no longer visible. Picture an immensity of flatness populated only by two immobilized women and two men in camouflage, one of whom was rapidly disappearing. There was nothing to say. The Test Site looked exactly like the landscape outside, though we were now unable to stand up in it because of our shackles.

The second guard came back with a third man. While one guard walked behind me to make sure that I didn't attempt to flee, the other two picked her up, each taking one arm and one leg, and carried her. We progressed a couple of hundred yards in this way, when an older, red-faced guard joined our group of five. He snarled at the guards not to indulge her by carrying her. First he got them to drag her by her arms, then he got them to stop going around the obstacles. They began to drag her through thornbushes and over cacti.

He had convinced them to engage in a mild form of torture, and it didn't seem to have occurred to any of them that they could refuse his orders, though it was this kind of mindless obedience that the Nuremberg Principles she cited were made to combat. Finally she gave up and, near tears, asked them to stop. She began to walk, so she wouldn't be dragged. We walked to the dirt road that ran parallel to the Test Site periphery, where a big van was waiting for us, along with several of the other women in our group. The van was there to take us to the huge holding pens the Department of Energy had built a year or so before, next to the main gate. The guards cut off the plastic handcuffs we were bound with and rehandcuffed us with our hands in front, letting the cut pairs lie where they fell. My companion offered me a drink of water from the bota bag they hadn't confiscated, then she took off her hiking boot with awkward double-handed gestures and took out her Swiss army knife. I pulled out as many of the thorns in her foot as I could with the knife's tweezers. Some of them were huge, and one long one broke off deep in her foot.

✚ I HAVE TROUBLE WITH THE ABSTRACT AND THE CONCRETE. IN the abstract we were committing civil disobedience in the cause of peace and justice, making a gesture that echoed the gestures of Thoreau in Concord in 1846 and the trials in Nuremberg in 1946, the resistance of the Shoshone and of pacifists in many places and times. In the concrete we were scrabbling around in the scrub, playing tag with a bunch of mercenaries who thought that we were completely demented. My faith wavers. I always had trouble seeing the guards as representatives of U.S. military policy rather than as rednecks with limited career options, though I think many of the activists at the Test Site had the opposite problem, that perhaps the concrete didn't complicate their abstract ideals. The invisible background to all this, to our plastic handcuffs, to the thorn that broke off in her foot, to the helicopter pelting gravel and the men making a living by wearing camouflage and chasing pacifists, to the whole ramshackle peace camp and direct action, the background we would never see, was even harder to keep in mind: huge nuclear weapons detonations in preparation for international wars and as part of a local nuclear war nearing the forty-year mark.

There is a theory about lines of energy that traverse the earth, running through sacred sites, called "ley lines." The people who have developed this theory demonstrate it by showing the alignment of important sites along straight lines. I'm not sure about ley lines, but I believe in lines of convergence. These lines are no more visible in the landscape than ley lines, and I am not even proposing that they have any existence at all outside our imaginations—

which are themselves crucial territories. These lines of convergence are the lines of biography and history and ecology that come together at a site, as the history of nuclear physics, the Arms Race, anti-Communism, civil disobedience, Native American land-rights struggles, the environmental movement, and the mysticism and fanaticism deserts seem to inspire in Judeo-Christians all come together to make the Nevada Test Site, not as a piece of physical geography, but of cultural geography, not merely in the concrete, but in the abstract. Such places bring together histories which may seem unrelated—and when they come together it becomes possible to see new connections in our personal and public histories and stories, collisions even. A spiderweb of stories spreads out from any place, but it takes time to follow the strands.

There's a strangely popular subject of speculation for hikers and explorers: whether they were the first people ever to tread on a piece of land. It comes out of the American obsession with virgin wilderness, which is itself a deeply problematic idea, and it speculates about the possibility of the utterly new, of an experience without predecessors. It is usually mistaken in its premises. There are few places in North America that were not first walked upon by the indigenous inhabitants of the continent, and even if one were to take out one's mountaineering gear and reach a peak literally untouched before by human beings, one is making a gesture that depends for its meaning and motives on a long history of such gestures. Though you may be the first to climb a peak in the Sierra and your foot may touch a place no human foot has touched, you are covering cultural territory covered by great mountaineers from Clarence King and John Muir onward. And the actual act of climbing a mountain depends for its meaning on the romantic cult of mountains, and so even if you have never read Shelley's "Mont Blanc," you have inherited it, and when you step on that piece of ground, you step where Shelley went, and where a wide road of meaning has been worn since. You may not know that the Italian poet Petrarch was the first modern man who climbed a mountain for the pleasure of the view, but you are treading in his six-hundred-year-old footsteps. New or old, it seems you should know where you came from to understand where you are, and only a true and absolute amnesiac could come from nowhere in arriving somewhere. We all carry the burden of history and desire; sometimes it's good to sit down and open the suitcases.

I want to be able to see the history of gestures behind even a voyage into the new, and I want more to be able to remember the lines of convergence that lead to a place like the Nevada Test Site. This is the abstract whose weight I have tried to feel behind every concrete gesture at the Test Site, a place that however few may see it, however invisible it may be, is the hub of so many crucial lines of our history. But it was hard to remember all this while pulling thorns out of someone's sweaty foot with my hands cuffed together.

✚ However foolish and futile this antinuclear activism seemed close up, at a distance it commanded respect. Maybe it was an accident that we helped inspire an extraordinarily successful movement on the other side of the globe, and maybe it wasn't. The fact remains that on February 12 and 17, 1989, underground nuclear tests vented radiation into the atmosphere in Kazakhstan, the central Asian republic where the Soviets tested most of their nuclear weapons and where the environment and human health had suffered terribly from radiation over the decades. And on February 27, the Kazakh poet Olzhas Suleimenov appeared live on television and instead of reading his poetry as scheduled, he read a statement condemning nuclear testing and calling for a public meeting. The next day 5,000 people came to the Hall of the Writers Union in Alma Ata, the Kazakh capital, and named themselves the Nevada-Semipalatinsk Antinuclear Movement, in solidarity with the antinuclear and indigenous activists of Nevada—an extraordinary line of convergence running from test site to test site halfway round the globe.

Local officials were members of this movement, along with distinguished professionals and many, many writers. On the confident assumption that the Test Site activists had the same kind of entrenchment in local institutions, the Nevada-Semipalatinsk Antinuclear Movement sent statements of solidarity to Nevada government officials, who must have been bemused to find that Communists thought they had a lot in common. In October, two huge Soviet tests triggered demonstrations of tens of thousands of Kazakhs, the republic's miners threatened to go on strike, and more than a million people signed the Nevada-Semipalatinsk statement opposing nuclear testing. However bleak the political situation, the culture was enviable, one in which a poet had such power and the public could join together so effectively. By October 21, 1989, the Soviets had stopped testing, begun a unilateral moratorium, and agreed to close the sites down altogether by the mid-nineties.

The people of the Nevada-Semipalatinsk Movement had timing on their side, of course. They began in the midst of the reforms sweeping the Soviet Union, when the nation was in fragile condition, when all things nuclear still recalled the meltdown at Chernobyl for most Soviet citizens, when civil disobedience and public demonstration had become a powerful new tool for them and for Eastern Europeans. Kazakhs would say, "We realized nuclear testing was bad, and so we demanded that our government stop it, and so they did. We don't understand why you don't do the same thing." Then the U.S. activists would try to explain the military-industrial complex, the sabotage of democracy by money politics, and the way that the U.S. government has successfully ignored popular protest, realizing that trivialization and obliviousness are its most effective weapons, the way the media overlooked us and everything else that took place in the state of Nevada.

That year, 1989, the year of the cactus thorns and of Suleimenov's statement, law-enforcement officials arrested 1,090 people for trespassing in one fell swoop, unloaded us into the special cattle pen they'd built for us, left us there with a canister of water and a portable toilet for the afternoon, then loaded us onto buses. They used the same buses for us that they used to transport the workers from their homes in Las Vegas to Mercury, air-conditioned coaches with tinted windows, reclinable seats, even toilets. It was a peculiar experience, sitting on the soft upholstery provided by the Department of Energy, watching the scenery roll by at sixty or seventy miles an hour on the way up 95. My first year there, 1988, they'd taken all 1,200 of us nearly 200 miles north to the remote town of Tonopah, and I had worried that they wouldn't take us that far unless they planned on hanging onto us for a while. It was a long enough ride, on that strange road as the sun set, to imagine many things. But every year they just hauled us north to inconvenience us, unloaded us a few buses at a time, snipped off our cuffs, and told us to go away and not come back. (Usually we were dumped in Beatty—"gateway to Death Valley"—a former mining boomtown that had restaurants with fingerbowls and tuxedoed waiters in 1906, but was more of a corn-dog kind of place by my time, and was the town where the Princesses had been held.) By the end of the ten-day event in 1988, 2,000 people had been arrested from among the 5,000 participants—and no charges were pressed in the vast majority of the cases. It was one of the biggest civil disobedience arrests in U.S. history, and it barely made the local news.

In 1988, the nuclear bombs exploded at the Test Site were named Kernville, Abeline, Schellbourne, Laredo, Comstock, Rhyolite, Nightingale, Alamo, Kearsage, Bullfrog, Dahlhart, and Misty Echo. Most of them ranged from 20 to 150 kilotons (Hiroshima was laid waste with 15 kilotons, Nagasaki with 21), as did 1989's bombs: Texarkana, Kawich, Ingot, Palisade, Tulia, Contact, Amarillo, Disko Elm, Hornitos, Muleshoe, Barnwell, and Whiteface. They didn't make the news either.

✚ THE REASONS WHY WE DIDN'T GET MORE SEVERE TREATMENT had to do with money and land. The land of the Nevada Test Site is itself under considerable dispute. The U.S. Department of Energy (DOE), which operates the Test Site, has an agreement whereby the Nye County authorities are responsible for legal aspects of the security of the site. It's supposed to have been a tradeoff for the economic benefits of having a major employer in the county. But Nye, the second largest county in the U.S., has a population in the low ten thousands, and though the DOE subsidizes Nye County sheriffs arresting activists, it doesn't pay the county to put activists through the legal system. So every year they've rounded us up and hauled us away and tossed us out with a reprimand or two: As long as they don't prosecute us, we serve as an additional light seasonal income for the county, rather than a burden on it. It resembles a cattle roundup more than a criminal arrest process, what with the quantity of people, the logistics of large-scale cuffing and busing, and the general lack of animosity between parties. Some people said that Nye was trying to annoy the DOE into patrolling its own premises by letting us off so lightly.

The land shouldn't really be controlled by any of these authorities, however—local, state, or federal—because legally the Nevada

Test Site is part of a much larger expanse that never really became part of the United States. U.S. claim to the land is based on the Treaty of Guadalupe Hidalgo, the 1848 treaty by which the U.S. concluded its war with Mexico, the war Thoreau went to jail to protest. It was that treaty, and a $15 million sweetener, which transformed northwestern Mexico into the southwestern states of the United States, from western Texas and New Mexico to California. What was then called Utah Territory was of little concern to either side at the time. Utah was named after the Utes, a linguistic and cultural subgroup of one of the continent's major indigenous groups, the Shoshonean people. From the Wyoming Rockies to the Sierra, and from Idaho to California's Mojave, tribes including the Western and Mountain Shoshone, Bannock, Utes, and Northern and Southern Paiutes lived for centuries before the first Mormons and mountain men wandered in. It was a Wind River Shoshone woman, Sacajawea, who with her newborn baby in her arms led Lewis and Clark on their journey across the continent in 1805–1806 to find a way to the Pacific and to begin the national imagining of a sea-to-sea United States. And it was Shoshonean peoples who learned how to live within the severe limits and delicate balances of the Great Basin, who made it a home and named its places long before Fremont and the Death Valley Forty-Niners applied the morbid appellations of their eastern imaginations to the place.

Nevada means snowy, a sign that Nevada was settled from the western, Sierran side, and it only became a separate territory, and a territory settled by non-Mormon whites, when it turned out that Nevada was full of gold and silver. Much of Nevada still belongs to the Western Shoshone. The Western Shoshone do not believe that land can be sold, and they have never sold their land. Nor have they given it away, or leased it, or been conquered as a nation by the nation of the United States; for all intents and purposes, they have never ceded their land, and nothing has superseded the treaty they signed with the U.S. in 1863 (and the Treaty of Guadalupe Hidalgo also asserts that prior land ownership would be respected by the new government). Called the Treaty of Ruby Valley, for the lush region in northeastern Nevada where it was signed, it describes the vast expanse of the Western Shoshone Nation and states the terms by which the Shoshone might cede their land and become reservation Indians. The reservations and other treaty terms were never met, however, and the Shoshone never ceded their land, and they are still fighting for their right to it today. The federal government has admitted their legal ownership of the land to the extent of trying to force the Shoshone to accept payment for it, but the paltry sum allocated still sits in a Department of the Interior bank account, where it has more than doubled since the government granted itself permission to purchase the land in the 1970s. And the Nevada Test Site is in the southwestern corner of the 43,000 square miles of the nation the Western Shoshone call *Newe Sogobia,* and nuclear testing, along with many other military and industrial assaults on the environment, violates Shoshone religious beliefs. So the Shoshone have become active in the international struggle against nuclear testing, and they issue permits to be on their land, and one of the pleasant things that can be said to one's arresting officer is that he, in fact, is the one who is trespassing.

✙

There's something profoundly American about getting arrested at the Nevada Test Site: The very issues are, not cowboys and Indians, but land, war technology, apocalypse, Thoreauvian civil disobedience, bureaucratic obscurity, and Indians, part of the great gory mess of how we will occupy this country, whose questions are as unsettling as its land is unsettled. Then, of course, after being unhandcuffed and thrown out, the obvious thing to do is to celebrate, which in Beatty means going to one of the diner-cum-casinos for drinks and American food. To start the day in the deadly cold of a desert morning, sitting on rocks and drinking coffee, to fill one's water bottle and mill around with friends and acquaintances as the day gradually creeps toward hotness, to sit through a sometimes stirring and often dull rally of speeches and music (folk to punk and back again), to commit the fairly abstract act of climbing under a wire fence that separates the rocky expanse of cactus and creosote bushes from the rocky expanse of creosote bushes and cactus, to be confronted by hired help in the wrong-colored camouflage (as though they, not we, had a use for stealth), to go through numerous pairs of disposable plastic handcuffs as we captives are rearranged, to idle in a sort of cattle pen built just for us, to be escorted after many hours in the sun into a special luxury bus and be given a tour of scenic Highway 95, to be interrogated by hard-faced sheriffettes with piles of teased hair who are irritated by anyone who wants to give a more complicated name than Jane Doe or Shoshone Guest, to be tossed out into a small town, to catch up on one's friends' well-being and head for fast food and ice cream in the middle of the night, to plunk quarters into slot machines while waiting for the food to come, winning the occasional handful of change, to retrace the pointless route as the liberated activists get driven back to the camp, to wander back through the rocks and thorns in the dark to a sleeping bag on hard, uneven ground under a sky more full of stars than almost anyplace else in the world—could anything be more redolent of life, liberty, and the pursuit of happiness?

✚ AND IN 1990 I GOT COWBOYS. FRIDAY AFTERNOON THE arrested roadblockers started to trickle back into camp and the workshops began. Every action included a day of workshops on issues relevant to the action, from the philosophy of nonviolence to the physics of radiation. I chose a workshop on Nevada and the military, which was scheduled to meet on a rise between two administration-center tents that afternoon, and when I got there I turned out to be the only one who cared about such concrete, local things. The workshop came with a lot of maps of Nevada, and it was given by an exuberant young Nevadan named Bob Fulkerson, who wore a Stetson hat over his strawberry-blond hair and spoke with a drawling verve. He had been for some years the executive director of Citizen Alert, a statewide group "working for public participation and government accountability in issues of concern to Nevadans," according to its mission statement, really a political group out to save the Nevada environment from the depredations of water-greedy cities, apocalyptic military technology, mining, and the indifferent administration of federal bureaucrats.

Bob is a fifth-generation Anglo-Nevadan, rare in a state that had no settled white population halfway through the last century; and one of his relations rode with the Jesse James Gang on its last holdup. A hellraiser with high ideals, he told horror stories without piety or grief, but with a cheerful hostility that made it clear he relishes his work. He told me stories about Nevada and the military all afternoon. In the course of them, I began to pick up the jargon: the DOE, MOAs (Military Operations Areas), FONSIs (findings of no significant interest), Secret Area 51, the Bravo 16 Bombing Range, the contamination of NTS Area 25, the proposed tank range at Tonopah Gunnery Range, the 1,389 live bombs and 123,375 tons of scrap ordnance picked up on public land by a Navy explosive team in what was called "Operation Ugly Baby." One story that stuck with me was about Dixie Valley in central Nevada, where the Navy decided to test sonic booms close over the inhabitants' heads, until finally it succeeded in driving them out, buying their homes for a pittance and burning them to the ground. Bob told me about a woman who used to raise thoroughbreds in Dixie Valley and works in a laundromat now. And he told me about nearby Yucca Mountain, slated to become the nation's first permanent high-level nuclear waste repository, the Groom Range to the east of us, and the Shea-hans who had been on the Groom Range for four generations. As we talked a dust devil ripped through camp, picking up hundreds of Shoshone guest permits—small white slips of paper—and spinning them fifty feet into the air. Then it lifted a huge black tarp and carried it over the camp, flapping loudly and looking like a pterodactyl. Its shadow crept across people, cars, and land, growing and shrinking like a separate creature as the tarp's altitude changed.

In the 1890s, the Sheahans began mining in the Groom Range, an area in southern central Nevada that has never had much of a white population. They stayed there for generations, mining silver and lead above Groom Dry Lake. An independent-spirited woman named Margaret Long, who spent much of the 1930s exploring the California-Nevada desert and tracing the routes of the Death Valley Forty-Niners, visited the Sheahans in what must have been the early years of that decade: "The Sheahan family was waiting with true desert hospitality to welcome the strangers whose car they had watched emerging from the mysterious distance across the great dry lake. They provided a fine supper, during which we listened to the radio. Across the same wilderness through which exhausted emigrants had steered this chartless course in 1849 came a distant discussion of the Boulder Dam bill from the Senate in Washington."

Two decades later, when Boulder Dam had backed up the waters of the wild Colorado dozens of miles and generated the electricity

that lit the casinos of Vegas, another guest showed up on the Sheahan doorstep. The polite man from the Atomic Energy Commission
(AEC)—a more candid name for what is now the DOE—said that
there would be some testing going on to the west, at Yucca Flat, in
what had been Nellis Air Force Range since 1941. The family then
consisted of Dan, who had inherited the mine from his father, his
wife, Martha, and their sons, Pat and Bob; and the mine—now solely
a lead mine—had just been improved with the construction of a
hundred-thousand-dollar concentration mill. The Sheahans stayed.
Before dawn on February 2, 1951, their house shook, the front
door burst open, and several windows broke. An 8-kiloton nuclear
bomb—about half the size of that dropped on Hiroshima six years
before—had just been dropped on Yucca Flat. Code-named Baker-
2, it was the fourth in the Ranger series of five nuclear weapons—
the fifth, a 22-kiloton bomb, would explode four days later.

In September of 1951, several months after atomic testing began
in Nevada, a delegation of AEC men arrived and told the Sheahans
that there was some danger from radioactive fallout. They said that
women and children should leave during nuclear tests, and gave Dan
Sheahan monitoring equipment with which to sample the effects of
the blasts. The fallout clouds kept coming, like rainstorms sweeping
over the valley, except that dust rather than water fell. The Sheahans
began to see cattle with silver-dollar-sized white spots on their
backs, found dead animals with the same white spots, and noticed
the wildlife becoming scarcer. Dan Sheahan once spoke of encountering a herd of horses that wandered east onto the Sheahan lands
with their eyes burnt out, left empty sockets by a blast.

All the tests took place when the winds were supposed to be east-
erly or northeasterly, because there were fewer people in that direction than any other. West of the Test Site is Los Angeles, south of it
is Las Vegas, northeast of it, closer than any other permanent dwell-

ing at that time, was the Groom Mine. During 1951 and 1952 the Sheahans continued their friendly relations with the AEC men who showed up to take the radiation samples and tell them when further tests would be conducted. In 1953, the Air Force began strafing the property with planes. That summer, while the family was having lunch, a high-explosive incendiary bomb hit the mill and blew it up.

Dan and Martha Sheahan died of cancer. They never told anyone about the bombing, because they were still trying to get along with the Air Force, though the photographs of the shattered mill have been published since. Their sons continued to try to work the mine. In early 1984 Pat Sheahan was driving to it when he ran into a roadblock. Armed men from the DOE and the Air Force told him that the land had been closed to the public "for national security reasons." That spring the Air Force claimed 89,000 acres of Nevada public land—144 square miles—and put it off limits to ranchers, miners, hunters, and anyone else who came along. The Groom Mine was in the middle of this vast chunk of Bureau of Land Management land, and neither the private nor the public land had been taken legally. Any parcel over 5,000 acres has to be withdrawn from the public domain by an act of Congress, but Congress only gave the seizure a meek and retroactive blessing with a four-year authorization. In hearings, an Air Force official acknowledged that the decision had been made "at the Secretary of the Air Force level or higher," meaning that the Secretary of Defense or then-President Reagan had authorized it. The Sheahans and a rancher were given permission to enter the now-restricted area, but they could no longer work their mine, since they couldn't bring anyone with them. The withdrawal was supposed to make a national security area more secure by preventing anyone from peeking into Nellis proper—it was a buffer zone, a zone of invisibility.

On June 15, 1988, the Congressional authorization expired, and on June 16 the withdrawal was extended, but during the hours when the land was public again Citizen Alert staffer Grace Bukowski and Nevada physician-activist Richard Bargen entered the Groom Range and staked mining claims. The Mining Law of 1872 allows mining to preempt all other activities on public land and allows anyone who stakes a claim to develop it. Theoretically, then, the two claimstakers had mounted a significant obstacle to closing off the lands again—which was their intention. On July 29, Grace, Bob Fulkerson, and two other activists came out to the Groom Range to mark the claims' borders. A helicopter monitored them as they moved across public land, and at 10:00 p.m., when they crossed the Air Force boundary line, heavily armed commandos surrounded them.

The part of the story that Bob left out, Grace told me later. While they were surrounded by invisible soldiers, Bob began to sing, and he held off the troops for an hour and a half by singing songs about Nevada—"And he never sang the same one twice," Grace said. She could see one soldier because his teeth gleamed in the darkness as he laughed. Finally, they surrendered, were taken to the tiny town of Alamo, cited for trespass, and released.

The Groom Range land is now part of Nellis, and insulates Secret Area 51 against public scrutiny. Although outrage over the appropriation of the tract has died down, another interest has arisen: UFO believers claim that the area is home for the "Black Project," a secretive, illicit program which tests alien aircraft and devices including antimatter reactors, gravity waves, and flying saucers. The tiny town of Rachel has a flourishing restaurant-bar called the Little A-le-Inn, which caters to those who make the pilgrimage to this remote site in hope of a glimpse of alien spacecraft. The area is patrolled by Wackenhuts, the same private security guards that patrol the Test Site.

Bob didn't delve into the UFO lore on Area 51. He was sufficiently preoccupied by earthly use of the land, and his story about the Groom Range ended with the 1988 mining-claim occupation. In 1990 he and Grace were still waiting to be tried, and they had offered to suspend their right to develop the mining claims for fifteen years if the Defense Department would add civilians to its land-abuse review panel and compensate Nevada acre-for-acre for withdrawn lands.

Like Moths to a Candle

✠ LATER IN THE AFTERNOON, DIZZIED BY BOB'S ACRONYMS AND horror stories, I set out due west for the mesas beyond the camp. (That year the Bureau of Land Management had driven American Peace Test out of the site it usually used, opposite the road to Mercury on 95, and so the camp was a few miles further from Vegas and closer to the Spring Mountains.) The camp was an anthill of people all purposefully heading in different directions: toward water, planning meetings, meals, shade, music. At its heart was the cluster of striped pavilions and huge army-surplus tents in which registration, meetings, first aid, and other community functions took place, along with a water truck and port-a-potties. There was always a women's encampment a little distance from this center, and other groups made their own little hamlets—the San Francisco and Seattle anarchists, for example, usually camped together under a black flag. The tents grew further apart as they moved away from the center, and from the roads where cars could go, and then the desert became itself again.

About ten minutes after I set out, on the fringes of the camp, I ran into the landscape photographer Richard Misrach walking an equally straight line south. He was unmistakable at a distance, for he was carrying his view camera—a mahogany box the size of a small TV on a tripod as tall as he was. A view camera, which makes huge negatives with an unparalleled sharpness of detail, was the camera with which the West was first photographed and is still the instrument of choice for many contemporary landscapists. I had met him for the first time at the Test Site the year before—I had been told to look for his camera, he for my pallor—and the first thing he said to me was that I should remember to put sunscreen under my chin and on my ears. He was himself burned brown and more at home in the desert than anyone else not born to it I knew: He explored remote and forbidden areas for weeks in his van and would walk around all day under a broiling sun hatless, in an undershirt. For the preeminent landscape photographer in the country, and for a man of immense drive, he was also very amiable—and an honorary Princess of Plutonium. That day, after we disposed of the topic of sunburn, we began a conversation about landscape and its representation that continues still.

He himself had been engaged with the subject far longer than I had. His early photographs, in the seventies, addressed social issues, and when they failed to have an impact he decided to abandon politics and return to nature. The ensuing images, of Stonehenge at night, of the rainforest as a turbulent jumble, refined his vision, and as he began to spend more and more time in the Mojave and Great Basin deserts, he found that the further he went into what was supposed to be wilderness, the more he found politics. By the middle of the 1980s, the work bore witness to an array of human follies in the American outback: manmade fires, floods, ruins, and abandoned settlements, tourists standing in a dry lakebed gawking at an empty sky where a space shuttle was supposed to appear. As time went on, the military in the desert became a central concern of his work, and he photographed the Enola Gay hangar in Wendover, Utah, where the pilots who bombed Hiroshima and Nagasaki trained, the Test Site and the actions there, and the illegal Navy bombings of public land at Bravo 20 Bombing Range. He called each series a canto, after Dante's cantos about Hell, Purgatory, and Paradise, and his last canto had been called *The Pit*. It documented a place near Fallon, Nevada, where ranchers dumped livestock that had died of diseases or unknown causes. The images gave a subject that would normally only be handled in the grainy black and white of photojournalism a monumental lushness and subtlety of color that made eyes linger on the atrocities. The animal pictures had taken landscape—or perhaps nature—photography beyond where it had ever been: eliminating the horizon and the distance, describing the bloated, twisted corpses of mustang foals and Herefords and longhorns in the poetic language usually reserved for the reassuringly beautiful. These bodies which had literally been thrown away took on the sensual immediacy of the warm-hued bodies of saints and concubines in baroque painting: A dead steer was foreshortened in the same way as in Caravaggio's painting of a man fallen into the foreground from his horse in *The Conversion of Saint Paul,* and carried the same revelatory weight. It was these pictures that had sprung to mind early that morning when I was watching the sheriffs drag the bodies of protestors off the highway—their frailty and vulnerability and the reality of their bodies as interventions in a huge, violent process.

This year, I was supposed to be writing about his work for a New York art magazine, and we'd been talking about landscape ideologies back in the Bay Area. I was overflowing with unripe ideas, and so the fruits of my research spilled forth. On and on I went, as I will go on for you presently. Finally Richard told me that he had to go because the light was perfect, and so he continued south and I continued west.

✢

The hour after dawn and the hour before sunset are called the magic hour by cinematographers and photographers, because it is then that shadows lick across the land with a velvety dark strangeness, light fills the air with something as palpable and rich as honey, and the earth seems to glow with all the warmth it had absorbed during the day.

The landscape that looks so homogenous at a glance, its plants scattered with the immense regularity dictated by scarcity of water and enormous root systems, changed as I walked. The rocks changed. I passed through a stretch where the rocks were crumbly, with rusty patterns that looked like petroglyphs running through them, then through a stretch where the desert pavement was dominated by great pink cobblestones of rose quartz. The cacti multiplied in size, and in variety, and number: The ecology had changed even by the slight rise toward the mountains I'd achieved—if they should be called mountains, instead of mesas, or hills, or outcroppings, or teeth of stone in the basinmouth. Geologically, they are uplifting mountain ranges, though many of them are no higher than hills. I saw small barrel cacti, beavertail cacti, and cacti like candelabra gone wild, some of them dead and reduced to gray skeletons. The ground is a maze of rocks and thornbearing plants, and weaving through the low obstacles can make you lose your course unless you pick out a sightline, as rowers do.

Halfway up the slope, the rock became crumbly and nearly black, the lava flow of an ancient volcano, and then it became a slatey stone, and I was scrambling through patches of scree. There were little caverns, lava porches really, further up. When I reached the top, I could see a volcanic cone far inside the Test Site that had always been invisible from basin-level and, in another direction, snowy peaks far away; even in the southeast a new vista of a flat expanse running all the way to the horizon opened up. The whole landscape which seemed so set and unchanging became something almost unrecognizable a few hundred feet further up. The rocks on top were neat little sandwiches of dove-gray and butter-yellow strata, and nothing like the rocks below. As the sun sank, the whole basin drained of color, but for the easternmost range, licked by the last rays into gold. The light was perfect, and then it was gone.

I went back down to the camp and brushed my hair and discovered something in the dark: It gave off showers of sparks with every stroke, as though my head were itself clad in a tiny theater of lightning. Moths flew into my small light, a Mexican votive candle whose side bore an image of the Virgin of Guadalupe with her cloak of roses, and these moths died too quickly in the molten wax to be rescued. Even this modest introduction into the natural world was fatally disruptive: The moths that navigate by night's celestial bodies were never prepared to actually encounter them, and so moths have no defense against flames. Once again I felt the force of scale in this place: the tiny radius of my candlelight within the thousands of miles of sparsely inhabited basin and range, the continuous sweep of the ground I was sitting on, like an ocean of rock, its waves become ranges washing east from here, scores of them between me and the Wasatch Mountains halfway into Utah where the Basin ends, all pressed under a black sky heavy with stars.

✚ I HAD NOT KNOWN WHEN I LIT THE CANDLE THAT IT WOULD kill those moths. Whether their deaths have had further repercussions on the environment I will never know. And I don't know now whether coming to the Test Site will kill me, whether some small particle of strontium or cesium in the dust will inaugurate a course of growth that will prove fatal. If you believe the statements by the men responsible for testing the bombs out here, they were no more intending the human deaths they would cause than I was the moths', though it may be merely that they count downwinders no more than I count insects. The death of a moth seems a small thing in this vast space, and the strength of a protest—of those blockaders on the highway that morning—seems a tiny thing against the power of the government. There were moths out there, navigating by the stars, however, before there was an atomic bomb, and we were out there in the hopes that there would be moths out there afterward, that this landscape would survive our history. I don't know what effect my coming to the Test Site so many years in a row had on the Arms Race, and I never will. The consequences are hard to measure, and are always discounted by the agencies and politicians they affect, but they are not therefore ineffectual. Coming here was an act of faith, a decision that whether or not I could ever quantify what I had done, I had at least done it. And it wasn't only an act of faith, for my coming here had begun to change me profoundly, an act of faith rewarded in a way I could not have foreseen.

An exploding nuclear bomb is a kind of star come to earth, and these bombs lure us the way my candle lured the moths. They are literally stars during a few moments of their explosion: As the temperature of the fission reaches millions of degrees, the physics of the bomb becomes akin to the physics of stars, though stars burn calmly for billions of years, and a bomb is only a star for a moment. The hydrogen bomb is a closer approximation of a star, for the vast energy that lets a star burn for eons without burning out is the energy of hydrogen being fused into helium at extraordinary temperatures: The hydrogen bomb is a fusion bomb, though the fusion is triggered by fission. There is something wondrous about the fact that humans have managed to make stars, and something horrible about the fact that they, or we, went to the trouble of making stars for no more interesting reason than obliterating other human beings, and the places around them. The artist Bruce Conner made a film of nuclear explosions when the footage of the first Bikini tests was declassified.

In his film, the bombs of the 1946 Crossroads series explode with a strange majesty, like roses in a time-lapse nature film, blooming and withering with a power that is fascinatingly terrible.

There is a term for my fascination, and for what I suspect is the fascination of many others: the sublime. In the eighteenth century when the taste for landscape and the vocabulary to discuss it precisely were both beginning to flourish, the sublime came into its own. Landscapes and phenomena that had previously been considered merely threatening or unpleasant—thunderstorms, mountain ravines, crashing waves, glaciers—came to be appreciated with a finely honed connoisseurship. The overwhelming scale of time, of the earth, of violent natural forces gave sublimists a pleasing sense of their own smallness. The major tract on the sublime came in 1757, from the pen of an Irishman in English politics better remembered for his political philosophy and his enthusiasm for the American Revolution, Edmund Burke. It was his first published work, and it bore the ponderous title *A Philosophical Inquiry into the Origins of Our Ideas of the Sublime and Beautiful*. In the middle of it, Burke's prose suddenly emerged from its intricate meanderings, and he declared, "Whatever is fitted in any sort to excite the ideas of pain, and danger, that is to say, whatever is in any sort terrible or is conversant about terrible objects, or operates in a manner analogous to terror, is a source of the sublime: that is it is capable of the strongest emotion which the mind is capable of feeling. . . . When danger or pain press too nearly, they are incapable of giving any delight, and are simply terrible; but at certain distances, and with certain modifications, they may be, and they are delightful, as we every day experience." Soon after, Burke enumerates some of the qualities of the sublime: terror, obscurity, power, privation, vastness, infinity, scale, difficulty, magnificence, light, sound and loudness, suddenness, the cries of animals, pain, darkness, solitude, and silence. It may be a measure of how much security eighteenth-century aristocrats had achieved, that they could enjoy those things which once only meant that slim chances at life were becoming slimmer.

Later, it became a Romantic taste for a violent, chaotic, overwhelming nature in the face of a relentlessly optimistic, productive, and increasingly industrial society. Gothic horror stories come out of this romantic reaction, and the paintings of J. M. W. Turner, and the rebellious fiction of the Brontes. The best description of the taste for it is in Charlotte Bronte's *Jane Eyre:* ". . . putting my ear close to the window, I could distinguish from the gleeful tumult within the disconsolate moan of the wind outside. Probably, if I had lately left a good home and kind parents, this would have been the hour when I should most keenly have regretted the separation; that wind would then have saddened my heart: this obscure chaos would have disturbed my peace: as it was I derived from both a strange excitement, and, reckless and feverish, I wished the wind to howl more wildly, the gloom to deepen to darkness, and the confusion to rise to clamour." Another woman, Mary Shelley, summed up the scientific sublime in her novel of 1818, *Frankenstein,* a story about what happens when a man takes God's or women's prerogative and creates life, a template for all further stories about creations gone out of control. The sublime is a taste that lives on, in science fiction, and horror movies, and in the contemplation of things—supernovas, for example—and places—the Grand Canyon, Niagara Falls—the Romantics would quickly have identified as sublime.

There is a casino on the Las Vegas Strip, The Mirage, devoted to the sublime as a neatly packaged novelty. In the mammoth fountain in front of the casino, a fake volcano belches water, steam, and gas-jet flame every twenty minutes from dusk till midnight, amid a great roar of prerecorded sound. Inside The Mirage, the resident magicians Siegfried and Roy perform a kind of miracle show with trained white tigers and illusions of death and resurrection. I am sure Burke would have enjoyed both. The secure enjoyment of those aristocrats is not a privilege of ours, however. Those eighteenth-century connoisseurs were happily poised between being at the mercy of nature and having nature at their mercy (and it may have been the increasing control over nature that provoked the increasingly destructive and morbid imagination of the romantic sublime, until that control itself went haywire in our time). The sublime they enjoyed came from natural phenomena or artistic representations of natural phenomena; the unnatural disasters of the present offer no such containment within the bounds of the natural—the oil fields afire in Kuwait, the mushroom clouds above Yucca Flat, the blood-red sunsets of Los Angeles—though they still compel attention. The atomic bomb—which it somehow seems right to speak of in the singular, as though it were a deity rather than a variety of weapon—is both the principal metaphor and fact of the problematic relationship between our power, desire, and limits.

It is this new, horrible sublime that Richard Misrach pursued with such brilliance and dedication, and that made his pictures so important for my own journey into the wars of the American landscape. His huge, formally stunning color images take on the subject matter usually reserved for photojournalism: Unnatural violence is his most perennial theme. He uses the vocabulary of landscape photography to address issues more akin to social documentary—that is, he refuses to respect the tradition in which the landscape is our refuge, is timeless, is serene, and he equally refuses to respect the tradition in which politics is represented in the hasty, grainy black and white of photojournalism. Imagine that Thoreau wrote *Walden* and "Civil Disobedience" as one book, so you had to understand solitary rapture and political confrontation in practically the same breath. Misrach's work provokes controversy in the West Coast photography community—so far as I can tell—because there is no ready correspondence between what is beautiful and what is good in his landscapes, in that what is beautiful is often deadly, damaged, evil, wrong, sick (it may be, too, a sense of moral prohibition about looking aesthetically at crimes, based on the belief that there is a non-aesthetic, noninterpretive way of looking—which brings us back to the conventions of documentary and photojournalism). Their reading is that Misrach is glorifying the wrong things. His reading seems to be that the relationship between appearances and values is a marshy, treacherous one (a particularly appropriate issue for ecologists, who deal largely in invisible poisons, systems, and places).

The beautiful and the good have a strained relationship. Otherwise things would be very easy. J. Robert Oppenheimer, the physicist who directed creation of the first atom bomb and opposed creation of the hydrogen bomb, said of the H-bomb afterward, "From a technical point of view it was a sweet and lovely and beautiful job."

The work is something else besides: a realization of the post-modern sublime—a category distinct from beauty: the sublime as the aesthetic of vastness, magnificence, power, and fear. These lush documents of political catastrophe point out that politics has invaded the landscape, that the landscape is now a victim of history, that history is not only the history of human actions, of causes, but the history of effects, of ecological damage. Thus, we see not the soldiers bombing the landscape—action pictures—but the landscape shattered by bombs. In representing violated landscapes—landscapes populated by dead animals or bomb craters—as sublime, he refuses too the neat before-and-after virgin-whore categories that both nature calendars and photojournalism prop up. Our morality is complicated by the fact that the sky above even the most demonic folly is often exquisitely colored, and its clouds as breathtakingly pure.

✚ THE WHITE EXPLORERS OF THE GREAT BASIN ALWAYS READ IT as a place of death and finality, as a terminal futurity, and though from aesthetic perspectives it might have been sublime, from the pragmatic outlook of invaders it was simply a hostile, useless place. It was the last part of North America to be explored, a blank on the maps that had long been filled in on the south and east and were rapidly filling in from the other directions. The last part of the Basin to be explored and mapped is what is now Nellis and the Test Site.

Jedediah Smith's fur-trapping party of 1827 was probably the first white incursion into the Basin, and the Goshutes (Gosh-Utes, in nineteenth-century parlance, or Go-Shoots) remember them: "The first white men they ever saw were three who staggered, almost naked, in from the western desert, and were half crazy from breathing alkali dust." The Hudson's Bay Company sent in a group of British trappers the next year led by Peter Skene Ogden. The British and American trappers were engaged in a territorial battle over the West. The British, through what was to become famous as their "scorched earth" campaign, intended to prevent American expansion into the Great Basin—the Hudson's Bay Company was out to destroy every beaver in the region and leave it useless, finished, for its purposes. It was a strange project, this fur industry, which had mountain men in buckskin roving the waterways of a pristine continent at one end, and gentlemen promenading in extravagantly impractical hats at the other—beaver fur was used primarily to make top hats. Ogden wrote while trapping along the Humboldt River from what is now Battle Mountain upriver to the Ruby Mountains, "The banks of the river are now lined with Indians. It appears on our arrival on this river they apprehended we were a war party, but now they are convinced we are come merely to wage war on the beaver. . . ." The trapping parties left the land permanently scarred by their horses, the rivers almost bereft of the beaver which had dammed up the waters and expanded the aquatic habitat.

Joseph Meek's party of trappers came through and did little of note, but for his murder of a Shoshone man who looked, Meek said, as though he were going to steal a beaver trap. When another party of Americans, Joseph Walker's, came through in 1833, it found nothing to trap on the Humboldt and named it the Barren River. The party continued west and encountered some Paiutes who repeatedly asked the trappers to smoke pipes with them. Walker became suspicious that the peace invitations were some kind of delaying tactic, so he and his party shot as many as they could. It is described as the first indigenous-white conflict of any scale in the Great Basin, though it was more like a massacre. The Walker party continued west, across the Sierra, caught what seems to be the first Euro-American glimpse of Yosemite, and so exits this story.

Trapping died out as an economy soon after when silk from the East replaced beaver felt, and the next significant incursion into the Basin was Fremont's, on his second expedition of 1842–1843. Fremont came looking for what may have been the last great mythological place on earth, the Buenaventura River. The Americas had begun their life in the European imagination as the land of marvels. Columbus speculated that the earth was pear-shaped, or breast-shaped, rather than round, and suspected that its nipple, the original Paradise itself, lay somewhere in Central America. During the next century Spanish conquistadors spent much of their time decimating Aztec and Incan civilizations and looking to plunder the treasures of the fabled Seven Cities of Cibola. They put Queen Califia's island of women warriors on the map where California is; claimed to have found the fantastic Patagons in Patagonia; saw mermaids in manatees; and generally remained so dazzled by what they dreamed that they failed to see what they had found. Yankees tended to fill in the blanks on their maps with development schemes; the Spanish populated them with monsters and wonders.

Certain vaguenesses of the Spanish and French expeditions into the southern and eastern regions around the Great Basin had given rise to belief in a great river flowing from its heart into the sea, and many maps showed a river like the Columbia running into San Francisco Bay. The saltiness of the Great Salt Lake seemed to confirm belief that the two places were somehow linked. "Among the trappers, including those in my own camp," wrote Fremont, "were many who believed that somewhere on its surface was a terrible whirlpool, through which its waters found their way to the ocean." Fremont had brought a rubber dinghy with him, and with it he rowed across the Great Salt to an island he christened Disappointment Island, because he had expected to shoot some game on it and didn't find any. Later it was renamed Fremont Island. He didn't give up on the Buenaventura until they'd gone to California and come back into the Great Basin's southwestern edge, near what is now Las Vegas. It was 115 degrees on the day they reached what would become Las Vegas (*las vegas* means the meadows, though the grassy oasis has since been sucked dry and paved over). The expedition got entangled in a conflict between some Mexicans and Southern Paiutes, and the expedition's guide, Kit Carson, set out with another member of the party and scalped the Indians, one while he was alive. Fremont's recounting of the event is one of the goriest moments in his expedition journals.

Fremont came into the Basin looking for a way to boat out of it, and instead realized that he had found a virtually unique geographical feature, a land of interior drainage. He wrote a few years later, in his *Geographical Memoir of Upper California,* "East of the Sierra Nevada, and between it and the Rocky Mountains, is that anomalous feature in our continent, the Great Basin, the existence of which was advanced as a theory after the second expedition, and is now established as a geographical fact. It is a singular feature: a basin of some five hundred miles diameter every which way, between four and five thousand feet above the level of the sea, shut in all around by mountains . . . having no connection whatever with the sea . . . more Asiatic than American in its character. Sterility is the absolute characteristic of the valleys between the mountains—no wood, no water, no grass, the gloomy artemisia [sagebrush] the prevailing shrub—no animals, except the hares, which shelter in these shrubs, and fleet and timid antelope, always on the watch for danger, and finding no place too dry and barren which gives it a wide horizon for its view and a clear field for its flight."

Even the most unprejudiced of nineteenth-century American explorers, John Wesley Powell, had trouble coming to terms with the desert, but we who can travel in an hour what might have taken them a week should be careful how we appraise them. The desert is prettier for having the oases of air-conditioned diners, and far smaller for cars and highways. In his account of his great expedition down the Colorado River in 1869, Powell described the deserts south of Vegas in a passage reverberant with intimidation: "The plains and valleys are low, arid, hot, and naked, and the volcanic mountains scattered here and there are lone and desolate. During the long months the sun pours its heat upon the rocks and sands, untempered by clouds above or forest shades beneath. The springs are so few in number that their names are household words in every Indian rancheria and every settler's home; and there are no brooks, no creeks, and no rivers but the trunk of the Colorado and the Gila. The few plants are strangers to the dwellers in the temperate zone. On the mountains a few junipers and pinons are found, and cactuses, agave, and yuccas, low, fleshy plants with bayonets and thorns.

The landscape of vegetal life is weird—no forests, no meadows, no green hills, no foliage, but clublike stems of plants armed with stilettos. . . . Hooded rattlesnakes, horned toads, and lizards crawl in the dust and among the rocks. One of these lizards, the 'Gila monster,' is poisonous. Huge rattlesnakes are common, and the rattlesnake god is one of the deities of the tribes."

The Mormons didn't mind the desert. It reminded them of the land of the Old Testament, and they were expecting the end of the world imminently anyway. It was they who named the largest species of yucca Joshua trees, seeing the trees as the prophet Joshua pointing the way to the promised land. In 1846 the Mormons had fled to the Great Basin from the midwestern frontier, becoming the first whites to actually try to live in the region. Brigham Young is said to have raised his hands above the Salt Lake valley and declaimed, "This is a good place to make saints, and it is a good place for saints to live; it is the place that the Lord has appointed, and we shall stay here until he tells us to go somewhere else." He was shrewd enough to know that the Great Basin was also the best possible refuge from governments and persecutors for his Latter-day Saints, who had been hounded off the Illinois and Missouri frontiers. Young chose the Great Basin over the more distant California, knowing that California wouldn't remain neglected by Anglo-Americans for long—and he was right, for California was Yankified and densely populated by the end of the 1840s, while the Great Basin today remains a sparsely settled Mormon-dominated area. The Book of Mormon was itself believed to have been hidden in Illinois by ancient Israelites who'd come to the continent somehow or other, and so their holy texts integrated the new landscape of the Americas into the old stories of the Middle East, and linked their anticipated apocalypse to a new story of origins. To them, their journey echoed the Exodus from Egypt, and they described themselves as a kind of reborn Zion.

Some of their other Old Testament names stuck—Moab, Jordan, and Zion itself—now a national park. They were attempting to set up a sovereign religious state called Deseret, but when the U.S. took the land from Mexico it made them back into Yankees.

The Easterners were fearful of the desert in the decades before the nation expanded into the arid West. The United States up to the Missouri Valley had been an experiment in transplanting European cultural and agricultural traditions to a new country. Further west the landscape—prairies and desert—became so different from that of Europe that the experiment seemed bound to fail. The yeoman farmer-citizen so dearly beloved of Jefferson was a figure suited only to the arable eastern lands, and the West even east of the Rockies was envisioned as "The Great American Desert," a realm uninhabitable but by nomadic pastoralists, roving hunters, and others who didn't fit the European picture of civilized man. As early as 1775 Edmund Burke, the sublimist turned political philosopher, seems to have foreseen cowboys: He warned the English government that, in the West, English colonists "would change their manners with the habits of their life . . . would become hordes of English Tartars." The explorer Zebulon Pike reported in 1810 that there was "a real value to this desert, in that it would be a bar to settlement and would prevent the reckless extension and perhaps disintegration of the Union." A traveler returned in 1817 to declare, "The prevailing idea, with which we have so much flattered ourselves, of these western regions being like the rest of the United States, susceptible of cultivation, and affording endless outlets to settlements is certainly erroneous. . . . A different mode of life, habits altogether new, would have to be developed." The critics of western settlement all saw the roots of their culture in agriculture, and speculated that it would not survive transplantation to the arid regions. After all, they were heirs to a tradition in which Cain had been triumphing over his nomadic herdsman brother for thousands of years, but here it was Abel who was fittest to survive.

The political desire to settle the West stifled these fears in a spurt of optimism and a sense of destiny. The question of whether a new landscape would create a new character seemed to fade: Although the frontier was universally acknowledged to generate rough and ready virtues, the long-term effects of the wide-open arid lands were left unexamined. And yet even today, the question is a valid one. At the hundredth meridian—a line that runs from the Dakotas to western Texas—rainfall drops below twenty inches a year, the level necessary to sustain unirrigated agriculture. Throughout most of the Southwest and Great Basin, rainfall is far below that—in Nevada, the most arid state overall, annual rainfall is under seven inches—and the culture is one of oases and ranches. The Mormons set up their own cooperative irrigation projects and abandoned yeomanly independence. Much of present-day farming in the West is dependent on government-subsidized water projects, while ranching often depends on cheap grazing on public land, dependencies that somehow fail to undermine the recipients' sense of a cowboy independence even more rugged than that of yeomen. The land and water and woods are being used up in most places—they are being mined, as metals are mined, in an unsustainable experiment of transplanting a way of life. The government fosters these projects for a number of reasons, and if they didn't the arid lands might be even more sparsely inhabited.

This is the kind of land that generates nomadic cultures—the hordes of Tartars of Burke's fears—and certainly the first inhabitants of the Basin were nomads, moving in a circuit governed by the seasons on a land that had plenty for them if they spread themselves thinly enough. "In the Newe [Shoshone] environment, there could be no wasted time, no aimless wandering, no 'guessing,' " says the

Western Shoshone's own history. Only cheap gasoline, predator control, groundwater pumping, public-land grazing, and barbed wire have made it possible for arid-land ranchers to live more like farmers than pastoralists following their herds across the distances. Even so, the West is a land of ghost towns, unsustainable water projects, and transient people: The flimsy trailer home is the most emblematic dwelling here, the superb interstates its counterpart. The land historian Roderick Nash refers to Western lifestyles as "maximum-impact camping." It may be that the land has realized all those early fears and made its people into wanderers, but even they don't know it. And it may be that we are approaching a time when this land will be grazed dead, drunk dry, gasoline will be prohibitively priced, and the only people who live out here will live within the limits of the land they're on, as they did before the mid-nineteenth century. Cain will be gone altogether and Abel at peace again.

Most Nevada towns during the nineteenth century, and many of them now, are mining towns that have fulfilled all the fears of the Easterners. They were rough places, quickly thrown up and quickly abandoned, and they left behind heaps of spent ore, the toxics of metal refining, tunnels into the earth, and piles of rubble. They bred a gambler's disposition in their population, a place in which wealth was easily gained and more easily lost, speculation in food and goods was a surer source of wealth than mines were, and nobody was planning on staying. Get rich and get out seemed to be the credo. At the end of the 1870s John Muir came through the Great Smoky Valley in central Nevada and wrote, "Nevada is one of the very youngest and wildest of the States; nevertheless it is already strewn with ruins that seem as gray and silent and time-worn as if the civilization to which they belonged had perished centuries ago. Wander where you may throughout the length and breadth of this mountain-barred wilderness, you everywhere come upon these dead mining towns, with their tall chimney stacks, standing forlorn amid broken walls and furnaces, and machinery half buried in sand, the very names of many of them already forgotten amid the excitements of later discoveries."

The Test Site had a real town on it once, before Mercury, before the men there began dispersing the heaviest naturally occurring element, uranium, and its heavier manmade relative, plutonium, when they were still gathering up another of the heavy metals, gold. In 1928 there was a mining boomtown out at the northeastern edge of Skull Mountain called Wahmonie, and for a season or so a thousand people lived there, trucking in their food and most of their water. The boom lined speculators' pockets but didn't produce much in the way of metal, and by the end of the year Wahmonie had become another ghost town, the last mining ghost town in the state. Nevada had more towns in the nineteenth century than it does today. Settlement spread from the Comstock Lode near the Sierra Nevada and along the Humboldt, so southern Nevada was explored and settled more slowly than the north. In 1900 Las Vegas had a population of 30, and the state had a population of about 40,000. The desert traveler Margaret Long called the land that is now the Test Site "the wildest, least frequented, and most desolate region of the United States." Now Nellis is the third largest settlement in Nevada.

By World War II, the sparse population of the arid West meant something else: open space for military installations, spaces big enough to fly warplanes across and test weapons in, and land considered worthless enough it could be poisoned and bombed to hell without much public outcry. There are vast tracts of land in New Mexico, Utah, southern California, and Arizona set aside for military purposes; Nevada alone has more than twenty percent of the military land in the U.S. Nellis Air Force Base was created in 1941 in what was one of the most uninhabited places in the country—but wasn't wholly uninhabited. A few mining families like the Sheahans were moved off, and nobody was counting the semi-nomadic Shoshone presence out there. Ethnologist Julian Steward estimated about seventy Western Shoshone lived in the Test Site region in the 1880s, and in 1993 there was still at least one man, Ted Shaw, who remembered how good the rabbit and deer hunting was on Whiterock Spring in the Test Site's northeast quadrant. The governing agencies have produced volumes of archaeological reports on the place, describing relics of mining shacks and travelers' wagons as well as Paiute and Shoshone artifacts. The open space had been noted before World War II, and a good map reveals something startling: Nellis overlaps more than fifty percent of the Desert National Wildlife Refuge, created in 1935 in what was then one of the least disturbed bighorn sheep ranges in the Southwest. Nellis was supposed to be a temporary installation, for the emergency of the war, but after World War II, the U.S. continued practicing and manufacturing for war, and the land was never taken away from soldiers and given back to tortoises and sheep. (Thus the right hand of federal government does not know what its left hand is doing: The Department of Fish and Wildlife is charged with protecting the wildlife on the same land the Air Force routinely bombs.) The Test Site was carved out of Nellis in 1951 because the early atomic tests in the South Seas were too far away for ready observation by physicists and politicians, and because the country was going into a heightened state of Cold War insularity—even its bombs weren't safe abroad.

The nuclear bombs exploded since then at the test site, all 953 or more of them, don't constitute the worst future ever prepared for the Great Basin, however. The Test Site was intended as a rehearsal theater for an offensive against another nation. That the DOE was in fact bombing within its own territory, over and over again, month after month, year after year, decade after decade, was intended to be incidental to the scheme, although it has introduced millennia of dire effects into this region. The MX missile scheme, launched in the 1970s and abandoned in the early 1990s, established the Great Basin as a target for enemy nuclear weapons—a sponge to soak up bombs in what may be the most preposterous military idea of all time, and one of the most peculiar follies ever designed for any landscape.

By the 1970s, U.S. and Soviet missiles had reached such a degree of intercontinental accuracy that they were supposed to be able to wipe out each other in their silos. The MX turned shooting out enemy silos into a shell game by basing each missile in twenty-three silos connected by a "racetrack" on which it would be moved from silo to silo. Because of this mobility, it was supposed to take many shots to take out an MX, rather than one, a decoy system that might ensure greater survival of the MX or greater devastation of their sites. In one of the longest-lasting schemes, MX missiles were to be sited across Nevada and western Utah, so that the Soviets could take pot shots at that area and spare all others. The Great Basin was being offered to the enemy as a national sacrifice area. A scapegoat in ancient Hebrew tradition was a goat burdened with the sins of the community and driven into the desert to die; MX turned the desert itself into a scapegoat for the political conflicts of the nation.

The Air Force Chief of Staff was said to have estimated that the area could absorb up to 5,000 nuclear warheads, approximately seventy percent of the Soviet arsenal at the time (twenty-three garages times 200 MX missiles equals 4,600 enemy warheads). That's five times as many as the Basin has absorbed already, and 2,500 times as many as Japan got from the U.S. at the end of World War II in an attack still regarded with horror. The Air Force estimated that this system of 2,000 warheads on 200 huge MX missiles would take up 10,000 square miles of land. The environmental groups that testified against the MX in Congress in 1979 estimated that the real figure was something closer to 25,000 square miles minimum, along with 15,000 miles of new roads, and that during the twenty years it was being built it would annually consume three times as much water as Carson City does. MX would have developed the Great Basin in a way no other place has been developed, as a monument to fear and a courtship of devastation, a great target incised across two states.

The Colorado journalist Ed Marston speculated that the recklessness of the U.S.'s nuclear programs has a lot to do with the spirit of profligacy the expanse of Western land inspired in Americans. He wrote, "Perhaps if Jefferson had never made the Louisiana Purchase, development of nuclear energy would have been confined to the eastern part of the nation, with its denser population and more settled and cautious culture. That might have avoided many of the mistakes that were made. But because nuclear weapons development ended up in the West, its managers were free to do as they chose in zealous pursuit of their twin missions. The West . . . had neither the interest nor the capability to provide the discipline and oversight the nuclear establishment needed. The West provided exactly the wrong climate in which to develop a technology that needed caution, attention to detail, and good housekeeping."

MX was, too, a big step forward in the Arms Race, one that was widely expected to prompt a similar response on the part of the Soviets. It was internationally opposed as an acceleration of the Arms Race, a move toward the brink of a nuclear war and away from disarmament, but in the Great Basin it was also opposed as an invitation to regional apocalypse.

Citizen Alert, the group Bob Fulkerson heads, was founded to fight the MX missile; and it was the MX that made many Western

Shoshone activists incorporate environmental issues into their land-rights struggle. They realized that there was no point in fighting to recover a land that might not live that long, and their desire to resume control over their traditional homeland is based in large part on their desire to take care of the land, a central tenet of their religion. And so among the fruits of the bizarre plan to turn the Great Basin into an intercontinental shooting gallery are the vigorous activism of the Western Shoshone and of Citizen Alert and the bond between them and with American Peace Test at the Nevada Test Site against further bombing of this land the government considers already worthless and lifeless. For every action there is an equal and opposite reaction is nowhere more true than in the course of political movements.

✚

Miners are unsettled by profession, and so are soldiers and their families, and mining and the military are merely the second and third industries in the state—the first is entertainment, which is yet more fickle. It's important here to distinguish between true nomads, who have no margin for "wasted time, aimless wandering, 'guessing,'" and drifters. The former migrate as regularly and faithfully as birds and live within the bounds of a known territory; the latter blow like tumbleweeds across places they never really know.

Tumbleweeds aren't indigenous to North America. They came as stowaways in nineteenth-century shipments of Siberian wheat.

✚ TO ME THE PLEASURE OF BEING IN THE DESERT IS A CEREBRAL one, and a sublime one, far from the sensual pleasure of being in a place where my body belongs. In the hilly coastal country where I grew up, you can walk to what you can see. Whenever I am driving across a desert, anywhere in the Basin and the Southwest, I find my-self looking at the nearest mountains and imagining what it would take to walk to them. At first it would just be walking, one foot after another, the simplest and purest of our acts of volition. Walking in its rhythm and naturalness is the closest of all the acts we choose to the acts we don't: to breathing and the beating of our hearts, the other rhythms that direct the rhythm of walking. Of all the things we learn, it is the most natural, like birds learning to fly, and of all of them the act that becomes most unconscious. Walking is the only way to measure the rhythm of the body against the rhythm of the land.

And so I picture myself walking, legs like a pair of scissors across a basin as flat as a paper map to the mountains pressed against the horizon, and I wonder how long it would take for those mountains, that horizon, to get bigger, and how big they would get before I would get near enough. I walk, and then become mesmerized by walking, and then exhausted by it, in that state of drunken calm that long exertion brings, and then come states of delirium and extrem-ity, where it is oneself rather than only the landscape that is beyond what's known. Where I come from, you can walk to what you see, because it isn't very far away, and because you can always find water, shade, or a road out. Here, though, I might die of thirst or sunstroke or the cold of night between the point where I begin thinking about the mountains pressed against the horizon and the point where I arrive at them—the mountains where there is shade, and where the aridity fades as the elevation rises. I might continue walking, but leave a dehydrated body behind me, between creosote bushes, where no one but the ravens and coyotes will notice. I know I am out of my element here, where my heart and my eyes are enraptured, but my body is afraid. This is not a landscape that tolerates mistakes or vagueness. You must know where you are going and how to get there, and there is usually far from here. When I eye the distances, my respect for the desert nomads grows. Part of what I see out there is my mortality.

✛

The early Americans feared that the arid lands would change the national character. The desert gives rise to a more intimate and individual fear, fear of its effect on the soul. Solitude, emptiness and silence, the forbidding climate and scale of the land, the slender margin for survival—all these things affect a mind used to a more crowded, lusher world, deprive it of the usual distractions. Here in the silence, voices that cannot be heard elsewhere, the voices of one's own fears and dreams and the voices of the geologic earth, the sky, the wind, and death, murmur to the traveler. For those in pursuit of such spiritual knowledge, the desert is the best place to hear the voice of the whirlwind; for those who aren't, it is a terrifying place.

People who've driven through Nevada often say, "There's nothing out there," and when I dropped by the University of Las Vegas one day to try to find out who was on the land that is now the Test Site before they began bombing, the research librarian kept saying, "But there isn't any information on it, because there's nothing out there. There's *nothing* out there." The walls around us were hung with old maps of Nevada, and the Test Site area indeed remained an area of nothingness on the maps as they gained detail in the course of approaching the twentieth century—one of them even used the region as the blank place to set a flowery inscription. There would be the Amargosa Desert marked to the southwest, and perhaps Forty-Mile Canyon, but few details. "It depends on what you mean by nothing," I told the librarian. For the religions of the Near East— Judaism, Christianity, Mohammedism—the desert in its absence of the things of this world manifests the presence of the next. That next world is a realm of abstraction, purity, of an absolute antisensuality that can be read in the relative austerity of the desert. The same silence and vastness and emptiness is an important spiritual territory in Buddhism and Taoism, the void, the notmind of Buddhahood, the emptiness of Zen. For any of these religions to read into the desert such a spiritual terrain, two things are necessary.

The first is a religion of transcendence, a religion which emphasizes the eternal over the mutable, the timeless over the live, there over here. The idea of a nonphysical realm of spirituality distinct from, even antithetical to, the natural world of bodies and biologies seems so normal that it is hard to remember it is not part of every culture's beliefs. The anthropological philosopher Paul Shepard speculates that the desert was in fact formative in the transcendent religion of the Jews, and he traces the evolution of a local storm god into Yahweh, who is usually distinguished by his absence, invisibility, and power. Perhaps only in the desert would it be possible to let one sky god take over all creation, to let a single male deity supplant a pantheon, and for that god to become *super*-natural, transcendent of his creation. . . . Shepard says, "Such a consciousness might include attention habitually directed to the sky, the relative insignificance of all things organic, the sense of hidden, invisible, unknowable power that seems more akin to the wind than to concrete things. Waiting, silence, emptiness, and nothingness seem to imprint themselves on the concept of truth, self, ultimate states. . . ."

In fact, the qualities of spirituality, of religion, and of the god they strain toward all overlap: the abstract, the absent, the austere, the immaterial become the marks of the divine. Abraham, Moses, John the Baptist, the Essenes, Jesus, Mohammed, the early Christian fathers all withdrew to the desert to test their souls and connect to this god, the same kind of place Brigham Young pronounced good for making saints. And a lot of them were expecting the imminent end of the world, and found the desert the right place to wait, not because they loved it for its own sake, but because they saw it as bereft of the things of this world—barren and desolate—and therefore a place to anticipate the next. Desert, after all, means deserted, empty. The Desert Fathers of the early Christian era pictured the world as a backdrop against which the individual drama of sin and redemption took place under the eyes of God, and this deserted landscape could be read as a physical counterpart to that mental picture, as a barren expanse in which a person stood out starkly under an unforgiving sky.

If the first condition for seeing the desert as a place of austere spirituality is a religion of transcendence, then perhaps the second is possession of something with which to compare it. The Near East was in many places not always desert, but desertified by overgrazing and poor agricultural practices, as much of Africa and the U.S. is being desertified today. Shepard speculates that this transformation generated a memory of a richer landscape, a paradise lost, and a standard against which the desert can be found harsh, forbidding, far from the motherly landscape of Eden. Shepard also suggests that in their transformation from the anarchic pleasures of hunting and gathering to the laborious round of agriculture, the ancients of the Near East lost a genuine paradise. Thus Eden is likewise a memory of a life in which gathering food was an adventure rather than a curse, and thereby in later eyes the paradise of childhood rather than the drudgery of adulthood: God says as he evicts Adam and Eve from Eden, "Cursed is the ground for thy sake; in sorrow shalt thou eat of it all the days of thy life. . . . In the sweat of thy face shalt thou eat bread, till thou return unto the ground; for out of it wast thou taken: for dust thou art, and unto dust shalt thou return." Cain slays Abel, and they're committed to farming and settlement.

Of course the indigenous people of the desert saw in it not a land of austerity and absence, but an abundance for those who were careful, attentive, and reverent. Death Valley was named that by the Death Valley Forty-Niners who nearly died there; the Western Shoshone who lived—and live—there knew what they were doing and called it Timbisha after a sacred mountain there. True dwellers of the deep deserts—the Australian outback, the Kalahari, the Great Basin—don't seem to believe that there is anything missing from their landscape. In fact while those in lusher landscapes were gathering bread in the sweat of their faces, these desert-dwellers were celebrating an unwalled paradise that had never fallen, a world in which nothing was lacking. Because there was nothing wrong with it, there was no reason to transcend it, either by leaving the body and the material world or by progressing, geographically or technologically: Their spirituality emphasizes a Creation and creators who are not profoundly separate from the world and its people, but part of a continuum, and in which the earth itself is full of spiritual power. And in a world where the beginning was never out of reach, the end remained out of sight (at least until Jedediah Smith came into the region). That is to say, they had little interest in history.

And the Hebrews had no interest in landscape. Despite all the journeys in it, the Old Testament reads more like a train schedule than a travel book: Few other books so completely lack a sense of place. The various patriarchs move through a series of places that are no more than names, abandon homes for unseen lands, receive territories from God as though the land were newly made for them, prepare the way for a world of poured-concrete trailer parks. Perhaps it was their ignorant detachment from the desert that made it a place of hardship for them, or perhaps it was truly a degraded environment that did not reward close attention. They were drifters, not nomads. Whatever the cause, their minds were on higher things, a sky-god, and they thought in terms of the finite line of history rather than the endless round of the seasons and lifecycles of the earth. They were in a hurry to move on, out of Eden, out of Sodom, onto the Ark, out of Egypt, out of Babylon, off the face of the earth. And even their religious stories took place in the linear time of history rather than the circular time of organic rhythms.

Everyone before only read this transcendence into the desert. It was first written upon the desert by the nuclear physicists who set off the first atomic bomb at the Jornada del Muerte (Journey of Death, a New Mexico desert that gave Coronado trouble as he set out for the fictitious Seven Cities of Cibola). If transcendence emphasized the importance of the individual soul leaving the world, history emphasized it for cultures. That is, proposed as a movement forward and above, history reached its logical conclusion in flight from earth, or in the end of the world. The atom bomb was the first device for actually bringing it about, and the desert was chosen as its natural place. Although the U.S. and France have chosen to test in the South Seas (something the U.S. gave up in 1962), the first bomb, Trinity, melted desert sand into radioactive glass, and most U.S. bombs since have attacked Nevada. The British began testing on Aboriginal land in the interior of Australia, the French tested in Algeria before that colonized land achieved independence, the Chinese test in the deserts of the Uigur people in far western China, and the Soviets concentrated on the arid plateau of Semipalatinsk in Kazakhstan, where the nomadic Kazakhs live.

Sometimes the desert spoke back, as it did when the physicist Freeman Dyson made plans to test a nuclear rocket at the Test Site. The rocket, Orion, would have been a far more effective way of leaving earth than conventionally fueled rockets are, but it posed enormous dangers as well. The Limited Test Ban of 1963 forbade atmospheric nuclear explosions, and so Orion was abandoned. Dyson was a great proponent of manifest destiny who believed that restlessness is an inevitable and valuable aspect of the human character. At the time of this rocket project, he believed that since the most restless culture had wrapped itself all around the earth, it needed to continue onward, into outer space. Dyson writes of the way his desire to realize Orion warped his views of a test ban. "In the summer of 1959, as my time with Orion was coming to an end, I tried to do what I could to improve the project's chances of survival. I made a pilgrimage with Ted Taylor to Jackass Flat, the desert area in Nevada where we hoped to carry out our first crucial demonstration of feasibility with a real bomb. I went for two weeks to Teller's weapons laboratory at Livermore and worked there with the team that was trying to design fission-free weapons. And I wrote an article for publication in the respected journal *Foreign Affairs,* arguing against the test ban with all the eloquence I could muster.

"Only once in my life have I experienced absolute silence. That was Jackass Flat under the midday sun. Jackass Flat was as silent as Antarctica. It is a soul-shattering silence. You hold your breath and hear absolutely nothing. No rustling of leaves in the wind, no rumbling of distant traffic, no chatter of birds or insects or children. You are alone with God in that silence. There in the white flat silence I began for the first time to feel a slight sense of shame for what we were proposing to do. Did we really intend to invade this silence with our trucks and bulldozers, and after a few years leave it a radioactive junkyard? The first shadow of a doubt about the rightness of Orion came into my mind with that silence."

April Fool's Day

✚ ON MARCH 31, 1990, THE PEOPLE'S COMPREHENSIVE TEST Ban was signed by representatives from Japan, East Germany, West Germany, and Holland, by Kairot Umarov for the Nevada-Semipalatinsk Antinuclear Movement in the Soviet Union, by Jackie Cabasso for American Peace Test, and by Raymond Yowell, Chief of the Western Shoshone National Council, who was there because the organizers recognized the Shoshone homeland of Newe Sogobia as a coequal sovereign nation affected by the Arms Race. My brother and representatives of some of these other movements would take it to the U.N. in January of 1991, where a Comprehensive Test Ban would be debated—and approved by every participating nation but the U.S. and Britain, which the U.S. had pressured into joining it in blocking the U.N. treaty (the DOE spent $20 million of public money lobbying to continue testing). The people's treaty suggested that, among other things, democracy meant initiating change rather than waiting for it to come up for a vote, and that citizens couldn't wait any longer for their leaders to lead them out from the shadow of the bomb.

The signing took place on an impromptu stage set up at the edge of camp, near the highway. It took a certain bravado to sign an international treaty on a little stage set up in the vast open space so far from any city, for a stage wants an audience, and the audience for this one was really part of the same dramatic performance. Who was watching? The DOE certainly was, although it tried to convince us we were ineffectual. (Later there was a scandal about the DOE's surreptitious photographing of activists in violation of its own regulations and the law.) The alternative media were, to some extent, and the Las Vegas newspapers. But really this signing served a symbolic function, gave a kind of heart to our actions here at the heart of the Arms Race, actions that reached far out into other communities, into the political bloodstream of this and other countries. Coming to the Test Site meant coming out of offices and into a place where numbers and prophecies had weight; we were here because this was the most real of all the nuclear places. And in that sense what was happening was not a performance, but a ceremony; the former depends on an audience, the latter exists for its actors. Ceremony is a conversation between the participants and their gods that can allow witnesses or shun them. Too, civil disobedience—c.d., in activist slang—asserts that we *are* the public, and that as the public we will be actors in history, not an audience to it. Direct action takes back history from the corridors of power and gives it to the public gathered in public places. This is what public places—city squares, the Capitol steps—are for, for the generation of a public, though it was more unusual for the public land of such a remote place to be put to such a use.

Every year the Western Shoshone participants had become more central to the spring actions, and every year there was a central arrest event; this year the idea was that the Shoshone would lead a procession down the road to the cattleguard at the main gate, then cross it to be arrested, and those of us who wanted to throw ourselves behind Shoshone land rights as well as against testing could follow them. I decided to follow them. I walked along the barbed wire fence of the Test Site boundary by myself. A lot of people drove the mile or so, but I didn't want to break the spell that tied together the camp and the cattleguard, so I walked.

On the fence were signs declaring that this was a habitat preservation area for the desert tortoise, which had been declared an endangered species the year before. The habitat of the tortoises has largely disappeared into a checkerboard of agriculture, developments, and military uses, and off-road vehicles and cows degrade what territory remains. A tortoise will often stay within the same square mile or so of land for its life, which may last as long as a century, and tortoises have been doing something like this for sixty-seven million years. More of a Mojave than a Great Basin desert creature, the tortoise seldom ranges much further north than the Test Site. The most crucial area for its survival is southwest of there in California's Ward Valley, where the Bureau of Land Management (BLM) wants to put a radioactive waste dump, near the sacred sites of the Old Woman Mountains. The DOE and BLM had claimed that the Peace Camp was bad for desert tortoises, but it was no doubt not quite so bad as nuclear fallout and the earthquakes created by the bombs. Nor can the dune buggies of the Wackenhut security guards, which were positioned at strategic intervals on the other side of the fence as I walked, do them much good. (Wackenhut is a private enterprise that rents out security forces around the world.)

It was hotter than the day before, and the sun felt menacing. I could feel the water rising up into the air from me, and the sun pouring down.

✦

The cattleguard is part of a more elaborate installation created in 1987, when the DOE moved the boundary dividing public space from forbidden territory a few miles further out from Mercury. At this current boundary, if you stand in the middle of the road looking toward the bombing grounds, you see to the right a platform on stilts. A huge white sheet of plywood partially obscures it, and on the sign is written in blocky black capitals,

YOU ARE NOW ENTERING
NEVADA TEST SITE
NO TRESPASSING
BY ORDER OF THE UNITED STATES
DEPARTMENT OF ENERGY

Behind the guard tower is a temporary-looking box that is the registration/security clearance station for the Test Site, a building that looks like it was towed in last week and will be towed out next. Maybe another nation would make its test site look more like a pillar of empire and less like a maximum-security RV park. Further to the right is an outcropping of hills and canyons, the tail of the Spotted Range, the first interruption of the flatlands around the entrance. Back a little way from the cattleguard to the left is the cattle pen built for protesters around 1988. And of course, during any action the foreground is crowded with sheriffs and Wackenhuts and security vehicles. The road runs straight into the distance, a perfect illustration of vanishing point perspective, though Mercury too is off to the right. The ridges of Red Mountain, Skull Mountain, and the Specter Range form the far horizon at the end of the road, and past that is what was to me the great unknown, the realm of the bomb craters that appear in photographs and even on the U.S. Geological Survey map (it was their appearance on the map that made me realize how monumental the craters are, big enough to be considered topography by the cartographers). If you look off to the left, you can see the dark crest of Yucca Mountain behind the Skull formations—which were named, I've been told, because the early emigrants through the region saw skulls in them as they approached them from the northeast, something hard to construe from the southwest of the Peace Camp and highway.

Like the stage, the gate suggests the vanity of human wishes in the vastness of the desert: Why people choose to congregate and clash in this narrow road when the whole landscape around them is so still and unoccupied would be hard to explain to an outsider. And it may be the openness of the site that makes the interaction between opposing sides so mild-mannered, so positively choreographed. Walking across the cattleguard always makes me feel like a participant in one of those Communist Chinese ballets of the 1970s, in which ballerinas in tutus with machine guns enacted a decorous interpretation of revolutionary history. Everyone here knows their parts as well, and the Chinese ballet could never have come up with a more ennobling and belittling setting for the dance.

I ran into Rachel and Richard in the knot of people to the side of the road to Mercury. Rachel, who is a photojournalist, was photographing the action. Richard was not. He looked at me and told me to drink some of my water, and drank some of it himself. We picked up where we'd left off the day before. He had told me that the old myth of the West was dead, and I was convinced that if I hadn't been so wrapped up in my own ideas, I would've found out his ideas about the new myth of the West. As the Shoshone elders were walking across the cattleguard, I was saying, "But Richard, you have to finish telling me about the new myth of the West," while he was saying, "You know, you really need to cross that line pretty soon if you're going to get arrested."

I offered no resistance as they put on the disposable plastic handcuffs and snipped off the ends, letting them drop into the dust. Probably the Test Site is littered with thousands of handcuffs and ends by now. They lack the ominous resonance of real handcuffs, looking less like appurtenances of crime and punishment than industrial fasteners, and they make it clear we're just being packaged for efficient processing. A friend who once saw a few pairs in my house took them for flea collars. They operate on a simple principle: the ratchety teeth at one end go through the geared slot of the other, so the cuffs can get tighter, but not looser—unless you happen to have a safety pin with which to push down the gear, which I did. Inside the dusty pen I liberated myself and then a dozen or so other women from their handcuffs, and squatted in the shrinking shade of the wall that divided us from the men's pen. This was the part of the dance where we threw ourselves into the arms of the authorities and then hovered suspended for hours—in the legal limbo before the lovely bus ride to Beatty where we would be cited, a limbo I always enjoyed. Having abandoned autonomy and freedom, there was little to do but wait for them to move, and move us—though the other women, heady with meetings and solidarities, usually tried to organize more of them in the pen, and if there was nothing to organize, they would sing and dance in circles. Sometimes there were people injured or isolated whose needs had to be addressed, and the meetings in the pen could result in an agreement to make our cooperation conditional upon that person being treated well. Sometimes there were other decisions to make.

Richard had told me that he has no theory of the American West, only that he thinks the old one no longer works.

✚ WHAT ARE THE MYTHS OF THE WEST? THE FIRST ONE IS THAT it is the West. North and South are absolutes, but East and West are places determined by the location of the determiner. The West is wherever the sun sets, the land of what is ahead, of destinations, while the East is the place of origins. But every place has its East and West. My West is the Pacific with Asia somewhere far beyond, and the American West is my East, part of what was formerly Mexico's North.

It's a larger problem, that the country has usually been looked at from the city, the West from the East. Even Thoreau yielded to this impulse, when he wrote, in that unavoidable passage, "Eastward I go only by force; but westward I go free. Thither no business leads me. It is hard for me to believe that I shall find fair landscapes or sufficient wildness and freedom behind the eastern horizon. . . . We go eastward to realize history and study the works of art and literature, retracing the steps of the race; we go westward as into the future, with a spirit of enterprise and adventure." This West has usually been represented as a place to go to, rather than to come from, a place to escape from problems or to dump them in, rather than a region in its own right, and one rattling with escapees. Thoreau's we is a we of Easterners, and the we of a race, the race that spread westward across the continent, and the we of Progress. Manifest destiny is only a suburb of Progress. I have been talking about Progress already, although I called it History.

I myself can't resist theories. After I got released in Beatty, I had a deep-fried burrito and a vanilla shake and some onion rings. That day 893 other people got arrested with me.

✦ SUNDAY MORNING I LOOKED ALL OVER CAMP FOR THE LOCALS from Citizen Alert who were going to take me on the tour of Nevada. Finally I saw someone who could help me, Bill Rosse, one of the Shoshone elders who had led us across the cattleguard the day before. He was shorter than me, and barrelchested, and silverhaired, and wearing a saucer-sized rodeo belt buckle and a grimy white tengallon hat with a beaded hatband, and when I came up and asked him my question he looked intently at me. We'd never met. Suddenly he gave me a bear hug, and asked whether my brother and I were twins, and so I explained my slight seniority. I teased him back about how I knew who he was; someone had hung a snapshot of him in the information pavilion with a note saying we should pray for him because he'd just had five bypasses. I told him that most people only had four valves, so his must be an unusual heart. And then, after a little digression on my brother's sterling qualities, he told me where to find the people I was looking for, and that he was coming along himself. Bill was born in Nevada's Big Smoky Valley, but his widowed father took him to Bakersfield when he was small, and he lived in California's agricultural region until retirement but for his stint in the military—he'd been injured in combat at Okinawa near the end of World War II. In 1974, he moved back to Nevada, to the Yomba Shoshone reservation, with his wife and eight of their nine children, and there he became tribal chairman and led them into activism against the MX missile and other threats to the land.

As I walked through the camp, Pauline Esteves, the other Shoshone elder who'd initiated the Shoshone-antinuclear alliance at the Test Site, yelled the same question about whether we were twins out the window of a parked car in which she was enjoying a cigarette. I had met her in San Francisco that February, where she gave the first talk in a speaking tour of the western states. My brother and Kairot Umarov of the Nevada-Semipalatinsk Movement were the other two speakers on the tour, and she taught them both to smoke Camels and called them her grandkids, since they were both 27 and she was in her sixties. All I remember from the first time we met is the way her hackles suddenly rose when she thought she was approaching a new-age group and the joke she told me afterwards: "Have you heard about the big new Indian tribe? They're called the Wannabees."

Within an hour I was back on Highway 95 rolling north toward Beatty again. This time I found out what I had been seeing on all those earlier trips. Chris Brown, head of the Las Vegas branch of Citizen Alert, drove me and told me stories about the landmarks out the window all that day.

When I was fifteen I was taken to England and saw my first Gothic cathedral. I can still remember wandering around a space that made no sense to me—it seemed as amorphous as a cave. Not knowing where I'd entered or how things were arranged, I managed to get lost in the building. I went back to Europe a few years later to study medieval art and architecture, and learned the universal floorplan of medieval cathedrals by heart. I learned that they are shaped like a crucifix, or a body with arms stretched straight out, that they always point east toward sunrise and Jerusalem, that the main portal was in the west, the end of things in Christian theology, and therefore often featured an image of the Last Judgment or the Second Coming. I became so attuned to the anatomy of churches that anything unusual—the decapitated head of Beauvais Cathedral (whose body, built too high, collapsed), the bad imitations of San Francisco—would throw me off balance, like a wrong note to a musician. In a way, I didn't see anything on that first trip, because I didn't know what I was seeing. I realize now that I had entered the north transept—or left arm—and turned right, away from the altar, then gone in circles. Since then I have always tried to travel in such a way as to gather the stories along with the sights, or to find the stories beforehand.

On that drive with Chris Brown and his wife, the landscape in which I'd ricocheted up and down so many times before finally took on meaning for me. We passed a sign for U.S. Ecology off to the west, and Chris told me about this radioactive-waste-management corporation and its employees, who mostly came from Beatty. The corporation had been called Nuclear Engineering before, and it had had a lot of trouble locally in the 1970s because the employees had

taken to selling equipment from the eighty-acre waste site, and some
of the equipment turned out to be hotter than the new owners imagined. Construction materials turned out to be radioactive, and so did
a livestock trough that had been a rad-waste shipping container, and
a contaminated cement mixer that had been used to pour concrete
for a local bar since shut down.

We passed Rhyolite, a ghost town from the Comstock era, and
the new high-tech mine there, which uses cyanide to leach gold from
ore too low-grade for nineteenth-century technologies—and econ-
omies. I saw a pretty gleam of silver away in the distance that Chris
said was the largest cyanide pond in the world; it had next to it a
mountain being digested into tailings for its gold. We passed Bullfrog, another ghost town named after the greenish cast of its gold.

Chris had already pointed out Yucca Mountain, a dark ridge a
few miles to the northeast from 95, not far past the Test Site boundary. Clouds hung over it, making it look even darker, and its bare
sides had eroded into gaunt ribs. Yucca Mountain is where the
DOE, with the BLM's blessing, would like to put the nation's first
permanent high-level nuclear waste storage facility. The ridge is several miles long, and about 1,500 feet taller than the surrounding
landscape, which makes it nearly a mile above sea level at its spiny
crest. Most of the mountain is tuff—densely compacted volcanic
lava.

✦ JUST AS THE MX MISSILE WAS GIVING UP THE GHOST IN THE
early eighties, Yucca Mountain succeeded it as a doomsday future
for the state of Nevada. The government, which hasn't been able to
make any conventional use of public, or Shoshone, land in Nevada,
seems hell-bent on making it useless for everyone and everything for
all time.

There always has been one problem with nuclear power, even had it worked the way many scientists envisioned it working in the 1950s and a few still dream it could nowadays. It was supposed to be an open-ended source of energy, cheap and without the output of pollutants coal- and oil-burning plants had. But it used quantities of a dangerous metal, uranium, and transmuted it into the most toxic substance on earth. The plutonium and other wastes weren't considered pollutants, since they didn't go into the environment—but where would they go?

Now, nearly half a century into the nuclear age, no one has answered that question, and as long as it remains unanswered, the nuclear power industry is in jeopardy. Much of the nuclear waste produced in weapons production has been unsafely stored—including rusting barrels in the ocean off the San Francisco coast and leaking storage tanks in Hanford, Washington, time-bomb monuments to the underestimates of the past. Spent nuclear fuel has been accumulating in the cooling tanks around nuclear power plants, where the operators are waiting for the government to make good on its promise to take this stuff off their hands. Spent is an ambiguous word: Although the uranium has outlived its usefulness for generating the subcritical reactions that fuel a nuclear power plant, it has partially mutated into more dangerous things—into strontium, cesium, and plutonium, and it is still very hot literally and radioactively. The half-life of the first two elements is short; but the half-life of plutonium is 24,000 years—and half-life means the amount of time it takes half of the element to decay into other elements, so it takes several hundred thousand years for plutonium to decay enough. As far as many scientists and activists are concerned, adequate storage is an idea that has not been realized yet, and may be unrealizable.

In 1982 Congress passed the Nuclear Waste Policy Act to initiate a quest for a long-term storage site for the rapidly growing temporary storage piles of nuclear waste. The initial plan was to have a site in the East and a site in the West, but several eastern states quickly shrugged off the duty. Three sites—one in Texas, one in Washington, and one in Nevada—were chosen, and political pressure eliminated two of the places, so in 1987 Congress passed what gets called the "Screw Nevada" bill, which prematurely settled on Yucca Mountain as the only site to be studied. Since then the state of Nevada has worked hard to keep the waste repository out, even though its senators and local politicians tend to favor nuclear testing (for the jobs, they say). The plan is to store 70,000 metric tons of high-level nuclear waste in the mountain, where the DOE has decided it must be isolated for 10,000 years to be considered safe (though the elements will be hazardous many times longer).

When I asked about Yucca Mountain, Bob Fulkerson sent me to talk to Steve Frishman, a geologist working for the state to prevent the waste repository from opening. Frishman, who worked himself out of a job when Texas defeated the proposal to site a repository there, told me that most of the country's commercial nuclear waste is produced in the population-heavy, resource-light East, and most of the plans for storing it point west. "In 1989 the state Senate passed a law that says in very few words that storage of high-level waste in the state of Nevada is prohibited. That's the major states-rights question that's going to be tested if the permitting process goes forward. It's maybe as significant a constitutional crisis as the Civil War, and Westerners are becoming more and more conscious of the fact that the East is eyeballing the West as a major dump site—for everything."

I asked him about what Bob had told me during that seminar under the sky at the Nevada Test Site: that the waste slated for Yucca Mountain is so literally hot it will boil for a thousand years. I had never heard anything like it besides medieval descriptions of the torments of hell. Frishman told me that Bob had underestimated both the temperature and the time. One of the plans for keeping water from reaching the waste, he said, is to place the spent fuel rods close enough together to keep the storage area above boiling temperature for millennia. This would succeed in vaporizing any water that might approach the area—but the rocks around would fracture from the heat, creating other problems.

I'd gone to visit Frishman in his office in Carson City a month or so after a major earthquake did a million dollars worth of damage to the DOE study buildings around Yucca Mountain, and he spent a whole morning telling me about geology, politics, and radiation in a Texas drawl, chainsmoking, and cackling at the madness of the plans. The main assumption made by the Department of Energy geologists is that Yucca Mountain is an ideal repository because of its low water table, and the main objection by its opponents is that the water table there is an unstable, even a mysterious thing. There are earthquake faults running all across the Test Site region too, and there has been volcanic activity in the area. Frishman said, "There's certainly a possibility of recurrence of vulcanism. When you drive along 95 the Lathrop Wells cone is pretty evident. As a matter of fact, the first time I was driving here from Texas, I was driving along 95, didn't know I was driving by Yucca Mountain or anywhere near it, I knew I was in that vicinity but I didn't even know that you could see it from the road, but I just looked over and said 'Man, there's a young volcanic cone—what's going on around here?' It turns out that the most recent activity associated with the Lathrop Wells cone could have been as recent as five to fifteen thousand years ago, which means it's very recent." And he told me that any volcanic or seismic activity could change the water table.

I asked him, too, why the DOE had chosen 10,000 years as the timespan for isolating nuclear waste, and he really hit his stride. "They did that for two different reasons. One is that in 10,000 years the level of radioactivity gets back to about the level of radioactivity of a fairly rich uranium ore, so it goes back to something that is no more radioactive than the most radioactive thing that someone would come into contact with in normal life. That was sort of an afterthought. The other thing that was the real driving factor is that if you're going to do a probabilistic risk analysis and you're looking out to some distance into the future, when you get out to about 10 to the 4th, meaning 10,000 years, you start vastly increasing uncertainty just because of our inability to predict geology and human futures and so on, our inability to predict climate. . . .

"Lake Lahontan was a significant lake for ten, fifteen thousand years. It's been drying up for the last 10,000 years or so; we're finding more and more evidence that it's been a cyclic drought. Most of the last 10,000 years has been very much wetter than now. We really don't know how to predict climate, but we have to assume that we're in an interglacial and it's going to get wetter again sometime, and sometime probably starting within the next 10,000 years. So you have to assume more rainfall. If you assume more rainfall, you have to assume more recharge to ground water, you have to assume some type of a rise in the water table. The DOE people have looked at it in terms of if we went back to the way it was 15,000 years ago how much would the water table rise? And in their very simplistic calculations you can see it rise about 400 feet, and that's about halfway from where it is now to the proposed depository horizon. The question is as simplistic as their calculation is, and the assumptions about infiltration; if they say it can go fifty percent what if they're 100 percent wrong, and the water's all the way up there?"

Another geologist, Charles Archambeau, told the *New York Times,* "You flood that thing, and you could blow the top off the mountain. At the very least, the radioactive material would go into the ground water and spread to Death Valley, where there are hot springs all over the place, constantly bringing water up from great depths. It would be picked up by the birds, the animals, the plant life. It would start creeping out of Death Valley. You couldn't stop it. That's the nightmare. It could slowly spread to the whole biosphere. If you want to envision the end of the world, that's it."

Lake Lahontan was a huge, shallow, salty body of water that covered much of northern Nevada, and its sister lake, Lake Bonneville to the east, was even grander. The Great Salt Lake is what remains of Bonneville, its minerals evaporated down to a brew four times as salty as the ocean. The first known culture in Nevada was made up of shore-dwellers around Lake Lahontan; and another lake to the south, Lake Manlius (after William L. Manly, one of the Death Valley Forty-Niners), filled up what is now Death Valley. People lived in the vicinity of Yucca Mountain too, though the *New York Times* article that quoted Archambeau described the place with the inevitable adjectives *barren* and *desolate*. Archaeologists have found stone tools around Yucca Mountain that suggest people were living there 12,000 years ago, longer than the DOE plans to isolate nuclear waste into the future.

The DOE expects that in 10,000 years our language and culture will be extinct, since none has ever lasted a fraction of that time. Marking the waste-deposit sites in such a way that the warnings will last ten millennia and be meaningful to whomever may come along then has been something of a challenge to the DOE's futurists. There were proposals, Frishman told me, to establish a nuclear priesthood, which would hand down the sacred knowledge from generation to generation. Others proposed forbidding monuments of a vastness that would survive the erosion of all those years, though any monument could attract curiosity and no inscription was guaranteed to make sense.

Western Shoshone and Southern Paiute elders remember Yucca Mountain as a place to gather chia and stick-leaf, and to hunt bighorn sheep. And they tell of a great snake that crawled down Forty-Mile Canyon and lies beneath the mountain still.

✚ WE WERE SLOWLY GAINING ALTITUDE, AND THE LANDSCAPE changed. There were more yuccas, and the rocks seemed somehow rougher, the land even more sparsely settled. There were no more towns on the hundred-mile stretch to Tonopah, except for the shrunken town of Goldfield, a former mining boomtown. Bob had told me that the Air Force wanted the Groom Range for, among other things, a secret area to test the Stealth Bomber, but the bomber had ended up around Tonopah instead. The Stealth Bombers, all 132 of them at $500 million apiece, were intended as first-strike nuclear-weapons delivery systems and as invisible planes for special military missions. They were used in their nonnuclear capacity in the Gulf War.

It was a strangely remote place, Tonopah, with the wide streets and low-slung buildings of places where land is plentiful, and unlike Winnemucca and a lot of other Nevada towns, too far away from anything to even have many chain fast-food outlets and motels. We stopped at the supermarket, where I found a display of F17 Stealth Bomber mugs and baseball caps. Beatty calls itself the "Gateway to Death Valley"; Tonopah is "Home of the Stealth." Other than the Stealth Bomber, it was hard to see what anybody made a living at in this town, although the bulletin board in front of the store advertised horse-breaking, housecleaning, and childcare, along with guns, undeveloped lots, and trailers for sale. It was exciting to see sweet rolls in cellophane wrap and refrigerated aisles of fresh vegetables and bottles of wine, almost as exciting as it had been to see running water. Bob bought a colossal pot roast, beer, bacon, eggs, fresh milk, all the substantial American food we'd been without.

In Tonopah, we turned east onto the Grand Army of the Republic Highway—not a very good advertisement for any army, since it was nearly unpopulated and not particularly grand—just two lanes running toward the vanishing point. There were bomb bunkers along the road at first—great massive earthworks designed to minimize the impact of accidental explosions. Chris told me bomb storage stories too, about the incredible quantities of decaying armaments stored around the state. Hawthorne, a little further north on 95, is the major armament storage facility for the country. It was set up after an ammunition depot in New Jersey blew up in 1926, and it became the staging area for most of the bombs, bullets, and other explosives in the next three U.S. wars. There are about 350,000 tons of ammunition there today, perhaps the largest such cache in the world. The range we crossed over on the Grand Army of the Republic Highway was bigger and lonelier than any I'd seen before, and the sign by the side of the road said it was a national forest. I didn't know then that national forests don't have to have trees, that the Forest Service is, like the Park Service and the Bureau of Land Management, simply one of the administrative arms of the federal octopus that controls most of the land in Nevada and much of the land of the West. We were about 200 miles northeast of Peace Camp at this point, and we were still circumnavigating Nellis Air Force Base and another of its subsidiary sites, the Tonopah Test Range, where the nonnuclear components of nuclear weapons are tested.

We passed a sign for Silver Arrow and Golden Bow, names whose allure could not be matched to anything visible past the sign. We climbed Sandy Summit and continued east. The landscape of ranges running north-south undulated as we went, and we seemed to be climbing or descending most of the time. The motion was rhythmic, like the bear in the song who climbs a mountain to see what he could see, and sees another mountain. After the descent, we would seem for a while not to be moving at all, and the range ahead would look like a permanent feature of the horizon, as though we were becalmed on a sea of sagebrush; then the car would begin to climb into the range, and reach the pass, where the next range came into view.

Seven mustangs loped across the road, five chestnuts, a bay, and a black, gleaming and fine in the glimpse we were given. Now, three days into Nevada and halfway across the state, I was beginning to forget where I'd come from and what I did there. The stories about military atrocities and the roll of the landscape mesmerized me, and the extraordinary spectacle of exuberant wild horses seemed of a piece with this expedition with cowboys and Indians into an interior world I'd never quite believed in, a West endlessly at war. Every time I've come since, the insular landscape has had the same effect on me: It feels like a place open to the sky and closed off to everything else. It is truly a basin, a rough bowl full of light shut off to the world outside its rim. The repetition of basin and ranges seems without end, as though there is nothing outside the hypnotic rhythm of the land, as though the outside world were just a story, a story that has nothing to do with this austere place with so few people, so little water.

I am used to my coastal world of edges, where the topography shifts from beach to chaparral to grassland to forest in the course of a mile, and foreign countries and international events abrade you every day. But here it was hard to imagine the places where nuclear weapons and Stealth Bombers might be used, and the reasons why. The strange, pointless war being waged against the landscape seemed unrelated to international politics, as though destroying was an end in itself and the land was itself the enemy. It didn't matter in this insular place that the Cold War was supposed to be ending: The generals said that withdrawing from Europe meant they needed more land at home; the bomb designers were quickly substituting the unstable regimes of the Third World for the Soviet Union and planning more bombs and tests; the nuclear industries were generating more tons of waste for Yucca Mountain. It didn't matter if the Arms Race ground to a halt, if a bomb was never used on a foreign country again, for the U.S. government had begun a war against the people and land here long ago and was going to lay siege to them until the half-life of the longest-lived radioactive elements was multiplied many times over.

✚ THAT AFTERNOON WE CUT OFF THE MAIN ROAD ONTO A DIRT road between the Hot Creek Range and the Pancake Range, up Hot Creek Valley. Chris pointed out signs of overgrazing as we bumped along. About fifteen miles up this road north, we reached our destination for the night, an abandoned Pony Express station in a cluster of dying trees. Built into a bluff was a handsome two-story stone and timber house with doors and windows open to the elements and half a dozen stone outbuildings huddled around it. The orchard of apple trees below was dry and nearly leafless, and the tall trees that shaded the house were brittle looking, though a stream ran through the pasture beyond the orchard. Spring had hardly made it to this place. There were real mountains in the distance, and the scale of the landscape had grown with the altitude. It was hard to believe that this had ever been a communications site, that messengers had stopped here on their breakneck rides with news from the East for California. It was completely quiet once I walked down a dusty path from the site, with an absolute silence only broken by birds and, once, by a pickup truck with a couple and two children in the cab and a trailer full of scavenged firewood bouncing behind.

There was a little bustle when I got back. Bob and Kit and a few others had built a huge campfire out of dead tree limbs, and they'd put the roast in a dutch oven. The vegetarians were making a stirfry off to the side, but by the time the sun had set, everyone was gathered around the fire. The rest of the caravan came in the darkness. Paul Rodarte came and told us in stricken tones that Kairot Umarov and Pauline Esteves had been arrested, and when he'd got us caught up in his story, he cracked up and told us it was April Fool's Day. Kairot came soon afterward with Bill Rosse. Beers came out, and a bottle of wine went from hand to hand. The wind rotated the heavy campfire smoke around the circle as reliably as a clock hand, but stepping out of the circle of light meant entering the bitter cold, and we all basted in the heat.

Bill took out his guitar and began to sing country-and-western songs. The music too was something of a revelation to me. Country music when I was growing up in a redneck town seemed mostly about truckdriving and reactionary Okies from Muskogee, and in the metropolises I moved to, it never intruded itself much on my consciousness. My parents were immigrants' kids, with no more relationship to the culture of the American outback than to the landscape in which they raised us. I had dismissed country as syrupy retrograde stuff, but the songs Bill sang had a wit and rancor that caught me by surprise. They were all bitter or melancholy reassessments of disastrously failed relationships, except for the ones about grievous bodily harm, and all of them relieved the nastiness of their view of human affairs with a rapturous litany of place names and topographies. Bill grinned through them all, explaining that it wasn't that he hated women, but that he loved the music. He sang "T for

Texas" (and for Thelma, who made a fool out of me), sang "Blood on the Saddle," a kind of coroner's account of an unsuccessful long-horn roundup, "I'm So Lonesome I Could Cry," and various others of Hank Williams's jaunty paeans to despair.

✜

I was supposed to be going to Oxford that fall, on a fellowship to continue researching the history and art history of landscape. When told I almost certainly had the prestigious thing, I began to think about living in Europe again and realized that I'd been a fake European most of my adult life. Mulling over my past, back beyond all the English novels and French poems and time in Paris, I remembered that I'd been a cowgirl growing up, catching bluebelly lizards, riding horses, and daydreaming impartially about Indians and any other culture living off the kind of land I knew, and that in those days my daydreams fit my territory. I realized that I had been a West-erner all along, and that though I'd come back to the West a long time ago, the fact had never imposed itself on my imagination. I re-alized that I'd spent my adult life living in the West as though it were an outpost of Europe, that I had always looked at it as a flawed copy of the original, and like the first white emigrants, longed for ruins, stories, and marks of my own ancestry, had lived in the West facing east. It was like crying for food at a banquet, and like trying to nav-igate the Sierra with a map of the Sussex Downs. For almost a de-cade I lived in a city where it never snowed without my realizing that every drop from my faucets was snowmelt, sucked out of a valley of legendary beauty that had been drowned by a dam. I realized then that I'd been living in a war zone my whole life without noticing the wars, since they didn't match any of the categories in which I'd been instructed. I realized too that the questions about landscape I was interested in were far more interesting in their branches than their roots, that rather than trace my culture back to Europe I might look at the ways that it had mutated, invaded, hybridized, mixed with the vastly different ecology and cultures of the West, and shaped and warped the vision of those making land policy and living on the land out here. I didn't get the fellowship, and I didn't want it by the end of the spring. I was meant for lower things.

✚ THAT MORNING I WOKE UP, CLENCHED WITH COLD IN MY sleeping bag on the second floor of the shell of a house at Moore's Station, filthy and smelling of smoke. Out the window, the sun was shining through the dying orchard, the mountains were clear in the distance, and birds sang, which they never did at the Test Site. People who were braver than I went to wash in one of the streams around the place, and people who were more skilled than I coaxed the fire back to life. The night had been so cold that the eggs froze, and we had to leave before they were scrambled. A group of us went to see the petroglyphs and the bomb crater, which were very near each other on offshoots of the road on which we'd driven into Hot Creek Valley, a conjunction too portentous to say anything about.

The petroglyphs were up a little canyon of crumbly pale rock running into the range that forms the eastern wall of the valley. At the mouth of the canyon there was a whole wall of them, and there were more within. They were beautiful complexes of rusty pattern on the pale face of the rock, strange figures and lines and jagged bolts and circles. One of them looked like a man with antennae, like a butterfly or a radio. They seemed such small things to find so far from anywhere, such faint signs of a culture and a relationship to the land they didn't evoke but only told us was out of the reach even of our imaginations. They seemed keys to a door that had been destroyed, and signs of a desire to shape oneself to the landscape rather than the other way around.

The crater too was strange. It's hard to talk about nuclear bombs without resorting to the numbness of numbers: For the crater here, the numbers included a date—January 19, 1968; a depth of the shaft, 3,200 feet; an explosive yield, somewhere between 200 and 1,000 kilotons. Even the DOE reports admit that there's a huge, highly radioactive chamber under the crater, which will contaminate groundwater—"not before 2000," they said when the next millennium seemed a comfortable distance away. When the bomb was set off, the DOE was still the Atomic Energy Commission, and Glenn T. Seaborg, the first person to make plutonium, was still its chairman.

The crater made by the explosion was a shallow basin about a hundred feet across where the earth had dropped, and the bushes growing in it were slightly paler than the bushes anywhere else. It was profoundly silent there, and the road, the crater, and the petroglyphs were the only traces of human presence we saw in the area other than our own. There was a plug sticking out of the center of the crater—a ten-foot-wide concrete cylinder taller than I am. The crater and the cylinder had become a monument to the event they evidenced, and there was even a commemorative bronze plaque on the concrete. I went up to read it. It said the test had been called Operation Faultless. And then I turned around and went home.

Trees

✤ On Memorial Day in May of 1990, a month after I got back from the trip across Nevada, my brother called me up from his home across town and told me, "Al Solnit's in town, and he'd like to meet us." I said, "No he's not, because he's our father and he's dead." My brother explained that the man who wanted to meet us was our father's cousin, a man we'd heard of, but never met. Our grandfather and his two brothers had all named their firstborn sons after their own father. This firstborn had seen David's byline on an article in a peace magazine and tracked him down. So when his son—also David—came back to Berkeley to get married, he called and invited us to the reception. We had a slew of relatives we'd never seen gathering in Berkeley that afternoon.

✤ The week had already been hectic. We had gone to a few Earth First! planning meetings for Redwood Summer that spring and were deciding—separately—whether we were going to get involved in their campaign to save the last of California's ancient forests from the logging companies. The cause was certainly attractive to me, and the strategy appealed to my brother. Earth First!, which had hitherto functioned as small cadres of guerrilla activists, was going grassroots. The organizers for Redwood Summer had publicly renounced tree spiking as a tactic (not that tree spiking had ever had much to do with the group in California, except in the lurid imagination of the media) and tried to form alliances with labor groups and loggers. Judi Bari, a Mendocino County carpenter and former labor organizer, had much to do with Earth First!'s new-found recognition of the ties between social and environmental issues. The lumber companies had convinced their workers that environmentalists and spotted owls were out to destroy their jobs, but the logging and milling jobs were largely being lost to mechanization, exports of unmilled timber, mills in Mexico, and the unsustainable rate at which northern California was being shaved bare. After all the steep slopes were logged, the companies were going to move on to easier terrain, and then it would be too late, for forests and for jobs. Thus Redwood Summer, a concerted effort of mass actions, grassroots outreach, and education intended to recall the Civil Rights Movement's Freedom Summer of 1964, which brought young activists from all over the country to Mississippi.

It was already a controversial program when a bomb exploded under Judi Bari on the morning of May 24. The pipe bomb loaded with nails had been put under her car seat, and it blew up as she drove across Oakland that morning. She had serious internal injuries and a fractured pelvis; her passenger was slightly injured. The FBI arrived almost as quickly as the ambulance, and Bari and her passenger, Darryl Cherney, were charged with possessing and transporting dangerous explosives. The investigation from that point onward proceeded on the assumption that Bari and Cherney were responsible for the bomb, despite her emphasis on nonviolence in her public speaking. One of the official explanations was that they were transporting it to use on someone or something else; another was that they blew themselves up to drum up sympathy for their cause. Bari had already received dozens of death threats for her environmental work, and a logging truck had run her off the road a few weeks earlier, but all this was discounted. "If you turn up dead, we'll investigate," she said the local police told her.

Then a letter written by someone signing himself "The Lord's

Avenger" showed up at a Sonoma County newspaper, claiming responsibility for the attack on Bari and another failed bombing of a timber mill and containing confirming details about the bombs. Written in flamboyantly Biblical prose, the letter condemned Bari as a tree worshipper and a women's rights supporter—and linked the two activities as interferences in the ordained hierarchy of the Creation. "This possessed Demon spread her poison to tell the Multitude that trees were not God's gift to Man but that trees were themselves gods and it was a Sin to cut them. . . . Now all who would come to the forests and worship trees like gilded Idols have been Warned." Earth First! thought the FBI might have written the letter, and the FBI claimed that Earth First! could have.

After the bomb went off, I was asked to come to the emergency planning meeting by someone who mistook me for an important organizer, and then it was too late to sit on the fence and decide whether the details of Redwood Summer were right for me. I went to the meeting that Saturday morning and got caught up in the crisis. Jumping into a political crisis is like jumping into a flooded river: The power of the current sweeps you along with an exhilarating, heady sense of purpose, and everything else, including your own life and work, seems a faint, distant, trivial thing somewhere on shore. Some people find nothing else sufficiently demanding, and some loathe the turbulence. I am myself a shorebird who tumbles into such waters irregularly. I declared that what they needed was a new brochure addressing the bombing and asserting that Redwood Summer had not been stopped, and ended up volunteering to have 2,000 copies of it ready by the next morning.

That spring we were in the fourth year of the drought that was turning California and Nevada into a dust bowl, but the day that Bari was bombed the skies opened up and it poured all over the northern half of the state, at a time of year when it never rains much.

She took personal credit for the deluge. It was still pouring when my brother called to tell me that our cousins wanted to meet us. I pasted up and printed the brochure I'd written, and delivered stacks of them to the vigils at Bari's hospital, the Oakland Police Department, and to Seeds of Peace, one of the co-sponsors of Redwood Summer, and—afloat on the momentum of my work—went to meet the houseful of cousins in Berkeley.

There were several sets of cousins of my generation there, and their parents, my more immediate cousins. No one had ever hinted that there were even so many people with the same surname as myself in the world. I was introduced to all of them at once, and this throng of dark, substantial professionals—doctors and college professors, mostly—astounded me. I am myself pale and spindly and not much of a Jew, our mother being Irish Catholic, and my immediate family is made up of malcontents and eccentrics. My father had been eager to distance himself from his childhood in a Yiddish-speaking immigrant ghetto and from his difficult family. His father, who died when I was six, was a rogue, a gambler, a smuggler, and the black sheep of his family. It was the white sheep I was meeting, the descendants of my grandfather's older brother, a man who had prospered wonderfully and had been a pillar of the community.

Sometimes in my sleep I discover a new room or cabinet in my home, and realize that the place I have been living in is more and different than it seemed. Or sometimes in that dream house, I open the back door and see not the cement courtyard of an apartment building, but green hills rolling uninterrupted to the horizon. That day my family grew like a house in a dream.

I spent most of my time talking to my grandfather's oldest brother's oldest child—the first Solnit born in the Americas (around the end of World War I)—and the older sister of the Albert Solnit who'd called my brother—my cousin Mary Solnit Clarke. She was brown-eyed, slender, elegantly dressed in linen trousers, and outspokenly urbane about politics in a gravelly voice that reminded me of Rosalind Russell. For all her auntly warmth I could tell that she was as steely as her hair, and as I talked to her it became clear that she liked being in the thick of things, like my brother, rather than looking on from the shore, like me. I was still caught up in the aftermath of the bombing, and somehow we moved on from family matters to that. She surprised me by knowing all about the incident, and by having strong opinions about the FBI's involvement with the matter. She talked about the radical antiwar movements of the sixties and the various forms of federally funded sabotage of them, and she talked about her own work with peace organizations. She had been involved with a group called Women Strike for Peace since 1961. And as she told me about the things they had done, I began to be astonished. This cousin I had just met had been organizing against nuclear testing and war since the fifties and had begun demonstrating at the Nevada Test Site in 1962.

✛

Women Strike for Peace still exists, but its heyday was the early sixties. The fact that no one had told me, no one seemed to know, that there had been a national women's antinuclear movement run along anarchist principles of direct democracy so long ago seems typical of the amnesia of the culture. Those who don't remember history are doomed to start all over again from scratch, and I am still surprised that so many feminists and pacifists have lost their own radical predecessors so quickly. Perhaps as someone who misplaced her whole extended family, I shouldn't be.

Our family came over from Russia for the usual reasons. That part of the world was torn by pogroms against Jews, by wars and revolutions, and even between these violent tides, the climate of anti-Semitism in that Russian-Polish border territory offered little chance to flourish and few reasons to stay. Mary's father came first, and he brought over his two younger brothers and his sister. They all came straight west across the oceans and the continent to Los Angeles, which had a huge Eastern European Jewish community, and Mary never left.

✚ IN THE YEARS FOLLOWING THE FIRST NUCLEAR EXPLOSION above the Nevada Test Site, nuclear bombs took on a new meaning for the public. They had been framed by the Atomic Energy Commission as nothing but a bigger bomb, a more profound control of nature. But as the 1950s wore on, it became apparent that a nuclear bomb was not only an explosive device, but a kind of chemical or biological weapon. After the blast and far around it, there was radioactive fallout. And what had been destroyed by the blast could be described, but what was damaged by fallout was impossible to measure. It spread too far and took too long to take effect. Much of the fallout of the fifties is still working its way through the plants and bodies of the living things in the places it fell, or lying on the ground waiting to circulate through these living systems.

War was a men's issue, but contamination became a women's issue. The bomb was meant to be about control, about controlling nature and war and enemies, even controlling the citizenry through fear, but it itself proved to be uncontrollable. The bomb was supposed to be a weapon that could be directed against an enemy, but it proved to be a plague that touched everything. A bullet hit or missed its target, but fallout could blow in any direction, take decades or generations to register. Nuclear war became the bombs bursting over and over again in rehearsals for holocaust, and war became a mother's issue, because it was no longer on an international frontier or in a distant future. It was in the bones of children, and it might already be fatal.

Strontium-90, a radioactive isotope in fallout, first became a public issue in 1955. An element that the body mistakes for calcium, it concentrates in milk and then in the bones of milk drinkers, particularly the quickly growing bones of children. It was showing up in the milk of nursing mothers, as well as cow's milk. There are other radioactive substances that settle in the human body, but during the fifties it was strontium-90 that received the lion's share of attention. When fallout was particularly heavy over eastern Nevada and Utah, milk was one of the things the Atomic Energy Commission tested, though it usually didn't go so far as to tell people not to drink it, for fear of causing a panic. Even now the DOE's plans in case of another massive venting from an underground nuclear test include instructions about destroying local milk collected during the fallout period (though iodine-131, which also shows up in concentration in milk and warps the thyroid gland, causes greater concern now). The DOE's 1987 guidelines describe the procedure as "control milk."

Milk is no ordinary thing to fear. It is the essence of the bond between a mother and her child, a substance at once innocent, erotic, and essential. It is no coincidence that all those early landscape paintings have at their center a Madonna clutching a child to her bosom, that the Christian vision of a nurturing earth was summed up in a nursing mother. If a mother can't tell if her own milk will strengthen or poison her child, then the most primary bonds have been ruptured, the most intimate acts contaminated, and the entire future called into question. To have a child is to reach into the future, an act of faith in the continuity of things; and the strontium-90 in cows' and mothers' milk sabotaged even this. The bomb proposed not only an Armageddon, but a science-fiction future of mutated and deformed descendants, as though the Virgin of the Fields had become the Beast of Revelation.

Adlai Stevenson talked about strontium-90 a lot in his unsuccessful presidential campaign of 1956. The first large-scale antinuclear organizations, Britain's Campaign for Nuclear Disarmament and the U.S.'s National Committee for a Sane Nuclear Policy (SANE), both addressed the present dangers of testing as well as the possible dangers of the ever-developing nuclear arsenals. Eisenhower beat Stevenson in '56, but the issues Stevenson raised wouldn't go away. The president was deluged with letters from citizens concerned about the effects of fallout on children. Two-thirds of the writers were women. On the twelfth anniversary of the bombing of Hiroshima, August 6, 1957, the World Council of Churches called for a halt to the Arms Race, and twenty-five people staged the first protest at the Nevada Test Site. They argued Nuremberg Principles, and eleven of them were arrested at the gate, taken to Beatty, cited, and released. When the *New York Times* reported the event, it had to explain what civil disobedience was to its readers and misspelled Gandhi's name in the course of the explanation. The saintly Albert Schweitzer took up the cause from his leper hospital in Africa, and the scientist Linus Pauling joined in from the California Institute of Technology in Pasadena. British philosopher and pacifist Bertrand Russell got involved, and Soviet physicist Andrei Sakharov began his three-and-a-half decades of peace work and persecution for it with a warning about nuclear tests.

Though the most prominent voices were men's, the strength of the movement came from women. What fallout brought about seems to be not only a specific political movement, but a profound loss of faith in authority and a consequent spirit of insurrection in

the U.S. Cold War politics had redefined patriotism as silent obedience to a paternalistic authority, but the instruments of the Cold
War, the bombs themselves, were endangering the people they were
supposed to protect. Those who questioned fallout increasingly saw
the scientists and politicians who were responsible for nuclear testing and the accelerating Arms Race as not only callous and dishon-
est, but wrong. The strongest scientific voice in support of this
worldview was Rachel Carson's. In 1962, she published *Silent Spring,*
a warning against the destruction being wrought by pesticides and
fallout, and one of the first books to popularize the vision of the
world as an ecosystem whose balances had to be respected, rather
than a machine with which to tinker. Challenges came not only from
people who were accustomed to questioning authority—leftists, fellow scientists—but from those who weren't. The backbone of U.S.
movements protecting human health from environmental poisons,
from the milk scares of the fifties through the Love Canals of the
seventies to the myriad of threats present today, has been housewives. "The Lord's Avenger" who linked Judy Bari's feminist and
environmental activities was confirming with hostility something
that has often been affirmed as a positive link: Women find themselves politically allied with nature, because of their distance from
war and their childbearing, or lifegiving, and because in the binary
logic of Western society women are cast as nature to men's culture.
So the bomb which was supposed to prop up the authority of nations also undermined them from within.

In 1958, the Soviets challenged the U.S. to join in a testing moratorium. The day before Halloween, 1958, the U.S. set off a small
bomb named Titania at the Test Site and stopped testing for nearly
three years. Then came the Berlin crisis, the collapse in East-West
relations that led to the building of the Berlin Wall and led the su-

perpowers to the brink of war. When I was born in June of 1961, John Fitzgerald Kennedy was preparing for conventional and nuclear wars. A month later, Kennedy told the U.S. public that he was requesting new funds for fallout shelters, that any misjudgments "could rain more devastation in several hours than has been wrought by all the wars in human history," and that it would be the Soviets' fault if a nuclear war started. The Soviets resumed testing with a 100-megaton bomb. In September, the U.S. set off the nuclear bombs Antler and Shrew together, underground in Nevada. Antler's fallout reached the northeastern United States. On November 1 of that year, women in more than a hundred communities in twenty-five states across the country went on strike. They demanded that world leaders stop testing, disarm, and devote as much to preparing for peace as for war.

My cousin told me, as we sat in her house above the opaque air above the city, "Close to 100,000 women in various cities took action in different ways. Some demonstrated, some went to see their elected representatives. They did whatever was most natural for them in their particular area. We had the largest here in L.A.; 4,500 women showed up. We went down to City Hall at seven o'clock in the morning. We didn't know what to expect. Buses came in from as far as Santa Barbara, San Diego, San Bernardino filled with women, and we just stood there, our mouths wide open, because we had never anticipated anything like this." Nothing vaguely like it had happened in recent history, and the strike became one of the major news stories of the year.

Women's Strike for Peace (WSP) was as traditional as the Virgin of the Fields in its insistence that women were the guardians and nurturers of life and as such bore a special responsibility to stop the Arms Race and fallout. It was profoundly radical too, founded on a frustration with the chess-playing logic of the Cold War and the bureaucratic, hierarchical peace organizations that had come to resemble the powers they opposed. The reason WSP was born as a women's-only movement, Mary said, was that in SANE (ancestor of the nuclear-freeze movement) and other organizations, the men deliberated interminably, and the women were left out: "We were sick and tired of doing the work and having nothing to do with the decisions." Positioning themselves as housewives and mothers, the women of WSP gave voice to ideas that were considered dangerous, subversive, and unpatriotic when they came from other quarters. They would go even to Moscow and North Vietnam on their peace missions, refusing to recognize the political boundaries upon which war is premised and citing their gender as the grounds for their ability to see only children and victims where the policymakers saw enemies.

My cousin had been there all the way through. With a wealthy husband, a fearless heart, and her two sons already grown up, she was slated for political action. She told me, "My mother and father were very democratic people, and they never disavowed their roots, the whole thing of where they came from and how they got where they were, and were grateful. Along with loyalty to family we were imbued with loyalty to our country, but we owed more than just loyalty, we owed activity. Volunteer, or whatever. I think that because of their background of persecution, Jews have a special feeling about other people (I wouldn't say that's true in Israel now). Then I guess the big push for me was when I read the essay by John Hersey on Hiroshima. That stayed with me, it just devastated me, and it stayed with me for all those years until we were doing the testing here. I think I became conscious of the testing through the ads the Committee for a Sane Nuclear Policy ran, full page ads in the *New York*

Times, the *L.A. Times,* and so forth—toward the end of the fifties. And then I started looking for a peace organization to get into." She worked for SANE almost daily during 1959–61, but it had problems.

When Women Strike for Peace was founded in 1961, Mary became Southern California coordinator and part of the National Consultative Committee. Later on she wrote about those early years. "Dagmar Wilson was the woman who started it all by calling together six friends in Washington, D.C., when she became alarmed at the increasing danger of nuclear war. This small group sent letters to women across the country. They wrote, 'We believe that a lot of people across the country feel just as we do—but thinking they are alone, do not speak out. If we are going to go under, we don't want to go without a shout. Let it not be said that we participated or approved or that we accepted nuclear war passively.' Breaking all the rules and behaving with incredible disorganization, Women Strike for Peace continued to attract recruits until the movement numbers several hundred thousand. We are always being asked to explain our organizing techniques—how many members we have and who our officers are. When we answer, 'There aren't any,' we receive reactions of incredulity, suspicion, and disbelief. But it happens to be the truth." They worked very much as anarchists, with local groups sending representatives to national meetings run along consensus guidelines.

WSP took a new position in the peace movement by refusing to care or investigate whether some members were Communists, and when they were investigated by Congress for potential Communist infiltration, they made a national laughingstock of the House Un-American Activities Committee (HUAC) with their cheerful refusal to take any interest in communism and their simple, funny answers to complex insinuations. It was the beginning of the end for red-baiting and for HUAC. WSP picketed the White House in January of 1962 and got the President to admit the merits of its cause. It sent a delegation to the U.N. and another to the Soviet Union that year, and members went to the Nevada Test Site.

✚

WOMEN'S BAN-THE-BOMB SPEARHEAD HITS VEGAS, the *Las Vegas Review-Journal* headlines blazed on Thursday, July 12, 1962. The demonstration at the Test Site in 1957 finally had a successor, and Women's Strike for Peace garnered a lot of attention. WSP made headlines every day, and CBS News interviewed representatives as they were protesting at the Atomic Energy Commission office in Las Vegas. That Saturday night, WSP joined the throng milling around the casinos. They pushed baby carriages bearing signs, "Empty because of stillbirth" or cancer or leukemia. People walking by spoke up against testing in numbers that surprised the picketers, and other people came up and told them to go back to Russia. They had come prepared with answers for those who thought pacifism was akin to Communism, and with information about economic conversion from military production to peaceable activity. Five locals joined the picket.

The next morning, Sunday, July 15, WSP went to the gates of Mercury. The following day would be the seventeenth anniversary of Trinity, the first atomic bomb explosion in the New Mexico desert. The day before the forty-four women arrived, the DOE had set off a bomb called Small Boy. The official records now state "release of radioactivity detected off site," and some of the evidence suggests fallout reached the Colorado border. The day's *Las Vegas Review-Journal* was dominated by a huge banner headline: 'BAN BOMB' PICKETING AT VEGAS, ATOMIC TEST SITE. Beneath it was the story on Small Boy. "An eerie yellow-gold flash several times brighter than daylight filled the sky for a 20-mile radius in the

Frenchman Flat area of the test site as the device was detonated. Several seconds later, a yellow-brown mushroom cloud billowed skyward. As it passed the 10,000-foot mark, it turned light pink and formed itself into the shape of a cotton candy cone. Then the bottom part of the cloud began turning brown with sand and debris as its cap soared higher and turned snow white, changing into the shape of a huge pinwheel some 10 miles across. The big cloud was clearly visible in Las Vegas 65 miles away." The WSP women carried umbrellas, because it was 115 degrees that morning. Nobody knows what the fallout from the cotton-candy pinwheel of Small Boy may have done to them.

The following August, a few months before my brother was born and Kennedy was shot, the U.S., the U.S.S.R., and Britain signed the Limited Test Ban Treaty. There had been some momentum in the U.S. for a halt to all nuclear tests, but Kennedy backed down. This was only an agreement to put all future tests underground, and France continued to test above ground until 1971, China until 1980. It was a "Treaty banning nuclear weapons tests in Atmosphere, in Outer Space, and Underwater," but it permitted underground testing as long as the fallout remained within "the territorial limits of the state under whose jurisdiction or control such explosion is conducted." Out of sight, out of mind. Women Strike for Peace was given much credit for creating pressure for a test ban, but the Limited Test Ban Treaty infuriated antinuclear activists and deluded the general public into complacency and then obliviousness. Most Americans began to forget that atom bombs were regularly being exploded in their country. Pressure for a comprehensive test ban never achieved the same strength again. The ban significantly decreased the amount of fallout spreading across the globe, but it didn't stop fallout, or the Arms Race. One of the terms of the Limited Test Ban Treaty was that the signatory powers would quickly move toward a comprehensive test ban, and so that treaty too was violated.

Women Strike for Peace didn't give up its fight on testing. In January of 1964 it came back to Nevada, demanding a total ban on testing. Quick on the heels of the August 1963 Limited Test Ban came stories that underground tests had been venting. When a bomb explodes underground, it creates a cavern full of radioactive gases under extraordinary heat and pressure. Sometimes—often—it cracks the surface of the earth and spews gases into the atmosphere. Nuclear tests have vented regularly since the Limited Test Ban and violated it, with fallout reaching as far as Canada. The *Wall Street Journal* reported on illicit fallout in Canada and on iodine-131 in Nevada, Utah, and Idaho milk not long before WSP's 1964 demonstration, and WSP called attention to the continuing dangers. But around the time of the Test Ban Treaty, WSP was given covertly obtained footage of U.S. soldiers fighting in Vietnam, before the U.S. admitted it was at war, and from that time onward attention was divided between the hot war abroad and the cold one at home.

✤ REDWOOD SUMMER WAS A PECULIAR EVENT. ON THE ONE hand, few outside the northern and Sierran parts of the state even knew that California was a major timber producer until the ruckus of the bombing and the subsequent summer of actions. The surge of public awareness put the California Department of Forestry, the Forest Service, and the governor under considerable pressure, and significant reforms took place. The demise of the last ancient forests was slowed down. On the other hand, the actions themselves prompted me to coin the slogan "Earth First! Plan Later," and it was often said that some of the ill-groomed and confrontational participants had alienated timberland locals from the environmental movement and undone fledgling alliances. It may be that the direct action was successful, but not directly. Without the ruckus, the real issues would never have been covered in the media, and without this media coverage of the destruction of the last of the old-growth forests, the public pressure to reform would not have existed. I did some propaganda work at home and went along on a few of the disorganized events, however, and in the course of the summer, I saw hundreds of clearcuts and grew familiar with the exquisite fragrance of a chainsawed grove. I learned to see the difference between the complex world of an old-growth forest, the modest variety of second-growth, and the regimented monoculture of tree farms. I swam in the delicious waters of several rivers—the Trinity, the Mattole, the Tule—and made a few friends. Judi Bari learned to walk again while she was in hiding and later resumed her activist work. No suspect was ever named in the bombing after the charges against her were dropped.

✣

My cousin had gone to one of the Test Site actions in the 1980s, but she told me her arthritis, which made walking any distance painful, would prevent her from ever going back. One day, she mentioned her work with Leo Szilard, and my jaw dropped. Szilard had worked with the great founders of quantum and nuclear physics, had been part of the beautiful adventure that was atomic physics before physics became useful for war, had lived in the intellectual ferment of prewar Europe that was gone forever. What had seemed like such a set and distant history, the history of the bomb, seemed within reach with her stories.

My cousin Mary brought me another history as well, a family tree, done by a distant relation of ours in Buenos Aires. As big as a map, it went all the way back to the early nineteenth century and was studded with scholarly rabbis. Her own sons who had both died young were there, but my branch of the family had not been updated since my parents' marriage: My brothers and I did not exist on it. And a whole side of the tree had been hacked off fifty years ago, and there was a blank white region there. Everyone who hadn't emigrated to the Western Hemisphere ended up in Treblinka, the Nazi death camp in Poland.

Lise Meitner's Walking Shoes

✚ A SENTENCE, OR A STORY, IS A KIND OF PATH. IN APRIL OF 1851, five years after his night in jail and a century before the nuclear explosions in Nevada, Thoreau gave a talk in which he took his audience down a path that few had trod before. The talk was called "Walking," as was the rambling essay published eleven years later, in the midst of the Civil War and just after its author's death. It still stands as a kind of manifesto for wilderness and as Thoreau's most quoted piece—the place where he says, "In wildness is the preservation of the world," among other things.

Thoreau's "Walking" really had three subjects: walking, wildness, and the West. "I wish to speak a word for Nature, for absolute freedom and wildness," he began, but somewhere along the way his words ran away with him, and he lost sight of his original destination, or lack of destination. In the beginning, he says both a word for wildness, and many more in praise of walking, not as a way of getting anywhere but as a way of being somewhere—in the wild. Every walk is a sort of pilgrimage, he says, and suggests that in nature one has already reached a holy land, rather than that the landscape is an obstacle course one must pass through on the way to some built-up shrine or other. The landscape, any landscape, is itself holy land enough, and so Paradise is here on earth ("one world at a time," he said on his deathbed). And if Paradise is nothing more elusive than countryside, then one need go no further than the nearest field or forest to have arrived.

He praises what walking can do for thinking. Walking is nearly alone among all our human activities in its poise between doing something and doing nothing; it is not idleness, and yet as the legs move and the eyes gaze, the mind can roam with a kind of discipline and scope hardly possible in an armchair. As the rhythm of the walk is interrupted by the surprises and irregularities of the landscape, so ideas arise from lengthy concentration interrupted by epiphanies. That is, new ideas often arrive as though from outside, seeming more like discoveries than creations, but it is only long work that takes one to them, as the walk takes one to the landscape. And in walking in the woods, one is, as Thoreau says, "an inhabitant of nature, rather than a member of society," part of a world of larger scope. And so Thoreau speaks, a few pages later, against "all man's improvements," which "simply deform the landscape." He tells a fable of a miser who digs a posthole in the midst of paradise as the angels move around him, and whose land surveyor is the Prince of Darkness.

The miser's drama takes place on the unsettled prairie of the American Midwest in the 1850s. And thus Thoreau takes up the subject of the West, the direction he himself always chooses to walk. "The future lies that way to me," says the tourguide of "Walking," "and the earth seems more unexhausted and richer on that side. . . . Eastward I go only by force; but westward I go free. Thither no business leads me. It is hard for me to believe that I shall find fair landscapes or sufficient wildness and freedom behind the eastern horizon. I am not excited by the prospect of a walk thither; but I believe that the forest which I see in the western horizon stretches uninterruptedly toward the setting sun, and there are no towns nor cities in it of enough consequence to disturb me. I should not lay so much stress on this fact, if I did not believe that something like this is the prevailing tendency of my countrymen. I must walk toward Oregon, and not toward Europe. And that way the nation is moving, and I may say that mankind progress from east to west."

As one may reach the crest of a mountain in what looks to be wilderness and see a city on the other side, so Thoreau in his rhapsody about the wild and free suddenly joins forces with the march of progress which will spread cities, railroads, mines, and military bases across his vision of the West. It may demonstrate the power of the jingoism of the time that even so obstinately independent a citizen as Thoreau falls under its sway. Halfway through the essay, the guide who has set out to show us the glory that is absolute wildness is taking us on a tour of the marvels of progress, cultural and geographical. In fact, in the spirit of his time, he conflates the two in one tide of advancing civilization, one celebration of the westerly ascent of European man in America.

The citizens of the United States had labored under a mighty inferiority complex when they looked back at Europe. The European landscape was given meaning by the long history that could be read in its names and ruins and monuments. The American landscape lacked all that to its newcomers. Over the decades, a new Yankee credo arose, in which the landmarks of Europe were evidence that the place was weary, spent, used, soiled almost; the supposed newness of the U.S. demonstrated that it was fresh, young, pure, a child of promise with its history all laid out before it, a tabula rasa on which a heroic history would be inscribed. (Thoreau proclaims that his is the heroic age itself.) In 1835 the godfather of American landscape painting, Thomas Cole, laid out the thesis: "I will now venture a few remarks on what has been considered a grand defect in American scenery," he began as disarmingly as Thoreau began, "the want of associations such as arise amid the scenes of the old world. . . . But American scenes are not so much of the past as of the present and the future. And in looking over the yet uncultivated scene, the mind's eye may see far into futurity. Where the wolf roams, the plough shall glisten; on the gray crag shall rise temple and tower—

mighty deeds shall be done in the now pathless wilderness; and poets yet unborn shall sanctify the soil."

Thoreau chimed in from his podium in 1851. He suggested even that the sky was higher and the stars brighter in the Americas, the Mississippi was preferable to the Rhine, for its heroic age had just begun, while Europe's was exhausted, as was its mythology. "As a true patriot, I should be ashamed to think that Adam in paradise was more favorably situated on the whole than the backwoodsman in this country." The Old World mythology of Adam didn't trip up Thoreau, and Adam was the key figure in this new American credo. Not the Indian but the backwoodsman clearing the forests of Paradise is his hero, his Adam in this swampy midsection of "Walking"—the New World wasn't new enough to its natives. He doesn't note that with the backwoodsman swinging his axe and the nation heading toward Oregon the forests might not long stretch toward the setting sun. Nineteenth-century Americans had a hard time thinking of the continent as less than boundless. In this world that was just beginning, in which the pioneer was a new Adam, memory was of no use, the past was so much burden to be dumped. Thoreau calls the Atlantic a river of Lethe—forgetfulness—to be crossed in this march toward a higher civilization under a higher sky. He proposes a Society for the Diffusion of Useful Ignorance. And he proposes a Gospel According to This Moment, and gives us the credo of this religion which supplants that of the Bible: "I believe in the forest, and in the meadow, and in the night in which the corn grows." And then, Thoreau seems to forget his own strange detour and finds his way again, against the American grain and the war with Mexico and in favor of undeveloped landscapes.

The United States of America has, ever since this strange up-welling of nationalistic optimism, been distinguished by its amnesias, its sense of prodigious destiny—its looking ever forward and never back—and its frenzied transformation of landscape into real estate. Not Thoreau but Thomas Cole traced the impetus braided of these three strands to its logical conclusion. In 1836, he created a five-painting cycle called *The Course of Empire,* which traces a single landscape through aeons of human history. The first big panel is titled *Savage State,* and in it half-nude figures rush across a tumultuous, misty landscape. This savagery is succeeded by *Pastoral State,* in which the deer hunters and spear chuckers have become contemplative shepherds. It is this, rather than the next panel, *Consummation,* that seems to represent Cole's ideal, for in *Consummation,* the landscape but for a mountaintop has been obscured by a fairyland version of Imperial Rome, whose splendor is a little repellent. *Consummation* leads to *Destruction,* and the dubious figures of the previous scene begin to lay waste to the fairy city and to each other. *Desolation* concludes *The Course of Empire:* The landscape has returned, and a few ruins grace it. The people seem to have succeeded in extinguishing themselves, for the landscape that has emerged from the buildings is uninhabited.

✚ THREE YEARS AFTER THE END OF WORLD WAR II, THE POET W. H. Auden wrote an essay called "Arcadia and Utopia" in which he proposed the two places as categories of belief. Arcadians believe that Paradise was in the past; propose that we return to a simpler state, a lost state of grace; and distrust government, technology, progress, and anything that tends to uproot, to supplant the country with the city, the simple with the complex. Utopians reach for their shimmering vision of a perfectible future with all the authority and technology within their grasp. In "Walking," Thoreau is an Arcadian who briefly lapses into the Utopianism of his time. In *The*

Course of Empire, Cole interrupts his Utopian visions for the American landscape with a little pessimistic Arcadianism. Probably the most perfect example of the two philosophies come into conflict today is in the confrontations between antinuclear activists and nuclear physicists.

✚

Arcadia is a place, a mountainous region on the Peloponnesus peninsula of Greece. It was old when Theocritus set the first pastoral poems there before Christ was born, and its inhabitants claimed to be of a lineage older than the moon. When Roman Virgil took up Theocritus's pastoral mode, Arcady was no longer a rough backward part of Greece renowned for its singing, but an ideal. Virgil's Arcadian world was a refuge from the strife and intrigue of Rome, and he established the pastoral as a celebration of the simple over the complex and the rural over the urban. An Elizabethan pastoral poet, Sir Philip Sidney, summed up the setting of the pastoral as "a civil wilderness, and a companionable solitude," a paradoxical ideal. Pastoral comes from *pastor*—shepherd—and the pastoral is a poem or painting in which pensive shepherds converse of love and loss; the pastoral's principal themes are time and nature. Shepherding served the pastoral poets as walking served Thoreau.

The nature writer and Sierra Club founder John Muir—who took the thousand-mile walks Thoreau only talked of—spent his first summer in the Sierra among shepherds, and he was appalled by the brutish minds of his companions and their indifference to the glories around them. Still, you can't imagine Marie Antoinette playing at being a turnip-gatherer or a goose-girl rather than the shepherdess role she favored. The aristocracy of Europe kept up this involvement with the pastoral, and Virgil's pastoral poems were taught in high schools until sometime in the twentieth century. Virgil's shepherds are less true images of rural labor than counterimages to the city: ideals of an uncorrupted, natural intelligence. So in some sense the pastoral is not about the country, but what the country means to the city, and what the past means to the present. The pastoral celebrates a paradise lost, less that of Eden than the secular paradises of the Golden Age; on which a later age overlaid the classical past, the world from Plato to Virgil or so; and the Romantics, who were adamant Arcadians, added childhood, the last paradise lost for all of us. Arcadia is the land of a universal childhood in which the earth brings forth her fruits without toil, a generous mother to her blameless children. Though pastoral poetry has been out of vogue for half a century, its themes were taken up by children's literature—*The Wind in the Willows* is a superb example—and by landscape novels, from the exotics of W. H. Hudson's *Green Mansions* to the bucolics of Thomas Hardy's Wessex countryside.

Utopianism is of a more recent genesis than Arcadianism. Until the seventeenth century, the New Jerusalem stood at the end of history as Eden stood at its beginning (though humanity was still moving from a garden to a city). Only divine intervention could undo the Fall, and all the time between these paradisal landmarks was essentially static, or in mild decline. The seventeenth century was the century of Descartes, Bacon, and Newton, who brought us scientific method and a vision of secular progress through technological achievement—that is, through the control of nature. Earlier visions of improvement emphasized social rather than technological change, but the two gradually ran together in the Utopian visions of a rationally ordered society. (The word Utopia was coined earlier, by Thomas More, who cobbled it together out of Greek—*ou topos:* no place—and had mixed feelings about Utopias.) Most contemporary historians of science declare that the modern era began with one of those three men, and the scientist rather than the capitalist or the land developer serves them as the very type of the manipulative Utopian.

For example, Francis Bacon proposed that the purpose of knowledge was utilitarian—the domination of nature—as it still is to us, but to his predecessors knowledge was primarily for spiritual improvement. Bacon most audaciously suggested that "man by his fall fell at the same time from his state of innocency and domination over creation. Both of these losses however can even in this life be in some part repaired . . . the latter by the arts and sciences." In his model of knowledge, what had previously been considered a sacrilegious prying into the mysteries of creation was reconfigured as a morally neutral, even an innocent, act. The sciences he described were those of empirical knowledge and scientific experiment, the idea of containing and manipulating something to discover its secrets. Bacon is often credited with establishing the scientific method, as well as the pattern for scientific purpose. And he wrote a Utopian novel about a technocratic society.

Descartes, who was as much younger than Bacon—about forty years—as Newton was younger than him, was equally radical. He abandoned the whole edifice of classical knowledge to begin over again, and he established as a new foundation for knowledge reason and mathematics. Descartes tore a whole cosmos apart with his *Discourse on Method.* And by asserting that such eternal verities as mathematics governed the universe, he displaced God as an active participant. The earth was no longer the way it was because of providence—divine intervention—but because of the laws of nature. "God sets up mathematical laws in nature as a king sets up laws in his kingdom," he wrote, but it was the laws, not the king, he found, and the universe he described resembled the great wonder of his age, clockwork. The universe was a clock wound up by a God who was no longer involved. And having driven away God and the ancients, he proceeded to drive the mind out of the body: The body becomes another machine, and machines are controlled from without. Thus derives a cosmos in which the divine and the creation are separate, as are the mind and the body; and since mind is a quality of human beings alone, the mind and nature; and nature—this distinct, soulless thing—is the subject of the new science. The nuclear physicist Werner Heisenberg commented that Descartes differed fundamentally from the ancients in that they endeavored to understand things through connections and affinities, Descartes through isolations and divisions.

Newton is significant here as the man who realized much of what Bacon and Descartes proposed. He laid down the principles of classical physics, describing the laws of the universe—the design of the clockwork—with a mathematical certainty that had never before been attained and has hardly since been exceeded. Like them, he asked a fundamentally different kind of question of the universe than theologians and alchemists had: not why, but how, things were. And with such questions asked and others unspoken, Bacon's vision of the moral neutrality of science was established. In the work of these three men the vision of progress was born—a vision in which knowledge allowed rational man to exert increasing control over the earth.

As means, the scientific methods they established are of unquestionable value; as an end, they are more dubious. The desire to know is as often motivated by love as by hate. Lovers and interrogators have curiosity in common, and they have differences: The desire to understand the universe is not the same as the desire to control it. But the definition of progress came to mean not understanding but control, and not spiritual or social improvement but the advancement of power—which meant geographical manifest destiny in the

America of Thoreau's age, and means technological manifest destiny in our own.

Those antiseptic scenarios of optimistic science fiction—rational men and women dressed in rational uniforms, living in highly artificial circumstances and probing further into the cosmos—are the logical outcome of this vision. Like Bacon's and More's Utopias, they seem cultures in which children, dreams, poetry, idleness, and mystery have no place, and even the intricacy of the landscape itself has disappeared in a more efficiently human-oriented life-support system. Freudians might say that theirs is a world that does not acknowledge the unconscious; mystics, the soul. It is Cole's *Course of Empire* painting *Consummation,* without the capstone of *Destruction,* a destruction wrought by the urges that fester unacknowledged in a Utopian regime. For the Arcadians, nature is good enough and Paradise is at least a memory; for Utopians, Paradise is a *super*natural ideal waiting to be realized on the earth by men. Nature and the past are problems to be overcome.

Thus, Arcadians and Utopians.

✚

Picture a confrontation between nuclear physicists and antinuclear activists and you get the most vehement and extreme advocates of Utopianism and Arcadianism, staring each other down across an abyss of incomprehension. They don't often meet at the Test Site, for the physicists only fly in for bomb tests, but they have often run into each other during the protests at the nuclear weapons laboratories—Livermore Labs near San Francisco and Los Alamos near Santa Fe. The blockaders are a motley group, ranging from adolescents to elderly clergy and old leftists, perhaps including a Buddhist monk in saffron robes (Japanese Buddhists have been persistently involved in antinuclear activity), some antinuclear lawyers, a doctor from Physicians for Social Responsibility, but professionals are the exception in the U.S. direct-action movement (though not abroad). Most of them are poor—not born to poverty but middle-class people who choose to live modestly and devote themselves to the general welfare rather than personal security. Many of them look countercultural—during the eighties, a lot of punks were involved, and there's still a sizeable number of hippie diehards out there for TV cameras to zoom in on. "Everything should be as simple as possible, but not simpler," Einstein once said, and one of the besetting sins of these Arcadians is oversimplification. With their platitudes of love, these can represent some of the nadir of Arcadianism too. I often find it embarrassing to be associated with them, but I agree with their general principles if not with their style. They are liable to be singing, carrying banners and signs they've made, and trying to strike up a conversation with the sheriffs and security guards. At some point one of the arresting officers will ask who the leader is, and the activists will say that they don't have leaders, though they may offer up a spokesperson to negotiate.

The spokesperson may offer to halt the demonstration if the development or testing of nuclear weapons is halted. The activists seem unrealistic, for the adjustment they are asking for is enormous. It affects economics, foreign policy, and the very definition of national security, as well as the continuing employment of physicists by the defense industry. They might themselves say they are realistic on a larger scale, for they are concerning themselves with disasters that the bombmaking institutions downplay or deny: disasters whose chances are slim—accidental detonations—and disasters whose impact is a long way away—disposal of waste that will be dangerously radioactive for tens of thousands of years—and the disaster that the people who can deploy nuclear weapons are not adequate to the decision—no one is.

The physicists are more homogenous. They are government employees with security clearances, in their middle years between acquiring Ph.D.s and retiring, mostly white and male; they are paid extremely well for their work, and most of them seem to believe in the rightness of weapons design and deployment. They may refuse to discuss the issue on the grounds that nonscientists are unqualified to assess the dangers of the highly technical weapons (I have been told this myself). They may instead say that the weapons guarantee peace, that only the vast array of missiles has prevented a third world war, and that they need to continue building safer weapons—less likely to detonate accidentally, for example. (Although they say they need to continue nuclear testing for safety purposes, the tests—at about $160 million apiece—are needed only for developing new weapons, more destructive destruction.) They may refuse to believe that nuclear weapons are out of control or must be controlled, for to them, they—the designers—are the ones who control them. As engineers they may consider the worst-case scenarios as allowable risks: In the fifties Livermore Lab's founder, Edward Teller, used to argue that a nuclear war was winnable: "Perhaps twenty million might be killed . . . yet within about three year's time we should be back on our feet." They may argue that arms reduction is a political, not a scientific, responsibility.

Olzhas Suleimenov, the Kazakh poet and founder of the Nevada-Semipalatinsk Antinuclear Movement which shut down the main Soviet test site, once met with Livermore Lab officials. Many questions were asked and answered, and then Suleimenov asked what they were going to do about the waste. It took several reiterations of his question for them to be sure that the translator was not missing the point, and then the physicists said that nuclear waste was not their department, but that of geologists, and so they didn't think about it. This is as fundamental a distinction as any between the Arcadians, the amateurs at the gate, and the Utopians, the professionals in the control room. The former believe that the bomb is everybody's responsibility, and that plans need to be laid not for the next decade's national security, but for all time and the whole earth. The latter accept a division of labor, and a compartmentalization of moral responsibility.

Or the fundamental distinction between them could be summarized with a kind of symbolic geometry. Arcadians believe in cyclical time, in the eternal return of nature, Utopians in the linear progress of culture, and these forms emerge in many ways. The most common formation of the activists—for discussions or celebrations—is a circle, with everyone equidistant from the center and equal. The formation of the scientists could be envisioned as a pyramidal grid, with responsibilities divided and delegated according to a chain of command and a compartmentalization of expertise. And while the physicists may hardly touch ground as they are shuttled from their airplane to the windowless control room for nuclear tests, the activists will be out of doors for the duration of their time at the test site, living literally on earth, exposed to the elements—and radioactive isotopes thereof—and sheltered only by the tents of good pastoralists.

The physicists I have been discussing are in many ways technicians, applying the principles of physics to bombbuilding, not pure theorists. They seem to represent most of the values of the Utopians of the Scientific Revolution, and that moment of progress-worship that Thoreau fell into in the course of his meandering talk on walking. It wasn't always that way.

✚ IN 1900 THE PHYSICIST MAX PLANCK AND HIS SON TOOK A
long walk through the Grünewald, the forest surrounding Berlin.
He confided to his son that he had made a discovery of the first rank,
perhaps as significant as a discovery of Newton's. The conservative
Planck was reluctant to unleash a revolution onto the world, but after a summer of calculations he found no way out of his own conclusions. So, late in the first year of the twentieth century, he
presented his findings to the German Physical Society—findings
which, says a later physicist, "were so unusual and so grotesque that
he himself could hardly believe them, even though they caused intense excitement in the audience and in the entire world of physics."
Energy was emitted by vibrating particles in discrete quantities, or
quanta, Planck demonstrated, rather than in the continuous flow described in classical Newtonian physics. Not only did Planck change
the picture of energy, but he supplied the mathematical formula with
which to measure this basic unit of energy, a number that became
known as Planck's Constant. The physicist Arnold Sommerfeld sent
Planck a delicate compliment to his originality:

> You *cultivate the virgin soil*
> *Where plucking flowers was* my *only toil*

Planck had gone into physics, he wrote later, because "it is of
paramount importance that the outside world is something independent from man, something absolute, and the quest for laws
which apply to this absolute appeared to me as the most sublime
scientific pursuit in life." But Planck's Constant was the tool that
took physics in another direction, toward quantum physics and a
more complex picture of the universe. In 1905, the year he also published his Theory of Relativity, Einstein interpreted Planck's Con-

stant in relation to light and heat, with revolutionary results: Light behaved as though it were particles—quanta of light—as well as though it were waves, an apparent contradiction Einstein left for posterity to resolve. In 1913, Niels Bohr used Planck's Constant to remap the atom, describing the specific orbits and energies of electrons in terms of it. In Bohr's new theory, energy at the atomic scale was also no longer a continuous flow, but an accretion of discrete packages, of quanta. In contemporary terms, the universe which had been so long assumed to be analog was turning out to be digital. In terms of early twentieth-century science, it was the beginning of quantum physics.

A big, athletic man, a terrible writer, and famous mumbler, Bohr was, after Einstein, the greatest physicist of the era, remarkable not only for his intuitive brilliance but for a kindness.

It was the summer of 1922, and Bohr was taking a walk on the Hain Mountain above Göttingen in north-central Germany with Werner Heisenberg, a student who had just won his admiration by contradicting him in public, on their first meeting. Heisenberg had been the most promising student of Sommerfeld, who wrote that couplet to Planck and who brought his protégé to the University of Göttingen to hear Bohr speak. "My real scientific career only began that afternoon," Heisenberg declared.

The historian Richard Rhodes recounts that Heisenberg was a member of Germany's youth movement, whose members went on "hiking tours, built campfires, sang folk songs, talked of knighthood and the Holy Grail and of service to the fatherland. Many were idealists, but authoritarianism and anti-Semitism already bloomed poisonously among them. When Heisenberg finally got to Copenhagen at Eastertime in 1924, Bohr took him off on a hike through North

Zealand and asked him about it all." Heisenberg laid Bohr's fears to rest during their several-days walk, and the two began their great work together.

Between them, they established a basis for quantum physics that undid classical physics and alienated even Einstein (who refused to accept the tenets of quantum physics for the rest of his life). Heisenberg's greatest contribution came about in 1926; he wrote of it, "I remember discussions with Bohr which went through many hours till very late at night and ended almost in despair; and when at the end of one discussion I went for a walk in a neighboring park I repeated to myself again and again the question: Can nature possibly be absurd as it seemed to us in these atomic experiments?" Thus far atoms had been looked at as though they were tiny planets, and if the location and velocity of a planet are known, its motion can be predicted, as Newton first demonstrated with eclipse predictions. It could not be done with the atom: the same apparent cause could produce different effects, violating the principle of causality.

Heisenberg came back from his walk in Copenhagen's Faelled-park convinced that the results they were looking for could never be found: The atom was so small that the attempt to look at it via instruments disturbed it and thus dictated its behavior. To identify its velocity changed its location, to identify its location changed its velocity; measuring one aspect made the other uncertain. His conclusion came to be called the Uncertainty Principle, and its implications reached far beyond the experiments it explained; it subverted the entire scientific model of observation and set a barrier to one progression of discovery. There was no distinction between looking at something and affecting it on this scale. From the Uncertainty Principle, Heisenberg arrived at a redefinition of science and of knowledge. "Natural science does not simply describe and explain nature; it is part of the interplay between nature and ourselves; it describes nature as exposed to our method of questioning. This was a possibility of which Descartes could not have thought, but it makes the sharp separation between the world and the I impossible." Bohr added later, "After all, we are both onlookers and actors in the great drama of existence." And thus they undermined the absolute Planck sought in physics.

While Heisenberg had been pacing through Copenhagen, Bohr had gone off skiing in Norway to ponder a different conundrum. Heisenberg and another atomic physicist, Erwin Schrodinger, had each explained properties of the atom with beautiful mathematical formulae that began from different premises and used different methods but arrived at identical results. Schrodinger had abandoned Bohr's model of the atom altogether and calculated as though it consisted of waves of energy rather than of matter; Heisenberg had stuck with matter. Bohr stood up at a conference of physicists in Como in 1927 and announced that one could best proceed on the assumption that they were both true, even though they contradicted each other. The truth available from both descriptions was more complete than the truth either offered, and so they were complementary, rather than contradictory. Bohr's Principle of Complementarity, as he called it, and Heisenberg's Uncertainty Principle described a universe more complex and less easily knowable than the world of classical physics in which they had begun.

Bohr's theory seemed, too, to bear traces of the generosity and justness of its creator. Long afterward, J. Robert Oppenheimer wrote, "It was a heroic time. It was not the doing of any one man; it involved the collaboration of scores of scientists from many different lands, though from first to last the deeply creative and critical spirit of Niels Bohr guided, restrained, deepened, and finally transmuted the enterprise."

✛

It was 1927, and the young physicists Robert Atkinson and Fritz Houtermans were on a walking tour near Göttingen. As they strolled together through the German countryside they began to speculate on the nearly inexhaustible energy of the stars, and of the sun that shone on them. "Such was the origin of the labors of Atkinson and Houtermans on their theory of thermonuclear reactions in the sun, which later achieved such fame," wrote the physicist Robert Jungk, in his history of atomic physics, *Brighter than a Thousand Suns.* "The theory for the first time put forward the conjecture that solar energy might be attributed, not to the demolition, but to the fusion, of lightweight atoms. The development of this idea led straight to the H-bombs that threaten humanity today."

All the European physicists of this era were people of enormous cultivation, classically educated and concerned with politics, poetry, and music, as well as science. Their walks evinced a taste for landscape, for the Romantic and Goethean tradition of nature worship, and for the informal and unhierarchical Socratic tradition of thinking and talking while walking, rather than doing so in offices and classrooms. In the university town of Heidelberg there is still a famous path where several German philosophers did their thinking, and by taking such walks the physicists positioned themselves as philosophers of matter, not technicians, however much time they also spent in laboratories.

It seems that walking maintained their sense of human scale and thus of humanity even while they speculated on the activities of stars and subatomic particles. Their epiphanies and confidences in the landscape suggest the way they thought of themselves as innocents involved in a beautiful and morally neutral practice. They had shattered other worldviews, though, and their own was about to be shat-tered. The Soviets often considered the breakthroughs of Einstein and of quantum physics to be subversively bourgeois, and the Nazis and a few German physicists denounced them as Jewish physics.

A decade after his speculative walk near Göttingen, Houtermans, who was Jewish, emigrated to the Soviet Union from the Germany of the Third Reich, but the Soviets too were in the midst of an era of terror. He was tortured and interrogated by the secret police and then handed back to the Gestapo. And thus the Soviets mislaid their chance at having an atom bomb first. Houtermans spent the war working in the private laboratory of Baron Manfred von Ardenne and obscuring the details of how to make a bomb as far as he dared.

It was Christmas Eve of 1938, and Otto Frisch and his aunt, Lise Meitner, were taking a walk in the Swedish countryside near Göte-borg. Both of them were Austrians, physicists, and Jews. Frisch had been working at Niels Bohr's physics institute in Copenhagen, a sanctuary for a great many Jewish and dissident physicists until Den-mark was invaded. Meitner had stayed in Berlin until Hitler annexed Austria and made her subject to the German racial laws. Then she fled to the position her colleagues found her in Sweden, a bitter exile for her. Frisch and Meitner had spent the holidays together for many years, and their reunion in the midst of the turmoil of the time was a triumph. But Meitner was excited about something else.

Frisch had wanted to go skiing, Meitner had wanted to talk. She asserted that she could keep up with him on level ground, and so he skied, she strode across the snowy ground. Her curiosity had been set aflame by an experiment her longtime collaborator, the chemist Otto Hahn, had just written to her about, in which the element barium had appeared in uranium bombarded by neutrons. (A gentile, he had stayed in Berlin, but defied the Nazis in continuing to work with her.) Hahn was the preeminent chemist of his day, and so there was no possibility that the new element came from impure samples. As Frisch and Meitner went past the river and in among the trees, they became more and more excited. Finally they sat down on a fallen tree, and she began to calculate on scraps of paper. They used Bohr's model of the atomic nucleus as resembling a drop of water held together by surface tension—the binding energy of the atom. The formula Meitner used to calculate the amount of energy released had already become famous, Einstein's $E = mc^2$, energy equals mass times the speed of light, and with it they explained the odd events in Hahn's laboratory. When one atom burst into two, it released a quantity of energy enormous for a single atom—enough to visibly move a single grain of sand, Frisch later wrote.

They concluded something that immediately afterward became obvious to their peers: Hahn had split the atom. Atoms were not so stable and strong as Newton had envisioned them when he wrote, "God in the beginning formed matter in solid, massy, hard, impenetrable moveable particles . . . even so very hard as never to wear or break in pieces; no ordinary power being able to divide what God himself made one in the first creation." Atomic elements with very large and very small neutrons—hydrogen isotopes at one end of the periodic table, uranium at the other—were unstable, and more readily split, unleashing their tremendous binding energy. This is why no element heavier than uranium exists in nature—plutonium would first be created by Glenn Seaborg in the cyclotron at Berkeley in 1940 and in nuclear reactors thereafter.

Frisch wrote his mother, "Feel as if I had caught an elephant by its tail, without meaning to, while walking through a jungle. And now I don't know what to do with it." And he asked a biologist what the word was for the way a cell divides into two as its means of reproduction, and the biologist said *fission*. He named what had happened to Hahn's atoms fission, and the news that the atom could be split stirred physicists as few possibilities had stirred them before.

It was a hot day six months later, July of 1939, and Leo Szilard was in too much of a hurry to walk. He seems out of step with his peers in all the histories and reminiscences—while they walked musingly forward, he scurried around them, fearful they were approaching a precipice. Amnesia made belief in progress possible for Thoreau, memory made it terrible to Szilard. He says in his recollections, "Apart from my mother's tales the most serious influence on my life came from a book which I read when I was ten years old. It was a Hungarian classic, taught in the schools, *The Tragedy of Man*. . . . In that book the devil shows Adam the history of mankind, with the sun dying down. Only Eskimos are left and they worry chiefly because there are too many Eskimos and too few seals."

Szilard had foreseen the destructive possibilities of splitting the atom many years before—quite suddenly as he was about to cross a street in Bloomsbury, London, in 1933, and he had tried hard to prevent it then. When Eugen Wigner (like Szilard, a Hungarian, and a Jew—and therefore a refugee) had told Szilard the news of Hahn's experiment and Meitner's conclusion in January of 1939, his fears about fission came to life again. "I immediately saw that these fragments . . . must emit neutrons, and if enough neutrons are emitted . . . then it should be, of course, possible to sustain a chain reaction," he declared. That is, if neutrons could split an atom, and a split atom then emitted further neutrons, the splitting would continue. This is the chain reaction that makes the energy increase from the scale on which a grain of sand visibly jumps to the scale of a small exploding star which can make an island vanish from the face of the earth (as one vaporized the South Pacific island of Elugelab when the U.S. set off a fission-triggered fusion bomb there in 1952). Most of the physicists saw fission in a scientific light, and some imagined nuclear reactors, but few seem to have foreseen bombs: In the months after Meitner's and Frisch's Christmas walk even Bohr offered reasons why bombs would be impossible.

That hot day in July, Wigner and Szilard went looking for Einstein. The two physicists set off for the town of Patchogue on the south coast of Long Island in a car and, after searching fruitlessly for two hours, decided they must have been given the wrong address. Perhaps it was Peconic that Einstein vacationed in, and so to nearby Peconic they went, but there too they failed to find their friend. Finally, as an ironic aside, the perspiring Szilard asked a boy of seven or eight, busy adjusting his fishing rod, if he knew where Einstein lived—he had become quite famous by that time—and the child gave them directions.

Szilard wanted to use Einstein's prestige and his friendship with the Queen Mother of Belgium to try to prevent the bomb from being built. "The possibility of a chain reaction had not occurred to Einstein," he said later. But Einstein agreed to use his influence to see that a letter reached the Belgian government, warning it about the potential uses of Belgian stockpiles of Congo uranium. Szilard's letter grew through many stages, from a letter trying only to prevent a Nazi bomb to a letter encouraging President Roosevelt to pursue a U.S. bomb. "Through a paradox of fate," Jungk writes of the great pacifist Einstein, "he had decided to give the starting signal for the most horrible of all weapons of destruction." After he signed it, Einstein mused that for the first time humanity would use energy that did not come from the sun.

✚

It was late in the month of October in the year 1941. Bohr and his former protégé and collaborator Heisenberg were taking a walk together again, although everything around them and between them had changed. Bohr, whose own mother was Jewish and who would soon flee Denmark himself, had taken the lead in the Danish effort to rescue Jews. Heisenberg had stayed in Germany and apparently in the good graces of the Nazi Party. He was, in fact, working with Lise Meitner's former collaborator Hahn and a few others on the bomb Szilard had feared, though the ranks of German physicists had been reduced by the ethnic cleansings of the new Reich. Officially, he had come to Copenhagen to attend a scientific meeting.

They were walking near the house that Bohr had lived in since 1932, the House of Honor. It had been built by the owner of the Carlsberg Breweries and modeled after a classical Pompeiian villa, and then its builder had established it as a residence for Denmark's most eminent citizen. The house stood among tall trees, and a beautiful garden covered the expansive grounds. Heisenberg had come not to admire the gardens, however, or to philosophize. Out of doors and in motion they could speak with less fear of being overheard. What Heisenberg said on that night will never be certain, nor will his intentions. He himself said that he intended to reassure Bohr and through him the world of physics that the German physicists would never succeed in building an atom bomb during the war. The English physicist and writer C. P. Snow considered Heisenberg an outright Nazi. But Houtermans, the carefree youth who speculated on the energy of the sun and later lost all his teeth in a Soviet torture session, said he helped Heisenberg smuggle out a note to a friend in the U.S. in 1941, in which Heisenberg declared that he was delaying the program "as much as possible, fearing the catastrophic results of success." The preponderance of evidence is in Heisenberg's favor.

Bohr was a famous murmurer and mumbler, but it is strange that Heisenberg should be so unclear on so crucial an issue. Perhaps he was ambivalent about so definitively treasonous an act amid his long campaign of equivocal loyalty and mild sabotage. But the Danish physicist came back from the walk convinced that his former collaborator had told him the Nazis were successfully pursuing an atomic bomb, and he warned the Allies. His warning gave additional impetus to the U.S. bomb program, which succeeded where the Germans—perhaps misled by Heisenberg—failed.

It was August 7, 1945, and Heisenberg was walking in a rose garden with the physicist Carl Friedrich. They walked up and down it for hours, talking about the horrific news they had just heard. The rose garden was in an English country estate called Farm Hall, where the two walkers were kept captive with Otto Hahn and several other physicists. They had been captured as the Third Reich collapsed that summer, but few prisoners can have been housed in more pleasant circumstances. Heisenberg read the complete works of the Victorian novelist Anthony Trollope while he was interned, and Trollope's portrayals of the small crises of rural gentry must have offered an interesting foil to the forced tranquility of the "guests," as their warden referred to them. Every bedroom and living room had been bugged, and for six months the British recorded their every conversation indoors, even the noises they made alone. In 1992, the transcripts were declassified. As Bacon described nature taken captive and spied upon as the basis for experimentation, so these physicists had themselves become the specimens to be examined for information on the German bomb effort in the glass jar of Farm Hall.

On August 6, their warden had told them that the U.S. had used a nuclear weapon against the Japanese. He reported, "Shortly before dinner . . . I informed Professor Hahn that an announcement had been made by the BBC that an atomic bomb had been dropped. Hahn was completely shattered by the news and said he felt personally responsible for the deaths of hundreds of thousands of people. He told me that he had originally contemplated suicide when he realized the terrible potentialities of the discovery and he felt that now these had been realized and he was to blame. With the help of considerable alcoholic stimulant he was calmed down and we went down to dinner where he announced the news to the assembled guests. . . . The guests were completely staggered by the news. At first they refused to believe it and felt that it was bluff on our part. . . . After hearing the official announcement they realized it was a fact. Their first reaction, which I believe was genuine, was an expression of horror that we should have used this invention for destruction."

Later, in a private conversation with Hahn, Heisenberg made some astute guesses. He conjectured that the Allies must have used much of their two billion dollar budget on uranium isotope separation and estimated the amount needed to produce a critical mass—that is, the amount sufficient for a self-sustaining chain reaction—at about sixty kilograms. And then he told Hahn that he had never pursued that avenue, "as I never believed one could get pure 235." (Most naturally occurring uranium is uranium 238; only the rarer U-235, with three fewer neutrons, is readily fissionable.) Heisenberg was beginning to imagine the extraordinary effort expended at Los Alamos, where Oppenheimer had orchestrated the making of the atom bomb, and at Hanford, Washington, and Oakridge, Tennessee, where the U-235 and plutonium were refined. The conversation recorded by concealed microphones concluded with political speculation. "They must prevent the Russians from doing it," Hahn said. Heisenberg replied, "I would like to know what Stalin is thinking this evening. Of course they have got good men . . . and these people can do it too."

The report on the German physicists in Farm Hall on that epochal day concludes, "Although the guests retired to bed about 1:30, most of them appear to have spent a somewhat disturbed night judging by the deep sighs and occasional shouts which were heard during the night."

✛

It was 1959, the Soviets had had the bomb for ten years, and both sides had developed and tested hydrogen, or fusion, bombs. Teller had just succeeded in designing a nuclear reactor for General Atomic, and Niels Bohr had been persuaded to officiate at the dedication in San Diego. The physicist Freeman Dyson, who worked on the reactor, wrote in his memoir *Disturbing the Universe*, "Bohr became restless. It was his habit to walk and talk. All his life he had been walking and talking, usually with a single listener who could concentrate his full attention on Bohr's convoluted sentences. That evening he wanted to talk about the history of atomic energy. He signaled to me to come with him, and we walked together up and down the beach. I was delighted to be so honored. . . . Bohr told me that we now had another great opportunity to gain the confidence of the Russians by talking with them openly about all aspects of nuclear energy. The first opportunity to do this had been missed in 1944, when Bohr spoke with both Churchill and Roosevelt and failed to persuade them that the only way to avoid a disastrous nuclear arms race was to deal with the Russians openly before the war ended. Bohr talked on and on about his conversations with Churchill and Roosevelt, conversations of the highest historical importance which were, alas, never recorded. I clutched at every word as best I could. But Bohr's voice was at the best of times barely audible. There on the beach, each time he came to a particularly crucial point of his conversations with Churchill and Roosevelt, his voice seemed to sink lower and lower until it was utterly lost in the ebb and flow of the waves."

✚ THERE ARE TWO REASONS TO GO WALKING. ONE IS TO GET somewhere. The other is to walk. Thoreau displays for us both ways of walking, and the kind of thinking behind each one, the ways I have been calling Utopian and Arcadian. Like Thoreau, the physicists had set out to take one kind of walk and taken another. On their strolls through the stately forests of Europe, they had begun, slowly, imperceptibly, inexorably, to march toward the Nevada Test Site. Szilard knew it first, as he stepped off the curb in London in 1933, and he spent most of the rest of his life trying to wake his colleagues to the peril they were approaching. After the war, he abandoned physics and became a biologist and a peace activist.

Until I read their stories, I believed that the scientists who made the bomb were ruthless Utopians. The contemporary Department of Energy scientists I had heard and read had such a mindset, and it seemed safe to project it backward onto their founding fathers. I had often heard the story of their calculation of the chances that the first atomic bomb would cause a runaway chain reaction which would ignite the atmosphere and destroy all life, and I believed that they were such Faustian arrogants, taking it upon themselves to decide the fate of the earth. I believed that their scientific work was undertaken with the desire to control nature, and through it, to control culture. They often serve as symbols of such desire in contemporary writing, but only Oppenheimer in his immense ambition and Teller in his recklessness and dishonesty—the father of the atom bomb and the father of the H-bomb, as they were called—seem to deserve it. Oppenheimer thought that the bomb would make war so terrible humanity would advance beyond war, a strange Utopian belief that technological progress could so neatly bring about social transformation.

It was the gentleness of the other key physicists that struck me in their biographies, and their cultivation, and their penchant for thinking while walking. They seemed the uttermost incarnation of Arcadian shepherds in their long musing walks together, in the sublime beauty they found in speculating on the fundamental principles of the universe. The chessplayers' offensive of the Arms Race could not be further from the wonder and leaps of imagination that built up atomic physics before the bomb, and until Hahn's fission experiments took on practical possibilities their accelerating knowledge of the basic structures of nature seemed to have no practical use. Afterward, Oppenheimer explicitly compared the physicists' situation to paradise before the Fall: Science has known sin, he said, and standing in the dust of the Jornada del Muerte immediately after the first atomic explosion had taken place there on July 15 of 1945 he declared "I am become Death, the destroyer of worlds," a quote from the *Bhagavad-Gita*. And another physicist, Mark Oliphant, said, "This has been the death of a beautiful subject." It all changed at Los Alamos.

Los Alamos is beautiful. It is a mesa 7,000 feet above sea level, even now accessible only through narrow roads that wind along steep slopes and precipices, a fortress of rock thrust up into the deep blue ever-changing New Mexico sky. The mesa is part of the rim of a gigantic extinct volcano, one of the biggest in the world, and from it the Sangre de Cristo (Blood of Christ) mountains dominate the eastern view. One reason Los Alamos was chosen was that the laboratory had to be isolated, to keep the world from the scientists and the scientists from the world. The place had to be remote, but not near a border or coast, and it had to be defensible. Originally the U.S. Army looked for a canyon whose surrounding rim could be guarded, but it settled on this mesa, which also had abrupt edges that could be secured. And perhaps there is another reason. Oppenheimer played a part in the final choice, and he chose it as a theatrical space, a space whose austere magnificence and sweeping views would confer nobility on the work to be done there. He seems to have been trying to match the loftiness of his ambitions to a landscape, and in Los Alamos he found an ideal site. And with this, physics turned from philosophy to war technology, left the gracious European forests in which so many of its crucial ideas had been realized, and moved into the desert expanse that has been its terrain ever since. The desert is no place to meander and fatal to innocents: You must know what you are capable of and what lies ahead.

It was a strange instinct that took the bomb to the desert. It is possible to read the flight of the physicists to this remote setting as a kind of Exodus, as the Mormons read their own flight from persecution to the Utah desert a century before. It is like the westward march Thoreau describes in his detour through Utopianism, a mingling of geographical migration with technological manipulation of nature, a double forward step of progress. There are many echoes in this gathering up of the physicists in the wilderness of 1942. In 1492, the year that Columbus landed in the Americas, his patrons Isabella and Ferdinand also began to expel the Jews from Spain. They had to leave, convert, or die, but many of them chose to dissemble. For more than a century, the Spanish Inquisition attempted to root out secret Jews, and many of them went to the New World to escape discovery. The first European settlement of New Mexico was in large part a mix of Christians of Jewish descent and secret, or crypto-, Jews, and it was they who established Santa Fe. They had invaded Pueblo Indian territory, and in 1680 the Pueblos rebelled and expelled the Spanish. Reconquering the territory distracted the Spanish from their campaign of rooting out Jews in the region, and since then many Hispanic families have practiced Judaism clandestinely into the present day.

Los Alamos, too, was an incursion into Pueblo territory, one that the Pueblos have recently begun to fight back with lawsuits for radioactive and toxic contamination of the land and water still in Pueblo hands. And, as with the settlement of Nuevo Mexico, many of the physicists were also Jewish refugees. Some, like Oppenheimer's family, were from earlier waves of anti-Semitism; Einstein had been the first of the current wave to emigrate to the U.S.; Szilard, Wigner, and Teller came; Bohr came briefly with one of his five sons; Enrico Fermi came from Italy with his wife, who was a Jew and in danger; Otto Frisch, the mathematical genius John von Neumann, Hans Bethe all came. C. P. Snow commented that the refugees made the U.S. "in a very short time, the world's dominant force in pure science." So it is possible to see these two epochal events for New Mexico—the first European incursions and the first atom bomb—not only as manifest destinies, but as effects of the same smoldering intolerance in a distant land. And thus, it is possible to see the bomb and its quick and slow Armageddons as one of the by-products of Hitler's Final Solution.

Bacon had thought that science could redeem humanity's fall from grace, but that science culminated in the atom bomb, which Oppenheimer saw as the fall itself when he said, "Science has known sin." He never clarified what sin it—or rather the physicists of the

Manhattan Project—had known, whether it was the sin of believing that they were on an Arcadian excursion when they had been in fact part of a Utopian project; or whether their sin had been that of turning it from an excursion into a project, changing a disinterested international pursuit of truth into a race for national advantage. Only Bohr and Szilard saw ahead to the impending Arms Race they tried to warn the Allied leaders of, but their warnings went unheeded. "Any temporary advantage, however great, may be outweighed by a perpetual menace to human society," Bohr told Roosevelt, but Roosevelt died soon afterward.

It is said that the Chinese had gunpowder for many centuries but chose not to use it for war, and that the Maya put wheels on the toys of their children but chose not to build wheeled vehicles for practical use. In doing so it seems that they attempted to preserve their cultures in a state of equilibrium, rather than to push them down a road of progress toward an unknown destination, that they valued stability more than the unknowns that come with improvement. It is conceivable that if the physicists had been Chinese or Mayan, they could have realized the possibility of the bomb without ever building it. But theirs was a Utopian culture overall, and it took less than seven years, from Christmas of 1938—the day Meitner and Frisch went walking—to July 15, 1945, to fulfill the possibilities they realized in atomic fission. The bomb was made to fight the Nazis, but only one scientist dropped out of the Manhattan Project when Germany collapsed in late 1944, and the American scientists would become heirs to the cruelties and perversions of Nazi science as their nuclear experiments created more and more victims. There was no way the military was going to spend two billion dollars and have nothing to show for it, and so Oppenheimer's bombs at Hiroshima and Nagasaki were there to justify a budget as well as to fight a war. They were dropped for scientific reasons too: Even the Department of Energy's own handbook of nuclear tests lists those two explosions as tests. To call such an act a test clarifies how far the mindset of scientific control had warped the vision of those who would call all future bomb explosions tests, no matter what their effect on the world around them.

Perhaps the bomb was inevitable, but the Arms Race was born of the suspicion between Germany and its enemies and then between the Soviet Union and its former allies in the war against Germany. It is a great irony that for much of the Cold War, the U.S. and the Soviet Union stationed nuclear missiles in the divided Germany and planned limited nuclear wars on its soil; and another that some of the greatest resistance to nuclear weapons arose in Germany. But those who have suffered most from the nuclear wars of the Cold War have been elsewhere, in Kazakhstan and the Uigur province of China (China, not the China of fireworks but the China of Mao, has had the bomb since 1964), in the aboriginal lands of Australia and in Algeria, in the Marshall Islands and French Polynesia, and in the Great Basin lands downwind of the Nevada Test Site.

The anthropologist Hugh Gusterson studied nuclear physicists and antinuclear activists for several years and came to some interesting conclusions about the cultures generated by nuclear weapons. At the end of the Cold War, as Iraq began to replace the disintegrating Soviet Union in bombmakers' justifications, Gusterson wrote about the beliefs about nuclear weapons and their uses as a kind of story the nation had been told. "The cold-war narrative is simultaneously utopian and despairing about human nature, and it mixes a faith in the redemptive power of technology with an American sense of manifest destiny that is paradoxically reinforced by our government's crimes and failures. By adhering firmly to the belief that America, both morally and technologically, is a chosen nation, the cold-war narrative extends the myth of American exceptionalism—the conviction that America is a country apart, blessed with vast territories and tremendous wealth as part of its historical mission to redeem the fallen nations of the earth. The myth of American exceptionalism runs throughout the country's history, from the Puritan settlement of New England, to the settlement of the frontier, to the nation's rise to global empire. . . . We will not see deep cuts in military spending and a fundamental restructuring of the American warfare state as long as this narrative and the institutions that sponsor it remain powerful. . . . Displacing the narrative will require political organizing against the military-industrial coalition, of course, but it will also require the construction of a new peace narrative that is as compelling and authentically American as the cold-war narrative."

The physics that led up to the bomb, like the walks that preceded the march toward the bomb, seemed to be a path to a different world, a richer, more complex story. Einstein's Theory of Relativity, Heisenberg's Uncertainty Principle, and Bohr's Principle of Complementarity suggested a subtler model of truth than classical physics and Cartesian philosophy put forward. The scientific method had been premised on the clear separation of the true and the false, the observer and the observed. In these concepts, they began to blur. They suggested a model of the world in which what is seen is contingent upon where you look from, the objectivity of the spectator is undermined, observation becomes a form of involvement, and no position is detached (something the Nuremberg Principles would affirm in a vastly different arena). In recent years many writers have attempted to interpret quantum physics in terms of Buddhism, Taoism, and other mystic traditions (and when Bohr was initiated into the Danish Order of the Elephant and given a coat of arms, he chose the Chinese yin/yang symbol as his emblem). Heisenberg wrote, "It has been pointed out before that in the Copenhagen interpretation of quantum theory we can indeed proceed without mentioning ourselves as individuals, but we cannot disregard the fact that natural science is formed by men." He went on to say that science is not a description of nature, but of the interaction between scientists and nature, "nature as exposed to our method of questioning." In other words, science was a conversation whose answers depended on the questions, and the narrative, the account of the conversation, had to include the questioner. The pigeonholes which had been so central to ideals of scientific method could not encompass such a narrative.

Bohr had hoped that the implications of complementarity would be far-reaching. In a lecture to anthropologists and ethnologists in 1938, he used complementarity to undermine the intolerance of the Nazis: "Using the word much as it is used in atomic physics to characterize the relationship between experiences obtained by different experimental arrangements and visualizable only by mutually exclusive terms, we may truly say that different human cultures are complementary to each other. Indeed such culture represents a harmonious balance of traditional conventions by means of which latent potentialities of human life can unfold themselves in a way which reveals to us new aspects of its unlimited richness and variety." Bohr also extended the lessons of the Uncertainty Principle into a lifelong emphasis on the nonobjective involvement of the observer in what is observed, in the way what we see is conditioned by what we believe and what symbols we use to describe it. A friend of his recounts, "When one said to him that it cannot be language which is fundamental, but that it must be reality which, so to say, lies beneath language and of which language is a picture, he would reply, 'We are suspended in language in such a way that we cannot say what is up and what is down. The word "reality" is also a word, a word which we must learn to use correctly.'" Like Heisenberg he believed there was no story without a teller, no fact beyond the influence of its context.

It seems as though quantum physics should have left as its legacy an understanding in which the absolutes and pigeonholes of classical physics and objectivist philosophies became something more rich and strange. Perhaps the principle of complementarity could have reconciled the communist and capitalist worlds to each other. Perhaps the fantasies of control over the political future and the weapons themselves might have been dispelled. Perhaps. But the governments and their strategists took from the physicists not their ideas but their invention.

✠ I WANT TO TALK ABOUT THE PASTORAL ONE MORE TIME. THE physicists saw themselves as being on a pastoral excursion. In a pastoral nothing happens; Arcadia is a refuge from happenings, from history. But something happened, and they, and we, can never go back. Perhaps when they moved from the forests to the desert, or perhaps when they moved from ideas to inventions, they left their pastoral and entered a genesis, a time of creation that in their case included a fall into history—the sin that science knew in New Mexico. A story in which nothing happened—a pastoral—became a story in which an epochal change happened—a genesis—became a story of a stalemate with an apocalypse hovering behind it—the Cold War narrative. Or perhaps they mistook Arcadia for a sanctuary, rather than just an ideal—a peace narrative—with which to gird themselves against Utopia's seductions.

The bomb served the function it was intended for in the wake of World War II. It girded the superpowers against each other and gave each side an argument for trampling and terrifying and sometimes killing its own citizens. But it inadvertently served other functions as well, and in this it may have fulfilled the promise of quantum physics. The Bible describes a few occasions when the cosmology of the world changed: the expulsion from Paradise, the Deluge, the Resurrection. At these times the covenant between human beings and their environment, their expectations, possibilities, and metaphysics were profoundly altered. The bomb was such an epochal event, both the consummation of Utopian fantasies of control of nature and their end—Bacon's redemption and Oppenheimer's fall—and it is easy to imagine its story becoming in a thousand years a second Creation story tacked onto the Bible after the Book of Revelation. It changed everything: the notion of human scale—physicists had manipulated the subatomic to generate destructive power on an unimagined scale, brighter than the sun and deadly for half a million years; the possibility of morally neutral science; the nature of nature itself, with radiation's insidious effects on genes and health. Most significantly, the bomb seemed to close a lot of the divides that had organized the Western worldview: between observer and observed, between matter and energy, between science and politics, between war and peace—after the bomb, any place could be annihilated without warning, and the nuclear powers were permanently prepared for war. Finally, the potential effects of the bomb were so pervasive over time and space that notions of containment and separation collapsed.

The radiations of the bomb, along with the herbicides and pesticides developed from chemical warfare research, were the first quiet messengers that the earth could no longer be regarded as a collection of inanimate objects but must be seen as a network of intricately balanced systems—that is, the substances themselves first spoke out against the inadequacy of the Cartesian worldview, and Rachel Carson first gave them a voice: "In this now universal contamination of the environment, chemicals are the sinister and little-recognized partners of radiation in changing the very nature of the world—the very nature of its life. Strontium 90, released through nuclear explosions into the air, comes to earth in rain or drifts down as fallout, lodges in soil, enters into the grass or corn or wheat grown there, and in time takes up its abode in the bones of a human being. . . ."

She echoes the credo with which Thoreau returned to his senses: "I believe in the forest, and in the meadow, and in the night in which the corn grows." The understanding that everything is connected, which should have come as a vision of harmony, came as a nightmare of contamination instead, but it came, and it came from the bomb. And from this fear of contamination and of Armageddon and this distrust of nuclear authorities came the vast resistance movements of Britain, Germany, Russia, Kazakhstan, and the U.S., came the voices of opposition from Szilard to Carson to Sakharov to Suleimenov to Caldecott. From it came an antiauthoritarianism that would challenge the governments and their judgment and their legitimacy, that would put into practice the Nuremberg Principles that were likewise a legacy of the Third Reich, and that would bring the Arcadians to the gates of the Test Site again and again. And so if the great early physicists of the bomb were walking toward the Test Site without realizing it, perhaps a few of them were marching across the cattleguard before us, not landing in the government jets.

Golden Hours and Iron County

✠ I CAME BACK TO THE TEST SITE FOR THE SPRING ACTION OF 1991. It seemed that nothing had changed there, but everything had changed around it. The Soviet Union was crumbling, and it was clear that the Cold War was going to be history sometime soon. But in January our own country had vetoed the Comprehensive Test Ban and begun a war on Iraq, and there had been talk of using nuclear weapons in the Gulf. For older Americans, the war was terrible because it reminded them of Vietnam. But for those of us too young to remember Vietnam, it seemed at first like the beginning of the end-of-the-world war we had always been anticipating, and we waited for Israel to retaliate and its neighbors to be drawn in and the whole thing to escalate. During those early days I slept with the radio on so that when I woke up in the middle of the night, as I did most nights, I would know if the end had begun. As the showdown with Iraq dragged on, it became clear that developing nations and renegade leaders would fill the gap left by the Soviet Union: The U.S. would find justification to continue developing and testing nuclear weapons as long as its leaders wanted and its citizens acquiesced. Officials at Livermore Labs described new scenarios in which new nuclear weapons and Teller's Strategic Defense Initiative–Star Wars project would be vital, and it became clear the Cold War was as much a mindset as a situation.

Perhaps everyone felt fragile after the months of the Gulf War, for the action that year I recall as unusually tranquil. The days ran together. I was with my friend Tim, an ACT-UP (AIDS Coalition to Unleash Power) activist who wanted to see the landscape beyond the

Nevada highways he'd driven through, and we camped near the Seattle contingent. Every morning I made a gallon of coffee and a pot of tea for Tim, and my brother and other friends would come by with their cups and socialize before the day's business began.

The Seattle people were mostly longtime antinuclear activists in what had been called SNAG—Seattle Nonviolent Action Group. Perhaps because Seattle's activist community was smaller than San Francisco's, they had a tolerance I never found in the San Francisco anarchists, or perhaps they themselves should be given credit for the generosity of their hearts, and for the way their sharp sense of irony never decayed into bitterness or snideness. They invited us to go with them on the action they had planned, and so we went. They had decided that they wanted as peaceful and nonconfrontational an opportunity to trespass as possible, and so they had decided to walk in from one side.

A van or two drove us to our starting point at noon. We drove south a few miles toward Vegas on 95, then turned in at a dirt road whose barbed-wire gates we opened and closed. The dirt road took us a few miles into the hills I had always admired, the ones that loomed like a hunched shoulder to the right of the cattleguard. At the end of the road were mining sites—scooped-out trenches, a litter of equipment—in the pale earth. We began walking from there.

We walked up over a rise between two low ranges and then for much of the rest of the afternoon walked down a narrow arroyo. The walls of rock rose high around us, but as long as we moved along the dry waterway, we were moving toward the flat plateau of Mercury, and there was little to worry about. We seemed to flow through it as leisurely, as desultorily, as spring runoff. As we walked, people moved ahead, gathered into groups for conversation, meandered a little on their own. Around us, there was no sound, and the peace of the landscape seemed to have permeated our own mood. In the shade of an overhanging ledge, we all sat down and had lunch. Madeleine had brought a big slab of chocolate and passed chunks around, and soon everyone was sharing food.

Later on, the arroyo opened up and we climbed a rise. Atop the rise we could see again: the radio tower on a ridge within the cluster of ridges we were in, Mercury off to our right, and the cattleguard to our left as we looked down onto the plateau. Someone had planned a dance at that point, or perhaps it was spontaneous, but however it was generated, the group began to cavort and wave vividly colored banners and discard shirts with growing exuberance. Tim was taken aback, and I sat it out with him. I have never been graced with the ability to dissolve my doubts in such activities, born as they are out of a desire for the innocence of immersion in an experience, for belief. What surprises me is how often the people who engage in such acts of desire seem to fulfill them, seem to be able to create rituals that serve the purpose of ritual for them. They require a willing suspension of disbelief that seldom takes hold of me, though I like being around it when it's free of cant and artifice, as this was. And so I waited, and looked out over the landscape. Later we went down and were arrested uneventfully by the guards who had spotted us out by a boundary fence.

What I remember best from that time is a speaker that morning. American Peace Test had organized a testimonial by people affected by nuclear testing, a representative from Polynesia, a member of the Alliance of Atomic Veterans, and a downwinder from Utah, Janet Gordon. She was heavyset and sweet spoken, with flyaway blondish curls and ferocious, deepset blue eyes, and what she had to say riveted me. But her words seemed to float away on the breeze of the afternoon, to soak into the surrounding rock. Throughout my afternoon walk, I kept looking toward the east, where her story took place, and the north just over the ridge behind Mercury. I kept imagining her brother riding his horse just out of sight in those lands, as he did in her talk.

✚ ONE SUMMER DAY MY BROTHER AND I DROVE EAST FROM Vegas to Janet Gordon's home in Cedar City, Utah. The way there was beautiful: We had crossed out of the pale earth of southern Nevada, into the red sandstone lands of southern Utah, through the rugged gorge of the Virgin River, past Snow Canyon State Park, where fallout devastated the cast and crew of the 1950s movie *The Conquerors*. (Most of them died of cancer, including John Wayne.) It was so hot we drove with the windows all the way down and the wind at 65 miles per hour whipping my hair into a huge snarl. The gas-station mini-marts didn't seem to sell drinks in any size smaller than 44 ounces, and I drank all their strange sweet concoctions—drinks more distinguishable by color than flavor—without ever slaking my thirst or filling my bladder. The water seemed to be sucked straight out of my skin, which stuck to the seat of my truck. Janet Gordon told me the story again, over huge glasses of iced tea in her house nestled in shade against the desert sun.

I grew up in the downwind area, about 150 miles east of the Nevada Test Site, and I was twelve years old when the testing started, 1951. After it started . . . it was a fairly regularly scheduled thing: They would do them just before dawn or at sunrise, frequently every week when they were doing the test series. It got to be a regular kind of thing, and it got so that we locally would anticipate them and plan events around them. The school classes would go out to watch them and go out to a high place where they could get a better view. My sister was in St. George, 70 miles closer to the Test Site during the early testing. When she went down there to college, sometimes they would pack up a breakfast picnic and go out to the top of

Utah Hill because you could actually see the flash and the mushroom cloud from there, instead of just the sky light up, which is what you'd get in most of these other communities, 'cause of the mountains. If you were high enough you could see clear onto the site.

To give you a little bit of background about me and the family that I came from, I come from a pioneer family which settled in this country in the wave of Mormon pioneers. Actually the second wave. My ancestors walked across the continent to find religious and political freedom and half of the family was buried coming across the plains. They went through a great deal of hardship and hard work to settle in this country. My grandmother on my father's side initially settled down in Nevada, in the area that's now covered by Lake Powell called the Muddy Mission. They had so much suffering and so many problems; they buried half the population the first year they were there. They couldn't even keep milk till noon in the heat of the summer; you can imagine what it was like with no potable water—and it was just so awfully hot. When that mission was abandoned, they came to St. George, and instead of going like they wanted back to Salt Lake, they were called to go and settle in Long Valley, which is where my family still is. I would tell you that in my family there is also a very strong sense of the earth, a strong sense of the people who lived here before they came; I grew up with a tremendous sense of respect for the native people.

My grandfather and my great aunt Jane drove the first 300 head of sheep from northern Utah to southern Utah—it took them all summer long. My great-grandfather came down and built a home for his wives, and got settled in the United Order. And Grandfather and Aunt Jane brought those 300 head of sheep by themselves almost 400 miles—through a wilderness— Grandfather was seven years old and Aunt Jane was nine. So I come from a very tough stock, a very hardy stock. I grew up also with a very strong sense of protecting the underdog. I've always been a scrapper for the underdog, even when I was very little. So I came into the era of testing with some family history, with a great deal of love for the land. I was a tomboy growing up. I was my dad's sidekick. I spent a great deal of time out in the desert and in the mountains and in the canyons, and I have a very strong sense of nature.

My dad in the early 1950s was just changing from sheep to cattle. He was losing a lot of sheep then; in fact that's one reason why he switched: They had so many devastating losses and they couldn't figure out what was causing them. We didn't know about the effects of the testing, but we wondered. We didn't know what was going on, we were told that there wasn't any danger, that we were "very lucky to be a part of history being made," and we were quite excited about it. I mean, this was a rural area, nothing much was going on, and to have newsreels come on in the movie theater saying we were part of history being made, this was a very big deal. We were quite excited about it.

The testing series they did in 1953, that was when it really hit the fan for us. Up until then we were wondering what was going on, we were nervous, and there were already some effects with cattle and sheep, but nothing like what happened in the spring of 1953 when they did the Upshot-Knothole series. At that time my brother Kent, he was out at the sheep camp. There were eight other men at that sheep camp that spring—just above Bryce Canyon National Park and on the Glendale Bench east of Zion National Park. Kent came back into camp one evening and he was very sick, he had burns on his skin like a really severe sunburn, he was throwing up, he had a bad headache, and he wondered if it had anything to do with the test they'd set off over in Nevada. They saw the flash, they heard the boom. They knew there was a test, it had been on the radio, and Kent said that it was like a ground fog. Now the area where they were, the Glendale Bench, is a mostly flat area, but with breaks and with brush, the scrub oak brush that's so common in this country, and sagebrush. And he said that down in the low areas it was like a ground fog, when he would ride down into that, he could feel it on his skin, it had a metallic taste, it left a taste in his mouth, and it made him sick and it made his horse sick.

His horse would just get kind of groggy, couldn't hardly get along, then he would get up on a ridge where there was a fresh wind blowing and there didn't seem to be any of this ground fog, and the horse would seem to be OK.

Well, Kent was sick all night, he was throwing up, and he had these burns, and within a few weeks his hair began to come out in patches, in great big patches. He thought that it was rather interesting that the sheep's wool also began to come out in big patches and they developed sores around their muzzles, and the lambs were weak and many died, and the horse that he was riding died. He didn't have any apparent thing wrong with him, he was a young horse, beautiful, and he just laid down and died for no apparent reason within about six weeks. The veterinarian couldn't find anything wrong with him, couldn't find anything wrong with the sheep. What was happening over here in Iron County? At any rate, my brother was sick all night, his hair came out in patches, the wool came out on the sheep, the horse died. Of the eight men that were at the camp with my brother, six of them have died of some form of cancer. One of them, Uncle Joad, he died of pneumonia. My father, who was also at the camp, now has cancer. The only one of all the men who didn't get cancer is my other brother Norman. Norman and Dad slept inside the camp wagon, my brother Kent slept outside on the ground with the other men, in bedrolls. That was probably a factor.

When local people began to question what was going on, the AEC [Atomic Energy Commission, precursor of DOE] developed p.r. films, they began to bring them 'round our schools. I remember sitting on the gymnasium floor when I was in junior high school watching one of these films they made about testing. It shows a chaplain and a couple of soldiers—oh it's an excellent film—the chaplain is talking to these two soldiers who are waiting for a test, and the chaplain says, "What's the matter son, are you worried?" And the soldier says, "Well, just a little bit, father." And the chaplain says, "Well, there's no need to be. First you will see a blinding flash and hear the percussion. And then you can look up and you will see the beautiful mushroom cloud as it ascends to the heavens with all the wonderful colors of the rainbow. It is a wonderful sight to behold."

God and the U.S. government. As a child when I saw that, I was just filled with patriotism. Well, as an adult when I saw it again, it was a whole different matter, after I knew what testing was, after I knew what radiation effects were—. They didn't even tell us what radiation's effects were. They didn't tell us that my brother's hair coming out and his nausea were classic symptoms of radiation exposure. We only had one doctor in the region, he was just a country doctor, he didn't know what to do. In fact the doctor, when my brother's hair started falling out, he gave him vitamin shots. He said, "I don't have the vaguest notion what's causing this, I don't think it'll help but it can't hurt." In fact a lot of people were having their hair come out in patches, particularly people who were out of doors a lot.

So, anyhow, when I saw that film as an adult, in 1979—my sister and I had gone to a uranium conference in Wyoming; I had been doing a lot of work on environmental issues at that time, particularly on strip mining, and so I got invited to this conference. For the first time in my life I learned what radiation effects were, in 1979, and my sister and I turned to each other and said, "That's what killed Kent."

I mean all the things fell into place for us. That's what killed Kent. When I saw that same clip in the film, it made me furious. I'd had some psychology classes by then, and I could see, I could just see those guys sitting around a table and saying, "Let's use soldiers, let's use a chaplain, that'll be good; let's use 'mushroom cloud ascending into the heavens with the colors of the rainbow'—nice imagery." I could see it and it made me so mad, because I had to superimpose that view—that callous, deliberate, intentional brainwashing of my people—over the view of my brother lying in bed in my sister's home.

We kept him at home because there was nothing they could do for him in the hospital. He died by inches. He developed cancer of the pancreas *when he was 26 years old. He died in 1961, in September of 1961, and before he finally died that cancer had eaten into his stomach, into his intestines, food couldn't digest, but he was so young and healthy except for that cancer. It kept getting bigger and bigger, it was as big as a basketball finally, and he was so thin, the skin was stretched so tightly that his eyes couldn't close, his mouth couldn't close. He literally was starving to death, and it was a hideous, hideous way to die. And he knew what had killed him. He wondered at the time, and none of the rest of us had any presence of mind. For years we prayed for him to live and finally we began to pray for him to die.*

To superimpose the picture of my brother lying in that bed with this huge cancer—and his cancer was so big that he couldn't lay his legs out straight because the skin wouldn't stretch that far—it was just hideous, it was so awful. And then to think of the callousness of the professional p.r. people finding the best way to manipulate us. That made me angry. That made me angrier than I had ever been in my life. And it lit a fire inside of me that wouldn't go away, that still hasn't gone away, you can see it's still here. Years since, as we have fought battle after battle after battle, and as our resources to try to fight the whole government have taken their toll on all of us that are still alive as well as the numerous people I've been working with who've died in the course of this battle, I've learned that I have to keep this fire banked or it consumes me and I have no energy to keep on going. So I try to keep it banked inside of me now to fire me up to be effective when I can be in a position where I can be effective. And that's what keeps me going.

The AEC attitude isn't unique. It's happened since the beginning of this nation, from the time that white settlers first came to the Americas— that is, a throwaway exploitation of open spaces and of resources. I think that in particular we were susceptible to it here. They began testing in the region that they did for a number of specific reasons. . . . According to a declassified Joint Chiefs of Staff memo, the American public resistance to

*nuclear testing needed to be lessened, and the best way to do that was to
"put the bombs in their backyard so they would get used to them."*

*So they were looking for open space or public lands, and as far as they
were concerned Indian lands were free for the taking, as they had always
been. And they wanted a place that they could hope for some control of the
fallout. Now the only major East-West range in North America is the Uin-
tas. They intersect with the High Rockies and they form a box with the
Rockies which the experts felt would be able to scrub out most of the radiation before it went across the rest of the nation. So they could contain
their fallout within the Great Basin, within this sparsely populated region
of people who were extremely conservative, extremely patriotic.*

*When Mormons came West because they had literally been run out of
the East because of their religious beliefs, it was like they had to prove they
were better Americans than anybody else. When they came here, they actually raised money for the war with Mexico, even before we were a state.
They had left the United States. They settled in a neutral territory for all
practical purposes. And they worked very very hard, and in most Mormons'
psyches is this ultra-patriotic, ultra-conservative—in fact it's part of Mormon doctrine that the Constitution of the United States was divinely inspired. So Mormons are exceedingly patriotic and they're not going to
challenge a government program when they're told that it's needed for the
good of the country.*

*One of the reasons they did the testing in the area that they did is be-
cause this is a, and I quote,* "virtually uninhabited area." *The area immediately downwind is virtually uninhabited. Well, frequently the
indigenous people, the only reason they have to put up with what they have
to put up with and they lose the battles that they lose is that there's so few
of them. They just don't have the numbers to have the political clout to
keep that kind of thing from happening to them. So we're in the same boat,
we're virtual uninhabitants, the indigenous people of the region and the*

*general population—in other words we have no political strength, we have
a moral right, but we don't have any political rights, apparently.*

I remember going to the second Sane/Freeze convention; I went to that
meeting, I remember standing before that group who were our closest allies
and begging them to recognize that nuclear war is not an esoteric question,
nuclear weapons testing, preparation for nuclear war is a battle that is killing people *now*. Everybody said, "Oh yes, that's fine," and they went right
on with their scheduled program of preventing nuclear war. Nobody would
even listen. I was so frustrated and so upset, I went down the hall and
found an empty room, and I sat down on the floor in a corner and just cried.
I was so frustrated because I couldn't get anyone to recognize there were
victims already, and recognizing that could help the movement to prevent
a global holocaust.

If we recognize this and still don't try to make these changes, then we
deserve what we get. In my opinion, democracy and freedom are something
that has to be earned, and something that has to be earned every day. And
if we don't exercise the privileges that we have, to have some control over
our lives, then we won't have any control over our lives, and that means
we won't have an environment that we can live in, we won't have the right
to practice an indigenous religion, and we won't have freedom from fallout
or from nuclear accidents, from another Chernobyl, and believe me, that
will happen again and again and again as the nuclear facilities get older
and nuclear weapons and debris proliferate. It will only get worse.

✠ IT'S THE SKY THAT I REMEMBER FROM THE VETERANS DAY
action in November of 1991. As we drove across the Mojave again,
at night again, huge lightning storms lit up the landscapes ahead of
us. Great branches of electricity dashed to the ground, and as each
one flashed, the massed gray clouds above became visible. Each time

we were lifted for a split second out of our night world into a strange arena of violent vision.

It stopped raining when we arrived, and that time I slept in the open because the night sky was more brilliant than I had ever seen it, the air scrubbed clean by the autumn storms. I had not yet learned that the physics of bombs mimic the physics of stars, and so as I lay on my tarp each night under a Milky Way like a whitewater rapid, I did not see millions of slowly exploding nuclear devices in the blackness, only stars.

About a quarter million American soldiers were intentionally exposed to radioactive fallout at the Nevada Test Site and the other test sites. So far the Veterans Administration has turned down nearly all requests for benefits for radiation victims, and for their children born with birth defects and diseases. The vocally resistant members of the Alliance of Atomic Veterans, who had initiated this Veterans Day action, were a small minority. Many veterans felt compelled to keep their experiences secret, or only divulged them on their deathbed. Two friends of mine told me almost identical stories about their soldier fathers. Both fathers died of cancer, and both of them on their deathbeds talked about witnessing a bomb so bright they could see the bones of their hands through their closed eyes, and then would say no more of what they had seen.

The veterans sat in a circle on the ground and introduced themselves to each other. They ranged from World War II vets to Desert Storm vets, and some of the Desert Storm vets were due to become radiation victims too, because the U.S. had used uranium-tipped armor-piercing bullets and uranium-armored tanks out there. Many were still angry, some were still wearing their fatigues. Most of them had a story about a point at which the meaning of war changed for them and they turned their back on the military, and on war. For some the change came in combat or at a front, for some within the bureaucracy of the army, and for many only after they became ill and realized that they had been fighting to protect principles that didn't protect them.

Afterward came another round of public addresses on another impromptu stage near the gates of the Test Site. What I remember is Corbin Harney, himself a WWII veteran and the spiritual leader of the Western Shoshone, standing up against a blue sky on the stage. He was wearing a blue gimme cap and a lavender shirt that faded into the sky, so that I saw only his brown hands and face in all that dreamy color. Clouds sat above the mesas of the Test Site the way a tree or a mountain sits above its own reflection in the water, clouds as big and solid and craggy as the land, their undersides dark with the shadow they cast. They didn't look like vaporized water, but like something as solid as marble, a floating landscape above the landscape. Corbin spoke of the Treaty of Ruby Valley and the way nuclear bombing in Nevada violated it, and he said in his deep rasp, "The stones are alive here, everything's alive here. But the bombs are killing them. We are killing our mother today."

When the talks were over the action began: a walk across the cattleguard led by veterans including Bill Rosse and Corbin Harney. I followed. It was as delicate a transition as Alice passing through the looking glass. On one side of the grate across the road we were U.S. citizens on public land, on the other we were civil disobedients in a security zone at the mercy of the forces of the Department of Energy. On that far side, the guards seemed overawed by the men in U.S. military uniforms they were supposed to arrest, and they moved slowly. I looked around and saw several others who were waiting, sheeplike, to be arrested. We said to each other that there was no reason to stop, and so we went walking.

We walked up the gravel road that goes to Camp Desert Rock, the camp where so many soldiers were made to watch atomic bombs go off—including Priscilla in 1957—and then we strayed off the road. Like my spring walk, this one was permeated by a profound tranquility, by the quiet of the expanse and the beauty of the mountains, and by the fulfillment of political purpose we were achieving with so simple and so peaceful an act as walking. We walked for a long time at a leisurely pace among the yuccas across the forbidden ground of this strange place, long enough to begin to wonder what we'd do if they did nothing. We decided to go until Mercury, and we strolled on this peculiar Sunday stroll for another half hour or so until finally a handful of guards came out and met us halfway to Mercury. This time I knew enough about the landscape around us to turn our bus ride to Beatty into a guided tour of environmental disasters. I took off a handcuff and stood up and pointed out sites that Bob and Chris had pointed out to me—Yucca Mountain, the cyanide lake, the low-level nuclear-waste dump—and said a few things I had learned about the Treaty of Ruby Valley and the Shoshone land-rights struggle. For the rest of the ride the women sang.

Ruby Valley and the Ranch

✚ I HAD BEEN TO RUBY VALLEY THE MONTH BEFORE THE VETerans Day action.

For the Western Shoshone, the forty years' war at the Nevada Test Site was only an extension of an assault against Great Basin land and people that should have stopped in 1863, with the Treaty of Peace and Friendship signed at Ruby Valley that year. Dust had not settled on that treaty for them, nor had they entered into any new agreements with the Federal Government in regard to their land, but it was being taken away from them piecemeal by bombs, mines, and bureaucrats.

In the summer of 1991, the Bureau of Land Management started after the Dann sisters, who were Western Shoshone ranchers in north-central Nevada. The government had finally won the lawsuit against them that had begun in 1974, and it was out to get Mary and Carrie Dann's livestock, and with the animals, their land rights and their livelihood. Later, Mary Dann told me how their troubles began. "I was out checking on the cows," she said. "When I came back my brother said there was somebody waiting for me from the BLM office. So I took off my saddle and put my horse away and there he was waiting for me in the house, and we talked, and he says, 'Do you know you're trespassing?' I told him I wasn't. I told him that the only time I'd consider myself trespassing is when I went over onto the Paiute land. Then I would be trespassing, I says. I'm in our own territory, in our treaty. I told him about the treaty and I showed him the map and he told me, 'Well that's a big territory.' And I told him, *Yes,* and I said I'm still within the boundary. He asked me to come to the advisory board anyway, 'We might talk it over and give you a grazing permit,' and I says, 'Well why should I pay a grazing permit when it's our own land?' So I never did it and then they wrote a letter to us, tell us we were trespassing. We wrote back, I don't remember what we said, anyway we wrote back, and then they wrote back again and says well they're coming over to round the horses and cattle up and sell 'em at the sheriff's auction. So we wrote back again and told them to go ahead if it's their God-given duty to come round up our horses and sell them. That they won't be doing selling but they'll be doing something which is stealing. That's what happened, that's what all started this. We ended up in court in '74. And if they're so right, like they say, that they took it in 1872, why didn't they just show us the documents on that? That way we wouldn't be where we're at today. And maybe we could have gotten into something else. Now we're old and they're taking our livelihood away."

When the court case ended and the possibility of a direct attack began, several groups that had been involved in Nevada politics came to their aid: Citizen Alert, where Bob Fulkerson worked, American Peace Test, where my brother worked, and Seeds of Peace, the collective that did much of the feeding and practical organizing at Peace Camp. (Seeds was organized to feed the Great Peace March of 1986 and stayed together to provide logistical support to related activities, from Redwood Summer to this event at the Dann ranch.) Later, AIM (the American Indian Movement) and other organizations got involved, but during the early days it was just these groups that had come together at the Test Site. I had wanted to learn more about the history that led up to it all, and so when the Western Shoshone National Council was looking for someone to write a long story, without pay, on short notice, for a respected environmental quarterly, I jumped at the chance, and I continued to write about the issue afterward. But that first fall, I was waiting for a signal to get started.

✚

One morning at the end of September of 1991, Shoshone elder Bernice Lalo invited me to come and hear her coyote stories at the Ruby Valley Treaty Days Celebration, and so that morning I threw all the gear that had been sitting on the kitchen floor into my car and took off for Ruby Valley in far northeastern Nevada. Highway 80 goes straight from San Francisco across the Bay Bridge east, up through Truckee, Reno, and Lovelock to Winnemucca and Elko, following the Humboldt River from where it disappears in the Humboldt Sink to where it begins, near Wells and the Ruby Mountains. Before it was 80, it was the emigrant trail to California, and the route the Continental Railroad followed, and follows—the great road west—but I was going east and so was the weather. On the road that night a storm blew past ahead of me: Where the rain had fallen, the smell of wet dust and sagebrush drifted on the night air, and one cloud hovered below the Big Dipper, so that the lightning seemed to be pouring out of the Dipper itself.

I stayed in a motel in Winnemucca named the Golden Nugget or the Longhorn or the Sunset Corral, and what I remember of the town is the man in the burger stand wearing a sweatshirt advertising a Christian gym—"His pain, your gain," it said, with a picture of Christ nailed to the cross. Winnemucca was a Paiute chief, and Truckee was his father, but his daughter, the activist Sarah Winnemucca, is the most memorable of the three. Born before the whites flooded into Nevada, she died fifty years later, around the time that the historian Frederick Jackson Turner pronounced the American frontier closed. "When I think of my past life and the bitter trials I have endured, I can scarcely believe that I live, and yet I do; and, with the help of Him who notes the sparrow's fall, I mean to fight for my down-trodden race while life lasts," she wrote near the beginning of her autobiography, and while she lived, she traveled across the country on speaking tours to try to allay the attacks on her people.

Further along Route 80 in the morning I passed a dead coyote, ravens flapping slowly up from their meal at the car's approach, and began to wonder about Bernice's stories. Her directions took me to a road running down Ruby Valley, then the pavement ran out and the road became an interminable line of dry mud ribs, and then I arrived. The Ruby Mountains are where the Great Basin begins to become something else. Humidity softens the air, the range is more like mountains, the basin more like a valley. The Temoke Ranch, where the gathering was being held, was an old homestead surrounded by a screen of hedges and ancient apple trees. Green apples no bigger than walnuts and striped with fine lines of red littered the ground, and I pitched my tent in a sort of inlet in a bay of wild rose bushes covered with ripe red hips. I found Bernice, short and beaming and motherly, and said hello and then took a walk. Being the only white person there made me feel like an invader.

There was an orchard full of horses and ancient automobiles—beautiful, rust-immobilized Model T's and Packards—and then, further away, a house of white-bleached logs. Past that was a tiny rivulet flowing over smooth rocks. Its mossy banks quickly lapsed into dry grass and chaparral, but their brief expanse was as manicured and luxuriant as a Japanese garden. Further upstream there were thickets and clusters of willows, banks of wild roses from which I filled my pockets with hips, and by the time the tributaries joined the main channel I was in among aspens turning golden. In one grove were tree stumps like sharpened pencils pointing skyward, the work of a beaver, and then I found the dam. The Temoak homestead was long out of sight.

✛ WHITES HAD FIRST COME INTO THE AREA THE WESTERN Shoshone call Newe Sogobia in the 1820s on the famous "scorched river" campaign to trap out all the beaver, and none of the accounts had mentioned that the beaver survived it. After the trappers and their sporadic violence, the Western Shoshone were mostly left alone until the emigrant wagons of the 1840s started along the Humboldt for California and the miners of the 1850s and 1860s spilled back across the Sierra into Nevada. It never occurred to me during the innumerable scenes of wagon trains being attacked by Indians in the movies of my childhood that I was seeing an invasion being resisted; it was the wagon trains that provided movie continuity, the Indians that interjected random disruptions.

The U.S. had acquired title to Nevada through the Treaty of Guadalupe Hidalgo—insofar as Mexico had ever owned it—but those who administered the western lands didn't imagine their countrymen would have much use for the region, other than mining and maintaining thoroughfares, and the treaty guaranteed that those who'd held land under Mexico would hold it under the U.S. When the Civil War began, the gold and silver of Nevada did much to shore up the coffers of the North, and the soldiers who had kept the territory safe for emigrants were called to the East. So the territorial governor, James W. Nye, and a few Indian Agents signed the treaty of peace and friendship with the leaders of the Western Shoshone bands in the vicinity of northeastern Nevada on October 1, 1863. The treaty is full of unwieldy phrases, heretofores and to wits, and it is not clear how well any of the Shoshone signatories spoke English, let alone read it. Even so, it was not a bad treaty for them.

Frank Temoke, the current head of his family at the homestead below the beaver dam, is the great-grandson of a Shoshone signatory
of the Treaty of Ruby Valley. (The Western Shoshone were organized
into autonomous bands, and there was no central authority over
them.)

The reasons for the treaty are most clearly stated in an 1864 letter
I found among the papers of the CIA (Commission on Indian Affairs, now the Bureau of same, or BIA): "The country being a mineral one," wrote Jacob T. Lockhardt, the principal Indian Agent,
"entire peace with the Indians has been absolutely necessary to the
development of it. The territory in gold and silver bearing quartz is
fabulous in its extent and richness. Gold and silver are discovered
in many portions of the Territory among large bands of Indians, who
have recently had undisturbed possession of the country. These discoveries being known, miners move in and settle up the country in
a very short time. In this hurried manner of settling the country, of
course, many little difficulties arise."

The Treaty of Ruby Valley is unusual among U.S. treaties with
native peoples in that it repeatedly describes the Western Shoshone
as a nation and, rather than ceding land to the U.S. as most treaties
do, it grants only right-of-way and similar rights. The territory described in the treaty, which was negotiated with the northern bands
of the Western Shoshone, includes a considerable portion of the
present state of Nevada; the total expanse of Western Shoshone ancestral land—Newe Sogobia—forms a long angle that stretches
from Idaho through Nevada down into Death Valley and the Mojave
Desert in California. Much of it was not surveyed well into the twentieth century; and a considerable portion still has no residents or
federal use, despite the jurisdictional markings on the maps. Although the treaty contains provisions for creation of reservations,
none were formed within the terms and times framed in the treaty;

similarly, most of the stipulated payments were never made. The U.S. government violated the treaty immediately through neglect and indifference—in 1869 the CIA official who was supposed to see that the treaty was observed wrote to Washington admitting that his office had no copy of the treaty or knowledge of its contents, and an 1867 letter from a government agent mistakenly asserted no treaties had been made at all.

The payments specified in the treaty were compensation for lost food sources. The fragile ecosystem the Basin peoples relied upon had begun to collapse from overgrazing, pollution of rivers, and overhunting. Later, this damaged environment would push many Indians into becoming scavengers, dependents living on the outskirts of towns, and encourage them to take up white farming and ranching lifestyles. The order of Great Basin culture seems to have been invisible to most of the observers of the time, who saw instead of a cosmology and a way of life merely a rabble of outlanders waiting to be saved from themselves. Mark Twain got some mileage out of his encounters with Great Basin natives in *Roughing It,* where he holds begging Goshutes—a Shoshonean subgroup—up for comparison to James Fenimore Cooper's noble savages and finds them sadly wanting. It never occurred to Twain to wonder how the savages he described fared in the millennia before there were towns to beg in, and the literary loss was all his. *Roughing It,* his Nevada book, is a masterpiece of humor, but its scorn for the landscape and people of the region is depressing. He remarked in it that Nevada would make the devil homesick and moved on to California.

Twain—Samuel Clemens—had himself come west with his brother, Orion, in 1861 when Orion had been hired as secretary to the governor of Nevada Territory. Letters with Orion's signature are still among the papers documenting early white settlement of the region, papers that sketch a dry and sober picture far from Twain's rambunctious account of the miners' West. For the essay I'd promised to write, I spent days in Reno deciphering microfilm reels of such documents, all written by hand in the most exquisitely indecipherable curlicues and flourishes. The letters all began along the lines of "I have the honor to report to you," and the bureaucrats who had learned such beautiful copperplates in schoolrooms back East always signed themselves "your obedient servant." Looking back, it is clear that the treaty was violated and the policies enforced were tantamount to genocide, but in these remote functionaries' letters, no gleam of malice or greed emerges, only an unimaginative anxiety to carry out duties undermined by lack of funds and lack of interest from their superiors. In the weapons industry, nobody makes bombs: They just work on the plutonium trigger assembly, or the uranium mining, or the missile casing, or the research and development. In the Commission on Indian Affairs of the 1860s, it was the same story: No one was trying to wipe out the Indians, and a few seem sincerely concerned by the catastrophes they administered. Famine, plague, and murder drastically reduced the Western Shoshone population in the first decades of contact with whites.

Nine months after the Treaty of Ruby Valley was signed, John A. Burche, the Indian Agent for the Humboldt River region, wrote to James Nye, governor of the Territory, "Owing to the Ophirlike mineral richness of the Humboldt mountains as well as the productive qualities of the soil of the valleys and the almost irresistible inducement held out to the hardy and industrious miner and agriculturalist the country is fast filling up with settlement. The mountains, which all contain the precious metals, are now being thoroughly prospected and marked by the skilful miner, and beginning to yield a generous reward to the persistent toiler from this redundant wealth. The river bottoms and the cañons of the mountains are all taken up as ranches and garden spots and being put in a state of cultivation. The game of the mountains and valleys are being frightened away by the appearance of the white man in this wild region, and the continual crack of his unerring rifle. The pine nut trees are rapidly being cut down and used for building purposes or fuel. The bunch grass, the seed of which formerly supplied the Indians with one of their chief articles of food, and which abounds in the Humboldt Country now fails to yield even the most scanty harvest owing to its being eaten off as fast as it sprouts by the vast amount of stock which has been brought to the country by the settler. . . . Thus you will see that the means of Subsistence for the Indians of this section for the past year and for the whole future, have been greatly impaired if not completely destroyed."

As the environment deteriorated, assaults continued. Mary and Carrie Dann were told of their grandmother being raped in front of her children, whom she transported under the hay of her wagon for safety, and native women were frequently attacked by white men (Sarah Winnemucca talks of this too). The Danns and other Western Shoshones told me stories of prisoners at Fort Ruby in Ruby Valley forced to eat the flesh of their comrades, and of the celebration of the signing of the treaty turning into a macabre tragedy as the Shoshone were "served a kind of meat they could not swallow and had never tasted before—the whites did not eat it." One of the biggest Indian massacres in U.S. history, and still one of its least known, was a cavalry assault on a gathering of Shoshone people on the Bear River in southern Idaho: 250 men, women, and children were killed in a surprise attack long described as a legitimate battle. In the 1860s and 1870s, the *Territorial Enterprise,* Nevada's main newspaper, argued for "exterminating the whole race" and abolishing treaties. The Danns report that even recently many elders believed that the

Indian Claims Commission money was compensation for despoiled land and raped women, rather than payment for lost land, and at Ruby Valley Treaty Days I encountered a man who still believed it.

From the time of the treaty to the present, government efforts in Nevada seem a cumulative effort to reproduce the landscape and lifestyles of the East. The Indian Agents made sporadic efforts to turn the Western Shoshone, and the Paiutes of western Nevada, into settled farmers and ranchers dependent on nonnative plants and animals. A six-mile-square reservation was created in the relatively lush Ruby Valley itself, but the government did nothing to prevent it from being overtaken by whites, and it did not last long. The Temoke band in Ruby Valley was given a herd of 500 cattle in 1869, but the cattle were taken back in 1874. The Danns' own father had his crops burned and was otherwise harassed out of agricultural life before he took out a homestead in Crescent Valley. This was one of the Danns' arguments against the Bureau of Land Management's assault on them: They were after all carrying out Article Six of the Treaty. When the president deems it expedient, they shall "abandon the roaming life, which they now lead, and become herdsmen and agriculturalists." The historian Patricia Nelson Limerick remarks ironically, "The instincts of humanity required that Indians be liberated from savagery and advanced to civilization. It was the only way to rescue them from their otherwise fated decline. Causing them to give up hunting and gathering and to adopt farming would reduce the amount of land they needed. Liberating Indians from savagery thus had the happy side effect of 'liberating' their land and resources as well."

At first inadvertently and then at the hands of the BLM, native grasses and plants were replaced by introduced species. In the 1970s the BLM "chained"—dragged massive chains across—large expanses of land and replanted them with nonnative forage in an effort to turn sagebrush and piñon into grazing lands. Many turned to ranching in an attempt to stay out on the land after drastic environmental changes and settlements put a stop to their traditional lifestyle, and most refused to be resettled on reservations. "We all want to stay here . . . allowed to live in our own dear Mountains and Valleys as we have done in times gone," the Shoshone of east-central Nevada declared in 1873. "We have been born and raised here, these Mountains, and Valleys, with their Springs and Creeks, are our Fathers and Brothers."

✛

Mining was the major impetus for white settlement, and a major source of environmental damage. "With the mining industry closed down, even at this day, there would result such an exodus from the State as would leave those who remained mere tenants at will of the Indians," said Myron Angel's 1881 history of Nevada. Mountains of spent ore still abound near the Comstock mines of the 1860s, gouged-out hillsides may never heal, and the effects of chemical refinement of ore—mercury then, cyanide now—are woefully unregulated and underdocumented. Most of this mining still occurs on public land, and the BLM still presides over the land giveaway sanctioned by the 1872 Mining Act. Under the act, anyone may stake a claim on public land and either destroy and abandon it or buy that land at prices that have yet to rise—usually $2.50 or $5 per acre. The rich subterranean veins of the Comstock have given way to open-pit mining in which many tons of ore are dug up and processed to yield an ounce of gold or silver. Nevada currently produces more than sixty percent of the gold in the U.S., and twenty-five percent of that national total comes from the Elko district of the BLM, a seven-million-acre expanse that encompasses the Danns' lands. A full-fledged gold rush is taking place in that district, which now has the dubious distinction of possessing the largest open-pit gold mines in the country. The gaping pit menacing the town of Tuscarora recalls the country song: "Everybody knows that the world ain't round/It drops off sharp at the end of town." The mines around Cortez in the Danns' own Crescent Valley are operating again.

✚ WHEN THE DANNS WERE TAKEN TO COURT BY THE BLM IN 1974, the slowly grinding gears of the Indian Claims Commission (ICC) had nearly finished settling Western Shoshone land rights. One of the perennial issues was whether they could get the land itself back, or only compensation for the land.

The Indian Claims Commission allowed Native Americans to sue the government for compensation for lost lands. A dubious benefit for those who had truly lost their lands, it was a clear loss for those who still had a chance to retain those lands, a means for the government to claim title to disputed territories—as it did with the Western Shoshone lands. Throughout the decades many Western Shoshone would hold that their lands had not been lost and were not for sale while lawyers who had acquired the legal right to represent them moved toward a financial settlement (these lawyers would receive ten percent of the settlement, a perk written into the legislation by one of the lawyers who represented the Western Shoshone claim). Stories tell of illiterate and barely bilingual people rushed into decisions, given ultimatums by these lawyers, frightened and manipulated into cooperating.

Throughout the process, Western Shoshone groups attempted to halt the proceedings and make it clear that many did not seek compensation for land they believed was not lost and did not think the lawyers were representing their intents and interests. In 1976 the Temoke band fired the lawyer who was misrepresenting it and filed a malpractice lawsuit against him, but the ICC allowed him to continue the case through 1979.

On December 6, 1979, the ICC's Court of Claims awarded a \$26,145,189.89 judgment to the Western Shoshone. This sum included payment for twenty-two million acres of land at 1872 prices—a dollar and change an acre—after deduction of all the shoelaces and spoons supplied in the nineteenth century. The court had chosen July 1, 1872, as the date of valuation of the land, although no relevant event had taken place on that date, and the court's own argument of "gradual encroachment" contradicted this setting of a specific date. At this point the courts were inventing history, not interpreting it. Carrie Dann declared, "Is the U.S. recognizing that it gradually encroached on another sovereign nation? Is gradual encroachment the law of the land? If gradual encroachment is the law of the land, we have gradually encroached back." The Danns' lawyer, John O'Connell, commented, "The United States chose to leave these Indians where they were in the nineteenth century because the white man could see no value in their lands. The government simply forgot about them and never got around to stealing their lands. It now wishes to drive them off while pretending it happened a hundred years ago." Raymond Yowell, chief of the Western Shoshone National Council, points out that at the time the case was closed, the value of what the U.S. had acquired from the Western Shoshone was nearer the tens or hundreds of billions. The payment money sat untouched.

Abraham Lincoln once wrote, "A nation may be said to consist of its territory, its people and its laws. The territory is the only part which is of certain durability. One generation passeth away and another generation cometh, but the earth abideth forever." What the traditionalist Western Shoshone wanted and want in this case was not private property but the dimensions of their nationhood—to be a nation without a land base is arduous for any people, particularly for a people whose land is central to their religion and way of life. Once, I asked the Danns what would happen if the Shoshone land rights described in the treaty were recognized. Carrie replied that contrary to popular fear, they had no interest in driving white settlers away, only in having their right to the rest of the land recognized and in preventing further damage to it. "Not much would change," she said. "We would have to negotiate all use of the land. Nukes, nuclear dumping, gold-mining ponds, and the Test Site should be done away with. Wildlife should be protected. But the main thing is water. Can they prove that cyanide ponds don't go into the water system? One of our laws is that all life has a right. These days all that has a right is human. There's little creatures out there screaming, 'help me, help me.'" Mary added, "There's purpose for those little creatures out there," and Carrie concluded that the loss of those beings "leads to the extinction of everything."

The Nevada District Court ruled that the Dann sisters had not been in trespass until December 6, 1979, when the ICC judgment became final—suggesting that the Danns had been in the right for the first five years of their legal battle, and then became wrong. In 1980, a majority of Western Shoshone at a public hearing told the BLM they were opposed to accepting the judgment money. Just as the lawyers had played both ends of the claims settlement process to their own benefit, so the Secretary of the Interior as trustee for the tribe transferred funds from one government account to another and then claimed that the Western Shoshone had been paid for the lands they no longer owned. Carrie is particularly infuriated by that trustee-controlled payment scheme, which gives native people the status of children. (The Bureau of Land Management is a subsidiary of the Department of the Interior, which makes BLM harassment of the Danns another peculiar in-house exercise.)

The U.S. Supreme Court ruled that placement of the award into the Treasury constituted payment whether or not the funds were accepted by or distributed to the Western Shoshone. The Ninth Circuit Court afterward ruled that Western Shoshone tribal title had been extinguished in the nineteenth century (contradicting its own earlier decision), but specified that the Danns might be able to claim individual aboriginal title. To do so would have been to abandon the larger issues they had been fighting for, and through the end of their case in June of 1991 they refused to argue individual title. "They are throwing away $1 million in cattle and horses on behalf of the Western Shoshone Nation," commented Western Shoshone National Council chief Raymond Yowell. The BLM quickly served the Danns with a fifteen-day notice to reduce their herds or have them confiscated. At this point the legal entanglements halted and plans for direct action began.

✜

The fact that we were out there to defend cattle ranchers made the issues interesting, since raising cattle is not what ecological saints do and defending cattle raising is not what environmentalists usually do (nor are most of those environmentalists faced with the challenge of making some kind of living off the land). My brother liked to joke that after Shoshone land rights were secured we could think about protesting Shoshone cattle ranchers—but until then the issue is not grazing or grazing permits, but sovereignty and jurisdiction. In recent years the BLM had begun to suggest that the issue was overgrazing, which seemed to be an attempt to obscure the real issue and divide the environmental community from the land-rights community. The righteousness of the BLM was questionable in a region so rife with open-pit mines, a state where public land was so eagerly handed over to the military and the DOE, and a region where grazing permits were granted so liberally. I would rather see the Western Shoshone make the major decisions about land use in the region. They have been here longer, and they care a lot more. And the Supreme Court notwithstanding, it is theirs.

✦ WHEN I CAME BACK DOWN FROM THE BEAVER DAM ABOVE THE Temoak homestead, Rachel and some other women I knew from the Test Site had shown up. The old people had gathered in a tent and begun to play an intricate betting game, and more cars and trucks kept pulling in. Carrie Dann pulled up in one, and when I went over to say hello, she invited me to come to the ranch. One of the people with Bernice pulled out a .22 and shot a jackrabbit as dusk was settling in, and I saw the creature transformed in half an hour from a live thing running in the distance to a soft, limp bundle of fur to a skinned creature whose long legs made it look like a flayed saint to limbs on a fire to food that quickly disappeared into several mouths, a transmutation as impressive as alchemy. The drums and dancing went on into the small hours of the night, and in the morning I turned back west, to the ranch.

You can see the Dann place a long time before you arrive—perhaps ten miles, and it disappears for a while as the gravel road there goes around the dry hills. From a distance, it's only a dark spot at the western base of the central peak of the Cortez Range, and the range bows in to the east, so the ranch seems embraced by the open arms of the mountains. The darkness is the stand of old cottonwoods that surround the house, though up close their light yellow-green leaves gleam and waver in the wind. The spot dissolves into the dusty satellites of the house: the trailer homes, boxcar, sheds, cars, and farm vehicles.

From almost anywhere in Crescent Valley you can see at least twenty miles, up and down the two ranges—Shoshone and Cortez—that bracket it, unless clouds of dust or rain or snow or smoke from summer's forest fires obscure it. Not only the sights but the sight is peculiar to the climate: The dry air of the Great Basin allows for a range of visibility far beyond that of more humid regions, and so one is given a vision to match the landscape. The valley, tilted a little away from the north-south axis of the Basin and Range, is a great stage for the drama of celestial light. During the day the ranges look soft, grassy, rolling like hills, the glare of the sun through the high, thin air flattens out everything. But for an hour or so after sunrise, and again toward sunset, the light rakes across the ranges, throwing them into sharp creases of canyon-shadow and ridge-light, making them look huge, forbidding, and majestic.

I pitched my tent in the resistance camp Rachel and company had just left. There were only a few people there, all seasoned Test Site activists. I struck up a friendship that day with Lauri, who was wearing an old cotton dress and cowboy boots. She had joined Seeds of Peace some years before, and she had the hardbitten pragmatism of that group, which dedicates itself to sustaining the basic needs of an action—food, water, sanitation, media support—while the ideologues flutter. Mary Dann had sent down an elderberry pie that first day I was there. It tasted wild and sharp and delicious.

There's a hot spring on the Dann ranch, just a thin pipe coming out of a crevice in the Cortez Mountains draining into a round stock trough that spills over and flows down the hillside. It's about a mile from the camp, and half that from the ranch buildings, and during the encampment it was supposed to be ours in the morning. The first morning I drove up to it, the Danns were there washing Mark, Carrie's retarded son, and some clothes, and when I told them I needed to talk to them, they told me to wash up quick and meet them at the house: We would drive into Elko together.

We all got into the four-wheel-drive 4Runner, Carrie and I up front, Mary and Mark in the back. (Bob Fulkerson told me there was a cluster of Down's-syndrome children in the area, likely connected to fallout from the Test Site, but whatever made Mark different wasn't just that.) They told me many stories on the road to Elko, which at seventy miles away is the nearest real town. They told me about their grandmother then and many times after, what she told them about the grasses that disappeared, when the deer were gone and the people were hungry, about the smallpox plague in Austin, and about the pet fawn they themselves had when they were young and how it ran away. We had coffee in the Commercial Hotel in Elko after half the errands were done and talked about men and their foibles. Carrie periodically asserted that men are stupid. She has an abrupt, staccato way of talking, likes to make pronouncements, and tempers her fierceness with sudden laughter. Mary laughs more quietly.

They ran a few more errands, and we went out for dinner at the Stockman's Lounge, a hotel, casino, restaurant, souvenir boutique, and barber shop. Over our lettuce with ranch dressing, fried chicken, mashed potatoes, cinnamony corn fritters, and coffee, we talked about Creation mythology. I talked about the politics of Eden: the male creator, the fall into a flawed world, the hostility to earth implicit in that. Carrie disagreed with me and reinterpreted Genesis, emphasizing stewardship of the earth and explaining to me that the Creator is male in native cosmology because the earth is female: Life is procreated by the pair, and they have equal standing. From there we slipped into prophetic dreams and UFO stories, and they told me many astounding things about finding mutilated cows that the flies wouldn't come to and strange lights seen in the valley.

After we left I-80 on the way back from Elko, Carrie drove in the middle of the road for safety, there being far fewer cars than animals on the rural roads of Nevada. One rabbit did run into the headlights, and Carrie shouted, "Get out of the way you goddamned rabbit." After it disappeared under us, she said, "I'm sorry for hitting you, rabbit." The white moths in the headlights of the 4Runner shone like stars themselves, so that we seemed to be plunging straight into the sky.

✚ THE PICTURE THAT STAYS WITH ME IS OF CARRIE AND MARY sitting at their worn, patterned linoleum kitchen table. They give orders to their brothers and to the cowboys who are busy branding and castrating calves that week, talk and joke with me, yell at the house dog, Scarlet; they smoke in unison or share a cigarette and switch off using the fly swatter with deadly accuracy, looking as free and confident as a couple of queens with a scepter. Carrie jokes all the time and wears a gimme cap over her short hair that says "Don't Let the Bastards Get You Down." Mary is quieter, though when she interjects a comment it's clear in letting her little sister do most of the talking she's allocated a job, not relinquished power. They call her "The Boss." Sometimes she and her sister talk in Shoshone together and then come back to the conversation in English. Both of them still work with the cows and horses and do other hard work around the ranch. They have raised their niece and nephew, as well as Carrie's two children, and there are often several other children and young people around the ranch who call them Auntie or Grandmother, though the connection is not usually that lineal.

They sit on a window bench, their backs to the yard with its tall cottonwoods. The yard dogs pass back and forth under the trees, and occasionally people and trucks move further in the distance, among the ramshackle sheds and high corrals that are the ranch's work space. Chickens and goats are penned up further away from the main house, and a converted railroad car and some mobile homes house other family members and employees. Outside the small green patch of the yard, the vegetable garden, and the alfalfa fields they irrigate, everything is dry—the gray-green of sagebrush gives the landscape its color. The lush places are hidden in the folds of the hills and on the mountaintops. Most of the livestock is out of sight, though a collection of cows sometimes wanders through— pale beasts like the cows of Central America, Herefords, longhorns, what might be Black Angus, and unrecognizable mixed breeds.

The television runs all day in the room next to the kitchen, though no one watches it most of the time. On the wall opposite the TV are two hand-tinted oval photographs of their grandmother seated outside her tent. She never, they tell me, lived in a board house or slept in a bed: "She lived in a tent and the earth was her floor." Their grandfathers don't seem to have the same prominence in their stories, though an aunt often figures. Their knowledge of their own history seems to come from the stories these women told them, and they themselves are clearly the mainstays who hold their own extended family together. Their parents, aunt, and grandmother were active in the land-rights struggle before them, and Carrie has been vocal about it since the 1950s. Their two brothers who live on the ranch are quiet figures in the background; Cliff works as the ranch foreman and Richard lives his own life. I tell them of an argument several of us women had with a Western Shoshone man in Ruby Valley, and how he told us, "In the old days you wouldn't even be allowed to speak up like this," and Carrie flashes one of her brilliant smiles and says, "In the old days he would have said what the women told him to."

On another visit one summer morning I came back from the hot spring and ran into Carrie. I spent the rest of the morning ghostwriting a backlog of correspondence for her, including a letter to Manuel Lujan, then Secretary of the Interior. The first letter sent off six months before had been forwarded by the Secretary or one of his underlings to the Bureau of Indian Affairs, where a diligent bureaucrat had answered Carrie's fairly rhetorical questions straightforwardly and humorlessly.

Do you understand the relationship that traditional Western Shoshone have with the land?
My staff informs me that many Western Shoshones have a strong attachment to aboriginal lands and consider them sacred.

We went over the letters together. "I've got to look at an animal in one of the corrals," she said to conclude the meeting, and I trailed her out, a bunch of correspondence in one hand and a coffee cup in the other. She shouted into the work sheds out front, a shy German young man who'd come out to help emerged, and we all went through a few gates into a round corral made of high, irregular posts. There was a bay filly with four white socks tethered in one corner, a white colt in the other: "You want a pretty little girl?" she asked me as she went up to the filly, while the German untied the other horse. The animal was so skittish he couldn't lead it into the corral alone. Carrie took over and showed him how to break a horse. We sat in the dust of dried trampled manure for half an hour or so while she slowly worked the horse into a double hobble. She'd toss a thick, soft cotton rope around its legs, then use that to secure another rope to it, going through an interminable series of binds on the animal until finally it was secured, left front leg to right rear, right front to left rear. She talked as she worked, cursing and soothing the beast she called little man, then handed it over and went back inside to the kitchen, the hub of their world.

She and her sister seem unintimidated by their twenty-years' war, a war on which they have staked their livelihoods and their way of life, and a war they could have removed themselves from with little trouble—payment of the grazing fees. It's the dishonesty of the government rather than the danger it poses that seems to distress them, the double role of the lawyers in the past and the Department of Interior in the present. Carrie complains about being, as a Native American, under the jurisdiction of a department that otherwise manages "natural resources"—trees, animals, parks, and so forth. "I don't know if we're the human species or some other kind of species," she says in regard to the Interior's stewardship.

Mary says, "Endangered species."

✦ COYOTES BEGAN HOWLING BEFORE DAWN THE SECOND morning after I arrived, and their voices came from every direction as they moved around the camp. Later I found huge paw prints in the dust. The howling woke Lauri up too, and we unzipped our tents and stepped out in unison. We hailed each other, and it quickly emerged that we both had planned an early morning bath. I deferred to her and she deferred to me, and before our politeness became brittle, I proposed we drive up together and I make coffee on the hood of my car while she bathed. We listened to Dwight Yoakam's new album on the way up, and I left the tape on while I worked.

Lauri plugged the tub and dumped several buckets of the hot water from the trough into it, then a cold one from the barrel. It took forever for the icy drinking water to boil, and Lauri was out in time for the first cups of coffee, and while I bathed she poured me a second cup and dumped buckets of steamy, sulfury water in as my bath cooled. I cannot imagine what it would make a person to see this land and this light every day for a lifetime. I am convinced, every time I visit the hot spring, that it is from the strong, stark, and clear landscape that Mary and Carrie draw the courage to face down the world's most powerful government through their middle years and into old age. The sun rises behind the Cortez Mountains, and we could see their shadow retreat across the valley from the Shoshone Mountains in the west. The line of morning light reached my bath-water as I stepped out.

Bathing on a mountainside on Western Shoshone land with a cowgirl to serve me coffee and Dwight singing in the background may stand as one of the supreme moments of well-being in my life, or at least as one of the most emblematic ones. Talking to Lauri, another such moment came up: It was in West Texas, the point we'd reached on our return from a raucous New Year's in New Orleans. I was racing our travelling companions with the man I was besotted with riding shotgun, and because we mistakenly believed it was legal to drink and drive in Texas we made a point of doing so. We had a bottle of bourbon, and we were listening to Roy Orbison. It was late in the day, and the sun showed itself for the first time that year, shining from almost due south over the biggest landscape I ever saw. The man gave me a swig of bourbon, then a bite of chocolate, then a swallow of coffee, then the bourbon again, and Roy Orbison sang, and the gigantic hills far far away were lit up by raking amber sunlight, and I had an epiphany as much prompted by the peculiarly American iconography of the moment as by its galloping sensuality.

Lauri told me a story in the course of our bathtime conversation about love and travel that seems part of the same American landscape. When she was eighteen, she said in her hoarse Midwestern voice, she bought a pair of red cowboy boots and hit the road, hitch-hiking, camping, and Greyhound busing across the country. At the Grand Canyon she got caught in a thunderstorm, developed a fine case of pneumonia, and ended up in a Christian mission in Flagstaff. So did two boys she hit it off with, but the friendship went astray when she decided she liked one of the two better. The other one robbed a liquor store in his grief, then fell down and cut himself on a whiskey bottle, and finally showed up at their motel, bleeding and an outlaw. I think he was drunk. Suddenly the lovers were accessory to a felony, and so the two young men hopped a Greyhound bus, and Lauri took off in the other direction. At the last moment, the one she liked gave her his leather jacket, which she gave to her one true love, who wears it still and still doesn't know where it came from. With the Grand Canyon as backdrop.

At times like these, I like the friction between people and land, the tawdry and the sublime, out west. They counterpoint each other instead of harmonizing. When I think of England, it's a landscape that's enlarged its residents only as much as they've diminished it. Everything is settled, adjusted. Here, the white people are paltrier, at odds with their surroundings, and the project is unfinished. I know the incomparable majesty of the Grand Canyon, and I've slept in the tawdry cheap motels of Flagstaff, with their neon and sepul-chrally sunken mattresses and courtyards fringed by dead gladiolas. There's something secretly comforting in the incongruity. It's terri-fying that we may destroy the land before we learn to live with it, but the process of improvisation, and the murkiness of the future, are exhilarating: The one thing the American landscape promises is that the future will be nothing like the present. I like being part of an unfinished project, however disastrous it has been to date. Im-provising something better is an exhilarating challenge, and this is why I am happy to be another unsettled Euro-American rather than someone as well grounded as the Western Shoshone. Suddenly I find myself endorsing Thomas Cole's notion of futurity, of the meaning of the American landscape lying in its future rather than its past, as Europe's does. Cole wrote in the 1830s, "American associations are not so much of the past as of the present and the future . . . looking over the yet uncultivated scene, the mind's eye may see far into futurity. Where the wolf roams, the plough shall glisten." Cole's futurity was about development; mine is more about the necessity of further change, of American culture as a series of inadequate adjustments, settlings that have never yet ended the unsettled nature of the culture, and the abandonment of settlements: Where the plough now rusts coyotes shall howl.

Tourists go to Nevada only to huddle inside the neutral zones of casinos, where there is no day or night or distance. Maybe it's that the Nevada landscape is too uncomfortable, too unassimilated, too lacking in landmarks where you can say *this* is beautiful and *this* is what we'll look at: It has a continuous unbroken beauty, a good driving beauty. There's a tunnel in a hill past Emigrant Pass through which Highway 80 and the railroad tracks go while the Humboldt River goes around it. And on the other side, slender buttes emerge from the steep slope almost leaning over it like Egyptian monuments or Easter Island figures. Fog descended as I passed them on my way to Ruby Valley, but the sun glowed through it, so the whole landscape was silver and gold, with the gray road slicing the gold. On the eastern side of that tunnel, on a sandy bank of the Humboldt twenty miles from anywhere, someone had planted two pink plastic flamingos. It was a tip of the hat to that peculiarly American incongruity: kitsch showing its tawdry face as a way of acknowledging there is no adequate response in our vernacular to this landscape, that nothing can touch the authenticity around it—thus the neon of Vegas, the motels of Flagstaff, the diners of Elko, the pink flamingos on the banks of a river named after a German who never saw it. At the most breathtaking landscapes of the West, people usually say something profoundly banal or trivial, not so much because they are not impressed, but because they know their words can't measure up to it, and it is more respectful not to try. In some way, banality becomes a refuge from fear of the sublime, overwhelming scale of the land.

Only the splenetics of country music seems to describe it: The eternal story of country songs is about someone who took refuge in the house of love, only the house fell apart, and so the singer is lost in the vastness again, and alone. Never mind their obsessive boy-girl front—they're songs about the pain of freedom, the loneliness of independence, about aftermath, irretrievable loss, fall from grace. If you don't believe the lyrics, the violins and guitars will tell you so. Like pastoral poetry, country music (before positive thinking ruined it in recent years) is usually about the past, though the past seen more through bitterness than pastoral nostalgia. The singer is leaving, being left, or looking back, and the lyrics are full of midnight trains and lost highways, rambling men, walking after midnight, coming back to see their sweetheart wed another. A passionate love for geography is buried in all this bile, so that the songs of loss are rich too, rich in place names, travels, and atmospheres.

My first English teacher told me that Aristotle's definition of tragedy was the expulsion of the hero from society, and he said that we could deduce from that that comedy is the incorporation of the hero into society—that tragedy ends in death or exile, comedy in marriage. The basic gesture of American society is a kind of atomization, an expansion into what was always imagined as an expanding universe. That expulsion was tragic in all Old World narratives, and America was settled by outcasts for whom tragedy became opportunity. Even framed as progress and manifest destiny, that gesture is one of loneliness, and of conflict resolved by space rather than society—room to swing your arm. Tragedy, our ability to fall out of society and into the landscape, has been the content of American optimism.

✦ THE WESTERN SHOSHONE NEVER MOVED ANYWHERE. EVEN their myths describe them as the people who remained while everyone else scattered. Bernice Lalo told coyote stories to us in a tent at Ruby Valley, and her first one went something like this: In the beginning, she said, Apa, the Creator, told Coyote to perform a task. He had made a huge willow basket sealed at both ends with pine pitch, and Coyote was to take the basket someplace far away. There were four conditions he had to follow. He must not stop swimming (this seems to be a story about a time when much of the world was under water); he must not take the basket off his back; and he must not open it. I have forgotten the fourth condition.

Coyote swam a ways and then thought that Apa wouldn't mind if he took a little rest, since it was such a long way that he had to go. So he stopped. And then he decided that the Creator wouldn't mind if he took the basket off for a minute. So he took it off. He decided that he wouldn't mind either if he took a little peek. So he opened it just a crack, and all the people of the world jumped out. He looked in the bottom and only one people remained, and that's how the Shoshone got here.

✦

Chief Raymond Yowell told me later, at his home on the green South Fork Reservation, "The Creator placed us here in this particular part of Mother Earth, and we have no record of how long ago that was, so the best thing we can say is that from time immemorial the Western Shoshone have been present in this area. When he placed us here he also gave us certain laws by which to take care of Mother Earth. These are what you could call natural law. The sun comes up in the east, sets in the west, water runs downhill, these are things that no human being can change. Only the Creator can change this. So Shoshone law as the Creator gave it to us is not like the law of the United States where every year or almost every year Congress sits in session and makes new laws and does away with its old ones and so forth. Shoshone law once it's in place that's it, unless the Creator makes the sun come up in the west and sink in the east. Then we would change our law.

"The land cannot be sold. That is a religious belief. The Creator placed us here as caretakers of the land and he didn't say that at some point you can sell this for money. Mother Earth is too sacred to be taken in this fashion. So payment is out. That money can be turned into something else, damages or whatever may be acceptable to Shoshones. Until that's done then the money can just stay there. But we can make agreements on the use of the land. We cannot agree to them testing atomic bombs within Mother Earth; that is unacceptable. There are certain other things that we cannot agree to, because they're against the religion. We're not completely in line with the mining that's going on because again this is reaching into Mother Earth's skin, damaging her, and that damage as you can see can be longlasting. You take Carlin, one of the biggest areas, and you can see where a mountain has disappeared."

✚ I WENT TO SEE ONE OF THE MINES NEAR THE RANCH ONE DAY, where a mountain had disappeared, a chastening place to think about restlessness. There were organized tours of the Barrick Gold Strike Mine north of Carlin, the town one basin east of Crescent

Valley. The tour guide was a guileless young woman from the nearby junior college who couldn't answer any economic or ecological questions. The operation, in her eyes, was one of the wonders of the world. I suspected her employers found her blithely uninformed confidence, like that of many of the librarians, historians, and public relations people I was encountering around the environmental disasters of Nevada, far more valuable than any expertise. These people were there not to inform the public, but to buffer them from information. She was bursting with statistics as she took us from cyanide leach pads to the equipment yards to the quarter-mile-deep pit to the water treatment facilities. She seemed particularly attached to the haulpaks—huge spade-heads mounted on vehicles so big it takes a long ladder to reach the cab, and capable of hauling a hundred tons of ore at a time. Many of my fellow mine visitors took pictures of each other next to the eight- or nine-foot-high tires which, she told us, cost $20,000 apiece. From the rim of the pit, the haulpaks looked like ants by the time they had trundled down the earth ramps to its bottom. We saw everything but the gold.

The pit is now 400 feet below the water table, and the guide said they pump 50,000 gallons a minute to keep it dry (a miner told me it's closer to 70,000). The water goes to a reservoir, and some of it to a farm, though a fissure below the reservoir allows a lot of the water to simply return to the aquifer being disturbed. Springs, seeps, and creeks in the region may dry up—the technical term for the drop in the water table is a "cone of depression." The thirty-three wells with which they drain the area are called "dewatering wells." In the words of our guide, "Instead of filling it up [with soil]—that'd cost too much—we're gonna turn on the wells—it'll be a lake." So sometime in the twenty-first century, the short roster of Nevada lakes will increase by one: an 1,100-foot-deep pothole with little shore life on its steep rim, chilly depths, and, at the bottom, geothermal springs pumping hot mineral water into this dead soup. "Very low on organic content," said the BLM man I asked about it. "You wouldn't wanna be a trout in it."

The gold in the Carlin Trend is so dispersed through the earth it couldn't have been mined before the gargantuan earth-moving and ore-extracting technologies were cheap enough, and as it is Barrick and most of the other mines in the region operate twenty-four hours a day, seven days a week, to keep up with the massive capitalization costs of the equipment. They get less than a tenth of an ounce per ton of ore, another BLM man told me, and the profit mostly goes to overseas companies. The leach pads looked like the Painted Desert rearranged by a geometrizing fanatic: black and brown and pale and pink earths all dumped in tiers atop black polyethylene liners. Slender black hoses ran up the tiers, and the sprinklers were on at some of them, sprinkling one-percent cyanide solution over the ore to leach out the gold. Higher-grade ore was subjected to other treatments before being taken to the leaching pads: Oxide ore was crushed and milled, and sulfide ore was put through an autoclave— a high-heat and oxygen processing system which makes the ore more vulnerable to cyanidization.

Cyanide partially succeeded mercury in ore refinement and certainly is an improvement over it, but it is still a deadly poison that poses serious problems of its own to living things. It is an organic compound that breaks down in sunlight, and so the residue of cyanide leaching is usually set in huge ponds where the sunlight will break the compound down into nonlethal elements. Unfortunately, animals, particularly migratory waterfowl, tend to use these ponds, and a variety of methods are used to keep them away. Some mining operations simply net them over. The British-owned Newmont Mine, which partially surrounds Barrick, has the dubious distinction of being one of the two or three biggest open-pit gold mines in

North America. Employees there, I was told, are dispatched with air guns to row across its dead lake of poison and frighten away the birds.

The BLM man who told me I wouldn't want to be a trout explained to me that the mines "semi–self-police. Of course this leaves a credibility gap with the public." But, he added, many of the cyanide lakes "would be sublethal to a majority of birds." The BLM requires that mines post a bond for reclamation of the mine sites after they close—and most of them will close in a decade or a few decades, leaving huge piles of subterranean matter, huge pits, and unemployed miners. The reclamation bond is something like an apartment deposit, though since the mines always forfeit it they must be bad tenants. For Barrick's Betze site, the bond is $20 million. The money in trust goes to repair the land, or if it is irreparable, to improve or buy some other land, as though the destruction of one area could be compensated for by generous treatment of another. For the BLM and the Bureau of Indian Affairs in the Department of the Interior, the idea of place doesn't seem to exist: Everything is exchangeable for something else. Progress as it's taken shape out here is literally Utopian, about the desire for no place, for a world of abstractions in which everything is equivalent to everything else—of commodities to be brokered. Place is the opposite of abstraction; it is immovable, concrete, unexchangeable.

✦ I REMEMBER LOOKING DOWN THE LENGTH OF CRESCENT Valley and startling myself by thinking, "No one ever took the land. It's still here, it never went anywhere, only the people come and go." The idea of ownership begins to fall apart when it comes to land, for a possession is something under one's control and which one has a right to control: Land undermines both these concepts, being beyond control and above it morally. A person owns land in somewhat the sense that a flea owns its dog; land ownership is really more akin to having a patent on something: One derives the exclusive right to benefit, but the thing itself is a concept or an area, not a commodity. When land is sold, it is the people that move, not the land—the expression is that it has changed hands. And even the idea of a piece of land is an abstraction: No wall or ditch can break up the continuity of the surface of the earth; it does not really become pieces. Native beliefs usually obviate the possibility of land ownership: The land is not conceptualized as alienable, divisible objects but as a continuity, spatially and temporally. One of the great beauties of English common law is the precept that no owner may close down a path across his land hallowed by long use, so that the walker's open landscape of a network of paths takes precedence over the square enclosures of property.

Even in legal terms, land ownership is becoming an increasingly limited set of rights: Environmental law, zoning codes, neighbors' rights, all limit what the owner can do to what he or she owns. Without necessarily articulating an underlying moral principle, these laws assert the rights of the land itself, its surroundings, and its future users over the present owner. The land of Newe Sogobia has been clearly used and abused, but whether to use something means to own it is an odd question. The mines have assumed ownership, for in their hands—or rather their haulpaks—geography itself has been undone and whole landscapes have been reduced to piles of rubble in which the original lay of the land is irrecoverable.

The War

✠ THE WAR BEGAN SUDDENLY, THOUGH NOT WITHOUT WARN-
ing.

The man the Western Shoshone National Council had hired to
organize the defense project went into the store in the mobile-home
hamlet of Crescent Valley one day—there was only one store and it
didn't sell much besides potato chips, Spam, Kleenex, Gatorade,
and beer—and the woman asked him what all those sheriffs' cars
were doing outside the community center. The lot full of four-wheel
drives was news to him, early warning signs of a roundup at the
Dann ranch. They had released their cattle in March, although the
BLM's regulations didn't permit grazing on the range until April 15.

I heard about it that evening, April 9, 1992. I was planning to go
to Yosemite for Easter vacation with some landscape photographers
and then drive on over to the Dann ranch afterward (there was another spring action at the Test Site that week, but I didn't like the
New Age group that organized it). Instead, I called the organizer
and confirmed that the roundup they'd been waiting for since 1974
might happen in the morning, and then I called one of the photographers to say I'd changed my plans and packed the car. Within an
hour or so of hearing the alert, I was on the road for the ten-hour
drive to Crescent Valley. I had never volunteered to go off to a war
before.

In the dark I pictured the landscape as I passed it—the flatness
of the Central Valley, the great spreading valley oaks that begin to
crop up east of Sacramento, then give way to the live oaks of the
foothills, the pine trees that mix with the oaks as the road becomes

steeper, the chaparral level, then the pine forests as the Sierra begin; Emigrant and Donner passes went by indicated only by signs, the dazzle of Reno and then the strange dry stretch to the junction between Highway 80 and Highway 50—and I wondered what kind of trouble I was driving toward. It was three in the morning when I pulled into a vast truck stop at the junction town of Fernley and passed out for a couple of hours. At five, I poured another cup of coffee from my thermos, started up the car, and drove toward the sun coming up. Nevada is traversed by three major east-west highways, and rows of finer north-south lines run from one to the next. Even from maps without topography you could guess at the long ranges the roads go around. Instead of taking the long loop around on 80, I had decided to take 50, then head up 306. My map didn't indicate that, though the road had been distinguished with a secondary-road number, it hadn't been blessed with pavement, and so I had seventy miles of dirt to get through before I arrived at the ranch. My car slipped and slid on the dust and gravel and a great tan plume rose up behind me.

I saw a few buildings on the long road up, but no people. An antelope stood by the side of the road and I got out to look at it. It looked back at me for a minute with wild liquid eyes, then sprang off stiff legged and weightless into the sagebrush. I had seen antelopes in zoos, stuffed in nature-museum dioramas, filmed for nature programs, but I had never seen one where it belonged before, and so in some way I was seeing an antelope for the first time.

I got to the ranch at about ten in the morning on April 10, and there was no one there but a supporter operating a radio scanner for news from either side. He told me about everything but what I wanted to know: He told me what was wrong with American Peace Test and my brother, about black power, Nazis, the coming Armageddon, his survival skills, his immediate plans. My eyes felt like fried eggs, I had the scratchy, gritty, dried-up feeling that comes from driving all night, and I did not appreciate his insights. Finally he told me that the roundup was expected, that everyone else was on the range, and suggested that I go be a lookout. I pointed out that the hot springs at the base of the mountain were as good a place as any to watch from and he handed me a periscope. So I spent mid-morning soaking in a tub with a periscope next to my soap, taking in leisurely panoramic scans of the valley. When I got back to the ranch, the young man at the radio was still ranting, but he had no news. I left him in mid-revelation to go to the trailer that had been set aside as a bunkhouse for the activists and fell onto a couch. I woke up to see a palomino snorting just outside the window, its rider sticking on imperturbably, though every time it reared he disap-peared above the window frame.

I drove back to Crescent Valley town, where the Defense Project office was—a trailer with an antenna on top (the telephone line doesn't run out to the ranch, and so this was the closest point to maintain communications with the rest of the world). The organizer was glad to see me, and so was Carrie, sitting in a folding chair look-ing tired but satisfied. The roundup had nearly succeeded. She showed me the bruise from where the BLM man had grabbed her—on her dark well-muscled wrist I could see the faint shape of three fingers—and she laughed at me for bathing while history was made. Joachim, a German volunteer who came early in the struggle and stayed to do a lot of good, had videotaped the whole thing with the camcorder the Danns had bought for such situations, and that after-noon we relived the morning. History, which once happened the first time as tragedy and the second time as farce, now comes around again as videotape. I saw what I had gone to see, though not as I had intended to see it. We all sat under the photographs of Carrie's and Mary's grandmother: Mark rocking to and fro on the couch and the rest of us on the floor, Carrie's other child, the radiant and vivacious Disha, her fiancé Lance who had been the man on the palomino, Carrie's brother Cliff and nephew Shannon, the ranchhand Jesús, the organizer, a few other activists, and Carrie herself. Carrie lay propped up on one elbow and commented continually on how fat she looked, with an occasional comment on how fat the women on the roundup team looked.

It was a genuine range war with a lot of rustlers riding around on horses and Jesús, Lance, April, and Jason riding for the defense, and at times the footage of them all loping across the still-green grass looked like a commercial for Marlboro Country. But the real action took place on foot, after the cattle had been herded into a corral that had been thrown up for them. A loading chute made of the same high segments of steel-tube fencing led from the corral to the trailers to take them away. It was near there that Carrie confronted the BLM's Special Agent Joe Leaf, a man whose pallid high forehead sloped down to a pair of mirrored sunglasses. He towered over her.

"You know," she declared, "the government you're working for has never given us any written documents as far as the Western Shoshone land transfer goes. I want the records of the land transfer from the Western Shoshone to the United States. I want it and I want it in my hands *now.* If you can't produce it for me, then it's illegal for you to go up there and gather my livestock. Everybody in your department knows it. You're stealing my land today. You didn't take it in 1872. You're taking it now. And that's the basic truth. You're taking it now." She asked Leaf what he knew about the treaty, and he said he wasn't there. She asked him what he knew about Shoshone history, and he admitted that he knew nothing. She headed for the chute, and Leaf began to twist her arm.

"You're hurting me, you're hurting me, God damn it. You're

hurting me; let me go. You let me go. They're my livestock and I have a right to protect them."

Mr. Jones, the portly local sheriff, ambled over and said, "Carrie, there's ways to do this, Carrie, Carrie. . . ."

"These are my livestock. You're hurting my arm, Leaf."

"Carrie," said the sheriff as she tried to climb into the chute, "I can't allow you to do this."

"Sure you can," shouted April.

"You're endangering yourself," said Leaf as she struggled.

As she continued to tell him he was hurting her, she wrestled free enough to climb the fence, though he continued twisting her wrist while she was on the other side. She broke his grip and went and closed the gate between the loading chute and the corral. April gave a tremendous whoop. As long as Carrie was inside the chute, they could not load the cattle, except by letting them trample her. After she'd been there a little while, she yelled, "April, gimme a cigarette." The cows began to bellow.

The sheriff tried to follow her over the six-foot-high bars of the chute, and then thought better of it and went around through a gate. He had the air of a man who would rather be somewhere else, and who wanted to see as little happen as he could.

"Carrie," he said.

"You're making my life miserable too," she shot back. "It's the only way I can protect myself. I gotta protect my livelihood. They talk about the Constitution. There's no Constitution as far as I can see. It doesn't protect me, it doesn't protect people of my color."

"Don't you think this could be taken up in court?" he asked.

"They stopped the court system, they stopped the courts," she yelled at him. "We were arguing on the title question—we the Western Shoshone people. The Secretary of the Interior stopped the court system by acting as my trustee and accepting that money and saying payment has been made. Who has it been paid to? It's been paid to the United States of America. I don't want money. My land is not for sale. It's not going to be for sale tomorrow either. That's the way it is, Mr. Jones.

"If you can, Mr. Jones, come down with the Western Shoshone land transfer to the United States, I'll be more than glad to get off. Here's Mr. Leaf. He represents the United States government. He can have those documents faxed here; we can see them in a matter of minutes."

The documents don't exist, but Mr. Jones probably didn't know that.

The cowboys and agents released the cows and went away.

Thus two decades of legal battle came to their culmination. The federal government versus the Western Shoshone boiled down to Joe Leaf twisting Carrie Dann's arm. I had come to Nevada because of the great apocalyptic end-of-the-world war, a war of great bombs and technologies annihilating cities or continents or species or the weather itself, and it had changed into a man bruising the wrist of a fifty-nine-year-old woman over some cows, but it was still the same war, and in this round, she had won.

✛ I SLEPT IN THE OFFICE IN CRESCENT VALLEY TOWN THE night of the unsuccessful roundup, so that there would be a runner if Joachim saw anything suspicious on his morning drive along the back roads by the ranch. He called in an alarm, a report of cattle trucks out in the Dry Hills, and I jumped into my car and drove down the thirteen miles of dirt to the ranch house. Carrie didn't seem as alarmed as I expected. The family finished breakfast and gave me a cup of coffee. Carrie and Shannon and I got into the four-wheel drive and followed the two cattle trucks across the rolling hills north of the house. As Carrie drove, she told us the names of the plants we passed, about the grasshopper plague of 1988, about the insect that eats sagebrush. A tiny red plane appeared and buzzed the higher hills for cattle. There were no official vehicles, and I had no idea what was going on.

Finally we pulled up right behind the cattle trucks and I walked up and asked them if they had anything to do with the BLM. They said no, they were part of another ranch in the valley. Carrie came up after me and the older man settled down onto the flatbed of his truck and shot the breeze with her for awhile. He was rounding up his cattle, which were out before the official opening of the grazing season, lest the BLM go after him too. His son, in mirror aviator shades and gimme cap, sat in the truck cab with his feet dangling. He pulled out a packet of Red Man chewing tobacco and put a wad in his mouth, then unwrapped a stick of gum, dropped the wrapper, and put the gum in too. He sat there while Carrie and his father talked, shooting out streams of brown juice and paring his nails with a clasp knife, answering in monosyllables when Carrie pried into his love life.

The rancher said, "It's gonna be a long dry old summer," and she added, "And hot too."

"Better do a dance for us, Carrie," he said.

✛

More people showed up, including Alain, a Franciscan priest who had not lost his thick French accent during years of administering to skid rows and radical movements in Oakland and Vegas. He had a white beard cut along the jawline Mormon style, gentle blue eyes, and a clerical collar he put on when he wanted to impress an officer of the law. He was a friend of my brother. But nothing more happened during the week I was at the ranch.

About sixty horses were still in a fenced-off pasture, and I walked out and looked at them often. The Danns had a part-Arabian stallion, and their horses were beautiful bays, chestnuts, blacks, pale buckskins, sorrels, whites, palominos. While the grass was still young, they were fed hay under a dead tree whose jagged branches were full of ravens. The cottonwoods around the house and the apple orchard next to it were still in bud, the tender flush of green across the land was muted by the gray-green of sagebrush, and the plum trees were in flower. There was still snow on the peaks of the Cortez Range, and from out in the center of Crescent Valley it looked as though the alkali flats and the peaks were covered in the same stuff.

One day I walked up Cottonwood Canyon with Joachim, the environmentalist whose German accent was as thick as Alain's French. Cottonwood Creek ran through this canyon in the Cortez Range year-round, making it one of the long riparian oases cached all over this driest state. The canyon was full of groves of the trees it was named after, the bones of cows and deer, overhanging ledges of rust-colored volcanic rock, the marks of prospectors, and dark butterflies.

One evening Carrie drove Mary, Shannon, the organizer, and me south into Grass Valley where the Dorothy Legaratta Memorial Caravan was coming through on its annual tour, and I realized it was only two years since I had come through Nevada with them myself. Bob Fulkerson was at the camp by a hot spring, in a Stetson, with his daughter and his father, and there I finally met Joe Sanchez, Citizen Alert's Native American Program coordinator and an impressive environmental writer, who was with his wife and young son.

Carrie talked to the twenty or thirty caravaners about how soon after the Pine Ridge shootout their own government confrontation began, about the contradictions in the BLM and BIA positions in relation to the Western Shoshone. All the banter that characterized her at home was gone, and she was dignified, fierce, and impressive. Mary refused to talk, saying her sister had said everything, but she was drawn out when Carrie began to talk of her grandmother, and they told us how they were told that the sagebrush hears you lie even if no one else knows, and about how liars cast double shadows.

Once, in an effort to kill two birds with one stone—April's and my desire for an excursion and the need for a meeting—we gathered in the local tavern, The Flame. Made out of two trailer homes put together, it had a supremely awful jukebox, on which I played "There's a Tear in My Beer," "Your Cheatin' Heart," and many other doses of resentful schmaltz. I realized as the tunes warbled on that I was having a political meeting in a tavern in one of those towns you fly over at night and look down at the streets all laid out in a pattern like a TV antenna and wonder who could possibly have any reason to be in so godforsakenly remote a place, and that I was having that meeting with an old French priest, an under-age half-Shoshone, a rustic German, a wannabe demagogue from Vegas, a working-class young woman with a bad attitude, and·only one other child of middle-class white American privilege like me, and I leaned over to the other brat, the organizer, and whispered, "Edward Abbey would've never dared to make this up." We came up with a plan that was a model of organization, and then we went to tell it to the Dann sisters. Mary was knitting an afghan and Carrie was smoking, and they picked holes in it, and then the next morning April's alarm clock malfunctioned, and so our well-laid plans went astray. Things had been better the fall before, when the Seeds of Peace people were around, and they got better afterward, when members of the American Indian Movement and other activists joined up, but that spring was slapstick.

Another day in the calm after the attack we decided to find out where the cows were in case the BLM came back again. I got in the four-wheel drive with Carrie, Joachim, and Alain, and she drove us up Cottonwood Canyon, on the road that had looked nearly impassable when we hiked the canyon. This time we went all the way through the canyon into Pine Valley on the eastern side of the Cortez Range. Up high the ground cover became more lush, the sagebrush mixed in with lupine in bloom and many wild grasses. Carrie stopped and showed me some of the grasses, as appalled at the BLM's charges that she was overgrazing as though she'd been accused of committing a violent crime. She told us stories about when she used to run her father's sheep out here during the summer, when she was a girl, alone but for her horse, her dog, and the herd for long stretches of time. We drove along the rough roads of the lower slopes, running our eyes over the hills and finding a lot of deer—but no cows.

We drove further north, to ask the ranchers on this side to keep an eye out for the BLM. On the way to their place, Carrie told us about the children of that family who died, a generation or two back, down to their names and the diseases that took them. The ranch was pretty and simple, with far fewer buildings than the Danns had, and only two people living on it still. We ran into the son in his yard, with his truck full of little bags of dirt he had prospected in the hills, looking for gold. "I can eat a cow, but I can't eat gold," Carrie disparaged, and we went in to have coffee with him and his mother. They were talking about getting out of ranching after all the generations their family had spent in the region, talking about how taxes were driving them away, about how the government was destroying people like them. Their complaints rose into a shrill crescendo until

they frightened themselves with their vehemence, and they retreated, saying that ours was still the best government in the world,
as if to propitiate the listening spirits. They felt profoundly isolated
there, and I realized how much politics had brought the world in at
the Dann ranch.

We never spotted the cows, and on the way back we got lost.
Once there had been a single road back over the mountain, but halfway across there were suddenly so many new roads made by prospectors that Carrie couldn't recognize the route. White PCV pipes
were planted everywhere, the contemporary version of the claim
stake—intimations that all this too could be dug up and obliterated.
We drove for hours across beautiful hills and creeks and willow
banks and chaparral until finally we came back out onto the great
sweeping grass plain behind the Dry Hills and so to the road home.

I didn't get much done on that trip, or nearly as much as I'd
planned on the next one that August, when I brought my computer
out and wrote letters for Carrie and leaflets for the defense project.
Instead, I got caught up in rural time. Everything took longer to ac-
complish—washing a cup, passing along a message, buying grocer-
ies—and the shortest distance between two points always seemed to
involve a detour, a distraction, a conversation, and a lot of looking
around. Schedules and organization fell apart, and there was a great
deal to do that at the end of the day came under the category of
doing nothing. I got a sense of what life must be like when there
wasn't a war going on.

I saw a dawn where you could really pick out the violet field between the blue of sky and rose of sunrise, and saw that rose stretch
out across scudding clouds fanned across the sky as though they
came from the sun itself. I saw the lights of the mines down the valley

glow all night as though they were on fire with flames that didn't move. From the hot spring I saw lightning fill up the southern end of the valley while a waning moon rose in the northeast, first a brightness atop the hill, then a beacon, then a lopsided disk not long before midnight. And late one night I opened the door of the trailer in which I was writing defense-project brochures, just outside the front yard, and saw my kerosene lantern, which seemed so dim inside, throw my silhouette bold and dark onto the cottonwoods, tall as a tree and terrifying, a giant who stretched from my shoes.

The land of Crescent Valley owns me now, in some sense. For the month after my last long trip there in 1992 I dreamed about it almost nightly. The dreams were not significant for anything but the repetition of that landscape over and over again in my mind, as though it had taken possession of me: It haunted me, it wouldn't leave me alone. I found it hard to live in a city again, indoors most of the time, with a horizon occluded by buildings in all directions, hard almost in a physical sense, as an animal feels the bars of a cage press upon its skin. I had thought of cities as places that obliterate the livingness of everything but leave you the sky, but after this visit it was the clarity and expansiveness of the sky that I missed most. The moon rose over the house across the street hours after it rose above the horizon, and the sun did the same thing; the light-bounce of the city and its smog hid the stars at night. The valley had taught me a new grammar of scale between self and surroundings, one that could not be erased and that made jumbled nonsense of cities.

One night a woman's yells woke me up, as such small catastrophes have woken me up in my San Francisco neighborhood before. I lay there then in the bed I've slept in for ten years and wondered where I was the way I wonder when I wake up in the middle of the

night in a strange place. It's not unusual for me to wake up on the
road and piece together my location by thinking of what room the
bed is in, what building the room is in, what town the building is in,
and what state or country the town is in, to expand my mental map
until I know where in the world I am. It expands like the rings from
a rock tossed in water, till it reaches the limits of the body of land,
the world's geography, as the ripples reach shore. Sense of place is
the sixth sense, an internal compass and map made by memory and
spatial perception together; anyone who has ever had another place
return to them in an overwhelming whiff of unexpected smell—of
sagebrush, vanilla, cigarettes—knows how much this very abstract
sense is composed of sensual detail. But this night about two weeks
after Crescent Valley, I simply couldn't imagine an apartment building among other buildings in a city crowded onto a peninsula where
a continent ends and the vastest ocean begins. I couldn't believe, in
that suspended state between musing and dreaming, that I could be
any place but down in the middle of a plateau embraced by mountains, myself central but infinitesimal. It was as though my sense of
place had absorbed that terrain so profoundly it crowded out all others and lingered on long after I'd left, a phantom limb of location.

Keeping Pace with the Tortoise

✦ Two more things happened to me in Nevada in the summer of 1992.

The first was that I got to Ground Zero.

I did it the easy way. I called up the Las Vegas Department of Energy and said that I was a journalist and that I wanted a tour of the Nevada Test Site. They had me come out and meet Darwin at six in the morning at the DOE office near the Strip in Vegas.

Darwin was a large, blunt-featured, public-relations middle-weight who seemed sincere, but not fanatical, about his job. He was well disposed toward me, but he dropped a pointed reference to my brother in case I thought I could pass as a nonpartisan. In fact, David wanted to come with me, but I wanted to see how the Test Site was presented when the presenter wasn't being grilled, so I was alone. I asked some tricky questions, but didn't press any points. I wasn't out to make a convert or make him admit the error of his ways, only to see the place and scribble down the DOE's version of things (no recording devices were permitted on the tour).

The first thing that I noticed was that he always spoke of the DOE as "we," and that bombs were never called bombs, they were "devices." By the time we passed the entrance to Desert National Wildlife Range, the wildlife refuge that overlaps Nellis Airforce Base, I also noticed that Darwin would readily concede that the DOE had once lacked "preplanning," which had resulted in problems, but that he considered the out-of-control era strictly over. I heard a lot about animals. "Our biologists for the longest time have kept a running catalog of the wild horses, fifty or sixty of them. We know every

[204]

one there is. They move away from where we're working. We have very stringent rules. If you harm the animals, you lose your job. . . . All the employees have instructions on what to do if there is a tortoise. There is a federal law that no one is supposed to handle them." It seemed as though the Test Site workers displaced their anxiety about their work into elaborate care for the wildlife. But their acts of concern didn't allay the nature of their work. I remembered that Dan Sheahan once spoke of encountering a herd of horses that wandered east onto the Sheahan lands with their eyes burnt out, left empty sockets by a blast. And Citizen Alert was publicizing a warning to hunters that deer meat from the region might well be too radioactive to eat.

We drove across the cattleguard after Darwin showed a pass and on to a guard station. Inside, I got an identity badge that was also a radiation badge. It would measure how much radiation I was exposed to, and if they considered it too much, they would notify me. (They didn't.) There were handmade signs everywhere, jaunty letters on painted plywood with cursive script for emphasis. The first one after the sign that said the place was "An Environmental Research Park" said

DOING IT RIGHT THE FIRST TIME. . . .

We drove past two neat rows of wooden benches from which the scientists had watched the atmospheric tests, toward Mercury, which looked like just another industrial park, and which Darwin told me had been named after an old mercury mine out there, not the Greek god of messages and tricks—but the element was named for the god, so it's the same thing in the end. The sign said

DRIVE CAREFULLY
PRESERVE *WILD*LIFE.

The next sign said

RADIATION HAZARD
TOUCHING OR REMOVING
OBJECTS IS PROHIBITED.

On the way to the control room we visited a few scattered sites off to the right of the main road, in the Frenchman Flat area. Along with an area for testing hazardous chemicals, there was debris that had been subjected to nuclear explosions. Aluminum and concrete domes had been tested by the Priscilla blast of 1957, and a railroad bridge had been twisted by another bomb. A safe stood all alone at a drunken angle in the middle of all that space. "If there is a full-scale nuclear war the economy needs to survive, our bank records and gold and silver need to survive," said my guide. "So this is a conventional bank vault."

The control room looked a great deal like the ones in movie spaceships and "Star Trek." The lights were dim. There were three tiers of seats, comfortable revolving ones, on a carpeted floor, facing the vast screens—a central screen flanked by banks of TV screens on side panels angled slightly forward, like an altarpiece. The TVs seemed to have live feed of the current Ground Zero—but it was still very early for me, and perhaps they were reruns. On the central screen, where you would look out onto space in a spaceship, I was shown a short documentary movie: Underground tests were prepared with dozens of thick cables running from the mobile measuring stations down into the shaft in the ground to measure aspects of the explosion. A shaft may be from 600 to 2,200 feet deep, and four to ten feet wide. Bombs are lowered into such a hole, which is then "stemmed"—stuffed full of sand, gravel, concrete, and anything else that might prevent the radioactive gasses from leaking into the atmosphere. When the bomb explodes, puffs of dust rise up from the ground-shock waves. The waves roll onward, and when the test is large, they can be felt as far away as Vegas, sixty miles south. A cavern with walls of molten rock has been formed, full of radioactive gasses at extraordinary temperature; at some point after the explosion, the weight of the earth above will partially collapse the new cavern, and a crater will form on the surface. I saw aerial views of these collapses over and over again on the overexposed documentary footage: The earth shuddered or rippled as though it were made of thick liquid, but the ripple ran inward as though the film were running backward. Aerial photographs of the Ground Zero region show an arid surface pockmarked with depressions and crisscrossed by roads like long slashes, a surface that looks more like the devastated skin of an ancient plague survivor than the familiar surface of the earth. Under these pockmarks on the surface of the Test Site, one must imagine hundreds of spherical caves, like bubbles in ice, each one a nest of radiation, the graves of short-lived suns whose light no one ever saw.

Back in the van, Darwin told me about the safety systems, including plans for milk testing, infant thyroid dose testing, and massive evacuations, if a test vents—which of course most of them do, to varying degrees, though most of the ventings don't cause the safety systems to be implemented. He mentioned the "air surveillance network" that samples the air for fallout all the way to Austin and Salt Lake City, with standby sampling stations all the way to the Mississippi. I looked in the tour guide's scriptbook by Darwin's side, which listed potential questions and official answers. There was a question about the effects of fallout on downwinders, and the answer said that, yes, potentially tens of people had died as a result. International Physicians for the Prevention of Nuclear War estimates that, worldwide, nuclear testing will have caused 430,000 cancer fatalities by the end of the century, mostly in the Northern Hemisphere. Extended into infinity, says IPPNW, the fatality incidence approaches 2.4 million; "Because most of the exposure is due to carbon-14 [half-life 5,730 years], the majority of the deaths will occur over the next few thousand years."

We approached the pass of the ranges that had always defined the horizon of the Test Site I walked into, and crossed over it into a new landscape, the imagined landscape I had always been walking toward, the most bombed place on earth. The one thing that I had never expected was that the landscape beyond the reach of all my trespassing would be beautiful, and so unlike what came before. We came through the pass into what by desert standards is a lush forest of Joshua trees, each with the upright posture of a sentinel or a witness, and Darwin began to speculate with a kind of rough poetry about what wonders the trees had witnessed since the days when the Death Valley Forty-Niners came through. There were volcanic formations on our left, a granite mesa straight ahead at the end of a road that looked as if it were drawn by a ruler, flanked on both sides by telephone poles, receding straight toward the vanishing point.

The first crater was full of huge steel boxes partly covered by dirt, and a road spiraled down into it, as roads wind down into open-pit mines. Darwin told me that the boxes were full of disassembled buildings from the Fernald uranium processing plant in Ohio (though he didn't tell me that Fernald supplied ingots for nuclear weapons until it was shut down for contaminating the region) and that the Test Site also serves as a low-level radioactive waste site. The next crater we drove into ourselves—the drive-through crater. There was a ground squirrel scampering over the ground around the plug, and Darwin pointed it out and told me about a raven that builds a nest atop the plug every spring. The crater had been made by the 249-kiloton Bilby test in 1963, a year when there were forty-four announced nuclear tests out here. Bilby was exploded in the water table to see how radiation dispersed in it.

From Bilby we drove to Doom Town. The town consists of two houses spread far apart on a wide plain, built to see how America's suburbs would do in an all-out nuclear war. Of the five houses that had been built on a line extending from a Ground Zero, the closest three were destroyed by the test, named Annie. Annie was the first in the Upshot-Knothole series of spring 1953, the series that killed so many sheep in Utah and probably killed Janet Gordon's brother. Like the safe, the houses seemed strange in their isolation, flotsam from a conventional life never lived out here. We got out and walked toward the wooden house, whose doors and windows had been blasted off, along with the paint on three of its sides. I was queasy about the dust, but it was a dank, still day, a good day to be out in a contaminated area. Inside, the house had the floorplan of the tin dollhouses of the time. A central staircase connected two stories, each with four rooms. There was a basement too, and —"I've never seen this before," said Darwin—it was full of water from recent rains. I walked down to the waterline, about three feet above the floor, and saw something he didn't—a small animal's corpse lodged under the next, partially submerged step, but the place smelled of chocolate powder, not of death. When we came out, a pale bird dived at us from the rafters, chattering furiously. Darwin said she must have a nest in the eaves.

At the Sedan Crater, a lark swung by the rim at great velocity. I kept feeling that somehow the small animals had been planted to make the landscape seem reassuring, that I was in a nature movie about Our Friend the Atom. Sedan Crater is a hole 300 feet deep and 1,200 feet across, from an explosion that displaced twelve million tons of earth. The bomb that made it was part of Operation Plowshare, a spinoff of Eisenhower's Atoms for Peace. Considerable effort—including the underwriting of the nuclear power industry—had been made to demonstrate that atomic energy was not merely a tool for destruction, and Plowshare had been meant to show that even the bombs had peaceful uses. The name came from the Old Testament prophet Isaiah, who foretold that in the last days "the Lord's house shall be established in the top of the mountains" and "the nations shall beat their swords into plowshares . . . neither shall they learn war any more." There were fantasies then, in both the U.S.S.R. and the U.S., about using atomic bombs as earth-moving devices for engineering projects such as another Panama Canal. "We will change the earth's surface to suit us," Teller said, presuming that it didn't suit as is. But the contamination made such uses infeasible, and the huge sandpit of Sedan is a memorial to this strange dream. There were crickets chirping while I stood on the platform that overlooked the hole.

As we drove along the road again, Darwin apologized for the bumps, explaining that every test's shock waves ripple through the road and buckle it. He told me that there had been a farm at three o'clock—he used the military method for indicating direction—and he indicated Plutonium Valley over the range to the northeast. Plutonium Valley was intentionally contaminated with radioactive material in another experiment, and "cowboys herded beef cattle in areas contaminated by atmospheric nuclear detonation." The Environmental Protection Agency, Darwin told me, "built viewports into the sides of the cows to take samples of irradiated hay and alfalfa out." The experiment in Plutonium Valley was discontinued in the seventies, and now there are 3,000 acres of contaminated soil "we are trying to find a way to clean up." Like mercury, plutonium was named after a god, Pluto, the god of the underworld and of death, son of Uranus. Here Pluto and his manmade element had a valley to themselves.

We drove all the way to the northern end of the Test Site, to Rainier Mesa. At Rainier, they drill holes horizontally into the rock and explode more bombs. Dark green junipers and piñons grow here, even this far south, where the altitude approaches 8,000 feet, and the landscape begins to look like that around Santa Fe and Los Alamos. Darwin's own parents grew up in south-central New Mexico near the Jornada del Muerte, and he told me they both remember the ground-shock wave of the Trinity Test, though they didn't see its flash, which turned night into day and which even a blind woman saw.

The landscape of the Nevada Test Site was strangely innocent of its own history, even with all its craters and ruins. It was the stories that brought it to life for me, the stories of Pauline and Rachel and Janet, of the atomic veterans, the local people. When I had come to it from the Peace Camp, I had always been walking on a strong foundation of stories; now I was being wafted around on a tissue of tourism—on nuggets of curious information that painted no picture of the real effect of the 953 or so nuclear bombs that exploded in this place. It was strange after five years of walking toward the jagged teeth of the horizon past Mercury to finally arrive and be swallowed up into the shrouded landscape of the Ground Zeros, but it was the journey that gave the landscape meaning for me, not this arrival. I would be back, on my own terms and my own feet.

✠ THE OTHER THING THAT HAPPENED THAT JULY IS HARDLY more emphatic. I was staying with my brother in his little duplex house near the dusty old downtown of Las Vegas that July. From midmorning to dark it was too hot to enjoy being outside—usually over 100 degrees—but after sunset we would turn off the swamp cooler and open the windows and move back into a world that had become welcoming again. One evening during that visit we sat on his porch steps sipping bourbon over lots of ice and watching the huge black bugs crawl out of the hole in the straggling remnants that had once been a lawn, as they did at the same time every evening. Cicadas were rasping, a breeze was rattling the acacia that shaded our trucks during the day. Somewhere in the last few years we had mutated into Westerners, our ratty little Japanese cars had become American pickups, and we had been consumed by Nevada, each in our own way.

He said that there was going to be a comprehensive test ban sometime in the next few years because worldwide pressure was going to be too much even for the U.S. government, whose great excuse for testing had faded away with the dissolution of the Soviet Union, and he talked about what he would do afterward.

There is a paradox about arrival that Zeno proposed in Greece twenty-four centuries ago. In it, the great warrior Achilles is racing to catch up with a tortoise—for our purposes, we can imagine it as a desert tortoise. Zeno proposed that the swift Achilles could never pass the tortoise because in the time he goes a yard, the tortoise goes a tenth of a yard, in the time he goes a tenth of a yard, the tortoise goes a hundredth, and so on into the world of infinitesimal fractions, and since the measurements can be continued infinitely, the event is never completed, and the runner is always behind the crawler. Zeno's paradox illustrates something else, that logic does not necessarily describe reality, and that it is not anticipation but journeying that does often bring us to a destination. As I had come to the great secret heart of the Arms Race, the mesas and craters of the Nevada Test Site itself, the people in the movement against this race had come to the brink of the fulfillment of their work and dream.

WATER, OR FORGETTING THE PAST:
YOSEMITE NATIONAL PARK

The Rainbow

✚ I READ ONCE THAT THE MONO LAKE PAIUTES BELIEVED THAT there were two skies, each coming down to rest on the crest of the Sierra Nevada. It was an old unreliable book that I read it in, but the theory does much to explain the profound difference of the two worlds the Sierra divide: the wide-open arid spaces of Nevada, still so sparsely inhabited, and the riot of life—flora and fauna, particularly human fauna—that overruns California.

The two skies may be just a way of describing the rain shadow the Sierra cast over Nevada—as the clouds blow east, the mountains scrape them off the sky, keeping the western slopes wet and the east dry.

✚ THE ROCKY BASE OF THE MONUMENT FOR THE DONNER PARTY is twenty-two feet high, the height the snow was that winter of 1846–47. On top of this rugged pillar is a cluster of bronze figures facing westward. "Virile to risk . . . indomitable—unafraid," says the plaque in a paean that has nearly nothing to do with what made these travelers history. I stopped on June 5, 1991, on my way to Reno, to look at the monument, the museum, and the lake named after these unfortunate adventurers. I wanted to know why their names stuck to this alpine landscape, because names were beginning to loom large in my adventures.

Plant names had provided the keys to the place in which I grew up. The patterns of that coastal California landscape emerged with names, with milkmaids that bloomed first, brodia whose bulbs the

Miwok ate, miner's lettuce and thimbleberries that I ate, buckeyes that flowered when June's feral hedge roses did and lost their leaves first in the fall. From a jumble of green the natural world came into focus as a delicately balanced cycle of events I looked forward to, of dangers, uses, and niches. Place names didn't add much to this picture for decades, until I began reading Western history and realized the larger landscape was a crazy quilt of names of successive waves of culture, battles, heroes, and real-estate developers, most of them forgotten but for their names.

When I unfurled a California-Nevada map for my trip to the Sierra that summer, the names began to tell the story: Donner Pass for the stranded emigrants of 1846; Truckee and Winnemucca for two Paiute chiefs; Carson City for Kit Carson who explored California with Fremont and defeated the Navajo Nation; Walker Lake east of Tahoe for the trapper Joseph Walker who in 1833 seems to have been the first white man to look into the Yosemite Valley; Mariposa County in California's gold country from the Spanish for butterfly; the Merced River which runs through Mariposa after the Spanish for mercy; and Yosemite itself, whose name—a Miwok word—is the strangest story of all.

I had set out for the Nevada Test Site and circumstance sent me to Yosemite instead. I was on my way to Reno to see Mary and Carrie Dann's last day in court—this was how I first met them. And seeing this last day in court was part of a larger itinerary that had just been derailed. The Department of Energy was holding public hearings around the country on its policies, and I had signed up to make a statement at the Las Vegas hearing. Bob Fulkerson of Citizen Alert was going down to testify too, and I was going to drive to Reno— which is only four hours away from San Francisco—to see this day in court, and then go down 95 with Bob, and with my brother, who was driving up for the day. But Joe Sanchez, Citizen Alert's Native

American Program coordinator, had suddenly fallen sick with leukemia, so Bob was going to stay in Reno, and I didn't have a ride back from Vegas. I decided I wanted to see this day in court anyway and would return through Yosemite:

I spent my first night in Truckee high on the western slope of the Sierra, and I stopped at the Donner site beforehand. The late spring landscape had that clean prettiness highland places do: The streams ran icy and clear, and everything green but the pines was a young, tender green, a green that didn't remember the harshness of winter. From Donner Pass, Highway 80 goes to Truckee, where the Truckee River turns north on its short run from Lake Tahoe to Pyramid Lake. The same swift, slender river ran past the casinos and office buildings of downtown Reno, and the next morning when I asked for directions to the Ninth Circuit Court, everyone told me to just follow the river.

High up in the Federal Building, the courtroom's fluorescent light panels hovering overhead looked like rectilinear clouds diminishing toward the horizon. The ancient judge on his dais looked miles away instead of yards. He was tiny as a child, with a voice like a paper bag being folded, even when he was insulting the Bureau of Land Management's snub-nosed blond attorneys. Judge Bruce Thompson had been fairly young when the case began, the Danns' lawyer told me later; not long after this day Thompson died. The Danns themselves were almost hidden from view by the high backs of their red-leather swivel chairs. Bill Rosse came in and beamed at me; Chief Raymond Yowell came in looking gentlemanly in his corduroy jacket; the extremist Glen Wasson, as handsome as a movie star in his Western clothes came in and murmured "God save the Queen" when the court clerk opened the proceedings with "God save America and this honorable court"; and Bob and my brother came in late.

The Danns politely told the judge his court had no jurisdiction over them. Judge Thompson, hemmed in by appellate-court decisions that overturned many of his own, ruled against them. "I think the history of the relationship to the aboriginal people that occupied the 48 states of the U.S. before Christopher Columbus discovered this wonderful country is a shameful history. Anyone who's read that history knows it's a history of broken promises and broken dreams," he said slowly, and finally. "All the avenues which were open from time to time for miscarriages of justice have been closed. There is nothing more I can do."

I was Yosemite-bound, and since the weight of the U.S. government had come down on the Western Shoshone before noon, I had hopes of being there before sunset. After lunch with the Danns and their supporters, my brother, his friend Reinard, and I bid farewell to all our friends and set off down 395, along the spine of the Sierra. We stopped in Lee Vining on the shores of Mono Lake to stretch and buy provisions. Next door to the main grocery store in this one-street town was a little monument, a small cousin to the Donner monolith, out of the same rough stones, cement, and bronze. It stated, "The name of this community honors Leroy Vining. In 1852 Lieutenant Tredwell Moore and soldiers of the Second Infantry pursued Indians of Chief Tenaya's tribe from Yosemite across the Sierra via Bloody Canyon. They took back mineral samples and a prospecting party was organized. In this group were the Vinings, Lee and Dick." We charged west over Tioga Pass through the route that supplanted Bloody Canyon and into heights still covered with snow, stopping for a brief snowball toss. The sun was already setting by the time we reached Lake Tenaya, and we had to keep descending if we wanted to stay warm in our scant gear, though it was Lake Tenaya that I'd come for.

Lieutenant Moore and the Vining brothers' Second Infantry were better known as part of the Mariposa Battalion, after Mariposa County, where the battalion was organized. In pursuit of Indians, it became the first party of whites to enter Yosemite Valley, on March 27, 1851, and most of what we know about the expedition comes from a memoir by one of the enlistees, Lafayette Bunnell's *Discovery of the Yosemite and the Indian War of 1851 Which Led to That Event.* His is a strange account, switching back and forth from feverishly romantic response to the land to cool journalistic recounting of the war. The war and the landscape have nothing to do with each other in his history, except that the war leads them to the landscape, and geography shapes the war, which was made up mostly of tracking, ambushes, and escapes. By the end of Bunnell's book, Yosemite begins to seem an early Vietnam, though nothing in the popular representation of Yosemite hints at such violence. I was shocked by the way Bunnell could be lyrical and coldblooded at the same time. The views moved him to tears, he wrote, and the rocks reaffirmed his faith in the deity.

For me the inadvertent climax of the book, the passage that haunted me, was a scene at Lake Tenaya, after the old Chief and his people had been captured, just before they were marched to the flatlands of the San Joaquin Valley to live on a reservation. The passage runs, "When Ten-ie-ya reached the summit, he left his people and approached where the captain and a few of us were halting. . . . I called him up to us, and told him that we had given his name to the lake and river. At first he seemed unable to comprehend our purpose, and pointing to the group of glistening peaks, near the head of the lake, said 'It already has a name; we call it Py-we-ack.' Upon my telling him that we had named it Ten-ie-ya, because it was upon the shores of the lake that we had found his people, who would never return to it to live, his countenance fell and he at once left our group and joined his family circle. His countenance indicated that he thought the naming of the lake no equivalent for his loss of territory."

Usually annihilating a culture and romanticizing it are done separately, but Bunnell neatly compresses two stages of historical change into one conversation. Bunnell says, in effect, that there is no room for these people in the present, but they will become a decorative past for someone else's future. Part of what is horrific about this encounter is that Bunnell and the Mariposa Battalion had come to exterminate these native people not out of implacable hatred in the usual spirit of war, but in a blithe administrative way. They were opening up the land for economic activity—gold mining, mostly—and the Indians were in their way and had to be removed as the earth above the gold-filled fossil streambeds was, with no more reflection.

Pyweack means shining rocks; like most of Yosemite's original place names, it describes what is present rather than monumentalizing a passing human figure. Tenaya is a name given from outside, neither about the lake nor about the man, but about an unpleasant incident almost entirely forgotten by Yosemite's visitors. Bunnell claims to Tenaya that the new name will give the man a kind of immortality, but what he is really doing is obliterating Tenaya's culture from the place and beginning its history over again.

Twenty-five years later John Muir camped on the shore of Lake Tenaya, or Pyweack, and described it in a journal entry. "The lake with its rocky bays and promontories well defined, its depth pictured with the reflected mountains, its surface just sufficiently tremulous to make the mirrored stars swarm like water-lilies in a woodland pond. This is my old haunt where I began my studies. I camped on this very spot. No foot seems to have neared it."

A decade after that a newspaper article declared that the lake was "so high and so lovely in its surroundings that hunters and prospectors say they have heard angels singing in the New Jerusalem."

The Rainbow

✦ Yosemite National Park is the very crucible and touchstone for American landscape, and I thought that if I could understand what happened at this lake within it, I could begin to see into the peculiarities, blindnesses, raptures, and problems that constitute the Euro-American experience of landscape. Yosemite is one of the most famous landscapes in the world, and it is usually pictured as a virgin wilderness. Literally pictured: In most of the photographs that have made the place familiar to the world, there are no people. And for landscape photography it is one of the most important places in the world. Charles Weed made some photographs there at the end of the 1850s, just as photographic technology was becoming capable of such things, and Carleton Watkins established landscape photography as an artistic discipline with his mammoth-plate photographs of Yosemite taken in 1860 and 1861. Watkins's photographs were shown around the world, and with the paintings, prints, and literary panegyrics, made Yosemite an icon for landscape at a time when very few white people had ever ventured along the steep trails into the place. In 1864, Abraham Lincoln signed a bill setting aside the Yosemite Valley as a park to be overseen by the state of California. Yosemite was the world's first national park and the model for all that came afterward (although the U.S. national park system really began with Yellowstone in 1872, which could not be overseen by a state since Wyoming was still a territory with few white inhabitants).

Muir came to California in 1868 familiar with the descriptions of the place, and he headed straight for the Sierra upon disembarking in San Francisco. Yosemite reigned supreme in Muir's heart, and it was a crucial place for the Sierra Club he helped to found in 1892. The battle over Hetch Hetchy Valley, the next valley north of Yosemite Valley, was the first time Americans took such a stand against growth, progress, and development, and this battle transformed the

Sierra Club from a hikers' association to the country's first significant conservation organization. Ansel Adams worked with the Sierra Club and with the Yosemite landscape for more than half a century, and his photographs helped to define not only how people saw the place, but how they imagined nature itself. It is hardly an exaggeration to say that no place on earth is more central to landscape photography and landscape preservation. What has been left out of the picture, then, says a lot about how we understand landscape.

Nothing in any of these images or any of these agendas suggested that Yosemite was a battleground before it was a vacation destination. This is already clear in Bunnell's *The Discovery of the Yosemite and the Indian War of 1851 Which Led to That Event*. The war and the discovery are two different experiences for him. In the gap between them, Tenaya and his culture fall. Yosemite always looks like a virgin bride in the artistic representations, not like somebody else's mother.

What does it mean that these two parts don't intersect, that Bunnell expends all his humanity upon the scenery, not upon the inhabitants, that the images which shaped the popular view of the place are similarly segregated, that the gap between our view of landscape and of history is full of lost stories, ravaged cultures, obliterated names?

✦ THAT FIRST EVENING WE'D BEEN TOO LATE TO STOP AT LAKE Tenaya we drove down into the valley, failed to find my reserved campground or anyone who could help us find it, stole into a meadow, spread our tarps and sleeping bags, and fell asleep under a starry sky, perfect examples of the wrong kind of campers. Half Dome was looming over us when I woke before dawn and, when I woke up again, so were hundreds of cars and people. The other two, who had spent less time looking at pictures of the place, were astounded by how high the cliffs rose above us, and even I had thought at first that the great dark form against the night sky was a cloud blotting out the stars, not an earthly body. The mostly level valley is about seven miles long, from east to west, and up to a mile wide, surrounded on all sides but the western outlet by steep cliffs and slopes, from which a number of waterfalls plunge. Here the creek out of Lake Tenaya and the upper branches of the Merced come together to form the Merced River, which flows out the west end of the valley to join with its south fork and merge with the San Joaquin River and thence, along with nearly every other Sierran river, to the San Francisco Bay. Yosemite National Park has the world's most vertical rock wall, the sheer face of Half Dome rising 4,733 feet above the valley floor; the fifth tallest waterfall, Yosemite Falls, cascading 2,425 feet in a plunge and two bounces; five glaciers up in the heights; 2,700 buildings in the valley including a church, a beauty salon, a jail; and more than three million visitors a year. The whole park is 1,169 square miles, a little smaller than the 1,350 square miles of the Nevada Test Site, and bigger than that usual standard, Rhode Island.

There were plaques, maps, and road signs everywhere directing visitors to the principal sights. Tour buses and a peculiar roofless train of the kind used in zoos provided an even more regulated experience. The waterfalls were the main attractions, and the great rock faces—Half Dome and North Dome to the east, El Capitan to the west—came in second. I saw a foreign tourist taking snapshots of Yosemite Falls later that year, when there was no water in the waterfall, only a dark stain on the rock face. There was less emphasis on what was ubiquitous in the valley: the spreading black oaks, the luxuriant meadows, the meandering river, the buildings, and the other tourists. Photography itself has largely reinforced this phenomenon for the public. When Carleton Watkins took his sweeping landscape photographs, there were very few people and buildings to exclude; but by the time Ansel Adams arrived, structures and people hovered around the outer rim of his images, just out of view. By a strange extension, people have learned to perform this cropping-out operation themselves, seeing in the world what they have seen in pictures. Millions of people a year crowd together here to see virgin wilderness, a natural phenomenon they recognize thanks to cultural intermediaries.

There are two hamlets in this valley, one connected to the Curry Company's assortment of housing, the other a small collection of stores, restaurants, and Park Service museums surrounded by a scattering of employees' houses, Yosemite Village. I found a plaque in front of the village store that said the valley was first seen by Joseph Walker's party in 1833 and "next seen and described . . . by a group of volunteers—the Mariposa Battalion—who had been sent deep into the Sierra foothills to dissuade the native Indians from their violent attacks."

Afterward, I found the Indian Cultural Museum, further away from the heart of the village. This museum presents another story that contradicts the park's own main version of Yosemite's history, a second story that has never been assimilated into the first, which features discoverers, wildernesses, and so forth. It was a cluster of rooms full of baskets, ceremonially garbed mannequins representing individual Indians from Yosemite's past, photographs, and a diorama of native life in the late nineteenth century. Suddenly, one of the figures by the diorama moved and shocked me as though she were a ghost or one of the objects had come to life: Among all the glass cases and pedestals was a living woman in period costume, seated on a platform demonstrating traditional crafts. She had been so still when I came in that I had taken her for a display, not a demonstrator.

✚

When he renamed the lake, Bunnell said that there would be no room for these people in the present, but they'd become a decorative past in someone else's future: Here was that future—a contemporary woman seated among statues, dressed in the clothes of another century. It seemed time to get out of the valley, and so I went to what I suspected would be the quietest part of the park, Hetch Hetchy. Besides which, if the human body is seventy percent water, mine after a decade in San Francisco contains a high proportion of Hetch Hetchy. I'd wanted to see this drowned valley at the other end of my faucets for years. For a while I kept a U.S. Geological Survey topographical map of Hetch Hetchy Reservoir tacked up above my kitchen faucet, so that every time I did the dishes or filled the kettle, I would remember the system that links my plumbing to this alpine landscape.

The road to Hetch Hetchy goes north through a burnt forest, along the rough, rocky western face of the park. Toward the end, it turns east, and far away and tiny you can see two waterfalls on the southern side of the water and the face of the dam. The dam divides two worlds. One side is almost level with a tranquil lake; hundreds of feet below on the other, an angry jet of water spurts out sideways. Vehicles can only go as far as the edge of O'Shaughnessy Dam, and thereafter Hetch Hetchy is accessible only by foot. In Yosemite, you walk on the valley floor; in Hetch Hetchy you walk on a broad path carved out of the valley's side. I have heard that sometimes when the water is very clear, the trees on what once was the valley floor become visible. There was something as terrifying about the idea of a whole landscape drowned beneath the still, opaque blue waters of that lake as there had been in seeing a living woman on display in a museum: Both of them were evidence of something grievously dislocated.

I parked and walked to the middle of the reservoir, and where you might expect a monument, there was a drinking fountain. Dozens of twittering swallows skimmed the surface of the lake for insects, soaring and darting after their invisible prey. I could see a tunnel or cave blasted out of the rock on the other side of the dam, and when I went to look, it was a tunnel, and magical: a long, roughly faceted passage of stone whose three or four hundred feet of darkness were hardly interrupted by bare lightbulbs at distant intervals. On the other side, a trail began. Without meaning to go far, I began walking, but every turn revealed a new lure, and I walked all afternoon.

What remains above water of Hetch Hetchy Valley was more richly carpeted in flowers than Yosemite Valley, and infinitely quieter. (The San Francisco Water Department argues that its dam preserved Hetch Hetchy from the blight of excessive tourism.) People hailed each other the way they do in remote places, rather than ignoring each other as they do in crowds. John Muir considered it more beautiful than the other valley; he called them the Tuolumne Yosemite and the Merced Yosemite; and he died fighting to save the Tuolumne Yosemite from the dam.

Snowmelt was near its peak when I was there, and the waterfalls were glorious. The first was a slender, graceful plume that fell hundreds of feet and broke into rivulets that ran down a broad swath of smooth stone, forming pools and watering a wild rock garden of mosses and flowers. The second I heard before I saw. As I came around a bend on the trail, the air filled with a thunderous roar, and I turned again to see a rainbow that leapt from a torrent of white water to the lake below. As I got closer, it became a brilliant double

rainbow arcing from the rock walls to the water. The air filled with
spray, so that it was hard to see the cataract of white water. The water
pounded against the rocks, leaping upward again with extraordinary
force. The spray was so thick around the wooden footbridge across
the waterfall that it seemed to pass through the gentler periphery of
the waterfall. The temperature dropped. Water streamed across the
vibrating bridge, and the roiling water below was clearly dangerous.
As I walked across, the spray soaked my clothes and obscured my
vision: All I could see was the full-circle rainbow the cascade made
in front of me, like a halo around a secret.

Spectators

✚ I CAME BACK TO YOSEMITE AGAIN AND AGAIN, BUT NOTHING
ever happened to me there. It was a place where nothing was supposed to happen. I had become used to things happening, used to
Nevada, which has not yet come out of the freewheeling frontier era.
Nevada is an insular, unregulated place whose few real inhabitants
are fearless and openhearted, while California's crowdedness breeds
professionalization and the cultivation of privacy. It may also be the
difference between institutions and communities, for at the Test Site
I worked with communities of volunteers, while at Yosemite I met
almost exclusively with employees of the National Park Service.
(There were volunteers and activists working on Yosemite issues, but
they were concerned with preserving it as a natural environment, a
position that differed from the Park Service in degree, but not in
interpretation.) Some of the people I met there had the same passion
for the land and issues of Yosemite that the Nevadans I met had for
theirs, but they didn't share it: Everything was well administered,
and nobody was looking for participants. And I wasn't looking to
participate: Wars and contradictions as old and tangled as Yosemite's demanded a different kind of response.

I spent a lot of time in the valley, because all the information I
was looking for was there, and because the valley was at the heart
of my question of what this landscape, and landscape, meant. I went
alone, because most of my friends refused to stay there. They would
willingly go into the backcountry, but they saw the valley as a Dis-
neyland and despised it. In a lot of ways, it wasn't a great place to
go see Nature, whatever that is, but it was the best place to go see

people going to go see Nature, the Park Service presenting them with the official version of Nature, and the accretion of Nature's artifacts and souvenirs—human nature. It was a strange place, full of crowds of people—families, tour groups, gatherings—in the brightly colored clothes that signify leisure and pleasure, more intent on having recreation than on pursuing the sublime, or perhaps pursuing the sublime as a quick recreational interval. The more time I spent in the place the more it seemed like a suburb without walls rather than a wilderness with amenities, as though one weekend night all the fences and buildings had disappeared, but the residents went on as usual with their cards, their cooking, washing up, dozing, tossing balls, and scolding children. I rarely saw anyone else alone in the valley, except for a few people painting or fly fishing. The bustle and the congeniality made my solitude more intense, and I withdrew more and more into myself, felt stranger and stranger for not being a part of a group or a family. I stayed there for a week once, and I don't think I talked to anyone except on business. And nothing happened to me, except that I walked and looked.

Or the events that happened were so small they hardly bear repeating. I hiked up the steep trails and found that the milling crowds quickly evaporated as the altitude increased and the paths along the cliffs around the valley were actually peaceful places. I hiked to Old Inspiration Point, which is where the invaders first saw the valley, and then climbed up above it to New Inspiration Point—apparently it isn't the nature of inspiration, but the growth of underbrush that has caused the point to be transferred upslope—and halfway to Glacier Point before I decided the day was too short and my water bottle too small to go all the way. I went to Bridalveil Fall a number of times. A slender fall at the west end of the valley, it is one of the most surprising of Yosemite's waterfalls, shooting over an almost-smooth cliff rather than tumbling down a water-carved trench or a crevice.

The rock face to either side is stained dark and glistens, and on the well-watered ledges lodge ferns and other verdure. One late summer afternoon, the spray swayed and billowed in the wind as though it were as light as smoke or powder. It seemed to be anything but water as it hovered weightless, a transparent shape up high among the rocks, and only further down did it gather again and drop like water. It cascaded among the rocks at the bottom of the fall, and then became a stream that burbled past the huge boulder I sat on, high above the noisy children and the people rushing about with video cameras. There is something almost hypnotic about waterfalls. Something that does not move can be seen at once, and something that moves extensively moves out of sight or satisfies our curiosity, but a waterfall tumbles perpetually, promising change and surprise while it stays constant, a throbbing, swaying cord of water. It may be the way waterfalls, like the sea, seem to defy the nature of water itself, to settle and be still.

It seems odd that natural and historical time should flow side by side, and so little affect each other, that the water should float down like smoke regardless of whether Yosemite was an indigenous homeland, a battleground, or a tourist attraction, and that a place that had changed so profoundly in so little time should possess so many constants. Thinking about natural history and human history is like looking at one of those trick drawings—a skull that becomes a seated woman, a wineglass that becomes a pair of kissing profiles—it's hard to see them both at the same time. One doesn't usually write, "Washington crossed the Delaware, a south-flowing river whose animal populations include . . ." Yosemite has been defined in terms of geological time scales and natural wonders; it has become easy to believe that Yosemite has no significant human history; and thereby that human history is not part of the landscape.

✚ ON THE FIRST NIGHT THAT WHITE PEOPLE SPENT IN Yosemite Valley—March 27, 1851—they got as far as Bridalveil Fall and made a campfire. A few days before, the Mariposa Battalion's leader, James D. Savage, had told Tenaya that if he didn't give up, the battalion would come in and destroy every member of the tribe. And Tenaya had told Savage that the snow was too deep for horses to get into the valley, but the horses had, and fifty-eight men from the battalion with them. By May 22, the day that Tenaya and his entourage were captured at the high-country lake, the battalion's campaign was largely over, though there were skirmishes, murders, and manhunts for years to come. Bunnell's account was written nearly thirty years after the events he describes. In many respects it has been verified as accurate, but some of the conversations he recounts seem to be at the very least embellished. Whether they happened the way he says they did or not is an important question, but not necessarily one that determines the value of the material. If it doesn't reveal what really happened, it reveals what Bunnell thought should have happened, and so it is valuable as myth as well as anecdote. He fine-tuned his descriptions of his responses so that he appears not as the place's first visitor, but as its first appreciator. And so as literature, it has some fine comic moments of conflict between the hard-headed frontiersmen and the romantic vision of Lafayette Bunnell. Major Savage particularly serves him as a foil, a man whose practical purpose is never interrupted by scenic appreciation.

In one passage, Bunnell comes down from a tour of the scenery of the valley and meets Major Savage burning a cache of acorns (the Mariposa Battalion went on a scorched-earth campaign in the valley, burning the structures and food stocks they found). "The major looked up from the charred mass of burning acorns, and as he glanced down the smoky valley, said, 'This affords us the best prospect of any yet discovered; just look!' 'Splendid!' I promptly replied, 'Yosemite might be beautifully grand a few weeks later when the foliage and flowers are at their prime, and the rush of water has somewhat subsided.'" As Bunnell goes on, Savage begins to laugh. He explains that the prospect he referred to is that of starving the Indians out of their valley, which is "more agreeable than all the scenery in creation." Bunnell comes out mortified by that exchange, but it is Savage's vision that prepares the way for his, the war that leads to the park.

The story that begins with Bunnell's devout taste for scenery is a story about art, conservation, and appreciation that goes on to greater luminaries. It is an important story, the story of the birth of national parks, of landscape photography, of the conservation movement, but not the only story that can be told about the place. It is the most told story, however, and the one I came across first in my explorations.

The speed at which the valley was transformed from an indigenous stronghold to a war zone to a tourist attraction seems dizzying now, though those such as Bunnell who oversaw it don't seem to have found it unusual. In the terms of change in the nineteenth century it may not have been, but it's hard to imagine a twentieth-century site undergoing such a festively amnesiacal metamorphosis. Bunnell quickly recognized the possibilities of the place for tourism and in 1856 built a toll road to the valley with a partner. The first tourists didn't wait for the toll road to open up. In July of 1855, four years after the war broke out and white men first became aware of the existence of the Yosemite Valley, J. M. Hutchings and a party of tourists arrived, lured by the descriptions that had filtered out of the region. The party included two native guides, reputedly from among the original inhabitants of the valley, and an artist, Thomas Ayres. The guides seem to have influenced the party not at all, beyond helping them find their way around, and the artist influenced future events a great deal. Hutchings was an Englishman who realized, as many others did, that there was more money to be made, and made more pleasantly, from catering to miners than from mining. He had plans to publish a magazine about California, and its first issue was to include descriptions and pictures of the sensational landmarks of Yosemite.

Ayres drew a view of the valley and pictures of the falls, and though his light pencil technique tended to smooth and soften the texture of what he drew, the magnificent scale was still evident. His pictures were purest landscape in which the tiny figures in the foreground seem to have just arrived, as proxies for the viewer. In the fall of 1855, Hutchings published a lithograph from Ayres's drawing of Yosemite Falls, the biggest waterfall in the valley. The following summer, his magazine appeared, with four etchings taken from Ayres's drawings. Ayres came back a year later on his own, travelling on the road Bunnell helped build, and finding a party of tourists already in the valley, where Bunnell and company were building a hotel. In 1857, Ayres's views of Yosemite were exhibited in New York City. At a time when few had seen the original, many could see the representations of this landscape, and many did.

Already known largely through the mediums of words and pictures, Yosemite's fame spread around the world after the first photographs of the place demonstrated that the drawings and descriptions were hardly exaggerated. In 1859, Hutchings came back with another artist, the photographer Charles Leander Weed. Weed had already photographed the mining regions along the American River the year before, with the new wet-plate process. The pictures he took at the time depicted the mine operations rather than the surrounding landscape, illustrations of a burgeoning industry for the curious and the investors. Weed was working for the San Francisco photography studio that belonged to Robert Vance, who made most of his money in portraits. Not long before, the only commercial photographic medium had been the daguerreotype, which had severe limitations. A daguerreotype was a direct positive made on a polished metal plate; like a Polaroid camera it yielded only a single image, and like a Polaroid, it had practical limitations in size. Easily reproducible photographs did not come about until photographers turned to a negative-positive process, of which the wet plate was the earliest commercial success. With the wet-plate process, photography stopped being like painting—a means of creating a unique image—and became like printing—a means of creating unlimited originals from the same source, and therefore a means of distributing images widely around the world. With this the revolution of photography was complete. Even so, it was burdensome to transport glass-plate negatives to remote places, get them into the bulky cameras without exposing them beforehand, and develop them quickly after making the photograph. But the process was the beginning of landscape photography, the medium that has so profoundly influenced knowledge and expectation of remote places. It is hard to imagine the campaigns to save a remote mountain area or wild stretch of river without the photographs that make the place real and precious in the minds of those who may never see it: This practice begins in Yosemite.

Hutchings used Weed's 1859 photographs of Yosemite as the basis for a new series of engravings of the place for another publication promoting the valley. He had become more deeply involved in encouraging tourism in Yosemite and took over a hotel there himself in 1864. Weed's photographs were displayed in Vance's San Francisco gallery, where they helped feed a growing curiosity about Yosemite. In 1859, the first celebrity arrived there, *New York Tribune* editor Horace Greeley, whose editorials and essays had made his the preeminent opinion of his time in the United States and who coined the phrase, "Go west, young man." Greeley came for half a day, complained about the lack of water in the waterfalls, and still wrote, "I know no single wonder of Nature on earth which can claim a superiority over the Yosemite." By 1860, both Horace Greeley and Weed's stereoscopic photographs were proclaiming its wonders in New York.

Weed's images are more significant for the role they played in publicizing the valley and for their status as the first photographs than for their artistic merit. In 1861 the first great photographer arrived, Carleton E. Watkins, and with him began both the tradition of major artists working in Yosemite and of American landscape photography. He brought in a camera far larger than Weed's—a mammoth-plate camera that made negatives as large as the prints: 16″ × 20″, photographs on a scale that suited their subject, at last. Watkins's pictures portray the valley as seen with superhuman eyes: They take in vast areas with every wrinkle and crevice on the rock faces in the distance as sharp as the foliage in the foreground. (Botanists have used his pictures to identify the plants growing in the valley in the 1860s.) In other images, there is no foreground, as though the walls of stone were so high it was impossible to see the ground and the sky at the same time. They are pictures of a breathtaking majesty and stillness. Only sometimes the river blurs, because the water was moving during the long exposure. And there are no people. There may be practical reasons for this—the less sensitive film of the time required long exposures, which a person could brace for in a portrait studio, or pose for in a group portrait, but which made it difficult to capture people acting naturally. In the very earliest photographs of city streets, people who moved vanished, so that

the scene would look strangely abandoned. With wet-plate technology, it took so long to coat the glass-plate negative and get it into
the camera that candid photography of activity was virtually impossible: There was a built-in bias in favor of the immobile. And in some
of Watkins's Yosemite photographs, the exposure took an hour. In
the 1870s landscape photographs of the U.S. Geological Survey, a
figure sometimes stands in the foreground, as though establishing
scale and the presence of this group of explorers, but there are few
images of people going about their business until some years and
technologies later.

And the Yosemite Valley Watkins was in looked less inhabited
than it had before or since. The Mariposa Battalion had burned what
structures they found when they came in 1851, the Ahwahneechee
had briefly deserted the valley and then taken up residence again
cautiously and inconspicuously, and the tourist industry had not
crowded in. Weed took a picture of the one hotel when he came two
years earlier, but such things seem not to have interested Watkins,
at least for his mammoth-plate masterpieces. A decade after the
Mariposa Indian War, they suggest a place in which nothing has ever
happened and which no human has ever touched: They are the
birthplace of the photographs of virgin wilderness that feed the continuing appetite for exploration and for conservation. They speak to
eternity, not to current events. It was these images, and their descendants, that shaped my early understanding of Yosemite, and that
made it so stunning when I read about the war.

At the time that Watkins was taking these images, the great photographers of the Civil War—Matthew Brady, Alexander Gardner,
Timothy O'Sullivan—were at work, making images of troops and
generals posing hopefully before battles, and after, of the dead lying
haphazard as they fell. Nothing could seem further apart than the
battlefields and this paradisal valley, but it too had been a battlefield,

a few years too early to be documented as the Civil War and later Indian-white conflicts, such as the massacre at Wounded Knee, were documented. So it may be a historical accident or a technical limitation that made these still scenes the definitive images of the valley. Or it may be that the war was simply irrelevant to what the visitors were looking for, as the war and the landscape were distinct from each other in Bunnell's response. The war, it seemed, was utterly over, and the landscape was the story that continues.

It continued for Watkins. He came back and photographed the valley again several times throughout the 1860s, and when he opened his own photography gallery in San Francisco, he called it the Yosemite Gallery. His were among the first photographs to be taken as works of art, and their influence was wide. Watkins gave up the economic security of running a portrait studio for the uncertain possibilities of photographing remote places in the West and on the Pacific Coast. He received a gold medal in the Paris International Exposition of 1867 for his Yosemite pictures and became the most widely acclaimed landscape photographer of his day, but he never secured a good living out of his photography. In the 1890s, he began to lose his sight and lived on blind and poor through the early years of the twentieth century. Another photographer made the image that is the epitaph for Watkins and his work: an image of him as a stooped old man being led away from the ruins of the 1906 earthquake and fire, which had just destroyed all his archives of pictures and negatives. He died in the insane asylum at Napa in 1916 and was buried in an unmarked grave.

Another visitor who gave the place wide publicity came just before Watkins, the Unitarian minister Thomas Starr King. A slight, goggle-eyed, lank-haired young man of startling eloquence, King had been a celebrated sermonizer and public speaker in Boston. He shared in the liberal and genteel intellectuality of the transcendentalists of his region, and had already become well known for his scenic travel letters on the White Mountains of New Hampshire, which had been gathered into a book; he would be best known in California for helping to convince its citizens to side with the Union in the Civil War. In the winter of 1860–61, his letters describing his expedition to Yosemite appeared in the *Boston Evening Transcript* and were later collected into a book. King had a strong attachment to New England, and his account of the other side of the continent mixes wonder with distaste. He exclaims over apples ripe before July and deplores the countryside he passes through between San Francisco and Yosemite that dry summer of 1860. What to a Western eye appears to be good golden grass he calls "mighty swells of barrenness . . . a universal desert . . . this harsh discord of green [the oaks] and grey [the grass]."

On the way to the Sierra, King's party took a detour to see the other marvel of the Sierra Nevada, the mines. They went to Mariposa, a town which was at that time within the bounds of the Mariposa estate of John C. Fremont, who had acquired it by accident in 1847. Fremont had given a sum to Thomas Larkin, former U.S. consul to the Mexican government in California, asking Larkin to get him a Mexican land grant. The grants were lavish pieces of real estate that generally became ranches, and most of them were near the coast. For some reason, Larkin picked out a "floating grant"—a parcel with undefined boundaries—far from any town and in an inland area virtually unexplored. Las Mariposas was seventy square miles, and historians describe its size as that of a principality or a small empire. When gold was discovered in the foothills, that is what it became, though Fremont never made much of an emperor. After redrawing the boundaries of his floating tract a few times to include all the gold-bearing streams and hard-rock mines he could reach, Fremont failed to manage his property well. His creditors seized the estate—"this largest gold estate in California, and perhaps the most valuable property in the world"—not long after King came through.

King arrived at the Merced and exclaimed over it as the first clean river he had seen in California: "No placer or hydraulic mining on its banks have polluted it yet." But it did drive the huge stamp mills of Las Mariposas, which pounded quartz ore to powder from which the gold could be extracted, and it had been dammed farther down. From the largest stamp mines in the world, King's party proceeded onward to the largest trees in the world, sequoias, in the Mariposa Grove, which lies about a dozen miles south of the entrance to Yosemite Valley. He marveled at their age, an age that encompasses most of recorded history and stretched back into Old Testament times. He talked a great deal about how disappointingly small the trees looked, as they stood in groves so full of huge trees that none seems exceptional, and of how he took out his string and measured their diameters and found them gigantic after all—one was ninety feet in circumference. In good Victorian spirit, King remained preoccupied with measurements throughout his journey, and detailed all the heights of waterfalls and cliffs as he described the valley. Those descriptions, too, mixed humorous passages with scenes that "awaken wonder, awe and a solemn joy."

The painter Albert Bierstadt came in 1863, lured by descriptions of the place. His companion on the trip wrote, "If report was true, we were going to the original site of the Garden of Eden." Born in Germany and raised in New England, Bierstadt returned to Europe to build a career as a landscape painter, then set out for the American West. His paintings have been compared to operas for their melodramatic presentation of light and space, and they served as both entertainments and reports for American audiences in the East. Phenomenally successful in his time, Bierstadt displayed some of his largest canvases as though they were performances, charging admission, lighting them theatrically, and even recommending that viewers scan them through binoculars to heighten the sense of scale and realism. After his first month-long stay in Yosemite in 1863, he returned several times, finding in the place every element he pursued in his landscapes—freshness, majesty, gigantic scale, spectacular light. The east-west orientation of the valley provided him a great opportunity to paint the rich light of sunrise and sunset warming the color of stone and water. He improved the place according to his own standards: more light, more grandeur, more evidence of divinity, fewer people. In one of his paintings of the valley, there are, tiny in the middle distance, a few Plains-style Indians sitting on horseback admiring the view themselves. Bierstadt actually hired the photographer Eadweard Muybridge to make images of the indigenous people who were around in the 1870s, and Muybridge obliged with eight stereoscopic photographs, but these factual images of continuing indigenous life didn't seem to affect either Muybridge or Bierstadt's artistic works. Muybridge came close to Watkins's genius in his images of Yosemite, images dealing with the qualities of land, water, and light, not with people (though a few figures pose in the foreground of some of his Yosemite images).

The stream of visitors to Yosemite kept increasing, and the names began to include those of more and more famous Americans. In 1864 came Frederick Law Olmsted. He had first become well known as a journalist, writing about the South and Texas at a time when they were the exotic far reaches of the United States and supplying practical information for the argument against slavery. His tastes were unusual, combining an interest in scenery and landscape with a concern for social justice, and the ways he found to exercise them were often as unusual. In the 1850s, he designed Central Park in Manhattan with his partner Calvert Vaux, and he promoted a vision and a program to make the park a democratic arena open to all classes of New Yorkers. Throughout his life, he saw nature not as a refuge from culture, but a salutary influence on it, whether it was one made or found.

This perspective is what makes Olmsted so unusual a visionary. In the history of American landscape he is usually bracketed and overshadowed by Thoreau before him and Muir after him, but both those figures saw landscape—nature—as a refuge from culture and as an essentially solitary experience. Olmsted did not withdraw into the wilderness, but tried to see how the natural world ameliorated and influenced his society. Where Thoreau said, "In wildness is the preservation of the world," Olmsted would have said more modestly, "In gardens and parks is the improvement of the community." And he created natural worlds as well as observing them, carving the great vistas, groves, and meadows of Central Park out of the scrubby farmland on the northern end of Manhattan Island. Central Park was not an exercise in aesthetics and earthmoving to him so much as it was an experiment in social engineering and the democratization of open space. (Europe's urban parks were usually private, reserved for the upper classes or for admission-payers, modeled after the gardens and grounds of aristocrats' estates; the U.S.'s first public parks were ornamental cemeteries on the outskirts of cities.) While the Central Park plans foundered in city politics, Olmsted helped start the Sanitary Commission that cared for the Yankee wounded of the Civil War. As his patriotic work for the soldiers came to a close and he found himself with a mixed reputation and unambiguous debts, Olmsted took a gamble. He accepted an invitation to take over management of the Mariposa estate for the creditors who had seized it from Fremont, seeing California in its usual role as both escape and opportunity.

He took much the same journey King had—a steamer to Stockton and horses thereafter. And like King, he exclaimed over the awfulness of the landscape, calling it brown and dead, and remarking that toward the end of the first day's journey "the desolation was somewhat relieved by multitudes of children's graves"—which is what the slate outcroppings of the foothills looked like to Olmsted. Thereafter he reserved most of his dismay for the dire financial circumstances of the estate he was to manage, which had been disguised by the previous manager, and by the violence and barbarism of the miners' society around him. "A store has been robbed; two men have been killed with knives; another severely wounded in a fight; another has been stoned; and a plot of murder and highway robbery is reported to have been detected—all in the three days I have been on the estate." The scarcity of water limited the mine operations on the estate, and he concocted fabulous engineering schemes to bring the waters of the South Fork of the Merced within convenient reach of it.

Later that year Olmsted's family came to join him, and in August he set off for Yosemite with his wife, their several children, her cousin, and a governess. The foliage seemed familiar to him from pictures of Switzerland, the river reminded him of the Avon or the upper Thames in England, the mountains of the Alps and Apennines. The haze of a humid summer gave distances the indistinct softness of the East. Much of the rest of California was remarkable at that time for the transparency of the air, which made it possible to see clearly for dozens or even hundreds of miles. John Muir describes his first view of the Sierra across the Central Valley from Pacheco Pass in the Coast Range, a spectacle I have never seen in all my trips over the pass and doubted until I read analogous accounts—even from the Central Valley and in the foothills, the haze of air pollution and humidity of irrigation almost always obscure the mountains. For Olmsted the familiar was more beautiful, and so haze was better than clarity, and the green mountainscapes better than the drier scenery below: Yosemite was a superlative version of the East hidden in the alien West.

Olmsted had a peculiar interest in the place: The Valley and the Mariposa Grove had just been set aside by an act of Congress, signed into law by Abraham Lincoln on July 1, 1864. The bill had been introduced by California's Senator John Conness, who had never seen the place but had been sent some photographs of it, probably by Watkins. And so a man who had never seen the place induced more who had never been near the state to preserve it for a public which had hardly reached it. At the time, 1864, only the valley and the Mariposa Big Tree Grove had been set aside in this park to be managed by the state of California. In 1890, when it was redefined as a national park along the lines of Yellowstone National Park, the park was vastly enlarged—largely thanks to John Muir's lobbying. Olmsted chaired the commission that oversaw this initial 1864 preserve. Central Park had been a great leap of the imagination, a vast manmade urban landscape; Yosemite was a greater one, a tract amid unmapped terrain set aside for the same public. In the report Olmsted wrote soon after his visit, he enumerated the setting aside of Yosemite as one of the great works of art carried out during the Civil War, along with the building of the dome of the Capitol, of Central Park, the photographs of Watkins, and the paintings of Bierstadt.

In describing the park as a great work of art, he admired most the combination of elements. "There are falls of water elsewhere finer, there are more stupendous rocks, more beetling cliffs, there are deeper and more awful chasms, there may be as beautiful streams, as lovely meadows, there are larger trees. It is in no scene or scenes the charm consists, but in the miles of scenery where cliffs of awful height and rocks of vast magnitude and of varied and exquisite coloring, are banked and fringed and draped and shadowed by the tender foliage of noble and lovely trees and bushes, reflected from the most placid pools, and associated with the most tranquil meadows, the most playful streams, and every variety of soft and peaceful pastoral beauty. The union of the deepest sublimity with the deepest beauty of nature . . . all around and wherever the visitor goes, constitutes the Yo Semite the greatest glory of nature."

Olmsted went on to enumerate the benefits the locality might enjoy, speaking of the tourist industry in Switzerland and the way the English Garden in Bavaria attracted visitors. "It is a significant fact that visitors have already come from Europe expressly to see it," he wrote, and added that it was a duty of government "to provide means of protection for all of its citizens in the pursuit of happiness against the obstacles, otherwise insurmountable, which the selfishness of individuals or combinations of individuals is liable to interpose to that pursuit." Olmsted here slyly inserted the language of the Declaration of Independence—the right to "life, liberty, and the pursuit of happiness"—into this proposal for a national park. By implication, access to nature is a citizen's right and preservation of appropriate places a democracy's duty. He had grounds to speak of selfishness. J. M. Hutchings, who had come with the first tourists to the valley, and James Lamon had staked out homesteads in the valley and were busily fencing and planting and clearing. Hutchings also ran a lumber mill in the valley and one year cut down 400 trees (in 1870 John Muir worked in this mill, though he later insisted that he only milled downed timber). Olmsted's report proceeded to ask Congress for $37,000 to create roads, paths, bridges, cabins, advertising, and other incidentals to open it up as a public park. The money was never given and the whole report was suppressed and disappeared for a number of years. The most widely accepted explanation is that some of the other Yosemite Commissioners, like Josiah Whitney, were also involved in the California Geological Survey and feared that money that went to the park would come out of survey funding.

Later that year the Mariposa estate went bankrupt again and Olmsted returned to his work on Central Park. Afterward he worked on restoring the scenery around Niagara Falls, which had been devastated by tourist industries, and on getting Niagara protected as another national park. He also established the first managed forestlands around George Vanderbilt's North Carolina estate, and by the time he died he had established himself as the founder of American landscape architecture.

✛

Nearly all these men who shaped Yosemite's fate in the fourteen years after the Mariposa Battalion marched in were involved with gold mining. Bunnell was a miner on an expedition with other miners turned soldiers to make the southern mines safer to work. The party that in 1853 chased Tenaya's people across Bloody Canyon to the shores of Mono Lake—the Lee Vining crew—came back with ore samples and started the miners' move eastward, to Nevada. Weed and Watkins made a more secure income from documenting mines and miners than from their pictures of untrammeled landscape, and in many cases their funding for the latter came from the former. Trenor Park, the rapacious creditor who forced Fremont out of the Las Mariposas estate and helped bring Olmsted in, provided the financial support for Watkins's first trip to the region in 1861: Watkins was to photograph the Mariposa mines for Park and then went on to photograph the valley on his own time.

Watkins's extant pictures of some of the mines provide a strange counterpart to the Yosemite pictures, an opposite world. The most stunning are of hydraulic mining operations in Malakoff Diggings, northward, in Nevada County. The jets of water and cliffs of raw earth in his photographs strangely echo the waterfalls and sheer walls of Yosemite Valley. In these, the jets look like festive plumes, like decorative fountains spouting, like anything but the means of washing away landscapes.

"The miners impounded water in the high country, then brought it to the gravels in ditches and flumes," writes John McPhee. "In five years, they built five thousand miles of ditches and flumes. From a ditch about four hundred feet above the bed of a fossil river, water would come down through a hose to a nozzle, from which it emerged as a jet at a hundred and twenty miles an hour. The jet had the diameter of a dinner plate and felt as hard. If you touched the water near the nozzle, your fingers were burned. This was hydraulic artillery. Turned against gravel slopes, it brought them down. . . . A hundred and six million ounces of gold—a third of all the gold that has ever been mined in the United States—came from the Sierra Nevada. A quarter of that was flushed out by hydraulic mining." This was why King was so impressed with the purity of the Merced—it was the first river in California he'd seen that wasn't brown with the washed-away soil of this mining procedure. In the time that Yosemite was set aside, thousands of tons of earth were being moved from the foothills into the valleys, the rivers, the San Francisco Bay. Even the mouth of the Golden Gate was brown.

In this light, Yosemite becomes not merely a general respite from the cares of the world, but a specific refuge from the frenzied earth-moving of mining. It serves as a world of recreation in contrast to the world of work, a compensation. To say that Yosemite is Eden is to say that everywhere else is not. "This place shall we set aside and protect" implies "all other places shall we open up and use." So the national parks counterbalance and perhaps legitimize the national sacrifice areas, which in the nineteenth century meant mostly mining and timbercutting and now has grown to include waste disposal and military-use areas and places drowned by dams. The birth of the national park idea, usually considered the fruit of great enlightenment, was an attempt to prevent alteration in some small portion of the land being so rapidly overrun and transformed. Parks were an attempt to save a few places from the fate of the rest and to prepare an escape from the diminished beauty of the rest, a landscape of leisure apart from the landscapes of work. Interestingly, the Malakoff Diggings that Watkins photographed are so spectacular a feat of devastation—great bony ridges and valleys on which nothing yet has grown—that they have been set aside as a California state park, virtually the nation's only such tribute to environmental degradation. The mines were a place in which men toiled and all too much change happened; Yosemite was to be therefore a place in which no one toiled and nothing changed.

Framing the View

✚ LATE ONE SEPTEMBER AFTERNOON, I WALKED ALONG THE Merced. As I followed the river west through the valley, toward sunset, something surprised me every few minutes. The river bent, the valley turned a little more due west and a last ray of sun stretched toward me, a stand of trees gave way to a meadow, a space between the trees opened up a view of a sheer wall or the deep V of the west end turning rosy. The river is a gentle, neglected, beautiful thing, widening into broad mirrors, spilling over shallow falls and singing to itself, breaking into halves to encircle an island, writhing, turning, harboring beautiful groves of broadleaved trees, ripping the soil from under them to expose the great knot of roots like hundred-fingered hands all bare and knobby-knuckled as they clutch the earth, throwing up sand bars and long reaches of polished boulders, gentle backwaters, stands of marsh grass, ducks, a school of large fish hovering motionless in a pool in perfect formation like a fleet of submarines, developing shadowy depths, swimming holes, washing up whitened tree trunks in places it's hard to believe the spring rush must reach, turning in winter into a long skein of icy lace and open pools. No one walks the river but a few fly fishermen.

The landscape here plays hide and seek. It's inconstant, fickle, flirtatious, not like the desert, whose open expanses are slow to change, where you see far ahead, where the topography changes imperceptibly, even at interstate speed, and where it may take an hour or more to pass through a view and come upon another one. The faceted interior space of the valley forms an infinity of potential views reshaped by the shifting light and changing year and forever emerging and vanishing as you move among rock and tree. Yosemite is all vertical, tall trees, tall cliffs all around and hemming you in, tall waterfalls, dwarfing you and pressing on you with a claustrophobic intensity, outdoing your biped's verticality, making you a midget among a crowd of giants, while the desert makes you an ant alone in its luxuriance of open air.

As I walked back east I saw a woman hunched over as though stricken with grief, and then I realized she had a camera with her and was trying to shoot the moon. Most of the campers were already sitting around fires and lanterns, in a circle of light that substituted for the walls of home by making everything outside invisible once the eyes adjust.

All that comes from passages I scrawled one evening in the lobby of the Ahwahnee Hotel as a bat flitted around the huge room. The hotel is one of those unapologetic borrowings of cultural styles the early twentieth century managed so well. It's rough-hewn and a little like a hunting lodge, though its huge fireplace and roof beams make it as much a medieval castle, hung with Southwestern and Middle Eastern rugs chosen to suggest an internationalism of geometry and warm colors. In a huge plexiglass box in the center of the room is a Yurok/Karok basket from northwestern California grown gargantuan past any practical utility, inside which a person or two could curl. An old lady in a white dress with pink flowers on it enjoyed the bat; another lady kept nervously reaching for her purse and saying, "Somebody should complain," while her husband assured her that bats are good luck.

I like the hotel. It's uncompromising—it isn't halfway to camping or wilderness or anything else, but all-out luxury. I come here for breakfast sometimes and try to sit next to what I at first took to be a pristine meadow, a verdant mix of grasses of different heights and other plants. The sprinklers should have been a clue. Before it was a pristine meadow it was a golf course, and before that it was a corn-field. The cornfield, the golf course, and the meadow all reflect changing expectations of the landscape, to produce, to entertain, to inspire. They serve as a kind of parody of the idea of a climax forest, in which the various phases of forest succession are supposed to reach their mature state and stabilize. To inspire was the final destiny of the Yosemite landscape, the view that won out over Hutchings's claims and will probably triumph over the demands that national parks supply forms of recreation other than walking, camping, and looking. The American taste for natural landscape seems so perva-sive that most people tend to believe that the taste too is natural—and virtuous. It is a taste that is in fact as thoroughly carved out by European traditions as Yosemite has been carved by glaciers, a wholly cultivated taste for nature.

✤ IF THE EUROPEAN TASTE FOR LANDSCAPE AND ITS AMERICAN variations begin anywhere, they begin with a pastry chef's appren-tice who was born in the same country and decade as the mathematician-philosopher René Descartes. It says something for a culture that can produce the ruthless Utopian logic of Descartes out of the same material as the wistful Arcadian reverie of Claude Gelée. Gelée, or Claude Lorrain as he is called after the French province in which he was born in 1600, found his way to Rome and became a landscape painter, and he painted the Roman *campagna* over and over until he died at the age of eighty-two.

Centuries earlier the gold-leaf backgrounds of paintings of the saints had yielded to more earthly backdrops, and the scenes became more and more realistic as Western painting collectively taught itself perspective, shading, and all the other appurtenances that make a painting look realistic. There are exquisite landscapes behind the Biblical and historical figures in European paintings from the fourteenth century onward, but they are always backdrops, subsidiary to the figures in the foreground and the story that fuels the painting. The subject of the art is still human life, which was for a time thought to be the only subject for art, and then the most noble. Landscape entered as a Cinderella and stayed in the corner until the eighteenth century, and even today it is still called scenery, a word that comes from theater.

Nothing dramatically new happened in Claude's paintings. The figures have shrunk a great deal in relation to the ground, and the stories become less and less eventful. In some of his images, no one is sure what the story is and who the figures are, and Claude himself doesn't seem to care. Sometimes the stories are from Greek and Roman mythology, which gives him an opportunity to paint classical columns, and sometimes they are Biblical. Either way it is really always the Roman *campagna,* stately trees spaced about a green landscape lit by the palpable but delicate light of early morning or late afternoon, a theater without action, a landscape without history. It is a supreme expression of the pastoral as a place and a mood—a sweet melancholic world in which the sudden and the violent seem impossible—and it was enormously successful in Claude's own time, though no contemporary landscapist shared his success. All the popes who ruled during his working life collected his work, and so did many aristocrats. He never opened a workshop, with assistants painting in the easy parts, and he never turned to any other kind of painting for money. He painted the same landscape time after time—small figures in the foreground at the bottom of the picture, arches of scenery framing them from the middle ground, the delicate tints of sky and water in the distance—as repetitive as a dream, and as elusive in its charm.

There were great painters who seemed to anticipate Claude's breakthrough into the uneventful and the nonhuman: Giorgioni and Titian; and more painters who were his peers in Italy and who were very nearly landscapists: the Carracci brothers; the severe classicist Nicholas Poussin; and one landscapist peer, Salvator Rosa, whose scenes were as wild as Claude's were serene. But Claude's influence was supreme, and his work marks the dividing line between a time when art was about human events, and when it expanded to encompass the dream of a nonevent in landscape. In the eighteenth century, English aristocrats developed a passion for his work and for Poussin's, and bought everything they could get. When the National Gallery organized a huge Claude exhibition in 1982, a surprising number of the works had once been in the collection of British lords, and many still belonged to the Queen. The tastes of these long-dead gentry would be nothing more than a historical curiosity if they had not shaped our own. They began collecting the paintings. And then they began modeling their gardens after the paintings. And then they began to admire the world as they had the gardens.

The landscape garden begins with William Kent, an unsuccessful history painter who had spent time in Italy, returned to England in 1719, and apparently decided to translate Claude and Poussin into real terms—to make their paint and canvas into dirt, water, trees, lawn, and architecture. The aristocratic writer Horace Walpole wrote that Kent "leapt the fence and saw all nature was a garden." All gardens, formal or natural, are scale models of paradise, and the word *paradise* itself comes from the Persian word for an enclosed garden. Persian carpets are often aerial maps of the formal gardens of the region, with their symmetrically arranged borders and fountains. A garden makes up for what the real world isn't—it's compensatory—and sketches out what the world ought to be. For practical and psychological reasons the medieval garden was enclosed—in a turbulent time, it offered sanctuary from the outer world and within its high walls established a little kingdom of fruit, flowers, and peace. In the Renaissance in Italy and then all over Europe, the need for fortresslike great houses faded, and the gardens grew larger and more open. But they also grew more formal. The garden was still something other than and apart from the world— safer, more structured, more controlled. Louis XIV's Versailles is the climax of this tradition, a garden that vies with the world for scale, that reaches to the horizon, but also a garden in which trees are shaped like cones, in which water occurs in rectangular and circular pools, an exercise presided over by ruler and compass. The geometrizing Cartesian gardens of the seventeenth century proposed the imposition of an abstract order on an earth that was conceived as in need of rational improvement. The radical thing about the English landscape garden after Kent is that for the first time it suggested that the real world was, to some degree and in select places, what it ought to be.

Some of this taste for nature came out of the paintings of real landscapes, real trees, which found an order rather than inventing one. A little came from descriptions of Chinese gardens, and a little more from the English preference for empirical rather than Cartesian *a priori* thinking. A lot of it came from the optimism that creation was good. The eighteenth-century English who led toward the landscape garden and toward romanticism veered away from the dark view of Hobbes that life is nasty, brutish, and short and government is necessary to prevent a chaos of selfish violence; they moved toward the optimism that men are born good and only corrupted by society. Rousseau was one of the strongest proponents of the latter belief, doing much to establish the icon of the noble savage, the taste for landscape, and the belief in childhood innocence—all beliefs that the natural was good (and he asserted that the foundation of civil society and of inequality came with the "first man who inclosed a piece of ground and took it into his head to say: *this is mine,* and found people simple enough to believe him"—with the superimposition of real estate over landscape). The implications were profound. After all, the goodness of nature went against much of Christian doctrine, in which people were born tainted with original sin and needed the ministrations of the Church to redeem themselves, and in which nature had crashed into chaos after the disaster of the Fall and the expulsion of the garden—"cursed is the ground for thy sake." Earlier Europeans had looked to natural landscape as evidence of this messy post-Edenic situation and found their evidence: In 1681 Thomas Burnett proposed that the world was created as smooth as an egg and damaged and "deformed" by the Deluge, a later but equally definitive disaster. Seventeenth-century writers preferred cultivated and mild landscape, describing the Lake District, the Scottish highlands, and mountains anywhere as hideous, terrible, dreadful, and rough.

A century later Kent saw that all nature was a garden. It was an earthshaking discovery, the triumph of Arcadian over Utopian views. Although the English garden was still shaped by artifice, it shaded invisibly into the landscape around it, protected by ditches rather than walls. It wasn't set apart as the formal garden was: an excessive order that proposed the rest of the world as chaos. And the garden got more natural as the eighteenth century wore on. In the hands of Capability Brown, the greatest genius of the landscape garden, the spaces became vaster, the elements simpler, the architectural adornments began to disappear. As the century drew to a close, the garden returned to some of its formality—but it didn't matter. The aristocracy had trained itself to appreciate in the landscape gardens elements of painting that became more and more evident in the rest of the world, until they suddenly realized that such experiences always had been available in the world at large. The taste for the sublime had developed by midcentury, and connoisseurs began to enjoy landscape features like the Alps that had previously been perceived as signs of catastrophe. They had gone from looking at Claude's paintings to looking at gardens to looking at the larger world, and they had learned to look at it as an aesthetic phenomenon. This was the dawn of scenic tourism. Before that, the space between manmade curiosities was a blank, both to the eyes of travellers and in the accounts they left us.

It was hard for travellers to look without a great deal of mediation, however. Texts about landscape appreciation were immensely popular, the precursors of travel manuals, of Baedeker's and Fodor's. Some of them described specific places, and some additionally taught aspiring men and women of culture what to appreciate and how to categorize it as picturesque, beautiful, or sublime. There was landscape poetry (like James Thomson's best-selling, novel-length *The Seasons,* almost unreadable now) and more landscape painting. Travellers looked at the natural world as though it were a work of art, critiquing composition, color, and lighting. A little invention called the Claude Glass, a murky, concave hand mirror used by facing away from the view and admiring its reflection, reduced the world to the size of a picture, framed and even made dark as though through the accumulation of generations of candle soot.

The ability to appreciate scenery became a mark of gentility, and the language that developed to describe it is astounding now. In its most unconvincing manifestations, this taste for landscape was nothing more than an affectation of gentility, but for many the taste was heartfelt, and private letters as well as published poems describe the world of their authors with a remarkable eye for detail and effect. There are other languages which possess a great deal more vocabulary to describe a phenomenon—the classic example is Inuit words for snow—but English itself proved for a century or two to be a fine and subtle tool for depicting the appearance of the natural world.

For the aristocracy, the taste for nature had been a mark of gentility; for the Romantics, it signified a revolt. They sought out the immediacy of direct experience, of childhood and children, and of the remaining wild places in Europe, aligning themselves politically with the natural and rural against a society swallowing the Industrial Revolution whole, or being swallowed by it. But for the Victorians, and particularly Victorians in the United States, nature became a kind of religion. The sublime was no longer a passion for violent energies and fearful displays but evidence of the might of God. In the landscape, they mixed their taste for scenery with piety and sought hard for traces of a God who was becoming increasingly hard to find anywhere else. And with this, art, nature, and religion become interchangeable experiences, and the vocabularies with which they are described overflow and mingle.

In 1851, Bunnell looks at nature and sees a work of art that speaks of God (though what makes him so unappealing are the lackluster clichés of his descriptions; in relating his overwrought spiritual response, Bunnell seems to be primarily concerned with establishing his gentility). As Savage hustles him along, he says, "I have here seen the power and glory of a Supreme being; the majesty of his Handywork is in that 'Testimony of the Rocks.'" A century later Sierra Club President David Brower fought the damming of the Grand Canyon—whose promoters said drowning it would let visitors get nearer the rims—with a full-page *New York Times* ad whose headlines demanded, "Should we also flood the Sistine Chapel so that tourists can get nearer the ceiling?" (He was echoing John Muir, who had said of damming Hetch Hetchy, "As well dam for water-tanks the people's cathedrals and churches, for no holier temple has ever been consecrated by the heart of man.") The identity of great landscapes with great works of art and with churches was a given. The Grand Canyon is full of temples—Osiris Temple, Buddha Temple, Zoroaster Temple; Yosemite was often compared to a cathedral, and one of its rock formations has been named Cathedral Spires.

Several things made Yosemite irresistible to the Americans schooled in this landscape tradition. Its meadows and spreading oak trees bore an extraordinary resemblance to an English landscape park, and Yosemite was considered a great miracle of nature imitating the art of the garden. Then, all around this gentle park were the extraordinary rock faces and waterfalls, elements of the sublime and evidence of the Creator. Finally, the Victorians were preoccupied with geology. In the twentieth century, physics has spoken to many people who are not physicists, seeming in its description of microcosmic structures and events to propose a new model of the world valuable beyond the discipline itself. In the nineteenth century the macrocosmic realm of geology played the same role. It was the science in which great breakthroughs were being made, breakthroughs that changed people's picture of the universe. Emerging evidence about the great age of the universe, the enormous transformations of the earth's surface and of life on earth, and the sense of an internally generated series of metamorphoses made geology an urgent, exciting discipline for amateurs as well as professionals. Darwin's *Origin of Species,* inspired by fossil evidence, appeared in 1859, eight years after Yosemite was invaded, five years before it became a park. Geology was a practical science in this era of great mineral discoveries and the mapping of the American West, but it was also a kind of spiritual quest. Arguments about whether the earth had been created through catastrophism or vulcanism touched the basic beliefs of their proponents, and Josiah Whitney of the California Geological Survey argued with fervent passion against Muir's theory that Yosemite was formed through glaciers, a theory now accepted as correct in its essentials.

Fossils from oceans found in mountains suggested some of the radical transformations the earth had undergone, and the fact that the fossils were not those of creatures now on the earth helped support the theory of evolution. As the Copernican model had removed Earth from the center of the universe, so the nineteenth-century geologists had transformed humanity from the central event on Earth to a late walk-on part. In changing the timescale of the Earth, the geological quest changed the relative age of European ruins: The bare rocks that cover so much of the West gave a new kind of antiquity to the American landscape. They served as a kind of natural ruin, evidence of an ancient nature if not of ancient cultures, and they were often named after towers, cathedrals, castles, and the other architectural shapes that Euro-American explorers fancied they resembled. Sequoias provided a similar expansiveness for their great size and age among living things.

Yosemite satisfied several tastes. It gratified the taste for landscapes resembling those of the great English parks. Its rocks provided superb geological wonders. And it is important to remember that the age of Darwin was also the age of P. T. Barnum—the great naturalist and the great circus impresario were born a year apart, 1809 and 1810. Yosemite could also be seen as the greatest natural sideshow of the nation, with the biggest rock wall, the highest waterfall, the hugest trees—and Barnum himself came to visit in 1870. Yellowstone had a similar range of spectacles, ranging from pastoral meadows to sublimely sheer canyons to the geysers which were enjoyed by visitors as freaks of nature. Religion, science, and entertainment were all compacted into the visible wonders of the first two national parks.

✠ Probably the greatest voice for nature as a religion is John Muir, who spoke as a virtual evangelist of wild scenery and who found in Yosemite his temple. Muir had been born in Scotland, brought to the United States as a child, and raised on a farm. His father Daniel Muir was a hard man, driving his children and his land to their limits. The rich Wisconsin land he had to abandon several times in the course of his farming efforts—moving on from spent soil was a standard approach then—and most of his eight children managed to abandon him one way or another. John Muir stole away by degrees and then broke with the whole way of life he had been reared in with its emphasis on work and practical pursuits, after an accident in an Indianapolis mill that made carriage wheels. Muir had been well on his way to becoming a good industrialist, with a genius for inventing new machinery and streamlining production, when the accident happened. While tightening a belt, his hand slipped and the file he was using went into his right eye. A few hours later, his left eye went blind in a sympathetic reaction. He recovered his sight after a long and traumatic convalescence, he quit, he went on a walk that would take him down through the eastern United States to the Gulf of Mexico in Florida and continued rambling until he reached the Sierra and Yosemite, the place he spent the rest of his life exploring, describing, and fighting to protect. He came there in 1868, enlisted as a shepherd for his first summer, later worked for James Hutchings at his sawmill in Yosemite Valley, and eventually began to publish the essays that made him famous.

Muir's biographer Frederick Turner sums up his early reaction to the Sierra. "In his Yosemite years he would write of the Sierras as being as holy as Sinai; of mountains so aglow with soul and life it seemed they had died and gone before the throne of God; of mountains wearing spiritual robes and halos like the aureolas the old painters put around the heads of saints." In rebelling against the grim Calvinistic Christianity of his father, he rejected the content of Daniel Muir's beliefs, but not the form. In place of the Bible he had nature, and his writing is full of references to the landscape as a book, to reading and interpreting it. What he read in it was a pantheistic message of interconnection and interdependence within cycles of perpetual change and renewal, a message that ran contrary to the linear march toward judgment of his father's religion and that foreshadows the ecological vision of the present (and echoes cultures other than his).

The farm and mill as well as the religion may have shaped Muir's views: He liked his landscapes wild, transcendent, unsocial, and unutilized—as far from the working world as he could get. That first summer he wrote, "We are now in the mountains and they are in us, kindling enthusiasm, making every nerve quiver, filling every pore and cell of us. Our flesh-and-bone tabernacle seems transparent as glass to the beauty about us, as if truly an inseparable part of it. . . . a part of all nature, neither old nor young, sick nor well, but immortal. Just now I can hardly conceive of any bodily condition dependent on food or breath any more than the ground or sky." The wilderness he sought was an antidote to society and use. An acerbic woman at the Yosemite Foundation once joked that Muir was an anorexic, citing his fondness for mountaineering on minimal rations and perhaps for regarding the body as nothing more than a window between the soul and the scenery, the more transparent the better. He tried climbing without food altogether until he found that he would dream of bread those nights. "Once," says his biographer, "returning from a long scramble in the region of Lyell and Ritter mountains, he had a dream of bread that mingled and mixed strangely with images of the glaciers he had been studying. In the dream he saw a wide, glaciated canyon filled with a foaming gray torrent and on its far side a magnificent lateral moraine composed of fine brown loaves, thousands of bread boulders that stretched into the distance." Muir was attempting, it seems, to leave his body behind along with people and cities, trying to find a nature that spoke only to the spirit, through the eyes, a nature whose materiality was only visible spirituality.

In striving for such an encounter with nature, Muir was joining a long tradition. In his landmark essay "Nature," his friend the transcendentalist philosopher Ralph Waldo Emerson had written, "In the woods, we return to reason and faith. There I feel that nothing can befall me in life,—no disgrace or calamity (leaving me my eyes), which nature cannot repair. . . . Standing on the bare ground, my head bathed by the blithe air and uplifted into infinite space,—all egotism vanishes. I become a transparent eyeball; I am nothing; I see all." Perhaps a reason for the kind of nature interpretation Muir engaged in was his brief blindness, which made him forever afterward grateful for vision and entranced with light. Ansel Adams had a similar relation to the visual, becoming entranced with the idea of visiting Yosemite after an illness that required him to lie in darkness for weeks. Even more rigorously than his predecessors, he cropped out evidence that Yosemite was a working landscape as well as a sublime one. Although he made his living for several years by supplying Yosemite's Curry Company with pictures of vacationers in the ice-skating rinks and so forth, his artistic work represented it as a place untouched and beyond human reach. He argued that "people, buildings, and evidence of occupation and use will simply have to go out of Yosemite if it is to function as a great natural shrine."

It is our own peculiarities that are most hidden to us, and the peculiarity of the tradition that began with the connoisseurship of landscape paintings and moved on to generate landscape gardens, tourism, and national parks is its emphasis on the visual.

The effect of this history—the transfer of attention from paintings to actual landscapes—is everywhere apparent in the national park system. Most obviously, the parks themselves have been chosen for their outstanding beauty within the tastes of this tradition. Until recently many of them had signs along the trails which marked the scenic spots from which to make photographs: The frame had already been put around the landscape, and the tourist need merely make the photograph that had been isolated from the continuum of a walker's view. In many places there are telescopes that focus on spectacles in the distance, isolating and framing a detail. In Arches National Park there are simple metal tubes resting on bases with notches: If you put the tube in a notch and look, it will frame a little composition. But of all these picture-making devices, the most amazing is at the Watchtower on the south rim of Grand Canyon National Park. All along the rim of a raised balcony are objects like trays tilted almost vertical, and on the trays are slabs of black glass. Even the official handout on the Watchtower describes them as versions of the Claude Glass, the device by which eighteenth-century English gentry turned the landscape into pictures that were easier for them to recognize as artistic compositions. The Claude Glasses in the Grand Canyon make a dark rectangular picture out of the view and also make the place into part of the aesthetic tradition that began when a pastry chef's apprentice took up painting the Roman *campagna.*

It is a tradition in which nature is conceptualized as a work of art. Not any kind of art, not music, or dance, or a film which mixes the visible with sound and with action, but painting. If nature is a painting, then we are viewers: We look, and our understanding comes through our eyes. The eyes don't serve as forerunners for the other senses, for touching, tasting, smelling, inhabiting the natural world, but look across a void never to be crossed. Eyes connect us to what we see at the same time that they separate us from it: We look across a distance at something that is not ourselves and does not include us. Paintings are lifeless and inert: We do not enter into them and they do not change; and a museum is a place in which we do not live and are told everywhere "do not touch." (Harold C. Bradley and David Brower wrote in 1949 that the national parks were "a sort of synthesis of the public library, the art gallery, and the museum, out of doors and full of native inspiration for those who desire that sort of inspiration," and while it is true that libraries and museums precede national parks in history, the landscapes within them are profoundly older, and have had other lives than that of picturesque preserve.) By and large Yosemite has been preserved as though it were a painting. The boundaries of the park are the gilt frame around a masterpiece, and within the frame we are urged to take only pictures, leave only footprints. There are enormously important reasons to do so—there are too many people coming to the park to do it any other way—and yet I cannot help feeling something is sadly missing from this experience of nature. Looking is a fine thing to do to pictures, but hardly an adequate way to live in the world. It is nature as a place in which we do not belong, a place in which we do not live, in which we are intruders. A tourist is by definition an outsider, a person who does not belong, a stranger in paradise.

✚ THOSE WHO COME FROM THIS LANDSCAPE-VIEWING TRADI-
tion often consider people from other cultures insensitive to nature
because they do not respond to novel visual beauty in familiar ways.
In his Yosemite report, Olmsted writes, "The power of scenery to
affect men is, in a large way, proportionate to the degree of their
civilization and the degree in which their taste has been civilized.
Among a thousand savages there will be a much smaller number
who will show the least sign of being so affected than among a thousand persons taken from a civilized community." He does not go on
to imagine that his is only one way of appreciating nature; as a good
Victorian, he does not think of his culture as one among many that
coexist but as the first to finish the great race toward civilization,
with the other cultures representing slower runners and later start-
ers, doomed to lose or favored to be helped along. It would be unjust
and ahistorical to condemn Olmsted for being a Victorian, but there
are a great many Victorians still among us. And there are many other
ways of experiencing nature.

The Pueblo poet Leslie Marmon Silko explains, "Pueblo potters,
the creators of petroglyphs and oral narratives, never conceived of
removing themselves from the earth and sky. So long as the human
consciousness remains *within* the hills, canyons, cliffs, and the
plants, clouds, and sky, the term *landscape,* as it has entered the English language, is misleading: 'A portion of territory the eye can comprehend in a single view' does not correctly describe the relationship
between the human being and his or her surroundings. This assumes
the viewer is somehow *outside* or *separate from* the territory he or she
surveys. . . . Ancient Pueblos took the modest view that the thing
itself (the landscape) could not be improved upon. Thus *realism,* as
we now recognize it in painting and sculpture, did not catch the
imaginations of Pueblo people until recently."

In a culture which describes nature in terms of its cycles and rhythms and patterns, it may be the perception of patterns of time and activity that are the strongest and most moving evidence of the presence of nature. For such a culture—which has sometimes been European rural culture too—dance, music, and seasonal ceremonies might be a better way to describe this experience. Such descriptions would be of a nature that was dynamic, living, with rhythms which could be entered into, not the static otherworld of paintings. For such a culture the rising and setting of the sun may be more beautiful in themselves as evidence of a cycle than an isolated image of a particularly colorful sunset, and the rhythms of music or ritual may represent it more than a static image does. And for them, the familiar may be more profound and moving than the exotic: They may care more for what they know and belong to rather than what they don't. If you really think of the Earth as your mother, it's not her glamorous exoticism you value most. Nor are the most significant places necessarily those prettiest to the itinerant eye.

Too, for many cultures, nature is as evident in animal life as in landscape—one of the great peculiarities of the landscape tradition is its emphasis on the relatively passive and static elements of the natural world, on the forms of plants, earth, water, and rock. There may be deer in a Bierstadt painting of a Yosemite meadow, but it is the meadow, the rocks behind, and the light that are its crucial elements. The Alaskan anthropologist Richard K. Nelson addresses these versions of nature in an essay called "The Gift," a story about taking his young son hunting and about what he learned from the indigenous Alaskans he went to live among when he was a young man himself. "Watching deer is the same pleasure now that it was when I was younger, when I loved animals only with my eyes," he writes, and then he talks of the hunting peoples' close knowledge of their surroundings and ethic of responsibility to a nature they believe is spiritual and aware. In his story he kills a deer, thanks it, dresses it, prepares it to take home to his family, and thinks of how he would explain it to his son. "I would explain to him again that when we eat the deer its flesh is then our flesh. The deer changes form and becomes us, and we in turn become creatures made of deer. Each time we eat the deer we should remember it and feel gratitude for what it has given us. And each time, we should carry a thought like a prayer inside: 'Thanks to the animal and to all that made it—the island and the forest, the air, and the rain. . . .' We should remember that in the course of things, we are all generations of deer and of the earth-life that feeds us." Nelson describes for us a sense of natural religion far more intimate than the appreciation of scenery, one that includes communion, interdependence, and participation.

He attempts a worldview in which food is a principal means of experiencing nature, a means that is profoundly absent from such nature experiences as the official version of Yosemite, and from the way most Americans consume food. For John Muir the farm had been an appalling ordeal of forced labor, and it is not surprising that he found no pleasure in seeing the landscape as nourishment; it was instead an escape not only from the social but from the practical. (In later life the body took its revenge upon him: Muir married in 1880 and eventually took over his father-in-law's Martinez fruit farm, becoming a wealthy owner of orchards and dealer in fruits.) For most contemporary Americans, food appears in the supermarket from no place in particular: It connects them to no place at all, and yet to know where our food comes from is to know which landscapes nurture us and to know that we are made out of these landscapes. Perhaps our presumed alienation from nature cannot be alleviated by scenery, perhaps it requires a more profound engagement with the natural world as a system in which we are enmeshed, which feeds us and takes our wastes. Perhaps we should learn not to look at scenery but at simple things—at our water taps which connect us to the water of distant landscapes, our garbage which ends up in landfills, our food which comes from so wide a range of managed lands. Unfortunately, our food is as likely to tell us of corporate agriculture, aquifer draining, pesticides, herbicides, and chemical fertilizers as the round of seasons on a farm and its rituals of sowing and reaping, so we may prefer to let it remain silent.

Of course Yosemite had sustained a population that lived off the deer, the berries, the acorns, and the water there, but that is another story. They weren't part of the tradition of the sublime and the pastoral landscape, and so they fell out of the story about Yosemite as a great national treasure of scenery.

Vanishing (Remaining)

✦ CALIFORNIA WAS PROBABLY THE MOST DENSELY INHABITED part of North America before the Europeans came, and its inhabitants spoke more than a hundred different languages and led lives as diverse as the climates and terrains of the state, from the deserts of the southeast to the rainforests of the north coast. Human history in the region may reach back more than 10,000 years, but the history of European incursion and written history begins a couple of hundred years ago.

In 1769, when Franciscan missions began spreading up the coast, the population of the state was about 310,000. The missions were built a day's journey apart (if you look at a contemporary California map and read the coast for saints' names you can guess at what a day's journey was like then). The missionaries devastated the populations they reached, intentionally and unintentionally. They spread diseases to which the native people had little resistance; they disrupted land bases, lifestyles, and marriage customs, eroding the stable populations; and they enslaved many people as "neophytes" and hunted down those who escaped. The missions developed huge herds of livestock, which their neophytes tended, the beginning of cowboys in the West. This treatment took its toll: At Mission Santa Barbara, the museum lauds the things the Franciscans brought to the people of the region, but a small plaque mentions that 5,000 people are buried in unmarked graves in the courtyard—more a sign of a killing field than a model community.

Mariposa County (which contains most of Yosemite National Park) and the Merced River (which runs west from Yosemite Valley) got their names in a Spanish expedition that nicely illustrates the way spiritual and territorial goals intertwined. In September of 1806, a detachment of soldiers was sent out from Mission San Juan Bautista, near Santa Cruz. They were there to explore for a string of missions to be established in the interior of California (which were never built), and on September 27 they reached an area in the San Joaquin Valley they called the Mariposas, or Butterflies, for the great numbers of the creatures they encountered. Father Pedro Muñoz kept the journal of the expedition, and he describes the butterflies as a menacing cloud. "In the morning they become extremely troublesome," he wrote. "For their aggressiveness reaches the point where they obscure the light of the sun. They came at us so hard that one of them flew into the ear of a corporal of the expedition. It caused him much discomfort and no little effort to get it out."

After this siege of butterflies, they continued their northeasterly march and arrived at another bank of the river they had left the day before. They named it Nuestra Señora de la Merced, Our Lady of Mercy, after the feast day of the Virgin Mary on September 24. Muñoz noted that the river had "fine meadows . . . well populated with heathen Indians." They came upon two villages which had been deserted—the inhabitants had fled to the mountains at the approach of the Spanish army. Only an old woman remained in one of the villages, apparently unable to flee with the rest. She jumped into the newly named River of Mercy at their approach, and Muñoz describes how one of the neophytes on the expedition was "forced to pull off his clothes in a great hurry and pull her out in spite of her attempts to surrender to the rough waves rather than come to us." Muñoz took her soaking as a handy opportunity, and after she was fished out of the water, he baptized her.

The San Juan Bautista expedition notwithstanding, the Spanish and Mexican occupants of California had little direct impact on the northern and interior indigenous populations, though they did introduce horses and cattle to them, and mission escapees sometimes came to the foothills for refuge and spread the Spanish language with them. (Kit Carson encountered refugees from the Bay Area's Mission San Rafael in southeastern California.) During the 1830s and 1840s, huge herds of mustangs and wild cows roamed the San Joaquin and Central Valleys, and the ethnologist at Yosemite once told me that some think if it had not been for the Gold Rush, the Indians of the valleys might have developed a horse culture akin to that of the Plains Indians. But in January of 1848, James Marshall discovered gold at the lumber mill he was building for the inland emperor John Sutter, and by 1849, tens of thousands of men from the U.S., Chile, Europe, Australia, and elsewhere were coming to this new outpost of the United States.

When the Gold Rush began, the Indian population was around 150,000, nearly half of what it had been seventy years before. In the next decade, two-thirds of those people were wiped out by disease, declining birthrates, starvation, and the kind of petty war in which Bunnell took part. Or perhaps war is not the right word for these incursions by the immigrants against the original inhabitants: They were too unevenly matched, and the word extermination comes up too often. Meanwhile, the American population went from 2,000 when gold was discovered to 53,000 by the end of 1849, less than two years later. The Forty-Niners called the various native people of California "Diggers," and the idea that they and then the people of Nevada were extremely primitive creatures subsisting on roots— thus the Digger name—and grubs was widely promoted and believed. Shirley Clappe, in her famous and otherwise charming letters from the northern mines in the early 1850s, asserted that the indigenous residents of the Feather River area spoke a language of about twenty words. Even the California history book I learned my req-

uisite fourth-grade history from at the beginning of the 1970s per-
sisted in the Digger myth, describing a people so simple they
provoked no wonder. The native people of the Motherlode called
the whites Gold Diggers, after their most feverish activity.

For all their pious cruelty, the Spanish and Mexicans made room
for native people in their society, room at the bottom. The Anglo-
Americans were different. The United States had pursued a policy
of relocating the peoples whose land they overspread, moving them
away from the new society, rather than bringing them into it. The
great relocations had begun in the 1830s, when gold was discovered
on the Cherokee lands of the Southeast, and so the Cherokees were
marched to Oklahoma—then "Indian Territory"—on what became
known as the Trail of Tears. In California, the expansion came not
with a slow spread of farms, as it had on the Midwestern frontiers,
but with a quick scramble into the heavily populated foothills of the
Sierra. The policy had always been to push the natives west, ahead
of the expanding nation, but the uttermost west had been reached
in California, and there was no place ahead to push them but the
Pacific.

In a message to the legislature of the new state, Governor Burnett
said, "That a war of extermination would continue to be waged until
the Indian race should become extinct, and that it was beyond the
power or wisdom of men to avert the inevitable destiny." The government sent three Indian Agents west to manage things a little more
delicately, and at the same time, January 14, 1851, they made their
own appraisal of the situation: "As there is now no further West to
which they can be removed, the General Government and the
people of California appear to have left but one alternative in relation to the remnants of once numerous and powerful tribes, vis; extermination or domestication. As the latter includes all proper
measures for their protection and gradual improvement, and secures

to the State an element greatly needed in the development of its resources, vis; cheap labor, it is the one which we deem the part of wisdom to adopt, and if possible consummate."

This was what the Mariposa Battalion was there to realize: either the extermination or domestication of the tribes in the southern motherlode. These original inhabitants were interfering with the economic development of the area: They resisted incursions into what was left of their territory, sometimes by killing miners; they occasionally exacted tribute for use of their lands, sometimes by force; and they supplemented their declining food sources with the horses and cattle of miners. A specific incident—the killing of three men and destruction of goods at James Savage's trading post on the Fresno River—precipitated the war, which was to some extent a personal vendetta, Savage's war. Savage convinced his fellow miners and local officials that the native people were gathering for a massive effort to drive the invaders from their land, and it was this alarm that precipitated formation of the Mariposa Battalion.

The native peoples of the region—Southern Miwok and Yokuts—were supposed to settle on reservations in the valley, where they could be easily overseen by Indian Agents, and where they could be turned into agriculturalists. This is the origin of the policy of creating Indian reservations in the United States, and from the first they functioned as refugee camps for displaced people. The natives were supposed to become self-sufficient farmers and ranchers, but the supplies to tide them over and the tools to make the transition were usually insufficient or nonexistent—much money and equipment disappeared into the pockets of local Indian Agents and suppliers. The belief that agriculture and settlement constitute civilization is strong throughout nineteenth-century America, as is the belief that nomadism and hunting-gathering are intrinsically savage practices (even though many of the alleged savages migrated no more than wealthy Europeans, from summer to winter homes, and engaged in many horticultural activities). Bunnell himself says late in his book that Indians who have been made into agriculturalists require no other religious instruction.

The three Indian Agents in California intended to implement creation of agricultural reservations as the new Indian policy, and so the Mariposa Battalion and other arms of the government began encouraging, threatening, and forcing tribes out of the foothills and into the land chosen for them in the foothills and flats of the San Joaquin Valley. The people most resistant to leaving their homes were the Ahwahneechee, a Southern Miwok subgroup, who summered in the high country, wintered in the foothills, but were most attached to Yosemite Valley, and who recognized Tenaya as their leader. (According to some accounts, the group also included refugees displaced by white incursions.) Much of the Mariposa Indian War was dedicated to hunting them through the canyons, passes, precipices, and valleys of the region. Their predecessors had been there, according to the evidence, for about 4,000 years, and so they had an advantage in navigating the terrain.

Bunnell gives the general impression that the war was a success, though the details of his story don't quite add up to one. On the first incursion into Yosemite Valley, in March of 1851, the battalion under the command of Major Savage rounded up about seventy people, whom they escorted out of the valley, but these Ahwahneechee escaped before reaching the reservation established for them on the Fresno. Most of the several hundred members of the group were probably in winter villages at a lower altitude than Yosemite, which is why so few were caught there to begin with. Meanwhile, the Indian Agents were attempting to negotiate treaties, and on March 19 some Southern Miwok people signed the Treaty of Camp Fremont, near Mariposa Creek. It was among many treaties that the U.S. Congress chose to suppress rather than to ratify, and so it was never honored. The Mariposa Battalion under the command of Captain John Boling returned to Yosemite in May and captured thirty-five Indians on the shore of what the captives called Pyweack and Bunnell christened Lake Tenaya. The group was taken to the reservation, but some were allowed to leave—including Tenaya—and the rest slipped away unobtrusively. Tenaya and some of his kin took refuge with the Mono Lake Paiutes on the other side of the Sierra. The Yosemite Miwok had had a trading relationship with these Paiutes, of whom the other Miwok were suspicious, and Tenaya himself may have been part Paiute. The army returned once more when two miners were reported killed in a skirmish with Indians in Bridalveil Meadows in the summer of 1852; Lieutenant Tredwell Moore led this expedition, which resulted in the discovery of mineral resources near what is now Lee Vining and the capture and death of six Indian men.

Tenaya and some of his group were killed in an altercation with their Mono Lake hosts in 1853—over horse stealing, says Bunnell; over a gambling dispute, say some native accounts. When I first began looking at this material, I thought that this was nearly the end of the tribe, and that I had run across a tragedy of extinction. The first books I read were ambiguous. Bunnell himself said to some potential tourists, "The Yosemites were so nearly destroyed that at least, while they were mourning the loss of their chief, and their people, no fear need be entertained of them." Carl P. Russell, a park ranger who wrote a history of Yosemite in the 1930s, wrote, "The story of this last act in the elimination of the troublesome Yosemites was made known to Bunnell by surviving members of the tribe." Of course, the existence of surviving members undermines the emphasis on lasts and elimination, but the idea was a popular one. The Indian Museum in Yosemite National Park seemed to be a monument to an extinct way of life, with the live woman herself framed as though she were caught in the past like an insect in amber, a relic of something lost rather than a still viable way of life. I found a book about Yosemite by the photographer Ted Orland, which declared, "By 1900, almost all Yosemite Indians were old; after the 1850's 'they didn't make Indians anymore,' as the saying went, and you can often roughly date a photograph by the age of the Indian in it—the older the Indian, the more recent the photograph. The last full-blooded Ahwahneechee died in 1931."

A book about this full-blooded Ahwahneechee was published in 1932. Written by Rose Taylor, it was sympathetic, melodramatic, and brief. Titled *The Last Survivor,* it was about the return to Yosemite and death of Totuya, or Maria Lebrado, a granddaughter of Tenaya who was part of the group forced out by the army. "Life was nearing its close when To-to-ya returned from exile to live a few days in her home of earliest memories. Souvenir-loving tourists came to look at her as she sat shelling a pile of acorns; one of them offered a nickle for an acorn from her hands. With deep feeling and resentment she pushed the coin aside and cried, 'No! Not five dollars one acorn, no! White man drives my people out—my Yosemite.'" The author doesn't make it clear why Totuya/Lebrado waited until 1929 to return, when she had been living in its vicinity all those seventy-eight years. Taylor became her friend and came to visit her on her deathbed: "The lone tree, representative of a by-gone forest, stays the woodsman's ax by the strength and power of its aloneness. The Indian band driven out of Yosemite Valley by the Mariposa Battalion became intensely personified in Maria Lebrado, granddaughter of Tenaya, Chief of the Yosemites. As its last survivor she symbolized the history of her people. In her own lifetime she had experienced the tragic disintegration of the Yosemite tribe. Her death on April 20, 1931, broke our last link with Indian Yosemite."

When I first found Rose Taylor's book, my timeline grew a little: I believed that the Ahwahneechee had died out in 1931, not soon after the war, or in the early 1900s. I think that the constant threats of extermination in Bunnell's book influenced me, and the museum's mortuary air. It's true that with the death of Totuya/Lebrado, the last firsthand memory of Yosemite before white incursions died, a landmark for the retreat of experience into history. But rereading the book, it's easier to see how Taylor maximized poignancy by minimizing cultural continuity. When Totuya died at nearly ninety, four of her nine children were still alive, one from her first marriage to another Ahwahneechee—which belies the idea that she was the last full-blood—and three from her second marriage, to a Mexican miner. Her children had children, and cultural survival doesn't depend on blood anyway. On her deathbed, she was surrounded by family, and she may have conveyed much of her history and traditions to them. They gave her a traditional Miwok funeral, with a cry that went on for days.

Melancholy is secretly pleasurable, particularly when it's over someone else's problems. A doomed and dying race is stirring poetic material, a people with a talent for integrating change is not. And indigenous people are pictured as fixed in time, possessed of fragile and static cultures which crumble under the force of colonialist contamination. Contamination is usually how it's framed: The culture is imagined as pure, and purity is imagined as a steady state, a self-contained system without outside influences, an Eden ready to fall (or as blood purity, which is how Rose Taylor renders the intermarrying Ahwahneechee extinct). Once purity becomes the criterion, the culture can be pronounced dead if it evolves or adapts, as all cultures are always doing, a neat formula for extermination on paper. This is a popular conception, evident in the outrage with which tourists protest the presence of nontraditional materials at a native

ceremony or native crafts and the way the federal government demands documented racial purity of everyone who wants to be considered an Indian. The belief in lasts and extinctions may also be a
faith that the wars succeeded in what they intended, although there
is quite a difference between decimation and disappearance. And
finally, as people speak differently about someone who is dead or
absent, so they may speak of peoples and cultures they presume
missing, the speech of most anthropology. A person who is present
is a political being with a voice, rights, and membership; a person
who is absent is a curiosity. Assuming the disappearance of Native
Americans made it possible to speak of them entirely in the latter
way, made the injustice part of our great-grandparents' era, not our
own. Part of the horror of Bunnell's comment to Tenaya at the lake
is its explicit language of exclusion: Bunnell is describing a future in
which Tenaya and his culture will be outside the conversation.

The Yosemite Indian Cultural Museum does show postcontact
native people, who wear cloth and have guns, pots, and other metal
implements. The plaque says that because too little is known about
precontact culture, the displays depict the culture as it existed in the
1870s, as does the weird re-creation of an Indian village in the yard
behind the museum (until 1982, the museum tried to present 1850s
culture, but the skimpy clothes of preinvasion times and even skimp-
ier information made the task daunting). There are also mannequins
wearing costumes used to entertain early-twentieth-century audiences. But the language is incoherent about time. The re-created Indian buildings in the backyard emphasize traditional structures, but
the booklet shows some nontraditional ones. Its text says, "Culture
is always in the process of change," but leaves that change off in the
1890s with the sentence, "The story of the Ahwahneechee's relationship with their non-Indian neighbors of the 19th Century is but
one of many still unfolding." It's unclear whether they and their

neighbors entered the next century, or only their story did; and the Mariposa Indian War is omitted for the more anthropological phrase "after contact." Politics exists in time, and traditional anthropology seeks out the timeless. The museum is above all apolitical, neither blaming the Indians for the war as some of the other plaques do, nor raising questions about their grievances and rights in the region. Nothing states that the Indians here are extinct, nor suggests that they are still present. It is hard to tell whether the story breaks off sometime in the early twentieth century because there's nothing more to tell or because it's no longer of anthropological interest.

Instead, the museum speaks in the tense of past perfect, a kind of dreamtime, and it is more interested in tradition and routine than in disruption. Much attention is given to basketry. The contemporary women who display traditional crafts are themselves framed in this kind of time: Their nineteenth-century garb and their seat among the objects suggest that they themselves are contained within this time, rather than that they keep it alive in the present they inhabit, a present that contains both acorns and taxes, baskets and televisions. They become relics themselves.

Meanwhile, in the other, more central museum, they don't exist. Only the aeons of nature exist—the primordial forces that shape the rocks and determine the vegetation—and late-blooming culture— the 1851 discoverers and subsequent connoisseurs. There are no Indians, but there are paintings by Albert Bierstadt and artwork by contemporary artists. Culture addresses nature, but it doesn't shape it or influence it, nor is culture contained or generated by it. Culture comes by horseback and then by automobile and admires it. There is no history: The events of 1851 are simply discovery, an odd term for a military incursion: "Soon after its discovery in 1851, Yosemite attracted artists, writers and lovers of natural landscape," says a museum plaque, and their "interpretations of such scenic splendor helped awaken the public to its natural heritage." It is on the one hand a kind of segregation, and on the other, a kind of obliteration.

✚ I FINALLY GOT TO LAKE TENAYA, ON A WARM DAY IN AUGUST. The water was marvelously clear. Dead trees and fallen limbs were bleached to the same pale gray as the rocks. At the other end of the lake was a bulge of solid stone like a vast forehead, and much of the surrounding landscape was of the same curving, glacier-carved granite. I stood there, as far from traffic as I could go on a small lake along a road, and looked. Skeins of golden light slipped over the lake floor, and rounded boulders rose out of the water or hovered just below its surface. The water was so shallow and the lake inclined so gradually I walked far from the shore before it became deep enough to swim in. It was an uncanny place. It was hard to trust that this cold, clear substance would bear me up if I immersed myself in it, or that I would emerge the same as I went in. In the gravelly shallows, eddies of fool's gold rose around me at every step, glittering in the bright light of the mountains. As the waves lapped at my feet, I tried to picture Tenaya and Bunnell standing there on a cold May morning 140 years before and wondered which shining rocks had moved the Ahwahneechee to name the lake Pyweack.

In Miwok culture one shows respect for the dead by not speaking their names, so after Tenaya's death in 1853, the lake's name became a violation of religious belief as well as an attempt to obliterate the Miwoks' sense of the place. But it would be hard to say that the Mariposa Battalion won the war, and the more I looked, the less it seemed that the war had ever been concluded. Some of the Ahwahneechee had returned to Yosemite Valley upon leaving the reservation. When Hutchings visited in 1855, he reported there was "scarcely an Indian track to be seen," but his Ahwahneechee guides may have steered him away from the evidence, or he may not have been looking very hard. They were apparently there in 1852, when the altercation took place that resulted in the death of some miners and, subsequently, in Lieutenant Tredwell Moore's punitive expedition. And in 1854, a Belgian miner named Jean-Nicholas Perlot visited a camp of 250 Indians just west of Yosemite Valley, and three years later encountered a village of 100 within the valley.

About the Ahwahneechee he encountered little is recorded; about Perlot, a great deal. He wrote for his family a memoir of his United States adventures, which was found and translated into English recently enough that his information hasn't become part of the standard accounts. A modest, urbane man, he had been in Paris when the revolution of 1848 broke out and held radical views about priests and about private property as the origin of evil. Most Western accounts of the time are self-consciously heroic, from Fremont's invention of himself as the Pathfinder in his expedition journals, to Bunnell's history with its continual references to his athletic ability and aesthetic refinement. Without the prejudices of most white Americans of the time and without the frontiersman's burden of heroism to carry, Perlot tells a far more engaging and often comic story. He describes an occasion when he and his continental colleagues fearfully let a bear steal their ham from the cookpot, and another time when he could find no game but "an eagle, of a kind whose head is bare of feathers," which he tries to eat, but his dog scorns. When he kills a bobcat that surprises him near Hetch Hetchy, he has nightmares about "my dying victim and her terrible spouse thirsting for vengeance."

He had landed in Monterey on April 7, 1851, in the midst of the Mariposa War. But the California he describes is less a frontier than a marvelously foreign country, in which miners, Indians, vultures, bobcats, and all the rest are equally unfamiliar to him. Perlot soon became a confident prospector and went far up into the southern mines of the Fresno, Merced, and Tuolumne regions. Once, on the Fresno River, Perlot needed someone to hold his mule's reins while he reloaded the animal; he waylaid an Indian from a passing party, accomplished his mulepacking, and offered the man "a dram to drink and a bit of bread." Later, not far west of Yosemite, he met up again with this man whom he calls Flesno, after the Miwok pronunciation of the river, and they became friends. Eventually, he even learned their Miwok dialect, but in the interim a Spanish-speaking associate of Flesno, Juan, translated for them. Perlot took up their offer to show him the places where they found their gold. The Indians had taken to mining because the land had become poorer and their treaty with Savage forbade them to enter the area between the Merced and the Fresno—a bountiful area for seed and acorn gathering in the fall and a warmer place in the winter—so entering the cash economy allowed them to supplement their local food resources. Perlot himself was running low on food at the time of this visit, and he describes how Juan told one of the women in the group to give him something to eat. She "hesitating and with a visible repugnance, came to place herself beside me. Shortly afterward, she began to cry." Juan explains that she has no spare basket left to let him eat from, but that if she shares his they will be considered engaged according to Miwok custom. It is hard to picture any of Perlot's Californian contemporaries admitting that he stirred revulsion, not admiration, in a native woman's heart.

Not long afterward, Perlot participated in a skirmish between this Miwok group and their northern neighbors, the Tuolumnes of the Hetch Hetchy region. He learned a little of their language, too. Juan and his brother (whom Perlot called Scipiano, after the Roman general) were the sons of a Yosemite chief named José, whom he also met. Leadership apparently did not die out with Tenaya. In 1854, Scipiano protested that his Yosemite people had not conducted the raids which led to the Mariposa Indian War and showed him the treaty he kept in his quiver. The treaty guaranteed some protection to the native people, but Scipiano was afraid he would be killed if he went to the sheriff to ask that it be honored. Perlot offered to escort him and sent a letter in advance to the sheriff. The sheriff was on good terms with the Belgian miner, who had protested the death penalty for three men slated for hanging and successfully advised they be banished instead. As it turned out, Sheriff Bills was fluent in Spanish, and so he and Scipiano negotiated a local peace directly. "The agreement attained, Bills gave Scipiano a certificate of permission to travel, in virtue of which Scipiano, as well as his subjects of both sexes, had the right to circulate through the County of Mariposa. All and sundry were ordered to let them pass in peace, to protect them in case of need, but to inform Justice of any act contrary to law or morality which they might commit. 'The interdict against the natives being raised,' added the document, 'it is henceforth forbidden to take the law into one's own hands' "—that is, it was no longer open season on Indians.

After recounting his expedition with Scipiano to secure a peace, Perlot pens his longest meditation on the Indians he has met. It is a remarkable assessment for its time, making them out to be neither Diggers nor noble savages, but clearly indicating the writer's own politics: "This habit of judging without knowing each other is, I think, most of the time, the source of the wars which break out between peoples, whether they are savage or civilized," he says in conclusion to the treaty account, and then goes on: "We had built a false idea, certainly, of the Indian when we considered and treated him as a wild beast. . . . He is called savage, I hardly know why; whether by this word one means a ferocious, unsociable being, or simply living in a state of nature, it belongs in no way to the Indian. He has, just like us, his customs, his laws, his religion; only they differ from ours. . . . Doubtless, there is an institution which forms for so-called civilized peoples one of the bases—some of them simply say the base—of society, and which the Indian does not know: property. Is this a sign of inferiority? I will not decide the question. But who can tell us that the progress of civilization will not bring us, in this re-spect, to the point where the Indian is? In the meantime, the latter owes to this ignorance his living in peace in his tribe—and in his family: he does not know lawsuits. His laws and his customs proceed from his religious beliefs: the Great Spirit (God) himself is his leg-islator and his judge; but his action is exerted without any inter-mediary whatsoever. A theocracy without priests—there, truly, is the government of the Indians. An attentive observer of nature, the In-dian sees in the mighty phenomena it presents to him, the manifes-tation of the will of Nang-Oua, the Great Spirit, and endeavors to make his conduct conform to it; he obeys him and offers no other worship to him: the precepts of this religion, which the old teach the young, constitute his civil code and his penal code." They would come to know lawsuits soon enough.

By his own account, Perlot used his knowledge of the area west of Yosemite to help survey the route for a road there in 1857. His account of his first entry into the valley itself is typical. He came with several other men, including a band of musicians. "The inhabitants of the Indian Camp, numbering perhaps a hundred, themselves ap-peared to marvel not at the beauties of their valley, but at the spec-tacle we offered them. From that moment on and as far as the top of the valley, the Indians followed or rather accompanied the mu-sicians on the right and the left, in order not to lose sight of neither men nor instruments; they flanked them, stumbling, climbing over each other, falling, getting up, then running to regain their post, without an instant's interruption of their profoundly attentive and imperturbably serious contemplation of the objects of their admiration." As the party moved further into the valley, "We remained some time as in an ecstasy, and the Indians at whom we had laughed so much in the morning, could have taken their revenge, if Indians laughed. At last we set off, desirous of seeing the marvel [Yosemite Falls] from nearby. We went the whole way gaping at the waterfall; we stumbled; we fell on each other, we got up and continued on our way without paying any attention to our neighbors, with our eyes always fixed on the same object—absolutely like the Indians."

Perlot left the Sierra slopes soon afterward and established himself as a gardener in Portland, Oregon. At first he was a market gardener, supplying scarce vegetables to the city, but with no more preparation than boldness and a continental background, he became a landscape architect and gardener for the fine homes being built in the new city. After amassing the wealth he had not found in the gold mines, he moved back to Europe, married, and had children. In the 1890s, he sat down and turned his journals and notes into the eloquent, funny account cited here. No other nineteenth-century outsider wrote about the Ahwahneechee with the camaraderie and respect he did.

Afterward, the information is sketchier. There are birth, marriage, and death dates for many individuals—and baskets by many women—but not much to convey what they thought and how they got by. When he worked as a shepherd in the high Sierra in the summer of 1869, John Muir had native co-workers, and there were often Indian villages and encampments in his vicinity. He called them Diggers and left it at that. Park curators Martha J. Lee and Craig Bates wrote in their basketry history of Yosemite Indians, "Some visitors remarked on the relative scarcity of Indian people in Yosemite Valley from 1870 on, but one astute visitor commented that Indian life 'is so unobtrusive a feature of the Valley that the conventional tourist "doing" the Valley in three or four days will hardly know of its existence at all.' Estimates vary as to the actual Yosemite Indian population in the latter half of the nineteenth century. In the 1870s and 1880s, accounts of their numbers ranged widely from very few to several hundred. Visitors in the 1890s reported twenty to thirty-five native inhabitants. One woman, Lucy Hite, caused a sensation around the turn of the century when she sued her white husband for divorce and half his considerable property, and won. In 1870, she had married John Hite, a miner she met when members of her community rescued him when he fell ill. He later struck it rich with a mine on the south fork of the Merced, deserted her, denied their marriage, and entered a bigamous liaison with a young white woman. She may have been the half-sister of Totuya, and some of her basketwork is still around.

Many of her contemporaries lived in their own summer villages in the valley and in Wawona, gathered acorns and other food, and sometimes made a living working for the growing tourist industry. Some of the men sold trout and game to the hotels, where some of the women worked as domestics. Mono Lake Paiutes moved into the valley, and there were intermarriages (as there apparently had been before white incursions). The valley around them was changing; the number of tourists coming each year dramatically increased; and the men who had staked land claims were turning more and more of the valley into farmland. The apple trees James Lamon and James Hutchings planted then are old and gnarled now, but still standing—Lamon's orchard lends some grace to the Camp Curry parking lot. The hayfields have been returned to a natural-looking state. Eventually, the government had to pay these squatters off to get them to relinquish their claims and yield up their fields to public use.

No such transaction satisfied earlier claims on the place. Yosemite had never been legally acquired from its first inhabitants. In a secret session, Congress refused to ratify the 1851 and 1852 treaties establishing land reservations for California native people, and the treaties themselves were classified documents until the envelope containing them was rediscovered in 1905. In 1890 or 1891, a "Petition to Congress on Behalf of the Yosemite Indians" was written by a sympathizer with a flowery style: "When the long list of oppressions and outrages to which our fathers were forced to submit at the hands of the whites had long ended by the slaughter and dispersal of our tribes, no notice was taken of the few who remained, and who from then until now have continued to travel to and fro, poorly-clad paupers and unwelcome guests, silently the objects of curiosity or contemptuous pity to the throngs of strangers who yearly gather in this our own land and heritage. We are compelled to daily and hourly witness the further and continual encroachments of a few white men in this our valley. The gradual destruction of its trees, the occupancy of every foot of its territory by bands of grazing horses and cattle, the decimation of the fish in the river, the destruction of every means of support for ourselves and families by the rapacious acts of the whites, in the building of their hotels and stage lines, which must shortly result in the total exclusion of the remaining remnants of our tribes from this our beloved valley, which has been ours from time beyond our faintest traditions, and which we still claim."

The petition finally suggested that since the valley would never be returned to its original inhabitants, they would consider a million dollars as payment for their title. Nothing came of it. In 1929, the U.S. government finally decided to pay California's original inhabitants for the land that had been taken from them, at the rate of forty-seven cents an acre, minus all appropriations of goods made for all of the Indians of California since 1848. (When native people occupied Alcatraz in 1964, they offered to buy the land back at the same rate, $9.40 for the whole island; during a reoccupation in 1969–70, they raised the price to Manhattan's original purchase price, $1.24 an acre.) The value of the native Californians' land was set at $17 million, the value of the appropriations at $12 million, and a judgment of $5 million was awarded to them. By 1950, disbursements of $150 to each individual had been issued, and a few similar sums were handed out until the 1970s, when the government satisfied itself it had bought California from its first peoples.

At the time of the petition, the small reserve of the valley and the Mariposa Big Tree Grove was vastly expanded to include all the land now in the park, and the additions became national parklands. Muir had become concerned about the effects of sheepgrazing and woodcutting on this land, and it was largely his efforts that brought about the big new park. At that time, the military handled the national parks, and so the army came back to Yosemite and stayed until the civilian National Park Service was founded in 1914. In 1906, the U.S. Army burned down the Indian village on Yosemite Creek, in at least one case with all the occupant's belongings inside. In the teens through the thirties, the native population became a popular attraction as tourists stopped regarding Indians as threats and started enjoying them as curiosities. Many of the spectacles provided for their enjoyment had little to do with local culture and clothing, as do the Indian souvenirs sold in several places in the park today (including beaded belts with "Yosemite" inscribed on them and Southwestern-style turquoise jewelry). During these years, most of the remaining indigenous inhabitants lived in a village in what was then called Indian Canyon, a sheltered niche on the sunny north side of the valley floor (many others lived elsewhere in the county).

In 1929, Park Superintendent Charles G. Thomson decided that the village was an eyesore and an impediment to development of the new Yosemite Village and had it burnt down. A hospital was built in its place. Meanwhile Thomson had invoked racial purity to limit those who would be allowed to remain: Only those who could trace their ancestry to early inhabitants could move into the new village, near the current Sunnyside campground and further away from the center of visitor and administrative activities. The initial plan was to build houses in the style of Great Plains teepees, like the bizarre stucco-teepee motels now scattered across the West. Fortunately, the assistant landscape architect for the project backed off and built conventional, if diminutive, cabins. Each of the fifteen had three small rooms, regardless of the size of the families for whom they were intended. They were heated by wood stove, and a sink was their only plumbing: The villagers shared a central bathroom. Because the tourist economy dried up in the winter, some families were forced to leave the village to work, and when they did, the Park Service destroyed their homes on the grounds that they were abandoned. In 1969, the new Indian village was destroyed completely and its remaining inhabitants evicted. It was the fourth era of village destruction—the army had done the job in 1851 and 1906; the Park Service in 1929 and 1969. With it the original goal of the Mariposa Battalion was coming closer to realization: eviction of the Ahwahneechee from the valley after their millennia there. There was no longer room for anyone but strangers in this paradise.

I met some of Tenaya's descendants that first fall when I was trying to unearth what the confrontation at the lake meant and what had really happened afterward. They didn't live in Yosemite. Actually, the first I met, Zandra Bietz, was a high-powered consultant who lived in San Francisco and headed the board of a contemporary Native American art gallery there. She didn't have a great deal to say about the current state of things, except that she considered Yosemite Indian territory and resented the Park Service and, in the surrounding areas, the Forest Service, for trying to prevent native women from gathering acorns there. The black oak, as far as she was concerned, has a spiritual significance as well as an ecological one, and the one was as important as the other—and not in conflict. She told me I should talk to her father, Elmer Stanley, who lived in Tuolumne.

I drove there from Yosemite one autumn day, along the winding roads that descend and climb the steep ravines and hills of the upper foothills, and finally got to Tuolumne Ranchería. Though the various indigenous nations in California got very few reservations, they did get to keep some smaller areas as collective land, usually called rancherías. This place was very different from Yosemite, a place of grass parched summer gold and spreading oaks. Elmer Stanley's house was a handsome one, with a two-story-tall main room hung with family pictures I recognized from anthropology books. There was a picture of his great-great-grandmother on his mother's side, Totuya/Maria Lebrado, which also appears as the frontispiece in Rose Taylor's *The Last Survivor.* Stanley had himself been born under a tree by a stream that had long disappeared under the water of Hetch Hetchy Reservoir, he told me, and his mother had subsequently farmed this illegitimate child out to relatives and married one of the men building the dam. And he told me that when he goes to Yosemite Valley, "I just cringe." But mostly he was cagey, flirting with me and asking me questions about myself that forestalled mine about him. He told me he would come to San Francisco and take me out to McDonald's. In the meantime, he took me into the backyard and showed me the acorn-leaching equipment there—a screened table—which was full of acorns. And he gave me a bowl of acorn mush from a jarful in his refrigerator. It was very cold with a texture a little like custard or tofu, and I was too distracted to pay attention to its flavor.

I was told there were still at least two Ahwahneechee descendants living in Yosemite Valley itself. Ralph Parker and Jay Johnson had been born there, grew up in the village, and had taken jobs in the Park Service, so they were eligible to live there as employees when they were no longer eligible to live there as natives of the place. Ralph Parker was the husband of the woman I had seen demonstrating in the Indian Cultural Museum, Julia Parker. She is herself a Pomo, from the Sonoma County coast region, but she has lived in Yosemite since 1947 and been married to Ralph Parker since 1949. It was Parker's grandmother, Lucy Tom Parker Telles, who taught her much of what she knows about basketry and acorn preparation, and it is she who has kept alive many of the old ways, not just as a cultural demonstrator in the museum, but as a speaker and teacher around the state.

A local photographer told me I should talk to Jay Johnson in the park's forestry department. We met and spoke in the Indian village replica behind the museum a few times. A softspoken man who wore his uniform well, he looked younger than his years. He and his sisters were born in the old Indian village and raised in the new one. They live nearby and he has managed, with the interruption of Indian boarding school and military service, to stay in the valley his whole life, where he takes care of the trees and the trails. But he is due to retire, at which time he too will be evicted from his home in the valley, unless things change. He is working on the changes.

At the time I first spoke to him he was part of the leadership of the Mariposa Indian Council attempting to get federal recognition for the 2,000 Southern Sierra Miwok still in the area. The government did not recognize them as an entity with which it could do business, since it had never completed its treaties with them. Establishing their tribal status would make them eligible for the program funding and land base they had been denied since the suppressed treaties of 1851–52. The burden of proof was on the council members: They had to provide written documentation of continuous existence as a distinct group. It is a standard that ignores both the fact that such documentation is not part of oral-history traditions and that the government itself has done everything it can to dismantle such tribes, from outright wars to sending native children to schools in which they are forbidden to speak their language to forcing them off the land and out of their customary practices.

Johnson was also working on a plan to create an independent Indian cultural center which, unlike the current "Indian Gardens" behind the museum, would be controlled by Mariposa Indians who could shut tourists out when they used it for ceremonial purposes. In 1976, the Mariposa Indian Council had proposed establishment of such a center and asserted that the museum and Indian cultural programs should be run by native people alone (as well as that local indigenous people should be admitted to the park free of charge). Johnson laid strong emphasis on the spiritual significance of Yosemite Valley and the importance of being able to continue religious practices there. One of the times I talked to him, he and his son were working on the roundhouse in the Indian Gardens behind the Indian Museum; the roundhouse was being rebuilt, but still could only be used for ceremonies in the early morning, before visitors came. The 1980 General Plan for the park's future permitted the new village, but supplied no funds for it. Like Elmer Stanley and his daughter, he complained about his niece and other women being bothered when they attempted to gather acorns in Yosemite. And he told me about the traditional walk, from Mono Lake to the valley, he had helped to reinstate in 1990. "My sister went down the day before to visit one of the last few Indian elders that we have today, he's in his nineties, and I listened to the tape. . . . He came up, he's from Mariposa originally like my dad. She was asking him what he remembered of people walking over the hill to Mono Lake. Well, he says, 'I've been on that trail, I've been on horseback, several times back and forth.' He was telling her what transpired when he went over the hill—my sister, both of my sisters remember and have done the same thing. Here she was talking with this Indian man doing the same thing, early 1920s up through the years. The last three years we made the walk ourselves as a group. We call it our traditional walk. So this is our third year this year we did that. We walk from the valley—Mono Lake or Bloody Canyon just on the other side. This year we walked from a little place on the other side of Bloody Canyon, to here. It took five days to do it. We camped along the way. We had sixty to sixty-five people, at one time it got up to seventy. Some people joined us for a little while, some left. But it was a very spiritual walk."

Johnson told me that he intends to write his own version of these histories someday, and told me about an encounter he had with the official version in the nation's capital. "I think it was 1980, Julia [Parker] and four of us on business for our tribe went to the Smithsonian and found the California museum exhibits, then Yosemite. It's almost the same thing as the diorama down here in the corner. Down in the Smithsonian it was on the wall and it had a little statement on the side and it left off with 'It's very sad today. There's no more Yosemite Indians.' Period. I said, 'Let's go down, talk to the people at the desk about this statement.' So we went down there and this lady, she was at the desk, and I said, 'Ma'am, about that diorama about Yosemite,' and she says 'Oh, isn't that nice.' And I said 'It's nice, but there's an error in the statement,' and she says, 'Oh no, there can't be. Every little word goes through channels and committees and whatnot,' and I says, 'It's OK, but,' I says, 'It tells me that there are no more Yosemite Indians today.' She says, 'Well that's true, it's very sad but whatever's out there is true.' So I say, 'Well I hate to disturb you, but I'm a Yosemite Indian, and we're here on business for our tribe.' And she caught her breath and said, 'Ohhh, uh, let me call somebody,' and so she called somebody who was in charge of exhibits, and I went and told her the same thing. If there's a statement saying that there are descendants of the Ahwahneechees living there today, all of us natives would be satisfied. But it hasn't been changed—I don't think so.

"The written material states that there are no more Yosemite Indians. If they would ask us, they use a term like full-blood. We are descendants, that's not all we are, but we are. I go back to my great-grandmother who was born here in the 1830s, before the army and militia came in. We can't prove it, but we come from her daughter, our grandmother, who was born here, same as my grandfather on my father's side. I asked my uncle before he died; I said, 'Where did we come from, where do the Johnsons come from?' And he says, well, he asked his dad, and his dad said, 'Well, we come from there, the Valley, and from Mariposa.' His father was born in that area, not in written documents, but this is what we know. Going back I know that I'm a descendant of the Ahwahneechee tribe, and that's what I feel, and when I talk even to the schoolchildren, that's what I tell them." And Johnson sitting in the model Indian village in his green uniform, the huge black-oak acorns dropping around us as we spoke, told me, "I still tell people that this land is mine. One thing that they can't take away from me is my feelings."

Fire in the Garden

✠ ONE WAY TO GUARANTEE A CONVERSATION WITHOUT A CON-clusion is to ask a group of people what nature is. One person will assert that it's anything that is unaffected by human beings, anything out there, and then another will object that DDT has been found in the polar icecaps and nothing is that far away. Someone else will go for a more moderate definition of anything not made by people, and more hairs will be split over domesticated and selectively bred things like cows and cabbages, and over artifacts made from natural materials, such as baskets. An antiromantic might bring up the bacteria in last week's casserole in the back of the refrigerator and the more complex and sustained communities of microorganisms in our own intestines as phenomena neither domestic nor manmade, perhaps as natural if not as impressive and out there as the wolverine. It's likely that someone will insist that people are themselves biological phenomena, are nature, and therefore that as nature their creations are natural too. So the definition of nature may exclude even a wolverine with pesticide in its fat reserves or may include computer chips.

One of the most extreme voices for nature as the phenomena out there is Bill McKibben, in his book *The End of Nature*. It is a two-headed beast, half in-depth report on the possible effects of global warming and half elegy for nature as something independent of man. "We have deprived nature of its independence, and that is fatal to its meaning. Nature's independence *is* its meaning." This, the crux of his elegy if not of his argument, comes in the middle of a long passage about the world he proposes we have lost. He describes

"very nearly the last person to see any part of this continent unpol-
luted even by the knowledge that someone had been there before"—
a strange idea of what pollution is, one that seems more like misanthropy. He talks about when the Grand Canyon was a blank spot
on the map. He describes Thoreau as being the fifth white man
known to climb a certain mountain and laments, "We've reconciled
ourselves to the idea that we'll not be the first up any hill." He cites
the journal of William Bartram, an eighteenth-century naturalist
who went to "the Cherokee country, the Extensive Territories of the
Muscogulges, or Creek Confederacy, and the Country of the Choc-
taws," and then after some of Bartram's lyrical descriptions of the
abundant verdure, refers to Bartram as a traveler in an "untouched
world." And he talks about John Muir in Yosemite.

For McKibben, nature is separate from us. It's not paradise if
we're not strangers, and a hill is better for not having been climbed
before. He does sometime say who that *we* is when he clarifies that
Thoreau only knows of the *white* men who have climbed the mountain before him, and he obscures the presence of people who are
apparently not us when he sets Bartram down among the Cherokee,
the Creek, and the Choctaw and describes theirs as an "untouched"
world, or when he considers the heavily populated Grand Canyon
to have been unknown. Despite all the evidence, McKibben wants
to imagine this continent as uninhabited and untouched, as a nature
made apart from man, and he mourns for the end of its independence (in much the way that earlier writers lamented the vanishing
tribes). The implication is either very hostile—that native peoples
don't constitute a human presence—or very idolizing—that they
lived in such utter harmony they had no effect on their surroundings
at all, but either way they don't count. The other implication is that
if nature is only itself before it's touched, if it's a place where we
don't belong, then we can only experience it as it's disappearing, and

our presence alone is enough to make it something else (the Wilderness Act of 1964 describes wilderness as "a place where man is a visitor").

For McKibben, the question of what constitutes nature is a spiritual question, a question of what the world means to him when he goes outside. For the National Park Service and other land managers, it has been a very concrete question. Charged with preserving landscapes in their natural state, they need to make major decisions about what that natural state consists of: what to include, what to exclude, what to provide compensation for. They have the peculiar duty of managing nature to keep it natural. For the most part, they and other land managers seem to have imagined it as McKibben would, with unexpected results.

The ecologist Daniel Botkin relates one fine example, a sixty-five-acre forest in New Jersey which had been protected from clearing since 1701. It was visited by a botanist in 1749, who described it as "composed of large oaks, hickories, and chestnuts, so free of underbrush that one could drive a horse and carriage through the woods." By the 1950s, it was the only primeval forest in the state, and Rutgers University bought it as a nature reserve. The people who studied it thought of it in terms of the theory of the climax forest, the stable forest of the system in its mature state. But it began to change; the oaks were not regenerating, and sugar maple saplings flourished. The forest that would be there in another 250 years would not be the one whose mature trees began to grow 250 years ago. The Rutgers ecologist who was studying it, Murray Buell, "found that before European settlement in 1701, fires had occurred about every decade, but none had burned after European settlement, when they had been intentionally suppressed. Oaks and hickories, it turned out, dominated the forest because they are more resistant to fire than sugar maple. Other evidence suggests that the

American Indians occasionally may have set fires. The effects of fire were visible in another way: instead of the open woods that Peter Kalm had seen, the forest was a dense thicket of shrubs and saplings crowded against the tall trees. . . . The forest primeval was revealed as, in part, a human product."

Alston Chase tells a similar story in his book *Playing God in Yellowstone.* Apparently on the first day of the 1870 Langford Expedition into what is now called Yellowstone—the expedition whose report brought about its establishment as a national park—a member noticed a fire that he presumed was set by Indians. Chase goes on to describe the many uses and benefits of fire in modifying the landscape: It promotes greater diversity in plants and animals, releases nutrients into the soil, keeps forests clear of underbrush that hinders large animals (including humans), and halts or alters the forest succession. And he goes on to cite the considerable evidence that native people across the continent—and elsewhere—used fire to modify their environment. "It has been documented that at least one hundred tribes of North America used fire for at least fifteen purposes, but nearly all these uses dramatically affected the landscape and ecosystem. . . ." And he goes on to say that the virgin forest was not what European immigrants found in the sixteenth and seventeenth centuries, but what late-eighteenth- and early-nineteenth-century Americans created, in the landscape and in their imaginations. The popular idea that the forests had been so pervasive a squirrel could jump from tree to tree from the Atlantic to the Mississippi Chase modifies with a complementary image: that these forests were also so open and uncluttered one might drive a coach from the sea to the great river without benefit of a road. He even declares that the Great Plains were made in part by Indians and were being increased to extend the bison's range when its makers were interrupted by white incursions.

All this has a specific relevance for Chase's investigation of nature management in Yellowstone. From fire, he goes on to describe the hunting skills of North America's native people and suggests that they had increased in population and thus in their effect on the environment until European diseases reached them in the 1800s, so that first settlers, then historians and ecologists coming in the wake of the plagues, underestimated their numbers and their effect on the land. And in popular accounts and land management practices, their presence was dismissed altogether, and Yellowstone was made into another virgin wilderness of the sort McKibben mourns. Chase says that it is because Bannock and Nez Perce groups moving through the park in the 1870s alarmed its first superintendent, Phelitus Norris. And the Nez Perce had nearly captured Civil War hero William Tecumseh Sherman, and such dangers would be bad for tourism. So Norris lobbied hard for expulsion of all natives from the park and invented a story that they had always avoided Yellowstone because they feared the geysers. "He must have known that the Nez Perce were so unafraid of the hot springs that they cooked their food in them. Yet, contrived as it was, the myth never died. Ever since then, the story of the Indians and the geysers has been part of Yellowstone lore." The burning stopped, meadows were encroached upon, rare animals became common and vice versa. A century later the ecology of Yellowstone is unsustainable, unbalanced, and unlike what it had been when the Langford Expedition wandered in. "Touted as pristine, the policy required that we forget those whose absence diminished it." A Shoshone woman, Doris Yowell, remembers a similar history for the Great Basin: "They used to burn an area of sagebrush so that plants would grow where they burned. These plants they would then harvest . . . but they no longer grow anymore." In the southeastern U.S., the extraordinary lushness the botanist William Bartram encountered was probably the result not of the land being untouched, as Bill McKibben imagined, but being touched with knowledgeable care: Useful trees were encouraged and tended for several miles around Native American settlements, creating parklike environments. Degradation of a landscape imagined as natural or wild is as often the result of lack of human interaction as of ignorant or hostile interaction.

Yet the idea persists that nature in a natural state is nature without people, and this idea has been exported around the world. In Tanzania and Kenya, the Masai have been displaced by the creation of national parks, and their 3,000-year-old nomadic way of life has become unsustainable without this extensive land base. Wild animals leave the park boundaries to graze on their small new land base, but Masai cattle are forbidden to graze in the parkland because of the usual distinctions between the wild and the tame, between nature and culture. I've been told that the natives forced out of Canada's first national park, Banff, in the Canadian Rockies, ride through it every summer in a refusal to recognize its boundaries. In Death Valley National Monument, the Park Service has taken over the oasis the Timbisha Western Shoshone had always lived around, forbidden them to build traditional structures or hunt or move to their summer homes, forcing them into an inconspicuous trailer park with piped-in water—in short, rendered them invisible refugees on their ancestral land (for a brief interval in the 1930s, the Park Service attempted to convince them to become a tourist attraction and live in teepees unsuited to the place's heat). During the early years when organizations in the temperate zone's industrial nations were first beginning to worry about tropical rainforests, many of the would-be saviors believed they were trying to save virgin wildernesses: They pictured those faraway places in the terms national parks had taught them, as prehuman primeval landscapes. The realization that the Amazon, for example, had had a population of several million before the Europeans arrived, and that many indigenous and adapted people were still there, living sustainably, eventually generated links between social justice and environmental movements, then taught the temperate-zone activists to see the issues as one issue. In South and Central America, parks, debt-for-nature swaps, and preserves sometimes provide an excuse to displace indigenous and adaptive inhabitants, whose absence opens up the land for new exploitation. Susan Hecht and Alexander Cockburn, in their book on the Amazonian rainforest and its people, *The Fate of the Forest,* call such ecological preserves "Edens under glass from which the local populations are excluded, denied any role in the sustaining of the ecosystem. . . . Few conservation areas incorporated local populations, an approach which can be traced back to John Muir's Yosemite National Park."

✢

In Yosemite, the answer to the question of what nature is has begun to change in recent decades. During most of its career as a national park, its managers thought of fire as a purely destructive force. It may be that the still, calm picture of nature they cherished had no room in it for such force and such abrupt transformation. And in Europe, forest litter had long been gathered for fuel, so fire was an unnecessary evil. Olmsted had enumerated it among the dangers to Yosemite's environment in his 1865 report: "Indians and others have set fires to the forests and herbage and numbers of trees have been killed by these fires; the giant tree referred to as probably the noblest tree now standing on the earth has been burned completely through the bark near the ground. . . ." Later on, the fire orphans Smokey the Bear and Bambi became popular figures in educating the public to regard burning as unequivocally disastrous, and park policy was to suppress all fires. The longer they were suppressed, the more disastrous they became. Every year without fire piled the forest litter thicker, so that if a fire were to come, it would burn hotter and longer and fulfill every dread.

In the late 1960s, however, foresters began to wonder why the sequoia trees in the park weren't regenerating. It turned out that even these serene giants need to be disturbed to renew themselves. Sequoia cones often hang closed on the trees until the heat of a fire causes them to fall and burst and release their seeds; and a recent burn creates the rich mineral earth in which they best germinate and establish themselves. In the 1970s, a fire history of the Mariposa Grove since the sixth century A.D. was reconstructed with cross sections from dead trees. Fifteen years was the longest interval between fires until the late 1800s, and the study concluded that the frequency had kept fires superficial. In 1988, Yellowstone had devastating forest fires as a result of the long-term policy of fire suppression, and in 1990 Yosemite also had fires whose ferocity was brought about by a century of suppression and years of drought, serious enough that the valley was evacuated. Old trees that might have survived a superficial fire burned through in the huge flames fed on decades of accumulated litter.

Without fire, incense cedars flourished in Yosemite Valley, and much of the vistas and open woodlands had disappeared in these young trees—including more than half the meadow area in the valley. When Totuya/Maria Lebrado returned to the valley after seventy-eight years, she complained it was "dirty" and "bushy," for there were trees and shrubs where meadows had been, and undergrowth in the forest, and photographs reiterate what she says: The early ones show a patchwork of dark trees and lighter grasslands, while in the recent ones the light areas are islands in a sea of darkness. Finally, in the 1970s, controlled burnings were initiated. A plaque in a restored meadow says, "Two hundred years ago the Valley's meadows were much more extensive. Oak groves like the one across the way were larger and healthier. By setting fire to the meadows, and allowing natural fires to burn unchecked, the Valley's Native American inhabitants burned out the oak's competitors and kept down the underbrush for clearer shots at deer. With leaf litter burned away, it was easier to gather acorns—the Indians' main food source. Without fires incense-cedars are encroaching on the left side of the meadow and beginning to shade out the oaks. But now with controlled fires the NPS is reintroducing a natural process." The plaque proposes an answer to the question posed at the beginning of this chapter: It asserts Indians are natural, and so is their burning, and it begins to intimate that therefore the National Park Service can have hopes of being natural too. It represents a long journey from the definition of natural posed by McKibben.

The environment within the park has changed in many other ways. The rivers and streams have been stocked with nonnative trout for the pleasure of anglers; grizzlies, wolves, and bighorn sheep have disappeared (the sheep are being reintroduced, but the California grizzly now exists only in a few taxidermic examples and on the state flag). Nonnative plant species have moved in, particularly in the valley. In 1879, Park Guardian Galen Clark blasted away a natural rock dam at the western end of the valley, on the grounds that the marshy meadows around it bred mosquitos. As a result, the nearby water table dropped. The leave-only-footprints credo is apparently not good enough either. Heavily used trails in the meadows have compressed the earth to a depth of about three feet, creating a network of earthen dams across the valley that prevent subterranean water flow. Some of the meadows have been fenced off and the trails dug up to leaven the earth.

Sue Fritzke, a smart young plant ecologist in the Park Service who probably wouldn't even have tried to answer the question about what nature was, told me about the trails and other restoration projects one sunny day as we sat at a picnic table under an oak near her office. Steller's jays scolded around us, and squirrels darted at early acorns. Instead, she described the place as a living system, an ecology whose influences were wide, and which she wanted to see become healthy, rather than something so ambiguous and ideological as natural. She wasn't trying to get the environment back to anything at all, because that was impossible anyway. "We can't go back, we can only go forward," was the phrase that punctuated all her explanations. Her goal was not to try to re-create a lost state, but to work toward making the place into a more supple, self-sustaining system, one that could regenerate after flood and fire, and to allow the reestablished ecology to do the final restoration. "Our department is misnamed. It's the human management department: We mitigate human impacts," she told me. The Park Service was doing a lot of things—digging up and shutting down some of the compressed paths, burning the meadows, restoring the riverbanks, removing nonnative plants, and replanting native ones. But many of the changes are permanent.

Her own particular project had been black-oak restoration. Using old journals and photographs, she had been able to determine that black oaks only covered ten percent of their mid-nineteenth-century area. Lack of burning is a major factor, and so is the proliferation of deer, which have jumped in population thanks to lack of predators. "One of the major predators was the Native American," she said. In her picture, the relationship between the trees and the people was reciprocal: Their burning and hunting helped sustain the trees, and the trees provided them with acorns. And she was for acorn gathering, as long as the gatherers checked in with the Park Service beforehand. Her restoration project had been sponsored by Chevron, the oil corporation, which had recruited some of its employees to help her plant 750 seedlings in the winter of 1989. And the corporation took credit for its donation with signs all around the seedlings, which were encased in little openwork plastic tubes to prevent them from being eaten by deer or stepped on by people and made the park look tackier that winter. She had tried to teach a little in a roundabout way to the oil-industry employees she worked with, emphasizing that an oak is only as viable as the air and water it depends upon, is part of the global picture, not an island of naturalness (and Yosemite's pines are being damaged by air pollution from cars). She got frostbite on her kneecaps from the planting. And she had learned something from it. The Chevron seedlings of 1989 didn't do very well, but the Chevron money let them study the black oak's growth patterns. It turned out that they grow in generations thirty or forty years apart, and the generation launched in 1991 was thriving. As we finished our conversation under the oaks, we heard the whine of a jet overhead. "Navy," she said, and added that ground-to-air missiles ought to be part of her toolbox, since low-flying jets frighten peregrine falcons into abandoning their nests.

The Ahwahneechee, and most of the Indians of California, are usually described as hunters and gatherers. The term evokes simple activities whose effect on the environment is limited by low populations and limited technologies, as though they were simply skimming off the surplus of an ecology they left unaffected. This belief played a part in the nineteenth-century idea that the land was not really put to use (and could only belong to those who worked it) and the twentieth-century idea that the landscape was somehow untouched before white incursions, was still wilderness, or virgin, or natural, or any of those adjectives connoting independence. Burning begins to change this, to suggest that the people in question created the environment that sustained them. In this picture, they not only reaped the bounty of the land but helped to generate it—not only with burning, but with many other techniques which make it hard to regard agriculture and hunting and gathering as such neat opposites. The newest version to enter Euro-American culture portrays California's indigenous people as far more complex in their interactions with the land, and far more powerful—the land as not wilderness but something far more complex, and interdependent with its human population.

The ethnobotanist Kat Anderson has drawn up the finest revision of what gathering meant in the Yosemite area, based on years of studying plants in the region and talking to Miwoks who remember traditional ways. Yosemite exists in many different versions in its literature, from the most popular histories that relate the succession of great men in the unchanging beauty of the place, to the more specialized literature of anthropology, to this radical version of the long relationship between people and ecology. This last one exists mostly in unpublished college and professional manuscripts, conversations, a few magazine articles, and has always been around in the thought of the people about whom these documents report. Anderson describes a world in which hunting and gathering are wholly inadequate terms to describe the way the Ahwahneechee and the Southern Sierra Miwok interacted with the plants. Nor does agriculture quite define what she calls "a variety of horticultural techniques which enabled them to directly influence the diversity, quantity, and quality of plant resources. In fact, plant manipulations of the California landscape were so extensive, varied, and were conducted in a manner which allowed certain plants to regenerate so completely that virtually every settler, gold miner, ethnographer, and missionary was fooled into thinking that the land they saw was 'virgin.'"

Agriculture involves the eradication of one landscape for another, and the sowing of seeds which are then usually dependent upon continued involvement for their survival, which may not be past harvest. Its straight lines and segregated crops propose that the agriculturalist cannot find order in the natural world, but need write a simpler order over the original one. In *Walden* Thoreau speaks of making the land "say beans," but in the methods Anderson describes, the landscape isn't made to say anything new or alien, only to shift emphasis. These methods cause the existing plant resources to increase their productivity and, sometimes, their range, but do not domesticate them in the usual sense of the word. They are part of a long-term involvement in specific areas at specific times of year that does not fit in with the idea of wandering groups gathering the bounty where it may be found. It seems instead a supple and subtle way between gathering wild plants and cultivating tame ones. The activity involves not merely taking something from the plants, but giving something back: The plants that supply the stuff of life are tended and enhanced, so that the relationship is symbiotic. And this symbiosis affected a wide range of plants and environments.

The Miwok could, Anderson reports, "identify by name, describe the growth habits, and denote other characteristics of over 256 species of plants found in seven different plant communities, gathered for basketry, food and medicinal areas." Many of the plants they gathered had roots, sprouts, bulbs, and other portions that could be left behind to regenerate if they were collected properly. Digging itself could aerate the soil and increase reproduction of bulbs and tubers that were used as food. Arrows and baskets were made from plants whose shoots and branches had to be straight; otherwise the baskets would be crooked and leaky, the arrows wouldn't reach their targets. Burning and pruning encouraged the growth of straight new shoots which could be harvested for such purposes and are rarely found in untended plants. All the plants used for basketry and arrowmaking, Anderson states, "are sprouters. This means that if the branches are damaged or broken in some way through herbivory, a lightning fire, or flooding, the plant responds to the disturbance by vigorously sprouting branches and ground stems." And she goes on to write that the wide variety of horticultural practices were often beneficial to the plants used. Such was the belief of their users. "Often contemporary Indian gatherers mention that deliberate disturbance of the habitat is not only nondetrimental to certain plant species, but actually maintains or enhances the availability of certain plants. Today among the Indian families there is a feeling that using the plants and interacting with them is regenerative. When they are not used, they deteriorate in quality, and become senescent, depleted, or even eliminated."

Sue Fritzke had talked about these ideas too. The kind of plants growing in Yosemite Valley, she told me, was largely the work of its original inhabitants, but it would take about 400 full-time gardeners to maintain it as they did. Had it not been for them, the valley might have been nothing more than a dense forest of conifers. Which is to say that when Bunnell, Olmsted, and their peers rode into the valley and wondered at it for its resemblance to an English landscape garden, it resembled such a garden because it *was* one, an explanation that never occurred to them and their successors. Had it truly been uninhabited wilderness, they might have instead entered a forest so dense that the waterfalls and rock faces they glimpsed from above would not have been easily visible from the valley itself. And this is where Kat Anderson's use of the word *horticulture* in place of *agriculture* is illuminating: *agri* comes from an old French word for fields, but *horti* from the Latin for gardens. She is, in other words, calling them gardeners, and saying they had made for themselves a garden useful as well as beautiful, as nurturing to the body as it was to the eye. The touchstone for wilderness turns out to be an artifact of generations of human care. So the model for all the park preserves of wilderness or pure nature around the world turns out to be no more independent than any other garden, and the deterioration of its ecology is as much the story of a garden gone unweeded as a wilderness civilized.

Stories appear when we are ready to hear them, and this story of the American garden comes at a time when many are sadly relinquishing the idea of an independent nature. McKibben's *The End of Nature* mourns the end of a natural world apart from human beings, but it may be instead the end of a story that was only told for a century or two, a simple, pure story for the youth of the ecology movement. The idea of an independent nature was crucial to John Muir, was the premise of establishing the national parks and the conservation movement. It has grown up and broadened its horizons into something less concerned with putting picture-frame fences around the exceptional places than with recognizing the interconnection of all things, the world as an *interdependent* network of systems rather than a compendium of scenes of varying quality. In recent times, it has become hard to regard places and species as so neatly set apart from culture: Acid rain and fallout land on the mountaintops regardless of whether anyone has climbed them, fall on the forests and the towns alike. But if we have to give up this story of virgin wilderness at its end, the end Rachel Carson describes of chemical incursions into every corner of the globe, then it may hearten us to give it up at its beginning too. By giving it up, we can lay to rest some of the misanthropy of old-fashioned conservationists and recognize that culture does not necessarily destroy nature, and that the ravages of those in a hurry are not the only pattern in the book.

The Name of the Snake

✚ So the Ahwahneechee didn't disappear, they just became invisible. And perhaps that was enough, enough to write a new history over the old one in the region and a new version of nature over the old one—except that the new version didn't work, because it was missing a key element. Even if the histories were silent about them, the land spoke of them. Still, a great many believed the Ahwahneechee had disappeared, and even more people pledged their faith to Yosemite as a temple of virgin nature, so that they were erased from the past as well as the present.

These facts give a new meaning to Bunnell's confrontation with Tenaya at the lake he named after the chief. When Bunnell took it upon himself to name the lake, the valley, and the other landmarks he came across, he was symbolically ending one history and beginning another. The New World wasn't always new—it was old to its original inhabitants, and it was a foreign country to its immigrants, but in the act of naming Bunnell was transforming himself from an invader or immigrant into a discoverer, making the place new, making a beginning. One state begins where another leaves off, and the New World of America began where the Old World of the first nations left off. They didn't really leave off, or disappear, or end, or anything so convenient, but it was enough for most people to believe they had. If the vanishing Indian and the virgin wilderness are the characters and landscape of the popular imagination, then they occupy the crucial place for political decisions and cultural representations, whatever their presence or absence in the real landscape.

Being true means nothing in the country of the imagination, and being believed means everything.

Naming is a form of claiming. Parents name their children, priests baptize their flock, husbands confer their names upon their wives, explorers name what they come across—whether it's Fremont naming the Humboldt River after another explorer or Martin Heinrich Klaproth naming the element uranium after the god of the underworld. To name a thing is to assert that a new identity has begun, as a baptized person embarks upon a new life as a Christian, a woman as a wife, a hitherto unknown element as a subject for science. But for those who renamed the Western Hemisphere the Americas, the first epic of naming came in Genesis, when Adam named the animals in the newly created Paradise.

The sense of newness was crucial to American identity, particularly during the nineteenth century. The nation's newness which had been seen as a flaw, a lack of historical weight and tradition, was reinterpreted as a virtue, as the lack of stains, decay, decrepitude, as the mark of a nation looking forward and taking its meaning from its future. Having shrugged off the burdens of Europe, America signified a new dawn, a blank slate, a paradise regained. And the image of this New World as Paradise and Eden occurs over and over again in the painting and writing of the time. The literary historian R. W. B. Lewis identifies the hero of this New World. "The new habits to be engendered on the new American scene were suggested by the image of a radically new personality, the hero of the new adventure: an individual emancipated from history, happily bereft of ancestry, untouched and undefiled by the usual inheritances of family and race; an individual standing alone, self-reliant and self-propelling, ready to confront whatever awaited him with the aid of his own unique and inherent resources. It was not surprising, in a Bible-reading generation, that the new hero (in praise or disapproval) was most easily identified with Adam before the Fall. Adam was the first, the archetypal, man. His moral position was prior to experience, and in his very newness he was fundamentally innocent. The world and history lay all before him. And he was the type of creator, the poet par excellence, creating language itself by naming the elements of the scene about him."

It was that Adamic act which transformed explorers and invaders into discoverers, at least in their own minds. The newness of this hemisphere, like the emptiness of its landscape, had to be manufactured, and it was made by painters, photographers, writers, namers, and gunslingers equally. It explains why Euro-Americans so deeply believe that Indians have vanished and the landscape has been born again as a place that was always empty. It explains why Thoreau in his essay "Walking" insisted that the backwoodsman, not the Indian, was the true Adam. It explains why the uninhabited landscape is so crucial an icon in American culture and so rare elsewhere. If the composition of the landscape painting, and the landscape photograph after it, is of stage scenery, then the uninhabited landscape signifies the New World before the drama had begun. It is full of possibility, and its heroes are in the wings or in the East or, in some of the U.S. Geological Survey photographs of the 1870s, in the foreground about to start out for the expanse that lies before them like the future itself. In Ansel Adams's photographs of Yosemite, the Claudian composition is largely preserved: The forms of the land frame an empty space at center, but in his works the foreground is often missing, the camera seems to hover in the air, and the emptiness is so majestic it seems that nothing could ever fill it, that the stage will always remain before and beyond human drama, that the American landscape is the natural home of divinity alone. It is as though that breathtaking moment when one steps into an unfamiliar landscape, that glorious pause when memory and time itself seem suspended, was mistaken all through the incursions as an objective fact of discovery rather than a personal epiphany. It may have something to do with why men often want to be first into the wilderness and why they often imagine they have been.

In Genesis, Adam wants a helpmeet, but God instead brings forth all the animals for him to name, and only after the fowl of the air and the beasts of the field are named does his Creator get around to making woman out of his rib. According to Robert Graves and Raphael Patai's *Hebrew Myths,* naming is a euphemism or substitute activity. In the original version Adam couples with all the creatures in quest of a satisfactory mate, and when his experiments with the animals prove unsatisfying Eve arrives for his use.

Nowhere is naming as a form of sexual possession more evident than in the West. Invasion was described in highly erotic terms. The land was virgin, untouched, undiscovered, unspoiled, and its discoverer penetrated the wilderness, conquered it, set his mark upon it, claimed it, took possession of it with the planting of his flag or with the plough that broke the plains. "And here we are once more upon the prairies, and surrounded by nature in all her purity and her bloom. No plough has ever furrowed these fields, nor has the axe sullied the loveliness of these groves," rhapsodized James Henry Carleton in 1845. Wilderness made "a sublime mistress but an intolerable wife," declared Emerson in a letter to Muir. *Wilderness* comes from the same root as will and willfulness; the word means land with a will of its own—in Emerson's language, an independent woman who needs to be domesticated. The sexual possessiveness of the Victorian husband seems to have transferred readily to the landscape imagined as bride or concubine, and the contemporary desire that land be virgin seems to come out of that need to be the first (and early settlers often moved on when they could see the smoke of another's chimney). Like Huckleberry Finn afraid Aunt Sally was going to civilize him, explorers lit out for the territory where they could be Adam before Eve.

In this arrangement, the naming of places and obliteration of their earlier names can signify a marriage in which the bride takes on the identity of her spouse. And to see the land as bride rather than mother reinforces its newness, for a land that is a mother has created her sons, while these sons from a strange land attempted to create a landscape which would yield to their will and bear their names, a blank landscape waiting for them to begin writing a new history across her rather than read what was already there. If the land itself fulfills the role of bride or conquest, then it is possible to understand why women played so little role in this early phase: why they accompanied so few expeditions, why places were occasionally given women's names but they almost never did the naming. Women are superfluous, because the land itself fills our shoes, or nightgowns.

If the drama has not yet begun, then there is nothing to remember, and the American capacity for amnesia may be grounded in this view. I grew up in a town called Novato, named after a Coast Miwok chief who had been baptized with the name of the obscure Saint Novatus, but saint and chief and even the Miwok have been forgotten by the townspeople. Nor do the people of Kentucky reflect much on the meaning of the word, which means "dark and bloody place," or the Missourians on the origin of their state's name in a Lakota word for "water flowing along." Names spread and lose their original meaning: Canada was the name of a village that became a country; a town Cabeza de Vaca stumbled across in Florida, Apalachen, was the origin of the name for the mountain chain that stretches hundreds of miles northward. Like the Tomb of the Unknown Soldier, many of the names across the country are monuments to what has been forgotten. Tuscarora in northern Nevada is a mining ghost town named after a Civil War battleship named after one of the tribes in the Iroquois Confederacy of the Northeast. Spanish and Anglo-European names are nearly as obscure: In San Francisco, few think of Saint Francis presiding over the long-dead politicians whose names crisscross each other like conspiracies in the streets—Polk, who started the war with Mexico, Larkin his consul in the then foreign country of California, Stockton a soldier who led the U.S. Army against Mexico in the state, Sutter who lost by that war and the discovery of gold, Castro a Mexican-era governor. Berkeley was named by a gentleman who watched the sun set from there in 1866 and was inspired to declare, "Westward the course of empire takes its way"—a phrase of the poet-philosopher Bishop Berkeley.

And perhaps it is all right for names to mean nothing but themselves, for Flagstaff to stir no musing about flags but to call to mind only the Arizona city among the pines, for Elko to cease to be resonant with elk-hunting aspirations, for Los Angeles to live down its angels. Most of these names speak of the places themselves to us, and nothing else. Names grow old associations of their own, and Berkeley and Appalachia are resonant without the histories, part of a hybrid new language. The mix of slang and description and importation and aboriginal phrase rings on the ear like the strange compost of American culture itself.

But the scattering of names across the land is a cipher of its history. As Utah is sprinkled with the Old Testament names that gave resonance to the Mormon emigration there, so California is overlaid with the sanctifying names of the Spanish missionaries, from the sacrament itself in the state's capital to the list of saints trailing down the coast. Other Spanish names are descriptive: Mariposa for the butterflies that menaced Moraga's expedition, the Sierra Nevada for their snow. Anglo names supplanted the original sense of place and the religiosity of the Spanish with secular authority—kings and queens in Virginia, Georgia, Maryland; and after the U.S. war of independence, politicians and dignitaries. The names of the peaks in a western mountain range often sound like the roster of a board of directors. Josiah Whitney, director of the state's Geological Survey, named the tallest peak yet found by his men in the Sierra after himself, then hastened to transfer his name to the taller mountain that turned up afterward, the current Mount Whitney. One of his surveyors, William Brewer, wrote, "As we had named the other mountain Mount Dana, after the most eminent of American geologists, we named this Mount Lyell, after the most eminent of English geologists." Though Brewer's casualness is a little unsettling—people deliberate longer over naming pets—these geologists seem among the few figures who merit the ancient mass of a mountain named after them. It is they who in the pivotal years of geology opened up the back door of Genesis's 6,000-year-old Creation to reveal another several billion years stretching out behind it, expanding the time of a world whose space was shrinking.

It may be the speed of development and scope of travel that necessitated the quick naming of the continent, so that where European and Native American names seem to have grown up with a place, American names are often tacked on and don't always stay. The explorers and invaders didn't have time to wait for an appropriate name to come, nor were descriptive terms adequate for mapping a continent, however well they might describe the landmarks of a locality. They were more interested in imposing a history on the land than reading one from it. Lewis and Clark named the river that flowed northwest to the Columbia (named after Columbus) the Lewis River and a large stream the Clark. Clark's name stuck, but the Lewis River became the Shoshone, for the people at its southern end. Then it became the Snake, because Shoshone could be thus translated, though the river is usually thought to have been named for its sinuousness.

Shoshone is a name given to the Newe by another people; as Navajo, or thieves, was given to the Dine; Sioux, or snake, to the Lakota/Dakota by their enemies; and Eskimo, or eaters of raw flesh, to the Inuit. Later on, Indian tribal names became popular for many things, including cars, from the Chevrolet Apaches of the 1950s to the Jeep Cherokees of the 1980s, though the rocketships of the era got the names of Roman gods instead—Apollo, Jupiter, Saturn. A series of seventeen nuclear bombs dropped in the South Pacific in 1956 bore tribal names, from Apache and Erie to Yuma and Zuni. In recent years the old name Denali has been restored to the great Alaskan peak tagged with the name of a less great president, McKinley, like a divorcée taking back her maiden name. Native names were sometimes used very loosely, out of a nationalism determined to keep American places from becoming homages to the Old World. The British wanted to name the giant trees of California *Wellingtonias,* in honor of the duke who defeated Napoleon at Waterloo, but he got little more than rubber boots—wellingtons, or wellies, in English slang—to commemorate him. Yankees named the trees after the Cherokee scholar and educator Sequoyah, who invented an alphabet so that his people could become literate in their own language—though he had little more to do with the Far West than the British commander. This relocation of indigenous names to places seems to imply that the originals are gone and no longer need them, much as the giving of one's own name prepares the place as a monument, but McKinley is gone and the Cherokee are not.

Early settlers often left their names on the land as Lee Vining did at Mono Lake, and explorers sometimes named places out of sheer peevishness, as the Spanish did with the Jornada del Muerte in New

Mexico; and as Fremont did with the Great Salt Lake's Disappointment Island when he found it had no game on it (now Fremont Island); and as the gold seekers who took an unwise southern detour to Death Valley did. Bloody Canyon east of Yosemite was apparently named that because the horses used to pursue the Ahwahneechee were cut by sharp rocks, and equine bones littered the pass in the 1860s. Perhaps the nastiest name in Yosemite is Three Brothers, which Bunnell made up for a formation that had been called "Kompo-pai-zes." Bunnell recorded that name as "mountains playing leapfrog," since "a literal translation is not desirable." He was skirting the sexual meaning of the name, which apparently came from an interpretation of the formation—three stacked peaks—as resembling a copulating couple. During the 1851 Mariposa War, five Ahwahneechee men were captured among the peaks and held as hostages, including Tenaya's three sons. One of the brothers was allowed to untie himself by a guard who then shot him in the back for trying to escape. "From the strange coincidence of three brothers being made prisoners so near them, we designated the peaks as the 'Three Brothers.' " Bunnell coyly gives another place name in Greek for its apparent reference to pissing (because Victorians considered educated minds less prone to corruption, such words were translated into languages whose obscurity indicated their degree of obscenity).

Had the old names been kept, the newcomers would have been emigrants, not discoverers. The great charm of the Belgian goldminer Jean-Nicholas Perlot is that he came to the Sierra foothills as to a foreign country rather than a manifest destiny, came to it as a place in the middle of a story rather than waiting for one to begin, without the sense of himself as a new Adam or the Indians as obstacles to a new Eden. As befits an immigrant, he learned the languages, English, Spanish, and Miwok. Changing the names is a symbolic substitute for wiping out the people, and in looking at the language of the newcomers, particularly in Yosemite, the constant conjunction of the words *extermination* and *aboriginal* captures this. Exterminate comes from *terminate,* to end, ab-original means *from the beginning,* and so the phrase means to terminate the originals, end the beginning, and begin again in the middle, making Adams out of Europeans in an Eden wrested from some people who didn't fit into the new story.

Perhaps the greatest irony in this scheme of virginity comes in the policy that people not touch the plant life in Yosemite except for the apple trees planted by the squatters of the 1860s. Signs explain that the balance of nature requires that the wildlife abstain from non-native food and the humans refrain from native food, and visitors are urged, like so many Adams and Eves, to eat an apple from the gnarled old trees, themselves presumed intruders in that mock paradise.

The Ahwahneechee seem to have named places after stories associated with them or after the resemblance of a natural feature to a bodily part or an animal (which survives rarely in Euro-American names, such as the Grand Tetons and Great Neck). Yosemite Valley itself its inhabitants called Ahwahnee, or Big Mouth, for its shape; their name for themselves, Ahwahneechee, means People of the Big-mouth Valley. The name survives only in the name of the Ahwahnee luxury hotel, but it's a nice description. One evening I was walking in a big meadow near the hotel and looked up in one of the few really open places: I could see the north and south walls of rock curving together at each end and rouged by the setting sun—like lips, I thought, and then I realized *like a mouth* and stumbled back upon the sense of the name that way.

Yosemite itself was named at that campfire near Bridalveil—or *Pohono,* gust of wind—Fall the first night white men ever spent in the place. "Some romantic and foreign names were offered . . . a very large number were canonical and Scripture names," records Bunnell, who himself proposed Yosemite. As he said when naming Lake Tenaya, the name would commemorate the people who had been removed. One of the men said, "Devil take the Indians and their names! Why should we honor these vagabonds and murderers by perpetuating their name?" And another said, "_____ the Indians and their names. Let's call this Paradise Valley." The naming question went to a voice vote, and the place became Yosemite for them. Then Bunnell went and asked Savage what the name meant. Savage confessed that the local dialect gave him trouble, though he understood many other native languages of the region, and then he told them that the name meant Grizzly Bear. The name had been given to Tenaya's band because of their "lawless and predatory character," Bunnell tells us. Savage's translation is still almost universally believed and is still the version on all the park signage.

No interpreter thought to ask a native speaker for more than a century. The linguist Sylvia Broadbent did research on the word and came to very different conclusions in a study she published in the 1960s. Park ethnologist Craig Bates made this research slightly more available in the 1970s, as a footnote in a park brochure, but it remains a largely unknown correction. It is true that *uzumati* means grizzly bear, but Yosemite is apparently a version of another Miwok word, *yohemiteh,* which means *some among them are killers.* Nearly all literature, from the volume on park names to the plaque in the Indian village, still translates Yosemite as *grizzly.* The first source I found that translated it correctly claimed that the killers in question were the whites, which would be a tidy irony—the invaders unwittingly naming the area after their own savagery. But the term is a derogatory or hostile one that other Miwok used for the valley's inhabitants who had intermarried with the Paiutes around Mono Lake: They generally feared and distrusted Paiutes. Some-Among-Them-Are-Killers National Park: a place whose name is a monument to hostile incomprehension itself.

✚ IF A STORY IS A KIND OF PATH, AS I HAVE SAID BEFORE, THEN a group of stories makes up a spider's web of paths, a map. And the stories we hear first, the ones that go down like mother's milk and become the forgotten material of our bones, are the maps that guide us, whether we notice them again or not. Genesis, the Judeo-Christian story of Creation, is such a map, and long after Darwin and the geologists did in most people's literal belief in a seven-day Creation, the premises of Genesis are still with us. A great poem, it's unavoidable in understanding Judeo-Christian worldviews, but I think it's a misleading map for the American West. In explaining origins, a creation story explains the current order of things, but the order Genesis explains seems grounded in the world it came from, not the world to which it was brought. Eden was between the Tigris and Euphrates in Iraq, not Yosemite; Armageddon is in Israel, not southern Nevada.

The Western explorers, those would-be Adams, those namers and readers of the Biblical map, thought of the land they arrived in as new in the absolute sense, rather than new to them; a place waiting for them to invent rather than a place they needed to learn. Even now, many in the conservation movement think in a way that owes much to the story of the Fall: Their belief in a static natural order before the intervention of man—Eden on day four or five—is behind their efforts, and the photographs that support this worldview show only the before and after, the madonna and whore, of untouched perfection and manmade disasters, never the during of coexistence. Perhaps a few alternate route maps would dilute the Edenic and apocalyptic tendencies of its immigrant populace and help them imagine a place where the *during* might endure.

Read archaeologically, the first few chapters of Genesis explain much about the explorers, if not about the land they explored. Genesis's first three heroines disappeared as the story evolved. The monstrous goddess out of whose defeated body the world was made and Adam's first wife, Lilith, who was insubordinate, have disappeared altogether from the story, and Eve, whose name means *mother of all,* is framed as a bringer of death rather than life. (In some alternate readings of this pervasive Near Eastern story, the fall was fortunate and Eve was worshipped for her conversations with serpents and plucking of the fruit of knowledge.) So it can be read as a story suppressing and expressing ideas about the role of women, and of the feminine principle in the order of things, particularly the expectation that earth and matter are passive and inert, to be done to rather than doing—a worldview crucial to scientific ideas of controlling matter and nature. Viewed in this light, Genesis becomes a political treatise bent on reattributing creative and procreative power to immaterial and masculine principles.

"For thousands of years myths of the creation and philosophical discourse have subordinated matter, or the feminine, to form, or the masculine," writes the German theorist Gerburg Treusch-Dieter. "The radiating spirit shapes the feminine, that which is passive and conceiving." He proposes that this order came to an end at Chernobyl, with the catastrophic nuclear power plant meltdown in 1986. It may look that way from Germany, but from here it looks like that epochal transformation began forty-one years earlier, with the first nuclear explosion, with Trinity. The fall from grace serves as an excellent allegory for the making of the atom bomb, with the physicists tempted by knowledge and a power they thought they could control, and with this transition accompanied by an exodus to the desert of New Mexico. And it was a fall that changed the nature of nature and the place of people within it with a kind of Biblical violence, a sequel to Genesis that undid some of its assumptions. But it was an imported drama acted out on the deserts of the West. As the nineteenth century had read death into the desert, the twentieth century wrote it there, with the fallout of nuclear tests.

The early chapters of Genesis can also be read as an allegory of Near Eastern history, of the transition from hunting and gathering to agriculture. Thus it becomes a story about the charms of the hunting and gathering life, its freedom from laboriousness, if not from exertion, and from the relative misery of agricultural labor. If the Fall was into agriculture, then much of this continent was still Edenic—but the nineteenth-century Bible-reading Americans were determined to see it as their Eden and no one else's, even if they were importing the curse of agricultural toil (and for many such as Muir, it was a curse). The expulsion from the garden has also been read as a description of the degradation of the once-lush Middle East by millennia of overgrazing. In this case too, the importation of domesticated herds and the attempts to turn the native peoples of the Americas into "agriculturalists and herdsmen," as the Treaty of Ruby Valley puts it, is likewise an attempt not to bring the Garden to them, but to force them out of it. But as most of us learned in kindergarten, even the puritanical pilgrims of the *Mayflower* learned agricultural techniques and acquired new crops from the Massachusetts tribes whose land they settled on, so the idea of such an epochal rupture is too simple for what happened on this continent. The earlier inhabitants weren't anything so exotic as innocents or savages, just more products of old cultures. The constant quest for watersheds, whether it's an announcement of the discovery of a place or the close of the frontier or the capture of the last wild man, is itself symptomatic of a reading of history as made up of definitive discontinuities.

For Yosemite, Genesis has been pernicious: The landscape was nothing so static as Eden, nor was it a garden divinely made without the intervention of people. A lot of the problems that have bedeviled it as an ecology seem rooted in such Edenic assumptions. Such thinking prevented the fires and discounted the human effect on that landscape until the subsequent human effect was disastrous. The tendency Genesis encourages—to think in paired opposites—nature/culture, before/after, wild/tame, wilderness/garden, perfect/flawed—is itself a blinding factor. Yosemite existed in a middle ground as a tended wilderness with a long habitation which wasn't terminated by the Mariposa Battalion and shows no sign of disappearing from the region.

Histories of conquest are stories of disjuncture, and the great curse of Euro-American history is its shallowness, its failure to take root in a place so different from its place of origin. There are other countries which have absorbed their conquerors, but the States can't absorb an immigrant population which can't remember where it is or who preceded it to the place. It is conquerors and invaders, not the conquered or invaded, who have lost their roots, their ties, their sense of place. Amnesia is one potent means of overcoming the traumatic dislocation of the conqueror: Rather than lacking a personal past in a particular place, the amnesiac lacks the past. Invention is the other means, the means by which a place is covered up with decorative motifs and fantasies; and for the U.S. the Bible has provided many of the principal embroideries scattered across the continent that was so blank to its invaders. Pretending that the place is somewhere else, whether it means naming it Zion or "making the desert bloom" by redistributing fabulous quantities of water, has been one way of coping. But the inability to remember the past becomes the inability to imagine the future, and it is not surprising that a country with a ten- or hundred-year past can't make wise decisions about the long-term future. There are other maps.

✜

My friend Lewis deSoto, who is Cahuilla, gave me the Cahuilla creation story, which provides an elegant antidote to Genesis. Before this statement summons up visions of oral traditions passed along at campfires, I should mention that the story took the form of a photocopy from an anthropologist's transcription, and I was given it so that I could write an essay about his artwork for a museum catalogue. The art consisted of a series of rooms occupied by mechanical devices that retold the creation story in a present tense of luminous images and ambient sounds. In the course of the retelling, Lewis had assimilated all that technology—slide projectors, video monitors, speakers, sound dimmers—into Cahuilla cosmology. In the course of being asked to understand the story for his work, I began to find it very valuable for mine. "Genesis is a ceiling often mistaken for the sky," I wrote in one of the essays, but it was the story that gave me the clearest glimpse beyond it.

Cahuilla territory includes the mountains and desert east of Los Angeles, in which the Cahuilla people hunted, gathered, engaged in subtle horticultural activities something like the Ahwahneechees, and told stories in a complex, rhythmic language classified as Shoshonean. The Cahuilla creation myth—or song, since it's meant to be sung—begins with darkness, a fecund feminine darkness, which conceives a fiery egg that swings in the darkness. The egg fails to hatch, and the myth calls it a miscarriage. Darkness produces another egg, from which two brothers hatch. They argue over how to make the world—Mukat wants to make his people mortal so that the world won't become overpopulated, Temeyawat wants them to be immortal. Mukat wins the argument and his brother withdraws underground with all the creatures he made, except for the coyote, the eagle flower, the palm tree, and the fly. The story continues with incidents and misadventures, including the shooting of Mukat by his people, an act that demands neither redemption nor resurrection, just adjustment. The story grows without the kind of epochal ruptures of Genesis. It maps a very different world, one in which the acts of human beings don't despoil a static creation, but participate in a dynamic, ongoing, incomplete creation, a world where change is a given rather than an evil. As the darkness makes the gods, and the gods the creatures, so the creatures make tools and objects: Nature is not a fixed pattern, and the works of human beings are elaborations rather than disruptions of this flowing pattern.

Miwok creation myths seem similar in their lack of a central authority; instead the gods argue about how things should be, and the world goes on being made, not according to a master plan but through conversation and improvisation. Worldmaking is more like poetry and less like architecture. In Frank LaPena's version of an Ahwahneechee creation myth, six races are created in a series of misadventures that end in a deluge. Afterward Coyote decides to make a perfect people, the seventh, the human race, but he and Lizard fall to arguing over the right kind of hand to give them. Lizard wins the argument, Coyote walks across the earth planting two sticks in every place he gives a name to, and when the places are named, the sticks become men and women. The deities, Coyote and Lizard included, become animals, and the people are taught by these animal inhabitants of an intelligent, named world, a world where nature is culture.

And culture is natural in a genesis story of the Yowlumni, a southern Yokut group from the Tule Lake region of the San Joaquin Valley. The story relates how the first people lived for many years without language, and only the birds and animals could speak. These creatures taught the people language—Yowlumni—so that they might understand the world, and the language is thereby intrinsic to the landscape, not a casual addition, like the names Bunnell pinned on what he saw, or a means of control over it, like Adam's naming project. In the Yowlumni cosmology, forgetting of names is a tragedy for the things named as well as for the speakers of language. "Through learning the Yowlumni language and the teachings given them from creation, the people learned to pray, become ceremonial, and live good spiritual lives," says one of the twenty-five or so contemporary speakers, Matt Vera. "Through their prayers, the people found food-gathering areas, ceremonial sites, hunting grounds, materials for basket making and much other knowledge."

With such maps, the creation of the world is not finished on the seventh day, or ever; the creative process continues in a present that remains charged with danger and possibility; and there is room for the new as something other than a transgression. The gap between nature and culture is harder to find, as are a lot of simple opposites, and perfection is not a standard by which the world falls short. Without faith in perfection and its synonyms, the natural and the pure, the need to rush forward to Utopia and Armageddon or to strain nostalgically backward to Arcadian Eden vanishes like dew; the yearning for missing perfection which drives so much Euro-American activity is itself missing from this picture. They are tough, pragmatic myths that prepare their audience to engage with a flawed, lively present, not myths immigrant Americans can immerse themselves in as though no other cosmology exists, but ones that question the imported version beautifully.

✛

There is one more thing to be said about Genesis and Yosemite. Early in the Mariposa Battalion's pursuit of the Ahwahneechee, Bunnell remarked that "no doubt to Tenaya, this was a veritable Indian paradise." To which Major Savage replied, "Well, as far as that is concerned, although I have not carried a Bible with me since I became a mountain man, I remember well enough that Satan entered Paradise and did all the mischief he could, but I intend to be a bigger devil in this Indian Paradise than old Satan ever was; and when I leave, I don't intend to *crawl* out, either." He may have been a poor translator of the Ahwahneechee dialect, but he was a forthright interpreter of scripture.

Up the River of Mercy

✚ AT SOME POINT IN MY RAMBLINGS THROUGH THE WOODS AND manuscripts of Yosemite it occurred to me that Savage might be the thread that would tie all the various histories together, a touchstone for their ambiguities. An extraordinary character of great courage, recklessness, athletic prowess, linguistic talent, and unscrupulousness, he was famous—some said notorious—in his time. Now he is hardly remembered but as part of the first chapter of the Yosemite histories, a second false start, after the Ahwahneechee, to the main story.

As the ashes of the cremated dead are scattered to the winds, so the facts of Savage have been dispersed into a hundred brief mentions in memoirs on dusty shelves and more in manuscript collections, in letters in libraries, in gossip in the newspapers of the early Gold Rush. Much is missing, and he is hard to reconstruct from the dry fragments. A woman named Annie Mitchell wrote a short book for a local press on his relations with the native people of the San Joaquin Valley in the 1950s, and a worshipful young man self-published a less reliable one a decade later, which begins by transforming Savage from a man of modest stature into the "Big Jim Savage" of the title.

He was born in Indianapolis in 1823 and named after his paternal grandfather, an Irish mercenary. This James Savage had come over with the British to subdue the rebellious American colonies, and upon being captured at Ticonderoga switched sides. His namesake would play both sides in his own wars, the California Indian wars. His involvement with Native Americans began far earlier, though.

By all accounts, Savage spent a significant period of his childhood with the Sac and Fox, who lived in Illinois until they were pushed west after the Black Hawk War of 1832. In one version, he and his brother were captured, but in the 1851 newspaper version which seems to be his own, he went willingly out to join the "wild life of the aborigines" and stayed "long enough to learn their language and acquire their habits." Relatives queried in the 1920s—and it makes the 1920s seem less jazz-modern to realize that such things were remembered then—say he stayed until two girl cousins of his were captured and then made his escape. In yet another version, he rescued them too, including the one he married in 1845. He was already wild at heart, and among the family stories is one that he wouldn't go to church, but would ride up and make his horse kneel at the door while the children within stifled their laughs. A superb athlete, he was reputed to have been illiterate, though he spoke many languages.

A year after marriage to his cousin Eliza Hall, they joined the great westward migration, as did his brother Morgan. The year 1846 saw the trickle of wagons going all the way west become a flood: That spring there were 2,000 emigrants waiting in Independence, Missouri, for the grass to grow long enough to sustain the oxen across the plains. The Mormons had left early that spring, driven on to their Zion by persecutions and lynchings in Illinois and Missouri. Even the former governor of Missouri, Lilburn W. Boggs, was leaving, and the Savages joined up with the company he led. A man born the same year as Savage but utterly unlike him, the scholarly Boston Brahmin Francis Parkman went west too, and wrote a book about it, *The Oregon Trail*. He described Independence as crowded, full of shops sprung up to supply the emigrants and traders, "and there was an incessant hammering and banging from a dozen blacksmiths' sheds, where the heavy wagons were being repaired, and the horses and oxen shod. The streets were thronged with men, horses, and mules. While I was in the town, a train of emigrant wagons from Illinois passed through, to join the camp on the prairie, and stopped in the principal street. A multitude of healthy children's faces were peeping out from under the covers of the wagons. Here and there a buxom damsel was seated on horseback, holding over her sunburnt face an old umbrella or a parasol, once gaudy enough, but now miserably faded. The men, very sober-looking countrymen, stood about their oxen; and as I passed I noticed three old fellows, who with their long whips in their hands, were zealously discussing the doctrine of regeneration. The emigrants, however, are not all of this stamp. Among them are some of the vilest outcasts in the country. I have often perplexed myself to divine the various motives that give impulse to this migration; but whatever they may be, whether an insane hope of a better condition in life, or a desire of shaking off restraints of law and society, or mere restlessness . . ."

On April 9 the Boggs company left Independence. On May 13, President James K. Polk declared war with Mexico, news that wouldn't reach the emigrants until California. On May 19, the Donner-Reed Party, three well-to-do families from Springfield, Illinois, joined up with the Boggs company. The rate at which they went west was about a mile an hour, and twelve miles a day was a good steady rate, meaning that a week of their travel (Sundays off) was roughly equal to a speeding hour on an interstate now. They ate all the buffalo and antelope they wanted, and "we would hardly ever be out of sight of a band of from 100 to 1000 of these animals," records a member of the company, Jacob Harlan. "We proceeded very happily till we reached the South Platte. Every night we young folks had a dance in the green prairie." They reached it on the Fourth of July, three weeks after Fremont's men had attacked Sonoma, California, and declared the short-lived Bear Flag Republic, and the same month that Thoreau spent his famous night in jail for refusing to pay taxes to support the war against Mexico. Morgan Savage—after a disagreement with his brother, according to family speculation—had already cut north for Oregon, where he led the uneventful life of a farmer and raised twelve children; James stayed on the California trail. After the Platte, travel became harder. Parkman records, "No living thing was moving throughout the vast landscape, except the lizards that darted over the sand and through the rank grass and prickly pears at our feet. It is worth noticing that on the Platte one may sometimes see the shattered wrecks of ancient claw-footed tables, well waxed and rubbed, or massive bureaus of carved oak. . . . the stern privations of the way are little anticipated. The cherished relic is soon flung out to scorch and crack upon the hot prairie."

At Fort Bridger in Wyoming Territory, on July 18, the emigrants ran into Lansford Hastings, author of a guidebook to Oregon and California, who urged California emigrants to take a shortcut across the Bonneville Salt Flats, rather than the long loop around the Great Salt Lake. The Boggs Party continued on the longer route, but the Savages in one large party and the Donner-Reed families in another, smaller one took his advice and suffered horribly on their trek across the dazzling plain of pure salt. By the time the latter party had reached the Humboldt River they had fallen back seventy miles—nearly a week's time. Harlan describes the journey to the Great Salt Lake as "difficult and disagreeable" and worse afterward, when they encountered what must have been Western Shoshone people: "The Indians on the Humboldt were at this time hostile and very troublesome." The California-bound emigrants would have passed through what would later become the railroad town of Beowawe at the northern end of Crescent Valley, past the future Winnemucca, Lovelock, and all the other towns now strung like beads on the thread of the trickling Humboldt. Between the end of the Humboldt and the beginning of the Truckee was a waterless stretch nearly as bad as the Bonneville Salt Flats, and it was here, at a place called Steamboat Springs seven miles from the Truckee River, that Eliza Hall Savage died. Her husband buried her in an unmarked grave. Some accounts say there was a child, which died soon after, others that the child had died before its mother. Savage must have set out as a family man aspiring to nothing more than a farm in the rich and well-advertised soil of Oregon or California, indistinguishable from all the other young men trudging west. But he crossed the Sierra Nevada as an unattached adventurer, entering the world on the other side of the mountains with his plans abandoned and his prospects unknown.

In Sacramento on October 15, he enlisted for three months in Company F of the U.S. Army, which was engaged in a fight for California with no certain outcome. Pay was twenty dollars a month. Company A was the elite cadre, including seasoned and celebrated mountain men such as Kit Carson and other members of Fremont's expeditions. Company H's muster roll included 32 men with Hispanic first names and no last names—Indians with mission contact—recruited in the San Joaquin region, as well as some Walla Wallas from much further north, who became known as the forty thieves because their principal duty was to steal horses and cattle from the enemy. It was among these men of Company H that Savage is thought to have struck up the friendships that later eased his way into the San Joaquin Valley west of Yosemite. Savage's own company included two Shoshone men and was led by the same Lansford Hastings who had blithely sent the Donner-Reed Party on his disastrous shortcut. On October 24, the diarist of the Boggs company met up with Savage in San Francisco and sold him a pistol for $2.50. The next morning heavy rain fell. "This rainfall must have been that, which in the shape of heavy snow, stopped the Donner Party on the east side of the Sierra," Harlan wrote. They were too late by only days to cross the pass that now bears their name, and they were marooned through the winter by the snow mounting up until they were living in deep white wells.

Meanwhile Savage disappears from Harlan's account and makes only sporadic appearances elsewhere for the rest of the 1840s. In a recollection written in careful ink in an old exercise book, one of his fellow soldiers, William Swasey, describes the march of the alphabetical companies from Monterey to Los Angeles in the rainy season. To eat, the army had "but beef, and very poor at that, which diet affected a great many of the command with diarrhea, resulting in the death of one man by the name of Davis. . . . The day we buried Davis, we captured an Indian spy, and tried him by courtmartial, and he was sentenced to be shot, which sentence was carried out. This was approved [?] of by many of the more intelligent portion of the battalion, but a large majority of the men were actuated by a great feeling of bitterness, which in their undisciplined state it was dangerous to disregard. After marching and undergoing many privations and exposures during the campaign, such as exposure to wet, inclement weather, without tents or proper clothing, and no subsistence except beef, a great deal of dissatisfaction was felt by the men, which almost culminated in the defection and desertion of a considerable number of them. One of the worst malcontents was the notorious James Savage." He is said to have been courtmartialed on December 7, 1846, but there are no records of it. Another of his enemies was Heinrich Lienhard, who spoke with Savage in German. His diary notes that he came across Savage around this time "out on a spying expedition to find out where he could steal the greatest number of horses" and credits him with a murder in the course of his thievery.

By the day after Christmas, 1846, a relief party split off from the Donner-Reed Party had begun eating Patrick Dolan, and after they had finished the dead they went after the living, two Indians sent by John Sutter as guides, Luis and Salvator. One of the party warned them, and they fled, but were later found dying in the snow, shot, and eaten. On January 12, the party came across an Indian village further down the western slope of the Sierra and were fed acorns and piñons. On April 17, the final rescue party found the final survivors by what was later named Donner Lake, and that month the California Battalion mustered out its men, Private Savage among them. In May, Savage went to work for Sutter as a teamster, and it is highly likely that he re-encountered some of the recovering survivors there. Well-to-do at home, most of them were unprepared for the grueling emigration, and among the things they left behind in the Sierra are the dainty silk parasols and elegant salt cellars now in the Donner Lake museum.

Sutter's operation near Sacramento in the Central Valley verged on an empire, with its own fisheries, tanneries, extensive wheat farming, and livestock operations, its own army, its own semislave population, and a fortress in the lush grasslands. Sutter himself had been a man of no particular distinction. A native of Switzerland, he invented a captaincy in the French army to impress his new acquaintances. He talked the governor of California into letting him begin an operation using natives much as the Spanish did, as slaves for enterprises that resembled southern slave plantations (though these slaves, being local, had more opportunity to escape). Some workers lived in their own homes, others lived at Sutter's headquarters where they were locked up, men and women together, in a bare room at night. Sutter also rented out Indians for labor and according to his overseer, the same Lienhard who calls Savage a horse thief, kept a group of young girls for his own use. Sutter's wife didn't come out until 1850, and white women were scarce altogether in the West. (Some white men married native women, some raped them, and even the skinny adolescent Virginia Reed received marriage proposals soon after she was rescued from the snows.) Sutter used trade goods, food, and threats to maintain his huge labor force, which was called to work by a large bell. Historian Albert L. Hurtado writes, "Before Sutter, native people had heeded the cycle of the seasons, time was infinite, and life's rhythms were unchanging. The clang of Sutter's bell announced that time was money, that it marched onward, and that it waited for no man, including Indians in the 1840s. Necessarily the arrival of the modern sense of time coincided with the establishment of market agriculture, which in turn was linked with an international economic network . . . enmeshed in a web of debt, credit and trade that encumbered them."

Later in May of 1847 Sutter's diary notes that he has sent Savage out with James Marshall to build a lumber mill on the American River. That summer Thoreau left Walden, where he himself had escaped from the bell. He concludes his account of his two years in the woods, "The universe is wider than our views of it. What does Africa,—what does the West stand for? Is not our own interior white on the chart? black though it may prove, like the coast when discovered. Is it the source of the Nile, or the Niger, or the Mississippi, or a Northwest Passage around this continent that we would find? Are these the problems which most concern mankind? . . . Be rather the Mungo Park, the Lewis and Clark and Frobisher, of your own streams and oceans; explore your own higher latitudes,—with shiploads of preserved meats to support you, if they be necessary; and pile the empty cans sky-high for a sign. Nay, be a Columbus to whole new continents and worlds within you, opening new channels, not of trade, but of thought."

By the fall of that year, Savage had learned enough from Sutter to strike out on his own, and he went to reconnoiter with the San Joaquin Valley Indians he had met in the California Battalion. His business partner in later years, who variously appears as Thaler, Vinsonhaler, and Haler, wrote, "And this commenced his career with the California Indians. He undertook to dig the celebrated mill race of Capt. Sutter, in excavating which gold was found. It was from that circumstance he claimed to be the discoverer of the great Gold district lying under the western slope of the Sierra Nevada." Gold was found in January of 1848, and James Marshall is universally credited with the discovery. Savage may have gone back to work on the mill, or stayed where he was and made up the story later. Honest men are hard to find in the Wild West they were inventing, and becoming a self-made man was as much a literary opportunity as an economic one.

What is now the town of Big Oak Flat was for a while called Savage's Diggings, before Savage moved further south and further into the rolling hills and steep ravines that precede the mountains themselves, into the area west of Yosemite and north of the Fresno River. The region is now called the San Joaquin Valley but was better known then as the Tulare (after the tule reeds that covered its wetlands; the largest lake in California was the shallow Tule Lake which still exists in my 1901 atlas but has since disappeared, thanks to flow diversion for agriculture). Like Sutter, Savage was reborn as an emperor. He established new channels, not of thought, but of trade, in these regions unknown to other white men—one trading post only a dozen miles outside Yosemite on the banks of the Merced—and exchanged trinkets for a king's ransom in gold.

All through the centuries of their invasion of the Americas, Europeans had dreamed of finding fortunes of gold. Columbus forced the mild Tainos to bring him regular levies of gold on pain of mutilation (and they turned the tables once and sated this thirst literally by pouring molten gold down Spanish throats). Cortez found quantities of gold in the course of conquering the Aztec empire, as did Pizarro in his devastation of the Incas, but many more sought and never found the wealth of metal they imagined in their new world. Coronado rode all the way from Mexico to Kansas seeking the Seven Cities of Cibola, one of the versions of the El Dorado legend, and was disappointed. Our James Savage who didn't discover the motherlode and didn't inspire a major mutiny may not have made as much of a dent in history as his Spanish predecessors, but he lived out their dreams more thoroughly than anyone else, for they all had kings and companions to spread their treasure among and homes to go back to, but he stayed to enjoy it all for himself.

A contemporary, Cornelius Sullivan, came across him at that time and declared, "Never will I forget the impressions of the scene before us. Under a brushwood tent supported by upright posts sat James D. Savage, measuring and pouring gold dust into candleboxes by his side. Five hundred or more naked Indians, with bolts of cloth bound round their waists or suspended from their heads, brought the dust to Savage, and in return for it received a bright piece of cloth, or some beads." Another contemporary, Horace Bell, wrote in his memoir, "Whence he came no one knew; who he was, or had been, was a mystery. He was comparatively a boy, white, and an American. . . . Jim Savage was the absolute and despotic ruler over thousands of Indians, extending all the way from the Cosumnes to the Tejon Pass, and was by them designated in their Spanish vernacular El Rey Guero—the blonde king. He called himself the Tulare King. The respect, fear and superstitious veneration these rude people had for their mysterious king, was greater than that shown by the Aztecs for the Tonotiuh of conquistorial history. . . . The Tulare King might have been El Rey Dorado, for the reason that in 1850 he had more gold dust than possibly was ever possessed by one man, and could have been gilded therewith every morning of his life should he have lived his allotted time. Mr. G. D. W. Robinson, one of our most truthful and intelligent '49ers, (and where is the '49er who is not truthful in all gold stories) now resident of San Diego, informs the writer hereof that in 1850 he was at Jim Savage's Camp in the Tulares, and that he had a pork barrel full of gold dust, which enormous quantity would amount to nearly a million of dollars in value; . . . and also that this great treasure sat in his tent wholly unguarded except by the Indians themselves." A more reliable source estimates that at the height of his reign, Savage was accumulating $10,000 to $20,000 a day in 1850s prices.

It's not the gold he accumulated but the image he radiated at that time that fascinated me. I looked in another book and found, "The word 'ivory' rang in the air, was whispered, was sighed. You would think they were praying to it. A taint of imbecile rapacity blew through it all, like a whiff from some corpse. By Jove! I've never seen anything so unreal in my life. And outside, the silent wilderness surrounding this cleared speck on the earth struck me as something great and invincible, like evil or truth, waiting patiently for the passing away of this fantastic invasion. He had been absent for several months—getting himself adored, I supposed—and had come down unexpectedly, with the intention to all appearance of making a raid either across the river or down stream. Evidently the appetite for more ivory had got the better of the—what shall I say?—less material aspirations. . . . They only showed that Mr. Kurtz lacked restraint in the gratification of his various lusts, that there was something wanting in him—some small matter which, when the pressing need arose, could not be found under his magnificent eloquence. Whether he knew of this deficiency himself I can't say. I think the knowledge came to him at last—only at the very last. But the wilderness had found him out early, and had taken on him a terrible vengeance for the fantastic invasion. I think it had whispered to him things about himself which he did not know. . . ." Or perhaps, "The wilderness had patted him on the head. . . . it had taken him, loved him, embraced him, got into his veins, consumed his flesh, and sealed his soul to its own by the inconceivable ceremonies of some devilish initiation. He was its spoiled and pampered favorite. Ivory? I should think so. Heaps of it, stacks of it. The old mud shanty was bursting with it. You would think that there was not a single tusk left either above or below the ground in the whole country. . . . You should have heard him say, 'my ivory.' Oh, yes, I heard him. 'My intended, my ivory, my station, my river, my—' everything belonged to him. It made me hold my breath in expectation of making the wilderness burst into a prodigious peal of laughter that would shake the fixed stars in their places. Everything belonged to him—but that was a trifle. The thing was to know what he belonged to, how many powers of darkness claimed him for their own."

These are, of course, passages from Joseph Conrad's novella *Heart of Darkness,* another story about a voyage up a river. Written in 1902, it was initially prized for its rich symbolism and evocative language, and since then has been variously celebrated as an early exposé of the evils of imperialism and decried as a racist text. It seems a little surprising that it has also become standard reading for English classes, because its layers of ambiguity never resolve into neat meanings: In the book's own phrase, "the meaning of an episode was not inside like a kernel, but outside, enveloping the tale which brought it out only as a glow brings out a haze." *Heart of Darkness* may have no kernel, but it is structured like a Russian doll: An unknown narrator tells the reader of how Marlow, sitting on the deck of a ship on the Thames, tells him and some others a story about his voyage up the Congo at some indistinctly earlier date, and Marlow's tale takes up the rest of the book. Conrad too had made a journey up the Congo in 1890, and he and his fictive storyteller have a lot in common. At the time the author went, the Congo—an expanse about a quarter the size of the United States—was considered by Europe to be the private property of King Leopold II of Belgium, and the place soon after became famous for atrocities against the native population.

As soon as Marlow arrives, in Conrad's version of this place, the company men in the ivory trade begin murmuring about the marvelous Mr. Kurtz. They keep it up as Marlow journeys up the river to where Kurtz has established himself in the jungle as a mystical despot extracting ivory at a fantastic rate, though the company fears that "his method is unsound." This and Savage's scant biography are alike in being stories about men who ventured further up rivers in unmapped lands than any white man had before, established trading posts, acquired a huge weight of wealth and power, and earned the fear of the natives and the gushing admiration of their fellow colonialists, though one is the true account of a man who didn't quite make history, and the other tells of a fictional phantasm, the Kurtz who haunts Joseph Conrad's incantatory piece. Without Marlow's voice, a voice that casts a sinister mist of disgust and dread over the tale, the events would have been little more than an account of another economic venture in another colonial backwater. Instead its title subject shifts around so that the heart of darkness that was conventionally Africa itself sometimes instead seems to be Kurtz's spiritual condition or that of the civilization he represents.

It is easy to forget how far, in geographical terms, the Europeans and their white descendants were from their origins and their familiar world when they began to run amuck in the Americas, but when Savage takes on a resemblance to Kurtz, his territory on the Merced becomes Darkest California, a place that for all its current paved-over banality had its own beginnings in blithe violence and

uninhibited greed. When the California filmmaker Francis Ford
Coppola decided to reinterpret *Heart of Darkness,* he relocated it to
an equally exotic setting for Americans, to the Mekong River, and
made it serve as an allegory for the Vietnam War. The destruction
of Vietnamese villages had had its counterpart a few hours from
Coppola's home, though strangely enough the 1969 destruction of
the Yosemite Indian Village was not nearly as visible in the U.S. California history is part of the state's fourth-grade curriculum, and in
1970 it was taught as a pleasantly bland story, like forest succession
or evolution, in which the simple diggers were succeeded (how, we
did not hear) by the admittedly dark and Catholic Spanish who then
naturally gave way to the climax forest of Anglicization, the excellent
state in which we found ourselves. Americans have often liked to
believe that atrocities and extremes of injustice are themselves foreign, prefer to save the rainforests of Brazil to those of their own
Pacific Coast, to worry about tragedies that don't implicate them.
Heart of Darkness sets the task of the colonialist as local rather than
exotic—not as understanding the natives, but understanding one's
own origins: "Is not our own interior white on the chart? black
though it may prove, like the coast when discovered"—and it has
seemed to me that there is something in Savage himself—his lack of
restraint, of doubt, and of introspection—and in the fools, liars, can-
nibals, and opportunists that surrounded him—that brings this lesson home again.

To know a place, like a friend or lover, is for it to become familiar;
to know it better is for it to become strange again. Not novel in the
easy way of the new, but strange in a deep, disturbing way that does
not dissipate, an unsettling revelation of what should have always
been known, a revelation that implicates its belated discoverers. This
disturbance is what Savage and Conrad have to offer together. The
differences are obvious: The Belgians didn't emigrate to Africa as

the Americans did to the West Coast, and enough indigenous Africans survived the brutalities of the ivory trade and colonial wars to achieve independence from Belgium in 1960 in what is now the U.S.-supported dictatorship of Zaire. I wonder if it was the alienness of the tropics that made it seem so suitable a frame for Kurtz's evil, since Marlow and through him Conrad are clearly appalled by the intensity of life there: the denseness of the jungle, the abundance of crocodiles, the heat and humidity of the air, the strength of the wide river—which looked like a mighty snake on the map, they say. Yosemite's landscape is, on the other hand, where those unfamiliar to the West could trace resemblances to English gardens and Swiss mountains. There are also, it is true, enormous temperamental differences between Kurtz, a man of European education with a frail, emaciated body, only one native concubine, and a row of severed heads on spears around his hut, and subliterate Savage, whose blond vigor calls to mind another Western subspecies, the surfer. But their seductive speech brings them together again—Savage, who could speak so many languages, and Kurtz, who likewise dazzled his countrymen. And for all its erudition and eloquence, Kurtz's report on the Congo natives collapses into a single imperative—"Exterminate the brutes"—which is not so far from Savage's directive in the Mariposa Indian War. Nor are the fictional and historical so far apart. The private, musing Conrad kept his invention separate from his Congo experience, but the semiliterate, urgent Savage chose to invent himself as the hero of extravagant episodes that obey the fictional rules of his era: Savage inscribed his self-image of mastery and fearlessness across the landscape of the Tulare and in the hearts of his followers.

For Conrad, the unfamiliar was easy to come by. The stories of Western conquest have until recently been told by insiders, but Conrad was an early outsider, an aristocratic Polish exile who had been a French sailor for a while before he learned his third language and became an Englishman. He was in a good position to doubt the merits of colonialism and could therefore portray it not as a transaction in which the wild become civilized, but one in which the civilized go wild, and he certainly felt no allegiance to the Belgian enterprise in the Congo. The outrages perpetrated in the Congo drew the indignation of Europe and America several years after Conrad made his voyage up the Congo (which at the time inspired him to nothing more than the shortest of diary entries about weather and other annoyances). Mark Twain, who watched the sufferings of the Utah, Nevada, and California Indians so blithely, wrote condemnations of the Belgian Congo, as he had of slavery in *Huckleberry Finn*. At the time of the Mariposa Indian War, however, Thoreau had just delivered "Walking," with all its celebration of westward expansion, as a talk, and Harriet Beecher Stowe was writing *Uncle Tom's Cabin*, which appeared the following year. Her melodramatic antislavery novel sold more copies than any previous American book had (while the slaves were finding their own narrative in the stories of exile, suffering, and redemption of the Old Testament Israelites). It may be that the national imagination was so invested in the North/South moral conflict over slavery that it had nothing left over for the West but to imagine it as a great adventure and epic of progress, in which Native Americans played little more than the equivalent of the extras they would become in Western movies. And what comes across most clearly from the stories of the insiders such as Bret Harte and Twain is that the Gold Rush was fun, a boy's escapade and treasure hunt.

It is hard to tell if Savage was having fun, but he was having a great many other things. H. H. Bancroft notes of him in his *Pioneer Register*, "It is related of him that he made it a point to marry a chief's daughter in every tribe, exchanged hardware and whiskey by weight, ounce for ounce, with the Indians for gold dust, and bet his weight in gold on the turn of a card in San Francisco." William Penn Abrams wrote in his diary, "Returned to San Francisco after a visit to Savage's property on Merced River, prospects none too good for a mill. Savage is a blasphemous fellow who has five squaws for wives for which he takes authority from the scriptures." The marriages were partly diplomatic liaisons, but not entirely, and Totuya/Maria Lebrado recalled in the 1920s that Savage "did all of the tricks with the women the very first time that he was with Yosemite Indians." Bunnell also mentions that he had five wives, while the young Mariposa Battalion private Robert Eccleston noted in his diary that the number was thirty-three, and a Yokut man named Pahmit says that he acquired seventeen but ten ran away and seven stayed.

Born in 1831, Pahmit was interviewed by an anthropologist ninety-eight years later. Among his memories of the colonization of his homeland were some about how Savage achieved such sway in the region: "Major Savage, he say, 'I big medicine man with big father at Washington. You haf do what I say. I hurt you if I want to. I make all your people die. I make all fish go out river. I make all antelope, all elk go 'way. I make dark. You do what I say, nothing hurt you. But you no hurt me. You shoot me with bow, arrow, I live. . . . You shoot me with pistol, you no hurt me.'" Savage then put a white handkerchief on an oak tree and shot six holes in it with his six-shooter, then reloaded the gun—apparently with blanks—and gave it to a Yokut man and invited him to shoot it at him. He shot six times and each time Savage grabbed the air. When the shooting was over, he had six bullets in his hand. He poured oil on water and lit it afire, promising that he could also make the rivers burn; he used sleight of hand to win traditional gambling games; and he intimidated them further with a galvanic battery. Savage is said to have wired up a grizzly cub pelt and given electrical shocks to his audience and once electrocuted into unconsciousness a rebellious subject, then pretended to raise him from the dead. "What can you expect?" declared one of Kurtz's admirers, "he came to them with thunder and lightning, you know—and they had never seen anything like it—and very terrible. He could be very terrible. You can't judge Kurtz as you would an ordinary man. No, no, no! Now—just to give you an idea—I don't mind telling you, he wanted to shoot me, too, one day—but I don't judge him."

Savage inspired such unstinting admiration among his fellow white men (no white woman enters into his story after his wife died in Nevada). For the young men he seemed to be as absolute a hero as the characters in the dime-novel westerns that were beginning to appear. In January of 1851, a young man wrote to his father, "From his long acquaintances with the Indians, Mr. Savage has learned their ways so thoroughly that they cannot deceive him. He has been one of their greatest chiefs and speaks their language as well as they can themselves. No dog can follow a trail like he can. No horse endure half so much. He sleeps but little, can go days without food, and can run a hundred miles in a day and night over the mountains and then sit and laugh for hours over a camp fire as fresh and lively as if he had just been taking a little walk for exercise." In February, the *California Courier* reported, "Major Savage is a small but sinued man and probably does not weigh over 138 pounds. He has regular features, round face, light blue eyes, and his long yellow, silken hair hangs in ringlets like a girl's. He never heard of the word fear, can track an Indian or a deer from sunrise to sunrise again over the mountains, rivers, and valleys, and run either the one or the other down before he gives up."

Not only backwoods boys, but the worldly Sam Ward, an Eastern literary man and the son-in-law of John Jacob Astor (whose millions came from the previous boom, the fur trade), fell under Savage's sway. In 1850, Ward was talking to Kit Carson and the Indian Agent

Adam Johnston in a store on the lower Merced when the natives in the vicinity began to stir excitedly as a group began to approach. "It was easy to detect the leader, whose yellow hair hung profusely down below his shoulders and who had something of that air-Napoleon which the habit of command is apt to impress on those who wield it. . . . It may appear singular that in stature, air, and feature, he bore a marked resemblance to the effigies I have seen of Peter the Great. . . . After his departure, this singular personage was the theme of conversation and comment, from which I learned that he had been the companion of Indians since his boyhood, having commenced his experience of their romantic life on the other side of the mountains, and was by some persons supposed to have a streak of their blood in his veins, an absurdity flatly contradicted by his hair, which was as fair as the golden locks of Achilles. . . . He exercised over the tribes with whom he was in contact a magnetic and almost mysterious influence. His habits and nature were externally consonant with his name."

The Mariposa Indian War began that year, when Savage's influence began to wane. He had played the miners against the Indians to his advantage, but the hostilities he cultivated began to close in on him. As the serpent in the Merced region, he had occupied an equivocal position, intent on exploiting his hosts rather than eradicating them, learning the local languages rather than starting over, operating in a transitional space he would have made permanent if he could. "When the white men were trying to arrive at a compromise with their red brethren, he circulated untruths that made them appear hostile," said a contemporary. "On the other hand, he imparted information to the Indians that created in them a very hostile feeling against the miners and traders." In the spring of 1850, his wives warned him that the Indians were planning to drive the whites out, and the first raid was on his trading post high up the Merced, just outside Yosemite. He was forced to retreat to Mariposa Creek, nearer the other whites who had joined him in the region. In late summer of that year, he still felt powerful enough to threaten that he and his subjects would sack San Jose when that town was harboring two Mexicans who had murdered their comrades—friends of Savage's, evidently—during a cattle-buying expedition. In October he went to San Francisco to deposit some of his wealth and buy supplies. One account says that he and his entourage camped out in Portsmouth Square in what is now Chinatown, and they were there for the October 29 celebration of California's admission to statehood (which had taken place in Congress on September 9, but the news did not arrive until October). He is said to have had his picture—a daguerreotype—taken by the well-known photographer Vance, but no painting or photograph of him has ever been found. And it is on this trip that he is supposed to have bet his weight in gold on the turn of a card, but he wasn't as good a cheat at cards as he was at native games, and he lost—not his own gold, but gold he had been entrusted with by some Indians.

He had brought with him one of the local chiefs who had been his ally, José Juarez, to impress him with the power of the whites, but the plan backfired. Savage is supposed to have knocked Juarez to the ground when the latter—and perhaps the former—was drunk, and the chief arose sober and hostile. It may have been that single blow that changed Savage's fate, that as the U.S. war against the Western Shoshone dwindled down into Joe Leaf's grip on Carrie Dann's arm in the spring of 1992, so Savage's blow to José Juarez in the fall of 1850 extends into the Mariposa Indian War and on into contemporary history. When they returned, Savage told the natives he encountered, "If the Indians make war on the white men, every tribe will be exterminated; not one will be left." He called upon José Juarez to confirm the great number of white men he had seen, but

Juarez stepped forward to say instead that the people he had seen were divisive among themselves and would not come to the mountains, and he bitterly advocated a war to drive the invaders out.

Savage's wives began to desert him. In December, his Fresno trading post was destroyed and its three clerks killed, news a group of Indians shouted across a canyon to him. Savage realized that his fragile kingdom, built in the space between the advance of the whites and the disillusionment of the native people, was evaporating into thin air. By January the deposed monarch had assumed the disguise of a buffoon, travelling in, according to the *California Courier*, "horse hair beard and buffalo mustachios." What was thus far only a private quarrel was viewed—with Savage's help—as the beginning of the general war José Juarez had advocated, and it was thus that it became the Mariposa Indian War now mostly remembered as the occasion of the first white visitation of Yosemite Valley. For Savage, Yosemite was no focal point, but an inconvenient gorge on the border of what had been his little empire for so few years, and he never went back. Bunnell reports him as saying, "hemmed in by walls of rock, your vision turned in, as it were, upon yourself—a residence here would be anything but desirable for me."

It is hard to tell what Savage did want, what fears and desires entered his dreams at night, dreams he seems not to have remembered, for he feared little and found little use for what he acquired. Sleeplessness is one of the qualities of the indefatigable Savage his idolators celebrate. He seems to have moved too fast for the questions to catch up with him, always seeking that openness, that fantasy of the frontier that liberated and goaded the national imagination into its excesses and devastations, in that form of migration in which travel itself becomes a palliative to the vision turned in, the internal prospecting Thoreau advocated. He was not loyal to either side, and though he spoke so many native tongues, he used them to aggrandize his position as a would-be emperor, not to join their cultures. Among all his subjects he was profoundly alone, and indifferent to his solitude. He evinced no great attachment to his wives, found little use for his heaps of gold, and had no particular respect for the tribes with which he entangled himself. The only documents in Savage's own voice are the bills he sent to the government demanding reimbursement for his destroyed trading posts; everything else is impression and reminiscence. It may be that all his dreaming was done by others, his nightmares by the people whose king he would be and his daydreaming by the boys who idolized him.

He had passed close to history, but it was only in the Mariposa Indian War that he actually made history. The war itself has already been recounted here; from Savage's point of view, it went well enough. Afterward, he convinced the government to make him an Indian Agent and regained some of his sway, though he had dwindled from a lone imperialist to one white entrepreneur among many. By July of 1851, Savage and his partner Vinsonhaler, along with Fremont, had obtained contracts to supply beef to the tribes who had been coerced onto reservations. With the cooperation of the three Indian Agents, these beef contractors swindled both the government who paid for the beef and the Indians who were supposed to receive it: In one deal, the agents themselves would buy cattle from Fremont at double the going rate and issue receipts to Savage for twice the number of cattle delivered. Corruption around Indian agencies was widespread, but it is surprising that Fremont and Vinsonhaler were pursuing it together. A member of Fremont's Company A in the California Battalion, Vinsonhaler is remembered largely as the cowardly incompetent who helped make Fremont's foolhardy 1847–48 Fourth Expedition such a disaster. Fremont landed his party in the San Juan and Sangre de Cristo mountains of southern Colorado in the dead of winter. Vinsonhaler subsequently hoarded supplies and abandoned one of the parties, which then resorted to cannibalism—an incident that damaged Fremont's presidential campaign of 1856.

In November the *San Joaquin Republican* reported that Savage's wives had returned to him. In the spring of 1852, a Stockton newspaper reported that Savage "has proved that these tribes may be taught agriculture and civilization as effectively as any on this continent. The Indians all love him, to all appearance, and still he manages them in such a manner that they also fear him as much." Similarly, his partner Vinsonhaler reported, "They have reposed the utmost confidence in him, a confidence bordering on superstition. . . . He had also commenced teaching them to read and sing and had succeeded so far with one class as to learn them their letters, and they were beginning to spell. His singing Class were also making progress; they could sing tunes by note very well. Their voices were good and they appeared to have a good Ear for music. He was also teaching them agriculture." Of all the roles Savage took on, schoolteacher sharing knowledge is most incongruous. It was at this time Jean-Nicholas Perlot had a brush with Savage, whose name he took to be a title conferred on the commissioner-major for his linguistic prowess. (The word *savage* actually comes from the same Latin root as *sylvan*, as in forest, and what in Latin was *homo sylvestris* became in French *hommes sauvages*, original, primitive, or woodland man— eventually Rousseau's noble savage. In the latter tongue, wild animals are still *animaux sauvages*. The word's associations with ferocity and barbarism came later, in English.) That April, the huge swath of California that had been Mariposa County was divided, and Tulare County was created. It is said to have included three houses and "perhaps a dozen bona fide residents." County elections were held under an oak tree that July, since it was too hot to vote indoors, and nine men were elected to various positions. Savage had been appointed one of the four commissioners. The new judge, Walter

Harvey, had staged a raid on the King's River Reservation in the southern part of the county and killed several Indians two days before he was elected. The newly elected clerk was killed in a fight in Mariposa town, the treasurer was found dead in a swamp in suspicious circumstances, and another commissioner was shot to death. On August 13, a newspaper reported that Savage and his later partner Dr. Leach were administering medicine to Indians on the Fresno dying of an unnamed disease. By August 17, Savage was dead too.

The news that Congress at the urging of the California senators and representatives had refused to ratify the California Indian treaties hadn't yet reached the West when Harvey and his volunteers attacked the Fresno reservation. They were resentful that even such a large and attractive portion of the native peoples' original lands should remain to them, and were intent on squatting the lands. Some men—including Harvey in one version—had built a trading post and ferry on the reservation land and attempted to drive the native people off. Both the King's River and Fresno Reservation people realized that the protection promised them was not going to materialize, and white anxiety had risen to such a level that the regular army was called in. The leader of the troops, Major G. W. Patten, reported that a chief named Pascual "pulled down the United States flag which had waved in front of his wigwam, gathered all his people around him, and when asked where he was going, replied that he was going into the mountains to weep." These were the circumstances in which Tenaya and the Ahwahneechee had fled their reservation, realizing that they were better off on their own.

Harvey had been infuriated by the news that Savage had made "ungentlemanly" remarks about him (which seems to mean that Savage had denounced his violent attempts to retake the King's River land) and put out the word that Savage would not dare show up at his King's River trading post. Inevitably, he did and demanded that Harvey retract his own remarks, while Harvey pressed his charges that the rival trader had insulted him. According to Bunnell, Savage replied, "Yes, I have said you are a murderer and a coward." Savage knocked Harvey down, and in most versions Harvey didn't fight back until Savage's pistol fell out of his waistband, or he dropped it repeatedly (which suggests he might have been drunk). Harvey then shot him dead. It could be said that Savage redeemed himself by dying in the attempt to redress the grievances of the King's River people. But it seems as likely he died in defense of a reputation to which he knew he had no claim. Or perhaps it was both justice for the natives and pride in his name that made him seek the bloody judge out, and so he died as he lived, one foot in either world, neither a horror nor a hero, but an ambiguity.

The *San Francisco Herald* published a letter which described the aftermath in melodramatic terms: "He could do more to keep the Indians in subjection than all the forces Uncle Sam could send here. The Indians were terribly excited at his death. Some of them reached the scene of the tragedy soon after it occurred. They threw themselves upon his body uttering the most terrific cries, bathing their hands and face in his blood and even stooping over and drinking it, as it gushed from his wounds. It was with difficulty his remains could be interred. The Chiefs clung to his body and swore they would die with their father. The night he was buried the Indians built large fires around which they danced, singing the while the mournful death chant, until the hills around rang with the sound. I have never seen such profound manifestation of grief. The young men as they whirled wildly and distractedly around in the dance shouted the name of their 'father' that was gone, while the squaws sat rocking their bodies to and fro chanting their mournful dirges." Savage's partner Vinsonhaler, who would have been sensitive about the mention of cannibalism and who is more reliable a witness to these events, wrote more simply in the letter which I found in the archives of the U.S. Army, "After taking a look at the Corpse, they walked off, saying nothing would ever go right with them again."

Harvey was never punished for the shooting. A relation, Ida B. Savage, wrote in 1927 that Savage's estate "was given back to the State of California, as his offspring, half Indians, could not be located, and his brothers and sisters refused it." His trading post on the Fresno was taken over by Chinese merchants in the 1860s. Francis Parkman, who was born the same year as Savage and went west when he did, left off history writing on account of his delicate health and took up horticulture. He bred several new varieties of rose, published a definitive book on roses, and died in 1893 at the age of seventy, three years after Joseph Conrad journeyed up the Congo. Conrad never had any direct dealings with California, but when the writer Mary Austin visited him in 1909 he paid tribute to her generous vision of California's native population and deserts with a rose, which she pressed in a book. The rose, and the book, now belong to the Huntington Library and Gardens in southern California, a lavish institution built with the profits of the Central Pacific Railroad which was completed in 1869, its western portion built largely by Chinese labor. It made the arduous six-month trek of the covered wagons and the dull six-week stagecoach trip of Mark Twain's *Roughing It* into a four-day pleasure excursion from Omaha. Unlike Conrad, Prince Leopold of Belgium (later King Leopold II) came to California and camped out in Yosemite in the early twentieth century. His mother, Queen Beatrice, was a friend of Albert Einstein, and in 1939 the physicist Leo Szilard approached him to see if he would use his influence with her. They were concerned that Germany might seize her country's stockpiles of uranium from the Belgian Congo. The explosive potential of nuclear fission had just been discovered, and Szilard and Einstein's letter went through various stages, from one simply attempting to protect the uranium to the one which urged the U.S. to pursue an atom bomb of its own. But these stories are not really Savage's story.

Savage's Grave

✛ WE WERE TIRED, AND THE MEN AT THE NEXT CAMPSITE WERE annoying. There were five of them, and they were loudly recounting their dubious sexual exploits to each other as their heap of beer cans grew. Catherine and Dianne were upset by the one who was talking about trying to seduce a twelve-year-old. I hadn't heard him, but I came back in time to catch another story about cornering a woman in an elevator. I cheered up my companions with promises to make trails of aromatic food—Bac-o-bits were the leading contender—to their tents so that the bears would take them in the night, and we all regaled ourselves with the picture of predators suddenly become prey. Yosemite, even the valley, is bear country, and a bear was supposed to have ripped a car door off at this campground the night before. Unfortunately, the U.S., even the national parks, are man country, which has hindered my freedom of movement far more.

My friends had come to keep me company on another venture into the valley. Earlier that day we had hiked up to Glacier Point and back, on a trail that zigzags up through Little Yosemite Valley, past Vernal and Nevada Falls and keeps going up the places where the perpendicular walls lean back a little, a 3,300-foot ascent. It had the initial pleasure that all hikes out of the valley do, that of outdistancing the Coney Island atmosphere of the crowds. A thousand feet higher or so, people are far more scarce and much more civilized, and they keep improving with the altitude. The view kept changing, and the terrain, and as we walked Dianne told me stories about trekking in the Himalayas. About halfway up, we bathed in a cold pool in one of the streams, and small trout—too wild to know they're supposed to be wary, said Catherine—swam through our legs. Up high near the rim, we ran across a lightning-fire area full of young green growth, and a little further along sprays of ripe elderberries nodded over the trail, sweeter than any I've ever tasted. There were points where the trail was little more than a ledge along a cliff, and sometimes the cliff wall was wet and dripping with mosses and ferns. The path worked its way back west as we went, the rest of the valley gradually came back into sight, and Half Dome and North Dome kept shifting in relation to the rest of the view. But when we got to the top, which I knew mostly from old photographs, it was not what I expected. Glacier Point is a big, flat-topped rock jutting out over the valley, and in the early part of the century it was a popular place to photograph daredevil stunts—a car driven out to the edge, an acrobat performing on a bar jutting out from it, a dancer pirouetting atop it. A safety railing has been put around it, and a snack bar opened up next to it, and the people who had driven there re-created the atmosphere we had so laboriously outwalked. I was suddenly seized by a profound craving for an Eskimo Pie, but we had brought no money, as we had not expected to encounter civilization in its commercial forms. We started back down in that euphoric state where exhaustion yields to a peaceful languor and once-sore limbs become leaden but loose.

We had left late and by the time we were nearly back, the sun had disappeared. The light became dimmer and richer and more palpable, and the stark contrast between the gray rock and the green vegetation disappeared. As the day receded, everything turned blue until the whole valley seemed poured full of an intense hazy blue light, as though trees, rocks, and air were all sculpted from the same celestial material, and the atmosphere seemed as substantial as the objects seemed diaphanous in this blueness—blue like the blue light that streams through Gothic stained-glass windows, which themselves may have been intended to re-create moments like this. It was the first time I really saw the place as the kind of spiritual realm that had inspired all its artists and poets, and it made me think of them a little more generously. Then came the evening next to the would-be predators, and the next day Dianne had to go back to work and we who remained scrapped our plans for another Yosemite jaunt and decided to get the hell out of the valley. I had an idea.

The topography changes from the east to the west end of the valley: There are more deciduous trees, a richer, more expansive environment, and then vines and bushes begin to flourish as the road narrows. Poison oak shows up near this western boundary and then becomes common below. The old road that follows the river and runs past Savage's Merced trading post at the entrance to the park, Route 140, was lined with wild grapes, covering the ground in thick mats and climbing up trees and anything else in their reach. We stopped, and I filled my skirt with the grapes. Small and black, with a purple-gray bloom of dust on them, the grapes dangled in the shadows of the broad grape leaves, hard to see unless you knew what to look for.

The Merced itself in this canyon west of the park, with its spreading oaks, willows and buckeyes, and tangled vines, with its gentle reflecting pools and braided flow over the shallows and around the water-carved rocks, was in an expansive, tranquil mood that seemed altogether out of keeping with the deep ravine it passes through, and carved out. The slopes above the riparian riches are steep, rocky, and arid; trees and grass seem to cling to them only through great effort. We swam at a bend in the river, and the water was wonderfully cool, not chilling nor muddy and stagnant, but clear and soft and refreshing—merciful. It seemed unlikely that this tranquil, inviting water began as the icy waterfalls dashing against the rocks in the high country we had walked through the day before. The chaparral faded with the steepness of the slopes as we continued west, and the foothills began.

There is a pleasure of novelty and grandeur to the landscape of Yosemite, but below it in the foothills there is a pleasure more akin to satisfaction for me, satisfaction in the familiar hospitability and modest beauty of the oaks and rolling gold hills, in the roads that wind through them, in a scene that constantly changes without major surprises. The great landscapes I admire, but this is the landscape of my childhood that I love personally, familiarly. The hills curve and continue like the back of a beast, and when a wind comes up, the grass ripples like a horse's flank. Oak trees spread out their strong crooked arms far from each other and cast a sketchy shade, and bluebelly lizards sun themselves on rocks and fences. It isn't an epic landscape, a landscape to disappear into and call wilderness, but a rustic one, on the scale of an afternoon ramble.

We took back roads—Buckeye Road, Ben Hur Road, and roads identified by rural route numbers, passed brindled cows, a palomino and buckskin switching the flies off each other, a redtail hawk soaring low over the road, a vulture flapping slowly up from its gore at the last minute, and incredible numbers of squirrels darting across the road when we approached, the way jackrabbits do at night, but with their long tails undulating and a general air of exuberant panic. Datura—jimsonweed—grew everywhere along the roadside, the flowers like pale trumpets spilling off the tangled clumps of vine. I had never seen them in California before, although they are common in the Southwest, where they provide a powerful hallucinogenic for indigenous spiritual practices, and a fatal one in slightly larger doses. Georgia O'Keeffe painted them often.

Another painter, William Keith, after all his years of painting epic Yosemite landscapes, retired to the toes of the foothills of the Sierra, to the town of Raymond, where he died in 1908. We arrived there, where there was no town visible at all, only a few old buildings of obscure purpose and a combination general store and bar, with a gas pump out front. When I paid for the gas in the store, I heard alluring sounds coming out of the dimness of the bar. So we went in where a half dozen people were lolling and racks of antlers punctuated the upper atmosphere, put on Roseanne Cash's "Tennessee Flat Top Box" and Patsy Cline's "Blue Moon of Kentucky" and had a Bud apiece. The place was cluttered with ersatz new imitations of Western authenticity that undermined its genuine rough-hewn age, as though in its desire to be Western it had forgotten it was Western already. Such self-consciousness and self-invention seems to have arrived as soon as this part of the continent became the nation's West, from the way characters like Fremont and Savage wove heroic myths around themselves to the way contemporary cowboys seem to have learned how to be themselves as much from Hollywood westerns as from each other and their work. Or it may be that the grittily authentic and the absolutely insincere are the twin poles around which westernness revolves, each part of its identity. The bar had the beautiful stamped tin ceiling of early twentieth-century buildings, a recent addition of fake wood panels, stag head trophies, a boar's head over the bar itself, a bunch of reprints of nineteenth-century beer posters, a slew of snapshots of the locals frolicking with humorous captions appended, some backlit beer signs, cattle brands burned into the wood of the ancient bar, and a sign that said "No One Under 12 on the Pool Tables." A handsome man with gray hair came in with a substantial blackhaired woman and a plump boy of about fifteen and proceeded to play pool with this presumable son and flirt with us. He was so bad the cue ball ended up under my chair at one point, but he was cheerful and harmless. It was getting late, though, so we tossed the beers back and left.

The hills didn't seem to diminish as we moved away from the Sierra toward the flatlands of the San Joaquin Valley, but suddenly there was a sign for Hidden Dam and Hensley Lake. We were on a wild goose chase. All I had to go on was a newspaper clipping from 1971 that said the dam the U.S. Army Corps of Engineers was building northeast of Madera would flood Savage's burial site and the old trading post nearby, so the grave would be moved to higher ground. I didn't know if it really had been or if it would be where they expected it to be. The first site we stopped at was a campsite without inhabitants below the earthen bank of the dam. At the Lazy E Ranch across the way, roosters crowed and cows lowed. The second was a ranger station that was locked up until morning, but through it I could see a simple map with the boat dock, day use area, and "Major Savage Historical Monument" on the other side of the reservoir, the south side.

The slender white obelisk I'd seen in an old picture was there atop a hill as we pulled in. I dashed from the truck. Catherine called after me, "It isn't going anywhere," and I said, "But I am." I think I wanted to make sure he was real, and dead. There was another administration building at the base of the hill, and a comfort station next to the parking lot below; on the way up the smell of skunk was strong. The stairs were made of railroad ties, and as I leaped up them, it looked as though they'd reburied some other people with Savage, but the low stones that scattered toward the plinth turned out to be plaques relating his history. Savage was buried three times, and now it looks as though he has five graves. His own says only,

TO THE MEMORY OF
MAJ.
JAMES D. SAVAGE

saying nothing of his complicated history and death. The more recent historical plaque has his birthdate off by six years—1817 instead
of 1823. Catherine was surprised he'd died before thirty, and I said
that his crimes were all young men's crimes, crimes of exuberant ex-
cess.

He was first buried near where he died. The second time, his
partner Dr. Leach ordered the ten-foot-tall white obelisk with the
simple inscription, had him excavated, and reburied him under it
near one of his Fresno River trading posts. Then the dam builders—
the U.S. Army Corps of Engineers—dug him up and reburied him
above the waterline of the dam they were building in August of 1971.
The clipping said that the skeleton was incomplete, there were no
signs of a coffin, but a metal buckle from an "old fashioned leather
purse" and a rusty squirrel or gopher trap lay with the bones, though
it did not say whether these emblems of money and entrapment were
reburied too. The gravel around this third grave glinted with mica.
As I stood there and thought about the bones under this white erec-
tion, I saw that past it, toward the end of the reservoir, there were
trees sticking out of the water, that there was a drowned forest re-
emerging.

The reservoir—Hensley (so-called) Lake—was about twenty-five
feet below its high-water mark, and had left a series of ledges all
round it, on which a strange weed grew profusely—grew everywhere, in fact, lush, repellant, vivid green, juicy like a succulent, with
clusters of thorns at its stem. The whole place had a strange sim-
plicity in the late afternoon light: Blue water gave way to green shore
region to yellow hills, with only the brown ledges separating these

paintbox colors. Powerboats droned industriously through the foul-smelling water, and the passengers whooped victoriously. It took far longer than I expected to reach the eastern edge where the drowned trees were, partly because there were marshy fingers reaching out of the reservoir we had to skirt, where the weed grew taller and the ground became slimy mud. High above the waterline were buoys inscribed "DANGER." Tall rocks jutted out along the shoreline, the lichen and roughness of grassland rock outcroppings soaked off, so they seemed strange, foreign, like standing stones. At the other end of the lake was a rock island, and the shoreline undulated prettily, but for its lack of riparian life. We saw four men in turquoise T-shirts walking the other way, carrying tackle and a big string of fish: I worried for a moment about them approaching us, so far away from anything else in such a strange place.

When I looked back, Savage's plinth stuck up between a pair of silhouetted oaks, and the hill looked taller. It got quieter and quieter as we reached the trees, and the light got lower and softer. Finally we were walking across a vast mudflat, with the earth cracked into a maze of tiles imprinted with the handlike prints of raccoons, the delicate inscriptions of small birds, and the large three-toed calligraphy of herons or egrets. Deer had sunk through this pavement, leaving no prints. I realized, looking back at the shoreline above us, that where we were walking had once been far under water and earlier had not been lake bottom at all. Boats had once floated above our heads, and catfish had nibbled the land that cracked under our feet, but before that it had been grassland.

The trees were not oaks after all, judging by the lines of their limbs, but cottonwoods or some other wetland-loving tree. Some of them were standing on this flatland, entirely emerged, some were still partially submerged. It's not unusual to see fallen trees in water, where they are clearly already dead, or trees that have died where they stood and stand dry and austere, but these trees drowned in place were uncanny, terrifying. Their branches lifted up like imploring hands, their immobility was a curse where land and water themselves so often changed place. They had died of fidelity in an unfaithful landscape and then been buried and unburied, like something in a horror movie. In their highest branches dangled a fringe of dried waterplants and strands of fishing tackle. We kept on walking.

Suddenly we saw a dead catfish hanging by a fishing line caught in a branch. The fish dangled three or so feet from the ground. It was dry and eviscerated, and dry weeds were tangled around the line that held it. The fish looked not as though it were caught in an underwater snag, but as though it had been hung for a crime, hung the way men were hung in the Gold Rush towns to the east, its twisted stiff-whiskered face like theirs. I figured it must have been caught by an angler and then by a tangle in a tree limb before the water retreated. Perhaps the catfish had hung there still alive keeping predators at bay as the water retreated, or perhaps it hung in the air from a tree whose base was still immersed in the retreating water—for why else hadn't the raccoons eaten it? Had it died of hunger too far from the bottom or died of air as the water receded? The motorboats had stopped, or we were out of earshot of them, and the day had become completely silent.

As we walked still further east, we could see around the hill to where more trees had been drowned and bared by the rise and fall of the waters, and the water had clearly not been as deep—the shoreline was now only fifteen feet or so above the bottomland we walked across. There were stagnant pools in it, in which swarms of little frogs disappeared in alarm at our approach. Finally, the original riverbed of the Fresno River emerged again, mostly dry or reduced to a trickle that would hardly be called a brook most places. There were willows along it, perhaps grown up after the waters had receded to some degree, and the land was becoming normal again.

The sun was beginning to set as we turned back. Each tree was reflected in the silvery still waters, doubled. The thin strands of cloud were tinged with pink, and the sky along a long ridge of oaks changed color again and again—though color is hardly the right word for those delicate mother-of-pearl iridescences of sunsets, in which blue becomes red or yellow without any perceptible transition. I kept stopping to turn back, for the sun was setting behind us. One tree was full of birds with long necks drawn into hunched wings, silhouetted, and a white egret flew across the scene. There were clouds the color of red-hot iron, and the horizon glowed gold; the rest of the sky carried on a summer blue as though nothing were happening. Huge dragonflies wove through the air, and the midge swarms were so thick in places that it looked as if the air were writhing the way it does around great heat—the air hummed with them, and a cricket began to saw away. The water changed from silver to a molten warmth, the land behind began to darken, and as we approached the hill on which Savage's monument was still visible, Venus began to shine through the sunset's colors. There were pockets of colder air in the valleys, warmth rising off the grass, rabbit holes everywhere, and cottontails racing away at our approach. The jagged curves of oak branches were black against the sky. As we climbed the hill, thorny flowers I hadn't noticed on the way out tore at my bare legs and left a strange, sticky perfume on my fingers.

Full Circle

✚ ON THE FIRST DAY OF OCTOBER IN 1992 I SET OUT ON THE longest route to Las Vegas I could take without heading in the wrong direction, across the San Joaquin Valley, up through Tioga Pass in Yosemite, and all around the Test Site's north and east sides I had never seen before.

Of all the cardinal sins against the environment, driving long distances is the most seductive, the one that brings us back to otherwise inaccessible places, whatever the terms. I love long drives alone. The road is a place itself, or a border between places, a long narrow country without citizens whose only inhabitants are transients and strangers, a great suspended interval of privacy and peace between departure and arrival. And the road is a net dropped over the vastness of the continent, tying together all its distances into one navigable labyrinth of asphalt. Roads are the real architectural achievement of this century in the U.S., freeway overpasses and cloverleafs the greatest monuments to its beliefs, rather as the Roman roads of Britain are the major legacy of the centuries of Roman occupation. Roads are the architecture of our restlessness, of those who wish neither to stay in their built places nor wander in the untouched ones, but to keep moving between them. A road promises something else to us, though the promise is better fulfilled by travelling than by arriving.

And the road is an event in itself, as well as the ribbon that ties two places together, and the fact that a road can be described as an event indicates how roads differ from other structures. Only over time does the full shape of the road become apparent, and its slow revelation is what fascinates me. The long horizontal scrolls of Chinese landscape painting, meant to be rolled by a section at a time and made so that the whole cannot be seen at once, are the only visual art that corresponds to this, though all stories do. A road is itself a kind of sentence, or story. A real place, it's also a metaphor for time, for future becoming present and then past, for passage. A road that travels over hills is a long sequence of geometrical variations that describes the landscape it runs through, of s- and c-curves, rises and dips, bends, disappearances, distant reemergings, of a perpetual serpentine writhing in response to the contours that came before.

In our heads and on maps, a road is a line drawn through the landscape, but from the road itself its foreground appears as a kind of V eternally opening up to wrap around us as we plunge onward, a great crawling king snake devouring us into the world beyond.

✚ WHEN I GOT TO LAKE TENAYA, THE WIND WAS BITING AND the pinetops roared gently, the noise of passing cars occasionally rising above their chorus and then disappearing into it again. Although the water was clearer than glass, clear almost as mountain air, the wind scored the surface of the water with ripples and I saw mostly surface when I got close. Clouds dimmed the sun. I walked the perimeter of the lake south, and at a little stream that flowed into it, I looked for a place to cross. There were rocks in it like stepping-stones, and halfway across I saw there was something upstream, something that turned out to be the white page of a book. It rested on fine gravel in midstream, just out of reach from either side, and when I stooped to read it from the farther side, the constant flow of water made the words ripple and dance. Sometimes I thought I could make out phrases, but they were all conjecture. All I could be sure of is that the page number had three digits—it wasn't a leaf out of a brochure, but serious stuff. The longer I watched the words move like water themselves in the stream, the more it seemed like an omen or a talisman.

Hoping for some fine passage from *Moby Dick* or the like, I fished for it with a pine branch. As soon as I touched the page, it wrapped itself around the stick, and when I pulled it out of the water the paper looked dirtier than it had before. The underside was a chapter heading, and what I had been trying to read was the following page. The chapter was titled "A Child Shall Lead Them," and the story was a stilted one, about missionaries and violent natives, written from the missionaries' point of view. The fragment began, "Like wolves stalking their prey, savage men were closing in on the small Christian community." After a lot of bloodshed and conversion and references to the men who had thrown Nindik into the Heluk, it ended, "In addition to the example and the preaching of men who loved Christ enough to die for Him, the lesson of the Seng patrol struck a death-blow to Yali confidence in the power of. . . ." In fact it seemed to be evangelical literature, and I wondered what kind of a traveller tore out the page and tossed it into the High Sierra. Later on, in Las Vegas, I looked up some of the words and found that the Yali people it described might be the Dali of West New Guinea. Missionaries in the 1950s alleged that they were Stone Age headhunters in need of salvation, the same old story.

It seems strange now that I found this country's national Eden so full of disturbing surprises and its Armageddon so comparatively pleasant, at least for its wide skies and gallant resistance community. Once again, I fled Yosemite. At the eastern gate of the park, high up past Tuolumne Meadows, I wondered why they set the boundary there and in a few miles I saw: The smooth glacier-polished granite gave way to more conventionally crumbling mountain faces, and the color too was different. The rock above was sandy and reddish, and aspens and poplars were turning yellow below. It had become the generic high country of the West, not the exceptional landscape of Yosemite. The road followed a meandering stream, and as it descended into the canyon floor, I saw its water flowing *east*. After a lifetime in California where all water flows west, after a day of driving past the San Joaquin and all the other bodies of water seeking the Pacific, this little stream heading toward sunrise seemed as defiant a phenomenon as water running uphill or fish flying. I had crossed into the Great Basin, the land of interior drainage, and though the water was flowing east it couldn't be going far—Mono Lake, perhaps—and I stopped at what I looked up later on a map and found was Lee Vining Creek.

The landscape all around this stream had the dreamy, secretive sweetness of a fairytale. The clear, quick-running stream, about eight feet wide, had carved vertical banks in the powdery pale soil. The streambed was mostly gravel and at my approach slender fish darted away into its shadows. Everywhere there were thickets of willow, short, scrubby, a dead gray below and yellow-branched above, less like trees than hedges. It was the grass that was most wonderful, though, silvery gold grass that made the whole landscape dull, pale, and rich, grass as thick and fine as fur and bent like fur in different directions, as though stroked by some great hand. Like fur, it was darker or lighter depending on whether it stood up or was brushed down, and I bent to run my fingers through it: It felt stiff but smooth. Narrow paths that had thinned the grass, shortened and flattened it, but not worn it out, wove all across the meadows, along the banks and through the trees. Sometimes the trails led through dense patches of willow I had to bend double to pass through, or couldn't enter at all, as though something much smaller had made them.

The late afternoon sky was overcast with big white clouds, and only a few rays of light emerged to strike the rock faces above, bringing out their roughness. The aspens were small, and the stream meandered in oxbows and arcs through the valley enclosed within the cliffs. Near the campsites were whole groves of aspen with lovers' names carved into them, the startling black eyes of their slender white trunks staring indifferently past these chronicles. Leaves like yellow hearts already littered the ground. I went back to the car and drove away from the setting sun and onward toward Tonopah in a deep black night until I could drive no more, and I slept in the back of the truck among RVs at a roadside rest area.

Had I gone north instead of east at Mono Lake, I would have come to the small town of Mason in about the same amount of time and commemorated another anniversary, a centennial. Mason Valley is where the Ghost Dance religion originated with the Paiute prophet Wovoka, or Jack Wilson, though its greatest effects were felt elsewhere, among the Plains and Indian Territory tribes, the Cheyenne, the Arapaho, and most fervently among the Lakota. The Lakota had spent the winter of 1890 dancing almost to the exclusion of every other activity, and the army's tension over their refusal to surrender their land or their dance had built up until it snapped, and the soldiers shot 300 unarmed people dead that December at Wounded Knee. Worried about the revolutionary potential of the movement, the U.S. Bureau of American Ethnology sent a young investigator to Mason Valley. Perhaps because of his own commitment to Irish independence and cultural survival, the ethnologist James Mooney was fairly sympathetic to the Ghost Dance movement when he came out to talk to Wovoka. He looked up the prophet's uncle, Charley Sheep, and asked him to take him to visit. "It was New Year's Day of 1892, and there was deep snow on the ground, a very unusual thing in this part of the country, and due in this instance, as Charley assured us, to the direct agency of Jack Wilson. It is hard to imagine anything more monotonously unattractive than a sage prairie under ordinary circumstances unless it be the same prairie when covered by a heavy fall of snow. However, the mountains were bright in front of us, the sky was blue overhead, and the road was good underfoot. After several miles we noticed a man at some distance with a gun across his shoulder. . . . Sure enough it was the messiah, hunting jack rabbits."

That night, Mooney went to Wovoka's wickiup, where he recounted how he had fallen into a trance during an eclipse and came out of it with the message that if Indians danced for five days, they would be reunited with their dead friends and, says Mooney, "there would be no more death or sickness or old age." In some versions, game became plentiful again and whites vanished from the earth or fell into it in a cataclysm native people survived, a vision of time rolling back to before Columbus, and in others—the story seemed to grow as it moved east—Wovoka was Christ himself returned to the earth. Wovoka himself never said he was Christ, only that Christ had returned like a cloud to the earth. It was a strange religion, seemingly shaped both by Christian ideas about salvation and apocalypse and by the despair over the loss of freedom and plenty that had come with the same people who brought Christianity.

✛ IN THE MORNING, IN MY SOLITUDE, IT WAS HARD TO SEE Tonopah as the same town I had been hauled to after the Test Site action in 1988 and visited again on the Dorothy Legaratta Memorial Caravan in 1990; it looked diminished, and a gale blew down the dusty main street. The usual route from Tonopah to Las Vegas is down Highway 95, which runs past the main gate of the Test Site and the area that is Peace Camp, but I wanted to complete my journey around the periphery of the Test Site that I had begun two years before, so I was going to go east on 6—the Grand Army of the Republic Highway—and turn south on 93. I drove past a sign that said, "Next Gas 121 miles," and drove for hours, to the junction with 93 and then past the town of Rachel, forgetting until too late that Rachel is as close to Secret Area 51 and the Groom Range as you can get without getting arrested, past hundreds of miles of pale expanse more dry and uninhabited than any part of Nevada I had ever seen, windows sealed against the dusty wind that hurled whole bushes across the road and, probably, old fallout. I think of this kind of travelling as "filling in the map," since it isn't a way to know any place, only a way to see how the terrain metamorphoses between known places.

I didn't stop until Ash Springs, where there was a half-sized covered wagon on a pedestal, emblazoned with the motto "Circle Your Wagons," the same slogan I found on the gimme caps inside the combination gas station and grocery. There was a military surplus store next to it. I didn't see much I wanted there, but I asked the proprietor if it's true that people out here get notified of each nuclear test. "They don't tell us a thing," said the older man with bright blue eyes in a blue flight jumpsuit. "They have these monitor stations out here, but they just come and change the air sample bottles. Most of the tests leak, but they don't tell us a thing. It's a problem but people out here can't take on a thing like this. Even if their grandparents died of it, their husbands work there." A spray of fine white hairs spread out from the zipper of his blue jumpsuit like milkweed fluff. He told me he was in the army himself, "but it was fun." I pried a little, and he told me it was fun because he was in military intelligence, doing covert stuff in the jungles of Southeast Asia in the late fifties. "In Vietnam," he finally said, "when we weren't supposed to be there."

8

After Ash Springs I passed through an oasis, the Pahranagat Valley due east of the Test Site, settled early on by Mormons and still a defiant green amid all the aridity around it. The road south began to become a road west and I passed a sign for a mineral-extraction operation run by Kerr-McGee, the defense contractor Karen Silkwood was trying to expose when she died. When I pulled my truck in under the acacia tree in my brother's backyard in Las Vegas, he was having a meeting inside with five women from various organizations. Among his houseguests were Bill Rosse, Anthony Guarisco, the founder of the Alliance of Atomic Veterans, and our older brother Stephen, back in the States after five years in Central America.

That day, October 3, 1992, President Bush signed a nuclear-testing moratorium into effect, the first one since a three-year moratorium had come to an end in the crises of 1961, the first one in our memory. It was to last nine months, the length of a pregnancy, and at its end we hoped it might be delivered of a nuclear-test ban.

The moratorium seemed like an auspicious omen to the walkers who arrived the same day. They had walked across the continent in that modern version of the pilgrimage, the issue ordeal—the genre that encompasses local bikeathons for cancer, peace fasts on the White House steps, and long-distance endeavors to call attention to causes, though this ordeal was, like a traditional pilgrimage, self-fulfilling—the walk had stirred and educated the walkers as well as doing something for their issues. Their legs were leanly muscled, their faces were reddened by wind and sun, red like the faces of the pioneers must have been, and their belongings, water, and food had been carried in buses that accompanied the walks. There were two groups: Walk Across America for Mother Earth, a Belgian project organized by people who had heard Pauline Esteves speak about nuclear and indigenous issues over there; and the European Peace Pilgrimage organized in the Netherlands, which was likewise a walk in solidarity with Native Americans and against the array of nuclear threats. It was a kind of walk few have taken in this century, a walk longer than John Muir's 1,000-mile walk to the Gulf of Mexico in 1867, longer than the Oregon Trail which begins a good third of the way west in Missouri, as long as a medieval pilgrimage from Western Europe to Jerusalem in the days when people walked off their sins and took walking as a spiritual exercise, but these European pilgrims had not a holy site, but the Nevada Test Site as their destination. The Dutch walk had passed the Savannah River plutonium production plant in Georgia, the Pantex Nuclear Weapons Plant in Texas, passed near Los Alamos, gone through the Navajo and Hopi reservations with their uranium mines in northeast Arizona, crossed the colorful contaminated deserts of southern Utah, all at a rate of about fifteen miles a day.

They were supposed to be one walk, according to my little brother, but national animosities kept them apart, which made their concern over American racism a little disingenuous—but I was less interested in their internal squabbles than in what it was like to walk from February to October, to cover the breadth of a broad continent on foot, a continent most of them had never seen before. I asked some of these pilgrims what it had been like. A woman from the Belgian walk told me what it meant to see the Rockies rise up after so many days of the flatness of Kansas, and I got a sense of what it might be like to make the continent big again, big as nine months of change a day at a time. They all agreed that the walk had been extraordinarily spiritual, that walking itself became strangely addictive, that it was hard to do without it once they had begun, that it had transformed them, but that the spirituality, the transformation, was harder to describe. I who had just driven nearly a thousand miles in two days envied them.

On Monday, the walkers began to walk the sixty miles to the Test Site. It would take them four days to get there. They were setting out a week before the Quincentennial, the five-hundredth anniversary of Columbus's landing in this hemisphere, to the gathering the Western Shoshone National Council was hosting in commemoration of it. Huge official galas had been planned across the U.S. for the occasion, but indigenous Americans pointed out that for them 1492 was the beginning of half a millennium of invasion, extermination, and slavery, nothing to celebrate. The phrases "five hundred years of resistance" and "five hundred years of genocide" began to catch on as the anniversary drew near, and most of the galas collapsed. In Las Vegas, a promoter staged a mock wedding between Columbus and the Statue of Liberty, but the replicas of the *Nina,* the *Pinta,* and the *Santa Maria* that were supposed to arrive in San Francisco ran into problems instead. There were a lot of less-remembered anniversaries in 1992: 1492 had also been the year that the king and queen of Spain had expelled the Jews and Moslems who had been there so many years and made it such a center of learning; four hundred years later, a hundred years ago, James Mooney had visited Wovoka in Nevada while the Ghost Dance religion was still flourishing; fifty years before, in 1942, the Final Solution had been launched in Germany and the Manhattan Project in the United States.

While the walkers were walking to the Test Site, I drove out to the Desert National Wildlife Refuge, the place half overlapped by Nellis Air Force Base. I had intended to explore its remote reaches and perhaps stay a few days, but when I got out of the truck, I was so tired I just lay down and slept in its shadow in all that peaceable space. A terrible flu had gotten me, and I spent the next days wandering the air-conditioned library at the University of Las Vegas and listening to the swamp cooler go while all my brother's other houseguests were out being industrious. I was waiting for Thursday night, when my friend Dianne would fly in, and for Friday morning when we would get to the Test Site, and as I lay there utterly enervated looking forward to getting out of the ugly sprawl of Las Vegas, I recalled all my walks across the cattleguard. I think it was then I realized what the nuclear threat had meant to Americans.

✚ WHAT, AFTER ALL, IS THE AMERICAN IDEA OF A NUCLEAR Armageddon but that of the preservation and reinvention of the frontier? Bomb shelters, drills, and survivalist movies instructed the popular imagination not to prepare to die or for the end of the world, but to prepare for a new beginning of lawlessness, chaos, every man for himself, self-sufficiency, a world in which Daniel Boone and Kit Carson might well be at home. America had been without a past before, and seemed ready to be without one again (though the subterranean vaults for preserving congressmen and bank records promised that some vestiges of the destroyed world would return). It seems to have been for this reason that the explosive power of atomic weapons was exaggerated, their radioactive aftermath downplayed: Rather than the bomb as a lingering disease, it was the bomb as a phoenix fire. J. Robert Oppenheimer, a man with a sharp-honed sense of theater, named the first atomic explosion Trinity, he said in 1962, because one of John Donne's religious poems was running through his head:

> *As West and East*
> *In all flatt Maps—and I am one—are one,*
> *So death doth touch the Resurrection.*

That was fair enough for Christian theology and flat maps, but a dangerous way to look at a weapon—and yet Oppenheimer seems to have grasped the mythical meaning the bomb would acquire, whatever its real effects.

I grew up after the generation that had bomb drills in elementary school: We didn't need them because the bomb had already become part of the fabric of our beliefs—and though the drills were supposed to prepare for survival of a bomb, they really seemed to be drills in imagining it. I think everyone my age or younger has always been mentally prepared for this afterlife. I have always been plagued myself by an inability to plan for a future that forks so clearly: Up one fork, it makes sense to build a career in anticipation of a comfortable maturity; on the other, I should learn to scavenge and survive in the ruins of a devastated country. This clouded horizon shadows the decisions of most of my peers and unsettles the simplest acts. It was this possibility that made it so easy for many to take a third path: to become activists who pursued no personal comfort but the cancellation of the apocalypse.

As a child living in a bowl of hills filled with people who seemed hostile to me, I daydreamed fondly of the collapse of their world and their disappearance, cherished pictures of living on alone among their ruins, or sometimes I pictured living in the landscape as it would have been before their appearance. The before and after of their habitation seemed one and the same peace. And this nuclear apocalypse seems refreshing too, like the deluge that washed Noah's world of all its excesses and crimes. Most of America's zealots, from the Mormons to Manson (and the atomic energy program's followers, who have their own peculiar faith), have gravitated to the desert, understood as the natural landscape of apocalypse, as well as the blankest slate on which a new history can be inscribed. The nation renews itself by turning its back on the past, and the atom bomb is a giant eraser sweeping clean the blackboard of the continent.

I saw one of the fifties nuclear-horror movies once. Called *The*

Day the World Ended, it opened with documentary footage of a giant mushroom cloud and the title "The End" and moved on to a melodrama involving a handful of survivors. Radiation and Donner Party–style social Darwinism narrowed down the group to a young blond couple, and the movie ended with them walking off toward the horizon with little Boy Scout–style rucksacks and the title "The Beginning." The film had rewound us from the fifties to the frontier to Adam and Eve walking out of the mess into Eden; it was a vision of history running backward, with the bomb as the great fulcrum of redemption.

The old emigrants used up their land, burned it over and moved on; the nation has continued to burn and move on, but the world has grown small and round, with nowhere to go. Space has been one solution to keep this linear trajectory going forward—the final frontier, in TV terms, a last place to keep fleeing the waste and the memories. But what has always been described as an advance is really a retreat, a retreat from the past, from memory, and from responsibility. This is why walking into the Test Site over and over again is an act of trespass, trespass against U.S. policy, against the transient American spirit, against the idea that the world began so recently and could begin again. It is a refusal to merely flee, forget, and survive. To walk toward the problem is an act of responsibility, an act of return, and an act of memory. The walkers walk into that homeland with all its hundreds of bombs' worth of fallout to shoulder the burdens of the past.

✦ AT THE TEST SITE, I RAN INTO FRIENDS, BEGINNING WITH MY friend Dodge, who stepped out of the shadow of a tent to throw his arms around me a moment after I arrived. Soon afterward, I ran into Carrie Dann, Rachel from the Princesses of Plutonium, Dana, Sarah,

Doug, Lillian and the other Seattle anarchists who had taken me walking in the spring of 1991 and who had brought Dodge down with them, Bernice Lalo who had told me coyote stories in Ruby Valley, Skip and Lone Wolf, the American Indian Movement activists I had met at the Dann Ranch in August. Corbin Harney embraced me, and my brothers strode around the perimeter trying to keep everything running smoothly. It was a great oasis of friendship in that desert, and the Test Site across the road seemed almost irrelevant during that halcyon of the moratorium and the gathering, as though we had finished fighting it and started building something better. There were all the European walkers, people from Russia, from Kazakhstan, from the Marshall Islands where the U.S. had tested bombs in the 1950s, from Quaker, Catholic, and other Christian communities at this event led by Corbin as the Western Shoshone spiritual leader, activists from other Native American communities, including the Southern Paiutes of Utah, whose population had been devastated by fallout, the Havasupai, who were fighting to keep their small homeland on the southern rim of the Grand Canyon from being destroyed by uranium mining, Mormon and other downwinders, atomic veterans, and a lot of others who weren't so directly affected by testing but chose to care about it anyway.

On Sunday, there would have been an action, customarily, but Raymond Yowell announced that the Shoshone weren't going to lead us across the cattleguard because native people had spent the last 500 years in prisons and didn't intend to start the next 500 in one. The Test Site workers were worried about what was going to happen to their jobs if there was a test ban, and the speakers at the gate talked about the immense labor of cleaning up after the forty-two years of nuclear war on the land ahead of us and the need to make job retraining and employment part of our demands. Some people walked in and got arrested, but with the victory of the moratorium, it didn't make sense to do the same things over again. It was time to imagine where we would go next, and in the meantime, we seemed to be in exactly the right place.

Or the right place politically and spiritually. A lot of my friends were beginning to worry about what all the years of camping out in the hot dust of the Test Site was going to do to them, and when I found out that two young activists I knew had developed cervical cancer, I began to realize I might not be coming back myself. Telling stories—testifying, if you like—is what people did instead of walking across the cattleguard. They told us stories on Friday, and we listened, and on Saturday, we listened, went swimming at Ash Meadows near Death Valley, and came back and listened some more.

Sunday afternoon Dianne and I were reading in the shade of my truck, which cast a larger and deeper shadow than our tents. I had even given up on so energetic an activity as turning pages and was admiring a new composition: the Funeral Mountains as framed by the underside of the truck, a long, low-horizoned landscape with Death Valley on the other side. In the middle of the day it would become too hot to do anything. When I walked, the side of my body the sun was shining on would feel miserable, the other side fine. Even in the morning, I would take a slice of bread out of its wrapper to eat, and though it came out fresh, the last bite would be stale and hard. The dryness was almost frightening. I could feel my own flesh dehydrate without continual infusions of water, could imagine mummification coming in a matter of hours to any body that didn't fight back with its internal irrigation systems and with drinks. All through this stay I found myself falling into reveries about that sweet serpentine creek east of Yosemite.

A Dutch man came to ask if he could look in the truck's rearview mirror: I haven't seen my face in a long time, he said, and so I sent him to a side window for a larger picture of himself. Do you recognize that man? I joked, and the convivial man—Fritz, who organized the Dutch walk, I learned later—stayed to point out the shelter he had built for himself out of the dwindling supply of sweatlodge firewood. His hut reminded him of a story about King Rat, a folk figure in his country who is fattened up by all the other rats during good times, and eaten by them in lean times. We talked a little more about Old World beliefs, and it must have been in the midst of that conversation that he pointed out the standing stones on a conical hill in the distance.

Later, Dodge came up and sat with us, moving into the truck's shade too, and not long after that I saw Skip Mahawk and Lone Wolf's son going by on the road with Tim Dann, Carrie's and Mary's nephew. I raised my voice to call him, and the three came over. Tim said he had just got in. He was wearing only his work boots, Levi's belted with a length of yellow rope, and a headband, and he looked utterly at home there. The three of them were holding bottles of very warm Dr. Pepper. I offered them our canteen, and after they'd stood around talking to us for a while, I invited them to move into our shade: Only Tim declined. Dodge said that Corbin needed more wood for the sweatlodges, and that someone he'd talked to knew where to get some. While the rest of us conversed, he found the person who knew, came back, and proposed to us that we go get it. All along I had thought that we were holding our guests back from some important purpose, but it turned out that they wanted to ride into Indian Springs to get the firewood with us. We cleaned out the back of the truck and I loaded up these five passengers and took off down 95. Somehow this event seems typical of the laconic sociability of the camp this time: One event slid into another without effort, one group mixed into the next. We found the wood behind the church in Indian Springs across from the sheriff's station. They were slender sticks mostly, and five of us spent ten minutes making armloads to hand to Lone Wolf's son, who piled it all up neatly, on one side of the truckbed, so that there would be room for them all still.

We spent another fifteen minutes admiring the rows of refrigerated drinks in the gas station store. The convenience stores in Nevada always seemed to promise the bounty of a true oasis, and every time I was fooled into wandering through the air-conditioned aisles of beer nuts, disposable diapers, Gatorade, Cheez Whiz, Doritos, jocular license-plate frames, and gum on a quest for some rejuvenating nectar that I never found. This one didn't even sell spring water or any kind of fresh food. It was later than I'd expected by the time we turned back, and the moon was rising in my rearview mirror, the sun getting ready to set and blinding me in the meantime. By the time we'd unloaded the wood at the pile by the sweatlodges, it was nearly time to get in them. Made of slender branches covered with thick blanketing and capable of holding three dozen tightly packed people apiece, they were big domes a person could have stood up in had the center not been a pit for hot rocks. Corbin was leading the men's lodge and a young woman the women's. It was clear we were welcomed into the sweatlodge ceremony not as converts or initiates, but as guests whose hosts wanted to invite us all the way in.

The sweatlodge attendant who brought in the rocks was the Dutchman who'd told me about King Rat. The moon was still low as we got in, and a shaft of its light came through the door, motes dancing in it as they do in sunbeams; the fire where the rocks were heated was also visible from where I sat, sending showers of sparks into the sky. We sang, prayed, called for more rocks and for the attendant to open the door so that those who couldn't bear the heat and enclosure could leave, and we sweated. The AIM guys had invited me into the sweatlodge at the Dann ranch that summer, and so I had found myself praying out loud for the first time in my life.

There, the experience had been disturbingly intense. Here though, the group of women hadn't coalesced into any kind of community, for all their good will. When I got back to my things, my watch said it was 10:30; we had cooked and ceremonied for nearly three hours. I was restless and drained, tried sitting in camp, went back to the sweat fire, and was heading for my bed when Dodge approached.

I had wanted to walk toward Mercury in the moonlight ever since I'd arrived, but I was no longer interested in the possible consequences. He wanted to walk toward the hill where someone had erected the two standing stones. I had found them peculiarly satisfying as an apparently European way of responding to the landscape within reach of a camp where we were in danger of becoming strays in the Shoshone fold. We began to walk toward them in the same clear moonlight that had been shining all night every night since I'd arrived, and walked for a long time without the hill becoming larger or nearer. We speculated on whether it was a small near hill or a large distant one: Even in daylight desert distance is hard to gauge. The desert floor seemed to roll right up to it, but it could be that a dip of any width lay between us and the foot of the hill.

The journey was made more demanding by the constant necessity of weaving in among the thorn bushes and cacti: It was almost always impossible to pursue a straight course, nor could we go more than a few steps looking ahead rather than down. On the ground, the rocks were becoming larger, and the streaks of quartz that ran through them looked like petroglyphs. It was easy to see by the light of the moon. Everything was perfectly clear and shadows were sharp, but nothing was bright, and there was no color to this cold light. It was like a dreamworld or a land of the dead in which time seemed less certain.

We did get there eventually. It took far longer than I would have decided to go, and I gave up halfway up the hill. We had stopped to look back at the lights of Mercury and the peaks beyond and around the jagged horizon. The hill was made of a volcanic rock so rough it seemed to grab at you if you touched it: Tiny sharp surfaces of petrified bubbles braked the motion of skin. I cut my chin leaning on a ledge. Later I realized that it was the same hill I climbed at sunset in the spring of 1990, after talking to Richard Misrach, the year the camp had been miles closer to the hill. Mercury was still visible in the northeast, but the camp wasn't. We saw the constellation Orion near where the moon had risen, but most of the stars were drowned in moonlight. Dodge wasn't tired, and went up the mountain without me. I heard him whistling on the way down. The two markers, he said, were made out of stacks of flattish rocks, and a bell the wind rung hung from one of them. The pause had made me realize I was utterly spent. He tried carrying me a little way, and we rested a few times.

We had thought we pointed ourselves in the right direction, but when we expected to be at the camp we were in an uninhabited expanse. Perhaps they'd all gotten up and left us, I speculated, and Dodge proposed that we had been gone far longer than we'd thought. In that world of bright night and companionable solitude, it seemed perfectly plausible that a century or two had passed. Finally I saw a tent dome between us and the freeway, and then more became visible: a mushroom colony sprung up in the night country. The moon was high overhead and we had begun Columbus Day.

✤ WE BEGAN IT AGAIN BEFORE DAWN. MOONLIGHT ETCHED THE silhouette of small thorny flowers against the tent's western wall. Corbin started drumming his sunrise ceremony earlier than before, and we awoke even before that—if we'd really slept in that timeless night—to hear him beat and stop a few times. The sky was red along its eastern edge, the sun was nowhere, and the moon still ruled in a dark blue realm. The day before, the moon had been golden as it set near Skull Mountain, but this day it was silvery and chill. During those days of seeing the full moon rise in the east as the sun set in the west and then the sun rise in the east as the moon set a little way north of sunset's country, as though the two chased each other across the sky in an interval of perfect symmetry, I felt for the first time what I'd known as long as I can remember: that the earth is nothing but a sphere spinning through a space with other, brighter spheres in it.

The sun climbed in the sky and the day grew hot as a long, and eventually an awful, ceremony under the open sky gave way to an afternoon of storytelling in the great striped pavilion. All the speakers were natives on this day, this counterquincentennial or first day of the post-Columbian; the rest of us were listeners, and the stories ranged from personal testimonies and downwinder stories to talks about environmental issues from the Columbia River Basin to the Southwest. Bill Rosse got up and welcomed us all, talked about how he discovered Brussels, about getting rid of nuclear power and promoting solar power, about littering the moon, social justice, and homelessness. He wrapped up his quick soliloquy by saying, "I'll leave this world loving all of you. Seeing us all here united is wonderful. Tell them to honor treaties. Thank you all."

His words filled up the last page of the yellow pad I had been scribbling stories on since Lee Vining. Havasupai participants ended the session. More Havasupai elders had left their Grand Canyon homelands to be here than had ever left it before, but they let a child do most of their talking and then asked us to join in a circle dance.

Full Circle

What else is there to tell, but that the circle became so large its far side was out of sight behind tents and the rolling terrain, or that we left for San Francisco late that day, Dianne, Rachel, a woman from Seattle, and I. This time I was just going back, because I was already home.

Afterword to the New Edition

✚ AROUND NOON ON MARCH 29, 1999, BOB FULKERSON sent me to go walking among the petroglyphs at Grimes Point near Fallon, Nevada, while he wrote a eulogy for Bill Rosse, who, after surviving a war and many illnesses and accidents, had finally passed away three days before, aged seventy-two. The rocks around me were almost black and the faint diagram-like petroglyphs were easiest to see when you weren't looking for them. Military jets shaped like arrowheads and hypodermics ripped through the pale sky overhead, and I seemed to be back where I was nine years earlier when Bill and Bob invited me into Nevada: sandwiched between enigmas, glories and disasters.

Looking back on all that had happened since 1992, it seemed that everything and nothing had changed. The United Nations, under pressure from activist groups around the world, approved a Comprehensive Test Ban Treaty in September of 1996 (which the U.S. Senate has yet to ratify). A test ban had long been imagined as the beginning of the end of the arms race and nuclear proliferation, but new technological refinements make it possible for the U.S. and other advanced nations to violate the spirit and sometimes the letter of the treaty. Physicists can now develop new nuclear bombs without full-scale nuclear tests, relying instead on computer modeling, new simulation techniques, and the limited nuclear explosions of "subcritical testing" at the Nevada Test Site. Like many new technologies, these nuclear-testing ones are harder to explain, harder to see, and harder to resist than that which they supersede. The U.S. is still prepared for and spending lavishly on nuclear war. As the U.S. National Academy of Sciences concluded in 1997, "The absence of change in U.S. nuclear posture and practice to reflect the dramatically altered post-Cold War conditions weakens the credibility of U.S. leadership in nonproliferation efforts."

The day of Bill Rosse's funeral, the first nuclear waste shipment to the WIPP project in Carlsbad, New Mexico, was dispatched from Los Alamos; but the winter before Bill's death, a magnificent cross-cultural coalition defeated a proposal to build the Sierra Blanca nuclear waste dump in West Texas, and similar coalitions were still holding off the dumps proposed at Yucca Mountain, Nevada, and Ward Valley, California. American Peace Test, which organized the demonstrations and Peace Camp at the NTS, disbanded, but other groups continue to focus on the Test Site, and Shundahai Network continues to organize demonstrations at the Test Site. Citizen Alert (whose board I joined in 1996) continues to fight the reckless plans for the high-level nuclear waste dump at Yucca Mountain and cross-country nuclear waste shipments to the NTS. Western Shoshone activists continue to oppose this violation of their land and to seek recognition of the Treaty of Ruby Valley, and Carrie and Mary Dann continue to stand up for their rights in Crescent Valley. Though the Bureau of Land Management continues to harass the Dann family, gold mining has become the most immediate threat to their goals and beliefs. Before, the land endured no matter who held title, but now the land near the ranch is being eaten away on a vast scale, and the water table is being pumped out to get at the gold ore below. Western Shoshones did win a major land-rights victory in California's Death Valley National Park. After a long campaign for land rights, the Timbisha Shoshone were granted 300 acres of their homeland at Furnace Creek in the park's heart, exclusive use of another 1,000 acres there, a role in managing the 300,000 acre park expanse to be named the Timbisha Natural and Cultural Preservation Area, and about 6,000 acres outside the park, as well as acknowledgment that many plant communities and springs were suffering from a lack of traditional ecological practices, which should be resumed.

The Ahwahneechee of Yosemite were by no means so lucky, though they have made significant gains. Jay Johnson told me that they might have gained more had they achieved federal recognition as a tribe. In 1997, on the site of the Yosemite Valley Indian village torn down in the 1960s, they were granted—for fifteen years—six acres on which to build traditional structures in which to hold ceremonies and an annual festival, and to represent themselves to the public. They also secured special access to several hundred acres of national forest service land outside the park and plant-gathering rights inside. The National Park Service seems to be coming to an understanding that in many cases it manages homelands, not wildernesses. Yosemite National Park's Indian Museum issued a splendid new brochure on the indigenous inhabitants of the valley that uses more candid language about such matters as invasions, acknowledges that the descendants of the invaded are still present, and is bilingual—in English and Miwok. Johnson told me that when he was a boy his grandfather had said "When the last of our people have left this valley, then the rocks are gonna come down. The rocks and things like that are gonna be angry." Johnson, the last person to preserve the continuity of Ahwahneechee presence in the valley, retired in 1996 and finished moving out of his home on December 30th of that year. A day later, he notes, the colossal flood that washed out many buildings and roads began. But "as long as we're able to hold ceremonies, things will be okay," he told me from his home in nearby Mariposa. The nation seems more aware of indigenous peoples' rights than in 1992, but less so of the nuclear problems that still cast a long shadow over our future.

The other activists who loom large in this book continue to work for environmental protection and social justice, though many do so in other arenas. Joe Sanchez died of leukemia in 1993, but his partner M. Lee Dazey is northern Nevada director of Citizen Alert and raises their son. As she says, "activists generally know that the changes they promote won't all happen in this life, which makes a good case for bringing up children and balancing the outer work with the inner." Carrie Dann has three grandchildren living at the ranch. Bob Fulkerson left Citizen Alert to found a progressive alliance for Nevada (and, as Lee points out, leads his daughter's Girl Scout troop). Rachel, one of the Princesses of Plutonium, continues to work against the proposed nuclear waste dump at Ward Valley in far southeastern California and has a one-year-old son, while other Princesses have become environmental scientists and lawyers. David Solnit returned to the Bay Area in 1993 and cofounded Art and Revolution, a collective that, as he put it, "infuses art, theater, music, dance and creativity into grassroots struggles for social change." Looking back years later, I see that however grim the devastation of land and culture that is this book's background, the cheerfully heroic characters who crowd its foreground achieved great victories in building friendships and coalitions across continents, generations, and religious and racial differences, in standing up for their beliefs, and sometimes in changing history. Bill Rosse, with his love, fearlessness, music and jokes, was one of the greatest, but there are more coming.

Rebecca Solnit
1999

Sources

Some of the books that influenced me most form a kind of subterranean foundation for this book, rather than rising to the surface in citations. No single book was exactly central to its themes and issues, though many were important. Many of the ideas came from friends who are mentioned in the acknowledgments, and much of the particular history I gather here was also unwritten or unpublished.

Patricia Nelson Limerick's *The Legacy of Conquest: The Unbroken Past of the American West* (New York: Norton, 1987) has been a crucial reinterpretation of Western history for many people, including me. One thing I neglected is a clear exposition of the beliefs, strategies, and history of the contemporary direct-action antinuclear movement, which became an important force in American nuclear politics in the late 1970s. Barbara Epstein's *Political Protest and Cultural Revolution: Nonviolent Direct Action in the 1970s and 1980s* (Berkeley: University of California Press, 1991) covers what I left out with careful research and cogent analysis. Another superb source is Hugh Gusterson's *Testing Times,* a brilliant anthropological study of the nuclear physicists' and antinuclear activists' cultural mores as revealed through interviews and analysis of activities and imageries (Berkeley: University of California Press, 1994).

The best single source for factual information on the effects of the Department of Energy and the U.S. military on Nevada is the massive *Special Nevada Report* prepared by Science Applications International Corporation of the Desert Research Institute and released on September 23, 1991, a bulky compendium of facts and statistics; copies are available from the Office of Public Affairs at Nellis Air Force Base. There are many histories of nuclear testing and its effects, some of which are cited below, but the Nevada Test Site itself has figured in them as little more than an invisible source of radiation, rather than as a tangible expanse of land, and most of them leave off when testing went underground.

As for Yosemite, great forests have been laid waste to supply paper for all the books about Yosemite, yet they echo each other curiously. There is an enormous gap between the scenic rhapsodies of the many official histories and the hard dry facts of the few anthropological treatises. The best overall book on Yosemite I found was Margaret Sanborn's *Yosemite: Its Discovery, Its Wonders, and Its People* (New York: Random House, 1991). Carl P. Russell's *One Hundred Years in Yosemite* was published in 1932; it has been republished with many useful chronologies and documents (Yosemite National Park, CA: Yosemite Association, 1992). David Robertson's *West of Eden: A History of the Art and Literature of Yosemite* (Yosemite Natural History Association/Wilderness Press, 1984) is valuable and copiously illustrated.

I used the following libraries: the San Francisco Public Library; the University of California at Berkeley libraries, notably the Bancroft Library, which houses many crucial documents, manuscripts, and rare books; the University of Reno and University of Nevada at Las Vegas libraries; and the Yosemite Research Library, and I thank the librarians at all of them for their assistance, particularly Linda Eade at the Yosemite Research Library, who made many valuable suggestions of material.

FROM HELL TO BREAKFAST

p. 4: The Worldwatch Institute's Worldwatch Paper 106, *Nuclear Waste: The Problem that Won't Go Away* (December 1991) is a useful overview of the varieties of artificially generated radiation; the International Physicians for the Prevention of Nuclear War's publication *Radioactive Heaven and Earth: The Health and Environmental Effects of Nuclear Weapons Testing in, on, and above the Earth* (New York: Apex Press, 1991) is also very helpful.

p. 4: "I will show you fear" is from T. S. Eliot's *The Waste Land*.

p. 9: "The politics of prefiguration" comes from Epstein's *Political Protest and Cultural Revolution* (op. cit.).

p. 13: Sylvia Townsend Warner's comment was cited in the *New York Review of Books* article "Good Witch of the West" of July 18, 1985.

p. 16: The backcountry guidelines were published in American Peace Test's newspaper in 1990.

p. 19: Information on and quote about the Priscilla Test and the Plumbbob Series come from Richard Miller's valuable *Under the Cloud: The Decades of Nuclear Testing* (New York: The Free Press, 1986).

p. 25: The initial declaration of the NSAM was published in *Earth Island Journal* (summer 1989).

p. 28: Names of nuclear bombs here and elsewhere come from the Department of Energy's publication *Announced United States Nuclear Tests July*

1945 through December 1991. It lists 720 announced U.S. tests at the NTS and 23 British tests there. On December 8, 1993, the *New York Times* reported that there had been 204 unannounced nuclear tests there, about twice as many as outsiders estimated. There were 6 more tests in 1992, making a total of 953 bombs detonated on this land.

p. 29: The best book on Western Shoshone history I found was produced by the Inter-Tribal Council of Nevada: *Newe: A Western Shoshone History* (Reno, 1976).

p. 30: The Treaty of Ruby Valley is available as a government document in the published compendium of treaties and in Jack Forbes's *Nevada Indians Speak* (Reno: University of Nevada Press, 1967).

pp. 32–37: Some aspects of the stories Bob Fulkerson told me are documented in issues of Citizen Alert's newspaper from around that time.

p. 33: Margaret Long, *The Shadow of the Arrow* (Caldwell, ID: Caxton Printers, 1941).

LIKE MOTHS TO A CANDLE

p. 38: Richard Misrach's work is reproduced in his books *Violent Legacies* (New York: Aperture, 1992); in *Bravo 20: The Bombing of the American West,* a collaboration with Myriam Weisang Misrach (Baltimore: Johns Hopkins University Press, 1990); and elsewhere.

p. 43: As for an exploding nuclear bomb being a kind of star come to earth, see Miller's *Under the Cloud* (op. cit.), pp. 36 and 46.

p. 47: Oppenheimer's "From a technical point of view" has been quoted in many places, including Freeman Dyson, *Disturbing the Universe* (Harper & Row, 1979).

pp. 48–54: The chronology of white exploration comes from *Newe: A Western Shoshone History* (op. cit.), from Hubert Howe Bancroft's history of Nevada, from Gloria Griffin Cline's *Exploring the Great Basin* (Norman: University of Oklahoma Press, 1963, reprinted by University of Nevada Press), and from William H. Goetzmann's *Exploration and Empire: The Explorer and the Scientist in the Winning of the American West* (New York: W. W. Norton and Co., 1966).

p. 48: "The first white men" is from *Newe,* as is "the banks of the river."

p. 50: Much of Fremont's Great Basin travel is described by Cline; more appears in Fremont's own *Geographical Memoir of Upper California* and Andrew Rolle's *John Charles Fremont: Character as Destiny* (Norman: University of Oklahoma Press, 1991). Francis P. Farquhar's *History of the Sierra Ne-*

vada also describes Fremont's travels and his interest in the Buenaventura River.

p. 51: John Wesley Powell's remarks appear in the opening pages of his *The Exploration of the Colorado River and Its Canyons* (reprinted—New York: Dover, 1961).

p. 52: Much of the material on the Mormons comes from Wallace Stegner's book *Mormon Country* (New York: Duell, Sloan, and Pierce, 1942) and his mentor Bernard DeVoto's *Year of Decision: 1846* (Boston: Houghton Mifflin, 1941). Brigham Young's "This is a good place" appears in Terry Tempest Williams's *Refuge: An Unnatural History of Family and Place* (New York: Random House, 1991), an exquisite, moving book by a naturalist, Mormon, and downwinder.

p. 53: Edmund Burke's "would change their manners" and "The prevailing idea" are quoted in Henry Nash Smith's *Virgin Land: The American West as Symbol and Myth* (New York: Random House, 1950).

p. 53: Zebulon Pike in Stegner's *Beyond the Hundredth Meridian: John Wesley Powell and the Second Opening of the American West* (Boston: Houghton Mifflin, 1954).

p. 55: John Muir in his collection *Steep Trails* (Boston: Houghton Mifflin, 1918).

p. 56: Long (op. cit.).

p. 57: Ted Shaw's reminiscences appeared in the *Las Vegas Review-Journal/Sun* of February 21, 1993.

p. 63: Paul Shepard in *Man in the Landscape* (New York: Alfred A. Knopf, 1967) and in *Nature and Madness* (San Francisco: Sierra Club Books, 1982).

p. 67: Freeman Dyson (op. cit.).

APRIL FOOL'S DAY

p. 74: Thoreau in "Walking," included in many Thoreau anthologies; I used a freestanding version of the essay (Boston/Cambridge: Applewood Books, 1987).

p. 81: *The New York Times Sunday Magazine* ran the November 18, 1990, article by William J. Broad from which the quote by Charles Archambeau came.

p. 83: Western Shoshone and Southern Paiute elders participated in a cultural history of the Yucca Mountain region sponsored by the State of Nevada's Nuclear Waste Project Office: *Native Americans and Yucca Mountain: A Summary Report* by Catherine S. Fowler, September 1990.

p. 90: The DOE report on Operation Faultless appears in *Special Nevada Report* (op. cit.).

TREES

p. 93: The Lord's Avenger letter is cited in the *San Francisco Examiner* story of May 30, 1990. Women Strike for Peace remains poorly documented, and most of the information cited here comes from my cousin's own files. Amy Swerdlow of Sarah Lawrence College wrote an excellent unpublished analysis of WSP's "rhetoric and tactics," which I read, and has a book on WSP coming out with University of Chicago Press.

p. 97: "Control milk" and related emergency material appears in the DOE publication *Off-Site Emergency Response Plans and Procedures for an Accidental Venting or Seepage at the Nevada Test Site,* July 1987.

p. 98: Adlai Stevenson's concern with strontium-90 and other details in this paragraph about the mid-fifties response to fallout in the U.S. appear in Spencer R. Weart's *Nuclear Fear: A History of Images* (Cambridge, MA: Harvard University Press, 1988). Kennedy cited in *Nuclear Fear.*

p. 105: Wall Street Journal, September 27, 1963.

LISE MEITNER'S WALKING SHOES

Richard Rhodes's *The Making of the Atom Bomb* (New York: Simon and Schuster, 1986) and Hugh Gusterson's articles and a chapter from his Stanford University Ph.D. dissertation (forthcoming as *Testing Times,* op. cit.) were important sources. After reading Rhodes, I read many of the primary texts that were his sources. Carolyn Merchant's *The Death of Nature: Women, Ecology, and the Scientific Revolution* (New York: Harper and Row, 1980) and Barbara Novak's *Nature and Culture: American Landscape and Painting 1825–1875* (New York: Oxford University Press, 1980) were also important, along with *Virgin Land* (op. cit.) and Werner Heisenberg's *Physics and Philosophy: The Revolution in Science* (New York: Harper and Brothers, 1958).

p. 112: W. H. Auden's essay appears in Bryan Loughrey's anthology *The Pastoral Mode: A Casebook* (London: Macmillan, 1984).

pp. 115–117: My thumbnail sketch of Bacon, Descartes, and Newton owes much to *The Death of Nature,* along with Morris Berman's *The Reenchantment of the World* (New York: Cornell University Press, 1981), William Leiss's *The Domination of Nature* (Boston: Beacon Press, 1972), and J. B. Bury's *The Idea of Progress* (London: Macmillan, 1932).

p. 119: Teller's "Perhaps twenty million might be killed . . ." is cited by WSP member Dr. Frances Herring in an unpublished WSP history.

p. 121: Max Planck's walk is described in Heisenberg's *Physics and Philosophy* (op. cit.). George Gamow's history, *Thirty Years that Shook Physics: The Story of Quantum Physics* (Garden City, NY: Anchor Books, 1976) comments that his findings "were so unusual" and quotes Sommerfeld's couplet.

p. 122: Bohr's meeting with Heisenberg is described in Rhodes (op. cit.), among other places.

p. 123: Heisenberg's own description of his walk and the passage beginning "Natural science . . ." come from his *Physics and Philosophy* (op. cit.).

p. 124: Bohr's "After all, we are both . . ." from Ruth Moore, *Niels Bohr: The Man, His Science, and the World They Changed* (New York: Alfred A. Knopf, 1966).

p. 124: J. Robert Oppenheimer's "It was a heroic time" is cited in Robert K. Jungk's *Brighter than a Thousand Suns: A Personal History of the Atomic Scientists* (New York: Harcourt Brace Jovanovich, 1958) and in Moore (ibid.).

p. 125: Houtermans's walk with Atkinson and subsequent experiences are told in Jungk (op. cit.).

p. 126: Lise Meitner and Otto Frisch's walk is described in many places, including Jungk's and Rhodes's histories and Frisch's own memoir, *What Little I Remember* (New York: Cambridge University Press, 1979), as is his "feel as if I had caught. . . ."

p. 127: Newton is cited in Merchant's *Death of Nature* (op. cit.).

p. 128: Leo Szilard tells this story himself in *Leo Szilard: His Version of the Facts,* edited by Spencer R. Weart and Gertrud Weiss Szilard (Cambridge, MA: MIT Press, 1978) and talks about *The Tragedy of Man;* Rhodes and Jungk also tell versions of it. Further information on Szilard came from Michael Bess's "Leo Szilard: Scientist, Activist, Visionary," an undated publication of the Council for a Livable World, reprinted from the Bulletin of the Atomic Scientists.

p. 129: Einstein's letter appears in an appendix to C. P. Snow's *The Physicists* (Boston: Little, Brown, 1981), Einstein's musing in Moore (op. cit.).

p. 130: The release of the Farm Hall Transcripts and the painstaking research of Thomas Powers have buttressed Heisenberg's claims and put him in an altogether better light. Although Powers's monumental *Heisenberg's War: The Secret History of the German Bomb* (New York: Alfred A. Knopf, 1993) had not been published when I wrote this chapter, two valuable articles on the subject had appeared: "Saboteur or Savant of Nazi Drive for A-Bomb?" by William J. Broad, *New York Times,* September 1, 1992; and the lengthy "The Farm Hall Transcripts: The German Scientists and the Bomb" by Jeremy Bernstein, *New York Review of Books,* August 13, 1992.

p. 131: Farm Hall passages come from Bernstein article, above, except rose garden walk, which comes from Heisenberg's *Physics and Beyond: Encounters and Conversations* (New York: Harper and Row, 1971).

p. 133: Dyson, *Disturbing* (op. cit.).

p. 135: "This has been the death" in Snow (op. cit.).

p. 138: "Any temporary advantage" in Ruth Moore (op. cit.).

p. 139: Hugh Gusterson in the magnificent essay "Endless Escalation: The Cold War as Postmodern Narrative," *Tikkun,* vol. 6, no. 5 (September–October 1991).

p. 140: Heisenberg in *Physics and Philosophy* (op. cit.).

p. 141: Bohr on complementarity and reality in Moore (op. cit.).

p. 143: Rachel Carson, *Silent Spring* (Boston: Houghton Mifflin, 1962).

GOLDEN HOURS AND IRON COUNTY

Several books have been published on the downwinders; unfortunately many tend to suggest that the problem came to a close with the 1963 Limited Test Ban. The books include Miller's *Under the Cloud* (op. cit.), Howard Ball's *Justice Downwind: America's Atomic Testing Program in the 1950s* (New York: Oxford University Press, 1986); Harvey Wasserman and Norman Solomon's *Killing Our Own: The Disaster of America's Experience with Atomic Radiation* (New York: Dell Publishing Company, 1982); Terry Tempest William's *Refuge* (op. cit.); and the deluxe pictorial *American Ground Zero: The Secret Nuclear War* by Carol Gallagher (Cambridge, MA: MIT Press, 1993), which came out after this book was written.

RUBY VALLEY AND THE RANCH

p. 159: Mary Dann's statement made in a video interview with the author which also became part of "Newe Sogobia Is Not for Sale: The Struggle for Western Shoshone Lands" made by Jesse Drew of San Francisco's Mission Creek Video. Sarah Winnemucca's book is titled *Life among the Piutes: Their Wrongs and Claims* by Sarah Winnemucca Hopkins, edited by Mrs. Horace Mann (facsimile edition, Sierra Media, Inc., Bishop, CA, 1969).

p. 163: The "scorched river" campaign in Inter-Tribal Council of Nevada, *Newe* (op. cit.).

p. 164: The August 29, 1864 letter by Jacob T. Lockhardt appears in the National Archives' Record Group 75, Letters Received by Commission of Indian Affairs, Nevada Superintendency 1861–69, frames 371–376 of roll 839.

p. 165: "In 1869, the CIA official" in frames 1105–1107 (ibid.).

p. 166: John A. Burche letter of August 1, 1864, in Record Group 75, frame 377 (op. cit.).

p. 168: Limerick, *Legacy of Conquest* (op. cit.).

p. 169: "We all want to stay" in Jack Forbes's *Nevada Indians Speak* (ibid.).

p. 169: Myron Angel, *History of Nevada* (Oakland: Thompson & West, 1881).

p. 171: Abraham Lincoln, Second Annual Message, 1862, cited in Elizabeth Darby Junkin, *Lands of Brighter Destiny: The Public Lands of the American West* (Golden, CO: Fulcrum, 1986).

p. 185: Raymond Yowell, "The creator" from interview with author for *Newe Sogobia* video (op. cit.).

THE WAR

p. 194: Carrie Dann's conversations and statements here are transcribed directly from Joachim's video of the event.

KEEPING PACE WITH THE TORTOISE

p. 208: "Because most of the exposure is . . ." in *Radioactive Heaven and Earth* (op. cit.).

p. 209: Operation Plowshare, Atoms for Peace, and Edward Teller's "We will change . . ." in Weart, *Nuclear Fear* (op. cit.).

THE RAINBOW

p. 220: John Muir's "The lake with its rocky bays . . ." is a journal entry dated August 1, 1876, printed in *John of the Mountains: The Unpublished Journals of John Muir*, edited by Linnie Marsh Wolfe (New York: Houghton Mifflin, 1938). The primary book on John Muir I used, aside from those containing his own writings, is Frederick Turner's *Rediscovering America: John Muir in His Time and Ours* (San Francisco: Sierra Club, 1985).

SPECTATORS

p. 231: "On the first night that white people" in Bunnell's *Discovery of the Yosemite and the Indian War of 1851 Which Led to that Event* (Yosemite National Park, CA: Yosemite Association, 1991).

p. 233: J.M. Hutchings, *In the Heart of the Sierra: The Yo Semite Valley* (Oakland: Pacific Press, 1886), and in *Hutchings' California Magazine,* vol. 4, no. 4 (October 1859).

p. 235: I relied on Fraenkel Gallery's *Carleton E. Watkins Photographs 1861–1874 (Essay by Peter E. Palmquist)* (San Francisco: Bedford Arts Press, 1989).

p. 237: Thomas Starr King's *A Vacation among the Sierras: Yosemite in 1860* (San Francisco: Book Club of California, 1962).

p. 238: Information on Fremont and Las Mariposas comes from Rolle's *John Charles Fremont* (op. cit.), notes to King book, above, and the biography of Frederick Law Olmsted, *F.L.O.,* by Laura Wood Roper (Baltimore: Johns Hopkins Press, 1973).

p. 239: Bierstadt's companion quoted in wall labels to Albert Bierstadt exhibition organized by the Brooklyn Museum and accompanied by a catalogue (Hudson Hills Press, 1990).

p. 243: Olmsted's "The Yosemite Valley and the Mariposa Big Trees: A Preliminary Report" (1865), published in *Landscape Architecture,* vol. 43, no. 1 (October 1952).

p. 246: John McPhee in the *New Yorker* articles which later appeared as *Assembling California* (New York: Farrar, Strauss, Giroux, 1993).

FRAMING THE VIEW

The history of landscape exists in many versions. Among the books I have relied on in my interpretation of this lineage of landscape are Christopher Thacker's *The History of Gardens* (Berkeley: University of California Press, 1979), H. Diane Russell's *Claude Lorrain 1600–1682* (Washington, D.C.: National Gallery of Art, 1982), John Dixon Hunt and Peter Willis's *The Genius of the Place: The English Landscape Garden 1620–1820* (Cambridge, MA: MIT Press, 1988), Ann Bermingham's *Landscape and Ideology: The English Rustic Tradition, 1740–1860* (Berkeley: University of California Press, 1986), Novak's *Nature and Culture* (op. cit.), Estelle Jussim and Elizabeth Lindquist-Cock's *Landscape as Photograph* (New Haven: Yale University Press, 1985), Shepard's *Man in the Landscape* (op. cit.), Roderick Nash's *Wilderness and the*

American Imagination (revised edition) (New Haven: Yale University Press, 1973), Donald Worster's *Nature's Economy: A History of Ecological Ideas* (San Francisco: Sierra Club Books, 1977), and Kate Nearpass Ogden's "Sublime Vistas and Scenic Backdrops: Nineteenth-Century Painters and Photographers at Yosemite," *California History* (summer 1990).

p. 252: Walpole in *The Genius of the Place* (op. cit.).

p. 254: Thomas Burnett quoted in Keith Thomas, *Man and the Natural World: Changing Attitudes in England 1500–1800* (Harmondsworth, England: Penguin Books, 1984).

p. 257: David Brower's ad described in Nash's *Wilderness* (op. cit.). John Muir in the *Sierra Club Bulletin* (January 1908).

p. 260: Turner in *Rediscovering America* (op. cit.).

p. 260: "We are now" in Muir, *My First Summer in the Sierra* (San Francisco: Sierra Club Books, 1988).

p. 261: Ansel Adams in a letter to David Brower of January 6, 1957, quoted in Alfred Runte's *Yosemite: The Embattled Wilderness* (Lincoln: University of Nebraska Press, 1990).

p. 264: Olmsted (op. cit.).

p. 264: Leslie Marmon Silko, "Landscape, History, and the Pueblo Imagination," in *Antaeus*, no. 57 (autumn 1986).

p. 265: Richard K. Nelson, "The Gifts," *Antaeus*, no. 57 (ibid.).

VANISHING (REMAINING)

Major sources for this recounting of California history include: Alberto L. Hurtado's *Indian Survival on the California Frontier* (New Haven: Yale University Press, 1988); Craig D. Bates and Martha J. Lee's *Tradition and Innovation: A Basket History of the Yosemite-Mono Lake Area* (Yosemite National Park, CA: Yosemite Association, 1990); Bev Ortiz's book on Julia Parker and her involvement with traditional Yosemite technologies, *It Will Live Forever: Traditional Yosemite Indian Acorn Preparation* (Berkeley: Heyday Press, 1991); Robert F. Heizer and Alan F. Almquist's *The Other Californians* (Berkeley: University of California Press, 1971); James Clifford's *The Predicament of Culture: Twentieth-Century Ethnography, Literature and Art* (Cambridge: Harvard University Press, 1988); and the chapter "The Persistence of Natives" in Limerick's *Legacy of Conquest* (op. cit.).

p. 269: Pedro Muñoz's diary is quoted in Craig Bates's *A History of the Indian People of Mariposa County* (1975), a manuscript in the Yosemite Research Library.

p. 271: Governor Burnett in "Message to the California State Legislature," January 7, 1851, California State Senate Journal, 1851, reprinted in Hurtado (op. cit.).

p. 271: Indian Commissioners' address printed in *Alta California,* January 14, 1851. Carl P. Russell in *One Hundred Years in Yosemite* (op. cit.).

p. 275: Ted Orland, *Man and Yosemite: A Photographic History of the Early Years* (Santa Cruz: Image Continuum Press, 1985).

p. 275: Rose Taylor, *The Last Survivor* (San Francisco: Johnck and Seeger, 1932).

p. 280: Hutchings (op. cit.).

p. 280: Jean-Nicholas Perlot, translated by Helen Harding Bretnor, edited by Howard R. Lamar, *Gold Seeker: Adventures of a Belgian Argonaut During the Gold Rush Years* (New Haven: Yale University Press, 1985).

p. 286: "Petition to Congress on Behalf of the Yosemite Indians" in Yosemite Research Library, from an article with commentary by Ed Castillo.

p. 286: The prices offered for Alcatraz from a letter by Dave Raymond.

p. 287: In 1906 the U.S. Army burned: in Bates and Lee (op. cit.).

p. 287: In 1929, Park Superintendent: in Robert C. Pavlik's "In Harmony with the Landscape: Yosemite's Built Environment, 1913–1940," *California History* (summer 1990).

p. 290: Julia Parker, who is so sketchily represented here, is beautifully portrayed in Bev Ortiz's book *It Will Live Forever* (op. cit.), which is, among other things, her brief oral-history autobiography.

p. 290: Jay Johnson: see also Kat Anderson's "We Are·Still Here" cover story on Jay Johnson, tribal recognition, and the American Indian Council of Mariposa County in *Yosemite* (a journal for members of the Yosemite Association) (fall 1991).

FIRE IN THE GARDEN

p. 294: Bill McKibben, *The End of Nature* (New York: Random House, 1991), excerpted at length in the *New Yorker* (September 1989).

p. 296: Daniel Botkin in *Discordant Harmonies: A New Ecology for the Twenty-First Century* (New York: Oxford University Press, 1990).

p. 297: Alston Chase, *Playing God in Yellowstone* (San Diego: Harcourt Brace Jovanovich, 1986).

p. 297: Doris Yowell in *Newe: A Western Shoshone History* (op. cit.).

p. 299: See Jonathan S. Adams and Thomas O. McShane, *The Myth of Wild Africa* (New York: Norton, 1993).

p. 300: Susan Hecht and Alexander Cockburn, *The Fate of the Forest* (London, New York: Verso, 1989).

p. 300: Olmsted (op. cit.) Oak trees: see Eric E. Angress, "The Decline of Quercus Kelloggii in Yosemite Valley," 1985, unpublished manuscript in Yosemite Research Library.

p. 305: Kat Anderson's "Southern Sierra Miwok Plant Resource ·Management of the Yosemite Region: A Study of the Biological, Ecological, and Cultural Bases for Indian Plant Gathering, Field Horticulture, and Anthropogenic Impacts on Sierra Vegetation," c. 1989 by the author, in Yosemite Research Library, and her article on native uses of native plants in *Yosemite* (summer 1990).

THE NAME OF THE SNAKE

Two major sources for this chapter are *Names on the Land* (New York: Random House, 1945) and Jack Weatherford's *Native Roots: How the Indians Enriched America* (New York: Crown Books, 1991).

p. 310: R. W. B. Lewis, *The American Adam: Innocence, Tragedy and Tradition in the Nineteenth Century* (Chicago: University of Chicago Press, 1955).

p. 312: Emerson to Muir in Nash, *Wilderness* (op. cit.).

p. 315: William Brewer, *Up and Down California in 1860–1864,* edited by Francis P. Farquhar (Berkeley: University of California Press, 1966).

p. 319: The real meaning of Yosemite appears in very few places: I originally found the story mistold in a popular history of Yosemite, which suggested that the appellation "some among them are killers" was an Ahwahneechee description of the white men; I found it mentioned again in a footnote in the brochure *Yosemite Indians,* by Elizabeth Godfrey (revisions by James Snyder and Craig Bates) (Yosemite National Park: Yosemite Association, 1977), and I found the source: Craig Bates's two-page "Names and Meanings for Yosemite Valley" in *Yosemite Nature Notes,* vol. 7, no. 3, 1978, which footnotes Sylvia Broadbent's linguistic research.

p. 320: These commentaries on Genesis come from readings of *Eve: The History of an Idea* by John Phillips (San Francisco: Harper and Row, 1984) and the essay "The Beginning of the End: On the History of Radiation from Plato to Chernobyl" by Gerburg Treusch-Dieter in *Looking Back on the End of the World* (New York: Semiotext(e), 1989), and Shepard's *Man in the Landscape* and *Nature and Madness* (op. cit.).

p. 324: The xeroxes Lewis gave me include passages from William Duncan Strong, *Aboriginal Society in Southern California* (Banning, CA: Malki

Museum Press, Morongo Indian Reservation, 1972), Lowell John Bean, *The Cahuilla* (New York: Chelsea House Publishers, 1989), and Harry C. James, *The Cahuilla Indians* (Los Angeles: Westernlore Press, 1960).

p. 325: Frank LaPena and Craig D. Bates, with illustrations by Harry Fonseca, *Legends of the Yosemite Miwok* (Yosemite National Park: Yosemite Natural History Association).

p. 326: Matt Vera, "The Creation of Language, a Yowlumni Story," in *News from Native California* (summer 1993).

UP THE RIVER OF MERCY

Some of the context here comes from DeVoto's *Year of Decision* (op. cit.). The major sources on James Savage are Annie Mitchell, who wrote "Major James D. Savage and the Tularenos" for the California Historical Society Quarterly, vol. 28, 1949, and the book *Jim Savage and the Tulareno Indians* (Los Angeles: Westernlore Press, 1957), as well as later articles. The Yosemite Research Library possesses a copy of a very fine dissertation by Neva Jeanne Harkins Munoz, "Political Middlemanship and the Double Bind: James D. Savage and the Fresno River Reservation" (1980). There is also a file on Savage at the Yosemite Research Library and another in Bancroft Library, the latter consisting largely of correspondence with Savage's cousins by Lilborne A. Winchell in 1927–1930, for a biography he never wrote.

p. 329: Francis Parkman, *The Oregon Trail* (op. cit.).

p. 330: Most of the chronology of Savage's journey west comes from Mitchell, although some of it comes directly from fellow travellers' accounts—notably Jacob Harlan's memoir *California '46 to '88* (San Francisco: The Bancroft Company, 1888).

p. 333: William Swasey, handwritten manuscript in Bancroft Library.

p. 333: Heinrich Lienhard's diaries have been published; this is from the volume titled *A Pioneer at Sutter's Fort* (Los Angeles: The Calafia Society, 1941).

p. 335: Alberto H. Hurtado, *Indian Summer* (op. cit.).

p. 336: Thaler or Visonhaler makes a brief appearance in Rolle's *John Charles Fremont* biography (op. cit.) and Preuss's *Exploring* (op. cit.). He himself wrote a marvelous long letter-biography of Savage which is in the military records branch of the National Archives as an enclosure in a letter from G. W. Patten to M. M. Gardner, September 26, 1852, Records of the U.S. Army Continental Commands, Department of the Pacific, Letters Received.

p. 337: Cornelius Sullivan in G. H. Tinkham, *California Men and Events: 1769–1890* (Stockton: Records Publishing Co., 1915).

p. 337: Horace Bell, *Reminiscences of a Ranger* (Los Angeles: Yarnell, Castile, and Mathes, Printers, 1881).

p. 344: Maria Lebrado, unpublished interview with Carl P. Russell, Yosemite Research Library.

p. 344: William Eccleston's diary, published as *The Mariposa Indian War; 1850–51,* edited by C. Gregory Crampton (Salt Lake City: University of Utah Press, 1957), provides an excellent counterpoint to Bunnell's book, which benefits from the clarity of hindsight.

p. 344: Pahmit's oral history forms a chapter in Frank F. Latta's *Handbook of Yokuts Indians* (Santa Cruz: Bear State Books, 1977).

p. 344: "A White Medicine Man" by James O'Meara in *The Californian,* Yosemite Research Library.

p. 345: January 1851 letter quoted in Bunnell (op. cit.).

p. 345: California Courier, February 20, 1851.

p. 345: Sam Ward in the Gold Rush, edited by Carvel Collins (Stanford: Stanford University Press, 1949).

p. 347: Sacking San Jose in C. Gregory Crampton's manuscript "Opening of the Mariposa Region" in Bancroft Library.

p. 348: California Courier (op. cit.).

p. 350: Savage's wives had returned: *San Joaquin Republican,* November 18, 1851.

p. 350: Savage's conflict with Harvey is recounted in Mitchell, in Vinsonhaler's letter, and in Patten's letter (the cover letter for Vinsonhaler's) and Stockton, in Bunnell, all op. cit., and in the *San Francisco Herald* of September 4, 1852.

p. 353: Ida B. Savage's statement about Savage's estate is in the Savage papers assembled by Lilborne A. Winchell in Bancroft Library.

FULL CIRCLE

p. 369: James Mooney, *The Ghost Dance Religion and the Sioux Outbreak of 1890,* republished with an introduction by Bernard Fontana (Glorieta, NM: Rio Grande Press, 1973).

Index

Index

Index